Social Rights in Europe in an Age of Austerity

This collection of essays examines the promise and limits of social rights in Europe in a time of austerity. Presenting in the first instance five national case studies, representing the biggest European economies (UK, France, Germany, Italy and Spain), it offers an account of recent reforms to social welfare and the attempts to resist them through litigation. The case studies are then used as a foundation for theory-building about social rights. This second group of chapters develops theory along two complementary lines: first, they explore the dynamics between social rights, public law, poverty and welfare in times of economic crisis; second, they consider the particular significance of the European context for articulations of, and struggles over, social rights. Employing a range and depth of expertise across Europe, the book constitutes a timely and highly significant contribution to socio-legal scholarship about the character and resilience of social rights in our national and regional constitutional settings.

Stefano Civitarese Matteucci is Professor of Public Law at the University of Chieti-Pescara, Italy.

Simon Halliday is Professor of Socio-Legal Studies at the University of York, UK, and Professor of Law at the University of New South Wales, Australia.

Critical Studies in Jurisprudence Series

This series continues the 'Edinburgh/Glasgow Law and Society' series

Titles in the Series

The Anxiety of the Jurist
Legality, Exchange and Judgement
Edited by Maksymilian Del Mar and Claudio Michelon

'Integration through Law' Revisited
The Making of the European Polity
Edited by Daniel Augenstein

The Public in Law
Representations of the Political in Legal Discourse
Edited by Claudio Michelon, Gregor Clunie, Christopher McCorkindale and Haris Psarras

The Many Constitutions of Europe
Edited by Kaarlo Tuori and Suvi Sankari

Law as Institutional Normative Order
Edited by Maksymilian Del Mar and Zenon Bańkowski

Law and Agonistic Politics
Edited by Andrew Schaap

Public Law and Politics
The Scope and Limits of Constitutionalism
Edited by Emilios Christodoulidis and Stephen Tierney

Transformations of Policing
Edited by Alistair Henry and David J. Smith

The Universal and the Particular in Legal Reasoning
Edited by Zenon Bańkowski and James MacLean

Forthcoming titles in the series

Law, Obligation, Community
Edited by Daniel Matthews and Scott Veitch

Social Rights in Europe in an Age of Austerity

Edited by
Stefano Civitarese Matteucci
and Simon Halliday

Routledge
Taylor & Francis Group
LONDON AND NEW YORK

First published 2018 by Routledge

2 Park Square, Milton Park, Abingdon, Oxfordshire OX14 4RN
52 Vanderbilt Avenue, New York, NY 10017

Routledge is an imprint of the Taylor & Francis Group, an informa business

First issued in paperback 2018

British Library Cataloguing in Publication

British Library Cataloguing in Publication Data
A catalogue record for this book is available from the British Library

Library of Congress Cataloging-in-Publication Data
Names: Civitarese, Stefano, author. | Halliday, Simon, 1966- author.
Title: Social rights in Europe in an age of austerity / Stefano Civitarese, Simon Halliday.
Description: Abingdon, Oxon [UK] ; New York : Routledge, 2017. | Series: Critical studies in jurisprudence | Includes bibliographical references and index.
Identifiers: LCCN 2017001664 | ISBN 9781138700598 (hbk)
Subjects: LCSH: Social rights—European Union countries. | Social legislation—European Union countries. | Public welfare—Law and legislation—European Union countries. | Public welfare—Economic aspects—European Union countries. | Welfare state—European Union countries. | Civil rights—European Union countries.
Classification: LCC KJE3275 .C58 2017 | DDC 344.403—dc23
LC record available at https://lccn.loc.gov/2017001664

ISBN: 978-1-138-70059-8 (hbk)
ISBN: 978-0-367-19180-1 (pbk)

Typeset in Galliard by
Keystroke, Neville Lodge, Tettenhall, Wolverhampton

Goffredo Civitarese (1936–2016)
In memoriam

Contents

List of contributors

Michael Adler is Emeritus Professor of Socio-Legal Studies in the School of Social and Political Science at the University of Edinburgh, UK.

Alessandra Albanese is Professor of Administrative Law at the University of Florence, Italy.

Francesco Bilancia is Professor of Constitutional Law at the University of Chieti-Pescara, Italy.

Emilios Christodoulidis holds the Chair of Jurisprudence at the University of Glasgow, UK.

Stefano Civitarese Matteucci is Professor of Public Law at the University of Chieti-Pescara, Italy.

Francesco Ferraro is Lecturer in Philosophy of Law at the University of Milan, Italy.

Stefano Giubboni is Professor of Labour Law at the University of Perugia, Italy and the Fernand Braudel Fellow at the Department of Law, European University Institute, Italy.

Marco Goldoni is Senior Lecturer in Law at the University of Glasgow, UK.

Simon Halliday is Professor of Socio-Legal Studies at the University of York, UK, and Professor of Law at the University of New South Wales, Australia.

Jeff King is Professor of Law at University College London, UK.

Ulrike Lembke is Professor of Legal Gender Studies at the University of Hagen, Germany.

Jed Meers is a Lecturer at York Law School, University of York, UK.

Diane Roman is Professor of Public Law at the François Rabelais University, Tours, France.

Lars Inge Terum is Professor at the Centre for the Study of Professions, Oslo, Norway and Akershus University College, Norway.

Dolores Utrilla is Senior Lecturer and Researcher of Administrative Law at the University of Castilla-La Mancha, Spain.

Stuart White is Associate Professor of Politics at the University of Oxford, UK and Fellow and Tutor in Politics at Jesus College, the University of Oxford, UK.

Acknowledgements

This edited volume of essays would not have come to fruition but for the help of many people. We take the opportunity here to thank them.

The book emerged from a research workshop that took place at the University of York, UK, in September 2015. The workshop was generously funded by the research project on 'Democratic Institutions and Public Administrations of Europe: Cohesion and Innovation in the time of Economic Crisis' (PRIN 2010–11 – Italian Ministry of Education, University and Research).

Many of the chapters in the book were presented in their original form at the workshop. We are very grateful to all those who took part. The discussions and debates of the workshop helped the authors refine their arguments and assisted us, as editors, in our planning and development of the book.

We are also grateful to Louise Prendergast of York Law School who, characteristically, oversaw the practical planning stages of the workshop with great skill and efficiency. Thanks are also due to Jed Meers who, similarly characteristically, made sure everything went to plan at the workshop itself.

Alisha Matthew was a highly effective editorial assistant, taking responsibility for turning the raw texts into a manuscript ready for submission.

Finally, we owe a debt of gratitude to the editors of the Critical Studies in Jurisprudence series and to Colin Perrin at Routledge for their enthusiasm for this project.

Stefano Civitarese Matteucci, Pescara
Simon Halliday, Sydney
November 2016

Table of cases

Note: If the case is not named in the text the locator includes the text page and the endnote number. For example, 33(n36) refers to text page 33 and note number 36.

Court of Justice of the European Union

European Court of Human Rights

European Committee on Social Rights

France

Germany

Hungary

Italy

Portugal

South Africa

Spain

United Kingdom

United States

Part I

Introduction

Chapter 1

Social rights, the Welfare State and European austerity

*Stefano Civitarese Matteucci and Simon Halliday**

1. Introduction

Social rights have become a major focus for public law scholars in recent years. Such attention is important, albeit, perhaps, a little belated. Following the inclusion of social rights in the Universal Declaration of Human Rights (UDHR) in 1948, the world witnessed a significant rise in their inclusion in domestic constitutions.[1] But it was not really until the jurisprudence of the new Constitutional Court of South Africa at the turn of the century that the widespread interest of constitutional lawyers in social rights was achieved. Since then, however, there has been an exponential rise in this scholarship.[2]

Much of this work has focused on the developing world and emerging democracies,[3] inspired by the thought that social rights in domestic legal form may prove to be transformational. Perhaps, it is thought, social rights can offer a voice to the poor in the face of neglect.[4] Maybe, it is hoped, they will catalyse the reform of welfare policies that sustain gross material inequalities.[5] Thus case studies have emerged from a wide array of countries,[6] including: Angola,[7] Argentina,[8] Bolivia,[9] Brazil,[10] Colombia,[11] India,[12] Indonesia,[13] Malawi,[14] Nigeria[15] and, most of all, South Africa.[16]

From this initial focus on the developing world, however, an interest in the role of social rights in the constitutions of developed nations too has now emerged,[17] not least because the global economic crisis of 2008 impacted on a broad range of economies, directly threatening a roll back of social welfare provision.[18] Might social rights, then, in addition to carrying hopes of transformation in the global south, prove 'fit for purpose'[19] in offering protection for existing provision in the global north?

It is in this latter vein that this collection of essays was conceived. The core of the book comprises case studies of five 'old' European states: France, Germany, Italy, Spain and the UK. Each study examines welfare policy reform in the 'age of austerity',[20] as it has been called, focusing particularly on the period around the global financial crisis of 2008. The studies then explore and assess the attempts to use public law rights to counter these austerity reforms. Additional contributors reflect on the case studies from a range of perspectives in order to develop theory and to deepen our understanding of social rights.

Our focus on 'old' Europe, then, offers something of a contrast to the original thrust of the social rights literature and an interesting comparator for social rights research. The selection of the case studies additionally produces an element of variation within Europe. It does so in three main respects: legal traditions in relation to social rights, social welfare traditions and the impact of the great financial crisis on the national economies. As regards legal traditions, our five main case studies are spread across what have been described as three 'models' of constitutional incorporation of social rights within Europe:[21] the 'liberal' (the UK), the 'southern European' (Italy and Spain) and the 'moderate' (Germany and France). As regards Welfare State regimes, our five countries fall into three of the four Welfare State regimes[22] of developed nations that are commonly depicted in the social policy literature: the liberal (the UK), the corporatist (France and Germany) and the southern European (Italy and Spain). Finally, as regards the impact of the global financial crisis on national economies, our five case study countries, as Adler and Terum's chapter in this volume (Chapter 7) demonstrates, have had different experiences. The challenges experienced by Spain and Italy, not least by way of the prerequisites of international financial assistance, may be contrasted with the comparatively less burdensome experiences of France, the UK and, most of all, Germany.

In this introductory chapter, we offer an overview of the main themes and concerns of the social rights literature to date. Having done so, we then point to what we believe are gaps and vulnerabilities in the existing research agenda, especially in relation to industrialised nations such as our European case studies. In particular, we argue that the study of social rights will benefit from an approach that contextualises them within the wider study of public law's relation to welfare. Equally, we argue that it is important to acknowledge that constitutional social rights are just one aspect of the wider Welfare State and, accordingly, should be understood and explored against that background. A focus on the Welfare State permits one to contrast the relatively recent attention towards social rights from constitutional law scholars with an older socio-legal tradition of empirically examining the front-line operations of the Welfare State. Our suggestion is that the study of social rights needs both. We conclude our introduction with a summary of the chapters that follow in the remainder of this volume.

II. Legal research on social rights

Constitutional law research on social rights has quickly become rich and eclectic, often drawing on comparative enquiry. Nonetheless, despite its variety, the literature, we suggest, ultimately revolves around five basic research questions, albeit ones that connect to one another and overlap:

- How do social rights come to be included in constitutional settlements?
- What does the concept of a social right entail?
- How do courts adjudicate social rights?

- How should courts adjudicate social rights?
- How effective are social rights?

A. Social rights and constitutional settlements

This research theme focuses on the reception of social rights into constitutions (and sometimes their failure to be received),[23] asking why and how they have attained their status as fundamental rights. Although such work is, by definition, historical, the specificity of the historical enquiry varies. Some have adopted a case study approach, focusing on one or two countries.[24] Others have taken a broader sweep, focusing on regions rather than countries.[25] More ambitiously, a general theory has been proffered about the rise, on a global scale, of domestic constitutionalism, including social rights. Law and Versteeg have posited that such constitutionalism is somewhat parasitic on the growth of human rights instruments in the international arena.[26]

As we can see, Law and Versteeg approached the question at a macro level. However, the more focused, micro-level research (in relative terms) has perhaps been more illuminating, touching on issues of motivation and ambition, revealing the social and political realities of constitutional settlements. We can observe that while for some constitutional actors, the inclusion of social rights may represent a transformational political agenda, for others it may reflect ambitions that are far more conservative – much more profane than the notion of fundamental rights as 'values for a godless age'.[27] The articulation of social rights is often the result of constitutional bargaining between parties who approach the task with competing visions of the good society and how to achieve it. Social rights, then, may carry hopes of preventing something deemed more radically progressive: a buffer, for example, against socialism, as was the case in Ireland in the early 20th century,[28] and in Germany in the late 19th century, as Lembke's case study (Chapter 3) in this volume reminds us. Equally, they may be a kind of trade for the purpose of preserving property rights protection, an 'insurance swap' as Dixon and Ginsburg[29] have framed it. As we shall see below, this complicates, to some extent, the question of the effectiveness of social rights.

B. The concept of a social right

The starting point for this second research theme is the historical observation that social rights have come to prominence at a later stage of modernity than civil and political rights.[30] The theoretical enquiry, as Ferraro's chapter in this volume reminds us, is about whether a distinction between so-called 'first' and 'second' generation rights is meaningful at a conceptual level, too. Given the normative status of civil and political rights in common understandings of the good society, the claim that social rights are conceptually indistinct from civil and political rights, or that they complement one another,[31] would be a powerful one.

The view that there is no real conceptual difference between civil/political rights and social rights has now become a kind of orthodoxy in the legal social rights literature (although not, as Ferraro stresses, within the wider debates of political philosophy). Suggestions that civil and political rights require governments to refrain from action, whereas social rights require them to undertake action – a contrast between negative and positive obligations – have been countered by the observation that the enjoyment of civil and political rights is secured by an infrastructure created and sustained by government.[32] Likewise, the notion that social rights are distinct in requiring public expenditure is challenged by evidence of the financial costs associated with systems of civil and political rights, as Albanese (Chapter 4) in this volume affirms.[33] Differences may exist, then, regarding the degree of financial commitments involved, but these do not touch on basic conceptual structure, it is suggested.[34]

This orthodoxy, however, is not without its detractors. Perhaps, it is argued, given that social rights impose higher costs on government, welfare duties create distinct challenges for adjudication, making decisions comparatively harder for judges.[35] More radically, perhaps to permit the adjudication of social rights at all is to commit a category error, one that fundamentally subverts their social character. Atria, for example, has argued that adjudication transforms and reduces social rights (in)to 'bourgeois' law, de-socialising them in the process and robbing them of their socialist potential.[36]

As we can see then, the theoretical debate about the concept of social rights is rooted in a real-world concern for the welfare of the poor. To some extent at least, it is about the appropriate form through which social rights may realise their deemed transformational potential.

C. How do courts adjudicate social rights?

This third research stream also focuses on the concept of social rights, but from a doctrinal perspective. By analysing constitutional jurisprudence, often using comparative methods, scholars have built up quite a complex picture of the ways in which constitutions across the globe may or do articulate social rights as a matter of positive law and constitutional style. In particular, the approach of the South African Constitutional Court, whereby social rights are conceived as giving rise to policy programme objectives, the pursuit of which may be subject to reasonableness review, has received much attention.[37] In turn, this approach may be contrasted with that of the Indian Supreme Court, which Khosla[38] describes as a 'private law' model of social rights jurisprudence.[39] Equally, these conceptions may be contrasted with the 'minimum core' approach to social rights advocated by international human rights bodies[40] and adopted in countries such as Colombia.[41]

Such variations within global jurisprudence have triggered attempts to reduce the multiplicity of adjudicatory approaches to meaningful categories or types. Thus, in an analysis that quickly produced some terms of art, Tushnet contrasted the 'strong-form' judicial review tradition of the USA with the weaker-form traditions of other commonwealth jurisdictions.[42] Young,[43] however, offers a more sophisticated typology with a global reach. She begins with the different interpretive postures adopted by courts: (a) peremptory, (b) managerial, (c) experimentalist, (d) conversational and (e) deferential. From these interpretive styles, focusing on the combinations employed by courts, she produces a typology of constitutional dynamics observable in social rights adjudication: (1) catalytic, (2) engaged, (3) detached and (4) supremacist.

D. How should courts adjudicate social rights?

Doctrinal analysis, of course, rarely restricts itself to describing what is, quickly embracing discussions of what should be. Thus, in normative terms too, a minimum core approach to social rights[44] may be contrasted with a proportionality approach,[45] a reasonableness approach[46] and so on. Such discussions are informed by a familiar, though complex, weave of ideas and concerns. Debates focus both on the needs of the poor and those of the polity. Thus, arguments about the necessity of protecting a basic minimum of social provision for the sake of the poor,[47] particularly in times of crisis,[48] come up against concerns regarding how best to resolve reasonable disagreements within the polity about how to meet competing needs in society.[49] Issues of democratic legitimacy, judicial expertise and polycentric policy problems encounter moral imperatives to meet the threshold needs of society's most vulnerable.[50] Strategies of judicial incrementalism,[51] meaningful engagement[52] and institutional dialogue[53] are among the suggested ways by which courts may appropriately meet these challenges.

E. The effectiveness of social rights

For many scholars within the legal academy, the internal study of law as a hermetically sealed system of ideas is a barren enterprise that overlooks the nature of law as a social institution. This is, perhaps, especially the case for social rights scholars. A concern with the real-world effectiveness of social rights is, accordingly, a major theme within the literature too.

Yet, the research agenda within this stream is somewhat skewed, we would suggest. For understandable reasons – good, politically progressive reasons at that, we should stress – effectiveness research tends towards a conception of social rights whereby their purpose is to protect the poor's well-being. But as we saw above, the inclusion of social rights within constitutional settlements can be somewhat Janus-faced. For some it is about the promise of change, carrying hopes of social transformation. For others, it is about securing the status quo, soothing fears of a greater and unwanted social upheaval. We expand on these observations below when we situate the study of social rights within the broader Welfare State, noting that social welfare has traditionally been underpinned by quite mixed ambitions, being as much about the collective needs of the capitalist economy as about the individual welfare needs of the poor. And as the chapters of Bilancia, (Chapter 12) and Christodoulidis and Goldoni (Chapter 11) in this volume demonstrate, recent experiences in Europe have brought this dynamic into sharp relief.

Even among those who share a sense of social rights being somehow about the poor's welfare, the methodological question 'effective in doing what?' does not produce uniform answers. As we saw above in reviewing the normative doctrinal literature, some regard the purpose of social rights as being about securing a minimum core of provision for the poor. For others, it is about catalysing and supporting healthy democratic deliberation about the needs of the poor, and so on.

Accordingly, we suggest that this research agenda could be more nuanced and balanced, with greater exploration of the more diverse group of ambitions that are ascribed to social rights. For the time being, however, we explore work that focuses on the effectiveness of social rights in securing the welfare of the poor.

Much of the legal research takes a qualitative case study approach, focusing on one or two countries,[54] in contrast to some political science research, which includes large-scale quantitative work.[55] A number of legal scholars have suggested helpful schemes for analysing the effectiveness of social rights. Such schemes generally set out pertinent features of the social world surrounding social rights litigation. The contention is that these features make a difference to whether, or the extent to which, social rights matter for the poor in a given society. Thus, Brinks *et al.*[56] point to legal mobilisation, judicial response, compliance and follow-up. Gloppen[57] focuses on marginalised groups' voices, courts' responsiveness, judicial capability and authorities' implementation. Yamin and Gloppen, in relation to health issues, highlight processes of claims formation, adjudication, implementation and social outcomes. Young and Lemaitre,[58] similarly in relation to the right to health, suggest judicial doctrine, judicial roles, financing backdrop and civil society.

As we can see, there is a degree of similarity within these schemes, focusing, broadly speaking, on the generation and resolution of litigation, followed by the implementation of the judicial mandates. A notable gap – or, at least, an insufficient stress – in these analyses, however, is the issue of the poor's take up of welfare provisions. Policy implementation does not exhaust the process of translating legal victories into the real-world enjoyment of welfare. Although trite, it is worth reminding ourselves that welfare provisions are only worthwhile if taken up by those who need them. As Roman demonstrates in her chapter in this volume, there are a number of reasons why the poor fail to claim or receive their entitlements. This is an issue that we return to below in discussing more broadly the operations of the Welfare State. Before we do so, however, we must first explore the importance of situating the study of social rights within an understanding of public law generally.

III. Social rights and public law

The argument of this section is that the study of social rights will be enriched if we locate it within broader understandings of public law more generally. Perhaps the most obvious reason for this is that not all constitutions have entrenched social rights. The UK, one of our case study countries, is an example. Given its commitment to the doctrine of parliamentary sovereignty, it lacks a codified constitution. But this is not to say that it does not have social rights. It simply lacks *constitutionally entrenched* social rights.[59] The UK, as is well known, has an extensive system of social welfare rights that are contained in primary and secondary legislation. These, surely, are as worthy of study as the welfare entitlements in other jurisdictions that are variously underpinned or supported by constitutionally entrenched social rights.

But the UK case study offers us a more important observation. As Meers' chapter (Chapter 6) demonstrates, although the UK lacks constitutional social rights, this has not precluded the evocation of other features of constitutional law in the struggle to protect social welfare.[60] And as the case studies of France, Germany, Italy and Spain further demonstrate, the UK is not unusual in this regard. As Utrilla discusses in relation to Spain, for example, such public law rights can be more effective in challenging austerity welfare reforms than the entrenched social rights provisions of constitutional texts. So, although constitutional social rights may now be legion, they are not yet everywhere. And even where they are present, they are not the only game in town.

A. Austerity constitutionalism within Europe

A wider perspective on public law and its relationship to social welfare also offers us an additional insight that may at first seem to be counter-intuitive. In countries that enjoy mature welfare systems, as Jeff King's chapter (Chapter 10) in this volume affirms, we have become used to the image of constitutional law as having the capacity to act as a kind of shield, protecting the poor from excessive governmental incursion into their welfare. Yet, as others chapters in this volume suggest, constitutional law is also capable of acting more like a sword, undercutting welfare spending. A constitutional concern with social welfare comes up against constitutional mandates for budgetary balance and propriety.

Europe offers a particularly fertile laboratory for such an enquiry, despite (or perhaps because of) the European Union's (EU's) aspirations towards a 'Social Europe'. As Giubboni sets out in his chapter in this volume (Chapter 13), this was a project that promised a transnational dimension to social solidarity, captured in the notion of European citizenship. Much, however, has been made of the fading of this dream in recent times,[61] even of its death,[62] and some of the chapters in this volume continue in this vein. According to Giubboni, for example, the direction of travel seems grim in relation to social welfare within Europe. He sees a creeping return to the logic of the *Poor Laws*: a post-modern rediscovery of the expulsion of the undeserving poor whereby they are sent back to their place of origin from the countries where they claim assistance.

The role of European and domestic constitutional law in hastening the death of a Social Europe and in undercutting social welfare spending is a theme taken up by other contributors too. The case studies by Albanese (discussing Italy) (Chapter 4) and Utrilla (discussing Spain) (Chapter 5), for example, recount how rapid constitutional amendments were made in relation to budgetary and financial 'stability' following financial assistance from the 'Troika' (the European Commission (EC), the European Central Bank (ECB) and the International Monetary Fund (IMF)). These provisions cast a dark constitutional shadow over public spending, particularly social welfare spending (which constitutes a large proportion of national budgets), and weaken the purchase of entrenched social rights. But Christodoulidis and Goldoni suggest in their chapter (Chapter 11) that such developments are best regarded as instances of a wider and longer trend whereby neoliberal economics has been constitutionalised within the European Union. Similarly, Bilancia builds in his chapter (Chapter 12) on work that sets out the precise means through which austerity has been constitutionalised.[63] In addition to substantive constitutional rules about balanced budgets, such as those mentioned above, such means also include various institutional changes establishing independent fiscal councils to undertake analysis of public finances from a position a step away from ordinary politics, and various innovative procedures for the allocation of public resources, most notably through the development of spending reviews.

The result of the constitutionalisation of austerity within Europe is that European law and certain aspects of domestic constitutionalism enable a shift towards a different character of, and function for, welfare policy within the overall economy. Welfare policy comes to serve capitalism in a different way. The Welfare State and capitalism have always, of course, been locked into a mutual dynamic. As Garland has recently stressed,[64] the Welfare State, as a rationality of government, has always been Janus-faced, being both about the welfare of the poor *and* the health of capitalism. It is, he argues, a fundamental feature of any industrialised society, a necessary means of regulating capitalism's inherent capacity to self-destroy:

> [T]he welfare state is an essential basis for human flourishing in capitalist society and an essential basis for capitalist flourishing in human society.[65]

But the particular dynamic between these two concerns seems to have shifted in recent decades, supported by the constitutionalisation of austerity. Under the 'golden age' of the Welfare State in the decades following the Second World War, the welfare of the poor was protected through public spending so that capitalism would flourish. Under the more recent neoliberal Welfare State, however, the logic around public spending has shifted: the welfare of capitalism is more likely protected through a containment of welfare spending. Christodoulidis and

Goldoni, in their chapter in this volume (Chapter 11), suggest that such is the price to be paid when so much of State finance is dependent on the financial markets. States, they suggest, must demonstrate austerity in order to please the markets and their ruling institutions.

Of course, there is room for debate about the precise impacts of neoliberalism and austerity constitutionalism on the character and generosity of social policy spending within Europe – a debate that Bilancia and King take up in their chapters (Chapters 12 and 10) in this volume. This empirical question is complex and difficult to answer definitively. But the larger, methodological point to take from all this is that we should think carefully about the core research concern of 'social rights' scholarship. Our suggestion is that we should resist the temptation to focus too narrowly on constitutionally entrenched social rights. The risk to be avoided here is that we fetishise them and thus lose sight of the broader and more complex dynamics between public law, poverty and welfare.

IV. Social rights and the Welfare State

The argument of this next section, which runs in parallel to the argument above, is that the study of social rights will be further enriched if we locate them within broader understandings of the operations of the Welfare State. This is particularly the case for Western Europe, the geographical focus of this volume, where Welfare States are mature.

A. Macro-level change in the Welfare State

The first benefit of framing constitutional social rights as just one aspect of the broader Welfare State is that we gain a better perspective on their significance relative to other aspects. It offers a clearer sense of scale that, in turn, offers a deeper understanding of the limits of constitutional social rights. And as we will see, the macro perspective on the Welfare State additionally permits us to better contextualise the great financial crisis of 2008 on which this volume focuses.

According to Garland, the Welfare State as a form of modern government – a set of governmental practices that differs from and replaced those of the previous laissez-faire regime – has been remarkably resilient since its inception. It persists to this day, despite claims to the contrary.[66] Economic crises, including the recent global crisis of 2008, have done nothing to alter this. But this is not to say that the character of the Welfare State remains immutable. Although its core existence is essential to the functioning of capitalism, the precise nature of its social policies is subject to change in the ideological contests over what is a good society and how to achieve it under capitalism. Thus, Garland suggests a distinction between what he terms 'welfare state 1.0' and 'welfare state 2.0'.[67] The key change, approximately four decades ago, is marked by the coming to prominence of neoliberal ideas about how best to manage the economy.[68]

With this longer view of Welfare State developments, we may suggest that it is mistaken to frame the 'age of austerity' as having been triggered by the great financial crisis of 2008. The better view is that austerity is a feature of the Welfare State 2.0. Indeed, as our case studies demonstrate, austerity policies were well established prior to the 2008 crisis. The specific austerity responses to the 2008 crisis, then, are better regarded as a chapter in the neoliberal phase of the Welfare State, rather than as a major rupture.

This is the backdrop against which social rights adjudication in 'old' Europe has taken place. This is significant because, in many senses, social rights represent the economic philosophy that was replaced by neoliberalism. Social rights are like gravestones for an economic orthodoxy that has passed on. As Couso[69] has noted in relation to international treaties articulating social rights:

> International human rights law embodies an economic policy 'frozen' in time from the mid twentieth century (in the form of social-democratic, social-Christian, or 'New Deal' thought). This philosophy has been 'transported' into our time by the social and economic provisions of the Universal Declaration of Human Rights and the International Covenant on Economic, Social and Cultural Rights, which are now incompatible with some of the core principles of contemporary mainstream economic thinking.

Social rights litigation, accordingly, represents, in some senses, a clash of economic rationalities. In some countries, such as Colombia[70] and Hungary,[71] the clash has been distinctly combative, with policy being stopped in its tracks. In old Europe, however, our case studies suggest that the encounter has been more cordial and genteel – more like a PhD supervisor cautioning her student to think carefully. The case study of Germany in this volume captures the dynamic especially well. Lembke notes that, despite recognising a fundamental right to a subsistence minimum, the Constitutional Court has held that the articulation of the right's content is a matter for legislative discretion. In Europe, it seems, the courts are speaking softly, without at the same time carrying any big sticks.

Of course, for some scholars, including King in this volume (Chapter 10), the value of the court may lie precisely in such soft power, its 'weaker' forms of review.[72] He argues, on grounds of constitutional legitimacy and judicial expertise, among other things, for 'judicial incrementalism', a cautious and contained constitutional stance on the part of the courts. Among scholars who stress the importance of soft power, constitutional courts largely have an expressive role to perform in relation to the needs of the poor and the nature of poverty.[73] In articulating the constitutional significance of social rights, the courts catalyse, it is hoped, meaningful deliberation about these issues.[74] But the consequence of such a position is that it is important not to expect too much from social rights adjudication in mature Welfare States,[75] particularly when social rights, as an economic imperative, are being pitched against a contrasting and very powerful mode of normative and instrumental thinking about economic management. Under such conditions, the courts are whispering into the wind: sometimes the whispers are heard, but often they are not.

We must stress again, of course, that there is plenty of room here for disagreement about how we should assess this in general normative and specifically constitutional terms. And we see elements of these debates in the other chapters of the book that are summarised below. But before we turn to the chapter summaries, we must first draw attention to the benefits of an empirical perspective on the operations of the Welfare State.

B. Empirical perspective on the operations of the Welfare State

Our argument here is that an empirical concern for the 'law-in-action', in addition to the 'law-in-books',[76] is crucial to our understanding of social rights. It pulls us down from the heights of constitutional doctrine and debate to the depths of social policy delivery. It also draws our attention towards the wider context of the day-to-day operations of the Welfare State, encouraging us to attend to social rights, first as creatures of positive law and policy (not merely of constitutional texts), and then as the empirical outcomes of social policy implementation processes.

This latter move is particularly important, we suggest. It offers us a more grounded sense of the concept of social rights. We may borrow a basic insight here from the policy implementation literature: namely, that the 'ultimate policy-makers' are the bureaucrats who work on the frontlines (at 'street-level'),[77] as opposed to those who draft the policy manuals and guidelines.[78] In other words, policy is what is delivered, not what is written.[79] In the same way, we may suggest, social rights, ultimately, are not to be found in constitutional texts, not even in the texts of legislation or policy documents, but, rather, in the actions of the frontline workers of the Welfare State. The study of such actions is, therefore, essential to a full understanding of social rights.

In addition to 'street-level bureaucratic theory',[80] there is a relatively long history of socio-legal work examining the fate of social welfare law in the routines of frontline agencies,[81] including explorations of the factors that mediate the impact of court decisions on bureaucratic behaviour.[82] This is a rich seam of scholarship for those concerned with social rights. In keeping with street-level bureaucratic theory, socio-legal scholarship has similarly stressed the significance of officer discretion,[83] routinisation,[84] working conditions[85] and culture[86] to the nature of law-in-action produced at the frontline.

The issue of discretion is worthy of particular note. The existence of at least some discretion in implementation work is unavoidable,[87] although as Meers' study demonstrates, many aspects of the Welfare State, including welfare conditionality, are explicitly discretionary. Street-level discretion within the Welfare State is something of a double-edged sword. On the one hand, it offers some flexibility whereby welfare officers can be responsive to the needs of individual citizens.[88] Yet, on the other, it offers a space into which cultural morality may flow. Street-level law is, accordingly, as much a cultural as a legal phenomenon.[89] It can become, in Hawkins' words, a 'morality play'.[90] Law can enable as well as constrain cultural morality. And as the case studies of Meers (Chapter 6) and Roman (Chapter 2) suggest, such cultural morality can be highly objectionable, with inappropriate perceptions of moral desert infusing the exercise of welfare discretion.[91] Such is, to some extent, an expressive feature of neoliberalism under the Welfare State 2.0, perhaps as significant as its more tangible, instrumental aspects. Whereas social rights express the importance of meeting the needs of the poor in society, neoliberalism tends towards an association of welfare needs with social deviance, at least in relation to unemployment. It is a cultural narrative that stresses individual responsibility more than collective solidarity, whereby poverty is better explained by reference to agency as opposed to structure.

This narrative of poverty not only has an effect on the character of local discretion, however: it also produces social stigma. And, in turn, as Roman notes in her chapter in this volume (Chapter 2), social stigma can affect people's decisions about whether to claim their welfare entitlements. This is an important finding of the literature that has examined the realities of poor people's engagement with welfare bureaucracies.[92] Psychological impediments to the enjoyment of entitlements must be considered alongside the more practical and cognitive barriers to take up.[93] These are important issues for the study of social rights – ones that require continued research and discussion.

We conclude our introduction to this volume with a summary of the chapters that follow.

V. Chapter summaries

The next section of the book contains a number of case studies of social rights and austerity in 'old' Europe. The bulk of this section comprises general studies of single nations: **Roman** discusses France (Chapter 2), **Lembke** focuses on Germany (Chapter 3), **Albanese** explores Italy (Chapter 4), **Utrilla** presents Spain (Chapter 5) and **Meers** (Chapter 6) examines the United Kingdom. In each chapter, the national rapporteur: sets out the constitutional position of social rights in the country; examines recent changes, under the rubric of austerity, to areas of law and policy that pertain to social rights; and then explores the attempts through litigation to use public law rights to protect the welfare of the poor against austerity reforms. The chapters reveal that there have been some notable victories in social rights litigation and we can observe some differences of approach between the five countries, with the Italian courts, perhaps, being the most active. And yet, as we hinted above, despite differences in legal traditions, Welfare State traditions and economic challenges after the great crisis of 2008, from a high vantage point, a broadly similar set of dynamics reveal themselves: austerity reforms have often predated the crisis of 2008, although continue after it; attempts to challenge welfare austerity in litigation have drawn on a range of public law norms and rights, not simply on constitutionally entrenched social rights; and the courts frequently prefer to support and respect the discretion of the legislature on the substance of social rights, constraining their own capacity to intervene.

Following the single, general case studies, **Adler** and **Terum** (Chapter 7) adopt a multi-site approach to a single issue – welfare conditionality – examining the nature of conditionality policies in a time of austerity, and the success of litigation in challenging them. They begin their chapter by helpfully offering an overview of the general impact of austerity on the economies of the five national case countries in this volume, with the addition of Sweden. They describe the actions that governments took in attempting to deal with the consequences of the financial crisis by implementing spending cuts and/or tax rises. They also look at the impact of government policies on the economic and social well-being of individuals. Having set this scene, they then zoom in to the topic of conditionality, picking up its discussion within many of the previous chapters. Their approach is to systematically and empirically investigate the relationship between the extent of the impact of the 2008 crisis and the development of conditionality policies within their six nations. Although, as Adler and Terum themselves note, we must exercise caution in the interpretation of their data,[94] their conclusion is that conditionality policies have not developed in a way that correlates with each country's experience of the 2008 crisis. Thus, conditionality should not, on the basis of their data, be framed as a feature of austerity post-2008. Rather, it should be thought of as a feature of austerity over a longer time frame. As regards their review of the attempts to use litigation to combat conditionality policies, they find that litigation has been both sparse and largely unsuccessful.

The next section of the book seeks to build upon the case studies and develop theory around the topic of social rights and austerity within Europe. **White** (Chapter 8) begins by picking up the main theme of Adler and Terum's chapter: conditionality as a notable feature of neoliberal welfare policy within Europe. White's approach is theoretical. He addresses the question of the justifiability of welfare conditionality and explores a case for an unconditional minimum income, thus also connecting to both doctrinal and theoretical work on what the concept of a social right entails. White argues that, while conditionality may be justified under appropriate circumstances, there is always a significant risk that the relevant conditions will not hold, rendering conditionality unjust. In this important sense, he stresses, the justice of conditionality is itself conditional. Moreover, he notes, the dangers from unjust conditionality can be severe. He proposes a pluralistic response to this context of risk and danger within which one element is to work to diminish conditionality and to shift towards an unconditional minimum income.

Ferraro (Chapter 9) continues the exploration of the concept of social rights. The starting point of his enquiry is an acknowledgement of the fragility of social rights in times of economic crisis. The aim of his enquiry, however, is to challenge the view that such fragility emerges from any presumptive difference in the nature of social rights when compared to civil rights. He suggests that neither a contractualist understanding of social rights – which allows for their conditionality – nor an allegedly different structure of social rights exposes them to being emptied of their original meaning and neutralized by crisis-driven policies.

Instead, what exposes social rights to negative effects in times of crisis is the democratic option of resource allocation and the social dimension of all fundamental rights, both civil and social, due to a prevailing tacit ideology favouring an unrestricted free market.

King (Chapter 10) shifts the focus from the concept of social rights to the role of the courts in promoting and protecting welfare through social rights jurisprudence. Accepting the general finding of the case studies – that European courts' role in protecting welfare after the crisis has been limited – he raises the important question of how, as legal scholars, we should feel about this. King argues for the attractiveness of what he describes as 'judicial incrementalism' as a constitutional strategy in times of economic crisis. Its attractiveness arises, he suggests, not from its capacity to vindicate fundamental social rights in a context of financial crisis, but rather because it is the best one can (ordinarily) hope from constitutional judicial review in times of economic crisis. To ask for more, he suggests, is to risk more than one should reasonably expect to gain. Yet, at the same time, judicial incrementalism, he argues, may humanise the way in which sweeping reforms are rolled out, and keep social rights values in play as political values that may orient political debate in a helpful direction. As King notes in his final sentence, contrasting his approach to those of the chapters that follow, this still amounts to the glass being 'half full'.

The final three chapters, while continuing to explore social rights from the perspective of legal theory, do so specifically within the European context and consider the significance of European law and constitutionalism for the fate of social rights. **Christodoulidis** and **Goldoni** (Chapter 11) begin their essay with a challenge to the traditional province of constitutional scholarship on social rights, including the likes of King. Their assertion is that, rather than exploring the question of whether social rights are better protected through legislative, judicial or administrative means, constitutional scholars should instead face the reality that social rights constitutionalism has been all but defeated. It is, they suggest, the first victim of the regime of economic austerity rolled out to contain the sovereign debt crisis within Europe. European integration, they argue, has been a process of encroachment on social rights: first, market integration and the influx of financial products established market rationality as the main arbiter for managing welfare systems, part of a general restructuring of the global political economy; second, the single currency project was founded on the assumption that, in the absence of a lender of last resort, self-imposed frugality would ensure that the Euro would function smoothly. In an interesting twist and macro perspective on welfare conditionality, they suggest that all this has forced States into the contraction of public expenditure in order to appear as virtuous actors before international financial markets. We have thus witnessed a transformation of the role of the State vis-à-vis social rights because the State itself has to resort to financial markets in order to fund social services. In this way, they conclude, the decoupling of social rights from European citizenship has been fully realised.

Bilancia, in his chapter (Chapter 12), continues the theme of the constitutionalisation of austerity within Europe. He argues that economic policies within Europe have been subject to an increasing juridification in the wake of the financial and sovereign debt crisis that began in 2008. National governments are no longer permitted to deal with social and economic questions in isolation. In order to manage national government deficits and debt and promote financial stability, States can only use traditional counter-cyclical policies to alter revenues and expenditures, including welfare spending. Across the Eurozone, this leads to an asymmetric reduction of public expenditure in order to control the different levels of public deficit and debt. In turn, this causes asymmetric levels of guarantees of social rights, breaking constitutional solidarity within the EU. Within the Common Market, he concludes, a fragmented European territory is being constructed – especially fragmented at the level of enjoyment of fundamental rights and equality in the delivery of social services. The consequence is that we are witnessing European citizens attempting to exercise their rights of free movement in order to seek more generous social rights provision – countered, of course, by national governments' attempts to inhibit them.

In the final chapter of the volume, **Giubboni** (Chapter 13) takes up the theme suggested by Bilancia's analysis – the spectre of a territorial 'shopping' of welfare guarantees and its significance for the notion of European citizenship. He argues that the dream of transnational solidarity exemplified by the free movement of economically inactive persons is now becoming something of a nightmare. The crisis of 2008, he suggests, has destroyed any propensity of Northern-European member states to host EU foreigners in need in their (still relatively) generous welfare systems. Instead, he observes the emergence of two forms of citizenship within the EU: first-class citizenship is reserved, he suggests, for those who are active in the internal market or who can prove their economic self-sufficiency; second-class citizenship, essentially devoid of any transnational protective status, is for the indigent. This amounts to an erosion of the constitutional meaning of European citizenship. For Giubboni, Europe has turned from light towards darkness. Such is his 'melancholic eulogy' for transnational solidarity within the EU.

Notes

* We are very grateful to Ros Dixon, Jeff King and Theunis Roux who offered feedback on an earlier draft of this chapter.

1 Some constitutions contained social rights prior to this point, of course. But the exponential rise occurred in the second half of the 20th century. See Daniel M Brinks, Varun Gauri and Kyle Shen, 'Social Rights Constitutionalism: Negotiating the Tension between the Universal and the Particular' (2015) 11 *Annual Review of Law and Social Science* 289; David Law and Mila Versteeg, 'Evolution and Ideology of Global Constitutionalism' (2011) 99 *California Law Review* 1163, especially 1195 for figures showing that the 'phenomenon of rights creep' regards both negative and positive (social and economic) rights.

2 This is true of the English-speaking world, at least. Social rights legal scholarship has a longer pedigree in Latin America. See Javier A. Couso, 'The Changing Role of Law and Courts in Latin America: From an Obstacle to Social Change to a Tool of Social Equity' in Roberto Gargarella, Pilar Domingo and Theunis Roux (eds), *Courts and Social Transformation in New Democracies: An Institutional Voice for the Poor?* (Ashgate Publishing, 2006).

3 See, e.g., Varun Gauri and Daniel M Brinks (eds), *Courting Social Justice: Judicial Enforcement of Social and Economic Rights in the Developing World* (Cambridge University Press, 2008).

4 See, e.g., Roberto Gargarella, Pilar Domingo and Theunis Roux (eds), *Courts and Social Transformation in New Democracies: An Institutional Voice for the Poor?* (Ashgate Publishing, 2006).

5 See, e.g., David Bilchitz, *Poverty and Fundamental Rights: The Justification and Enforcement of Socio-Economic Rights* (Oxford University Press, 2007).

6 On social rights generally see, e.g., Malcolm Langford (ed.), *Social Rights Jurisprudence: Emerging Trends in International and Comparative Law* (Cambridge University Press, 2008). On the right to health specifically, see Alicia Ely Yamin and Siri Gloppen (eds), *Litigating Health Rights: Can Courts Bring More Justice to Health?* (Harvard University Press, 2011).

7 See, e.g., Elin Skaar and José Octávio Serra Van-Dunem, 'Courts under Construction in Angola: What Can They Do for the Poor?' in Roberto Gargarella, Pilar Domingo and Theunis Roux (eds), *Courts and Social Transformation in New Democracies: An Institutional Voice for the Poor?* (Ashgate Publishing, 2006).

8 See, e.g., Gustavo Maurino and Ezequeil Nino, 'Economic and Social Rights and the Supreme Court of Argentina in the Decade Following the 2001–2003 Crisis' in Aoife Nolan (ed.), *Economic and Social Rights after the Global Financial Crisis* (Cambridge University Press, 2014).

9 See, e.g., Pilar Domingo, 'Weak Courts, Rights and Legal Mobilisation in Bolivia' in Roberto Gargarella, Pilar Domingo and Theunis Roux (eds), *Courts and Social Transformation in New Democracies: An Institutional Voice for the Poor?* (Ashgate Publishing, 2006).

10 See, e.g., José Reinaldo de Lima Lopes, 'Brazilian Courts and Social Rights: A Case Study Revisited' in Roberto Gargarella, Pilar Domingo and Theunis Roux (eds), *Courts and Social Transformation in New Democracies: An Institutional Voice for the Poor?* (Ashgate Publishing, 2006); F F Hoffmann and F R N M Bentes, 'Accountability for Social and Economic Rights in Brazil' in Varun Gauri and Daniel M Brinks (eds), *Courting Social Justice: Judicial Enforcement of Social and Economic Rights in the Developing World* (Cambridge University Press, 2008); O L M Ferraz, 'Harming the Poor through Social Rights Litigation: Lessons from Brazil' (2011) 89 *Texas Law Review* 1643.

11 See, e.g., Rodrigo Uprimny Yepes, 'The Enforcement of Social Rights by the Colombian Constitutional Court: Cases and Debate' in Roberto Gargarella, Pilar Domingo and Theunis Roux (eds), *Courts and Social Transformation in New Democracies: An Institutional Voice for the Poor?* (Ashgate Publishing, 2006); David Landau, 'The Promise of a Minimum Core Approach: The Colombian Model for Judicial Review of Austerity Measures' in Aoife Nolan (ed.), *Economic and Social Rights after the Global Financial Crisis* (Cambridge University Press, 2014); K G Young and J Lemaitre, 'The Comparative Fortunes of the Right to Health: Two Tales of Justiciability in Colombia and South Africa' (2013) 26 *Harvard Human Rights Journal* 179.

12 See, e.g., R Sudarshan, 'Courts and Social Transformation in India' in Roberto Gargarella, Pilar Domingo and Theunis Roux (eds), *Courts and Social*

Transformation in New Democracies: An Institutional Voice for the Poor? (Ashgate Publishing, 2006); S Shankar and P B Mehta, 'Courts and Socio-Economic Rights in India' in Varun Gauri and Daniel M Brinks (eds), *Courting Social Justice: Judicial Enforcement of Social and Economic Rights in the Developing World* (Cambridge University Press, 2008); M Khosla, 'Making Social Rights Conditional: Lessons from India' (2010) 8(4) *International Journal of Constitutional Law* 739.

13 See, e.g., B Susanti, 'The Implementation of the Rights to Healthcare and Education in Indonesia' in Varun Gauri and Daniel M Brinks (eds), *Courting Social Justice: Judicial Enforcement of Social and Economic Rights in the Developing World* (Cambridge University Press, 2008).

14 See, e.g., S Gloppen and F E Kanyongolo, 'Courts and the Poor in Malawi: Economic Marginalisation, Vulnerability and the Law' (2007) 5(2) *International Journal of Constitutional Law* 258.

15 See, e.g., C A Odinkalu, 'The Impact of Social and Economic Rights in Nigeria: An Assessment of the Legal Framework for Implementing Education and Health as Human Rights' in Varun Gauri and Daniel M Brinks (eds), *Courting Social Justice: Judicial Enforcement of Social and Economic Rights in the Developing World* (Cambridge University Press, 2008).

16 See, e.g., Jackie Dugard and Theunis Roux, 'The Record of the South African Constitutional Court in Providing an Institutional Voice for the Poor: 1995–2004' in Roberto Gargarella, Pilar Domingo and Theunis Roux (eds), *Courts and Social Transformation in New Democracies: An Institutional Voice for the Poor?* (Ashgate Publishing, 2006); Rosalind Dixon, 'Creating Dialogue about Socioeconomic Rights: Strong-Form versus Weak-Form Judicial Review Revisited' (2007) 5(3) *International Journal of Constitutional Law* 391; J Berger, 'Litigating for Social Justice in Post-Apartheid South Africa: A Focus on Health and Education' in Varun Gauri and Daniel M Brinks (eds), *Courting Social Justice: Judicial Enforcement of Social and Economic Rights in the Developing World* (Cambridge University Press, 2008); Dennis M Davis, 'Socioeconomic Rights: Do They Deliver the Goods?' (2008) 6 *International Journal of Constitutional Law* 687; Rosalind Dixon and Tom Ginsburg, 'The South African Constitutional Court and Socio-Economic Rights as "Insurance Swaps"' (2011) 4 *Constitutional Court Review* 1; Anashri Pillay, 'Towards Effective Social and Economic Rights Adjudication: The Role of Meaningful Engagement' (2012) 10(3) *International Journal of Constitutional Law* 732; K G Young and J Lemaitre, 'The Comparative Fortunes of the Right to Health: Two Tales of Justiciability in Colombia and South Africa' (2013) 26 *Harvard Human Rights Journal* 179; Anashri Pillay and Murray Wesson, 'Recession, Recovery and Service Delivery: Political and Judicial Responses to the Financial and Economic Crisis in South Africa' in Aoife Nolan (ed.), *Economic and Social Rights after the Global Financial Crisis* (Cambridge University Press, 2014).

17 See, e.g., Mark Tushnet, *Weak Courts, Strong Rights: Judicial Review and Social Welfare Rights in Comparative Constitutional Law* (Princeton University Press, 2008); Katherine G Young, *Constituting Economic and Social Rights* (Oxford University Press, 2012); Jeff King, *Judging Social Rights* (Cambridge University Press, 2012); Jeff King, 'Two Ironies about American Exceptionalism over Social Rights' (2014) 12(3) *International Journal of Constitutional Law* 572.

18 Claire Kilpatrick and Bruno De Witte (eds), 'Social Rights in Times of Crisis in the Eurozone: The Role of Fundamental Rights' Challenges' (Working Paper No 2014/05, European University Institute, 2014); Colm O'Cinneide, 'Austerity and the Faded Dream of a "Social Europe"' in Aoife Nolan (ed.), *Economic and Social Rights after the Global Financial Crisis* (Cambridge University Press, 2014); Nicholas J Lusiani, 'Rationalising the Right to Health: Is Spain's Austere Response

to the Economic Crisis Impermissible Under International Human Rights Law?' in Aoife Nolan (ed.), *Economic and Social Rights after the Global Financial Crisis* (Cambridge University Press, 2014).

19 Aoife Nolan, 'Not Fit for Purpose? Human Rights in Times of Financial and Economic Crisis' (2015) 4 *European Human Rights Law Review* 358.

20 The notion of the 'new age of austerity' was popularised in the UK by its then Prime Minister, David Cameron, in a speech in early 2009: see Deborah Summers, 'David Cameron Warns of a "New Age of Austerity"' *The Guardian* (online), 27 April 2009 < www.theguardian.com/politics/2009/apr/26/david-cameron-conservative-economic-policy1>.

21 Mark Eric Butt, Julia Kübert and Christiane Anne Schultz, 'Fundamental Social Rights in Europe' (Working Paper SOCI 104 EN, Directorate General for Research, European Parliament, 2000).

22 Gøsta Esping-Andersen, *The Three Worlds of Welfare Capitalism* (Princeton University Press, 1990); Maurizio Ferrera, 'The "Southern Model" of Welfare in Social Europe' (1996) 6(1) *Journal of European Social Policy* 17.

23 See, e.g., Cass R Sunstein, 'Why Does the American Constitution Lack Social and Economic Guarantees?' (2005) 56 *Syracuse Law Review* 1. For a counter to the American exceptionalism thesis, see Jeff King, 'Two Ironies about American Exceptionalism over Social Rights' (2014) 12(3) *International Journal of Constitutional Law* 572; Helen Hershkoff and Stephen Loffredo, 'Tough Times and Weak Review: The 2008 Economic Meltdown and Enforcement of Socio-Economic Rights' in Aoife Nolan (ed.), *Economic and Social Rights after the Global Financial Crisis* (Cambridge University Press, 2014).

24 See, e.g., M B Vieira and F C da Silva, 'Getting Rights Right: Explaining Social Rights Constitutionalisation in Revolutionary Portugal' (2013) 11(4) *International Journal of Constitutional Law* 898.

25 See, e.g., Couso, above n 2.

26 Law and Versteeg, above n 1.

27 Francesca Klug, *Values for a Godless Age: The Story of the United Kingdoms' New Bill of Rights* (Penguin Books, 2000).

28 Thomas Murray, 'Socio-Economic Rights Versus Social Revolution? Constitution Making in Germany, Mexico and Ireland, 1917–1923' (2015) 24(4) *Social & Legal Studies* 487.

29 Dixon and Ginsburg, above n 16.

30 See T H Marshall, *Citizenship and Social Class and Other Essays* (Cambridge University Press, 1950).

31 See Cécile Fabre, *Social Rights under the Constitution: Government and the Decent Life* (Oxford University Press, 2000) 45–9.

32 See, e.g., Tushnet, above n 17; Jeff King, *Judging Social Rights* (Cambridge University Press, 2012).

33 See also Stephen Holmes and Cass R Sunstein, *The Cost of Rights: Why Liberty Depends on Taxes* (WW Norton & Co, 2000).

34 David Garland, 'On the Concept of 'Social Rights'" (2015) 24(4) *Social & Legal Studies* 622.

35 Gustavo Arosemena, 'Retrieving the Differences: The Distinctiveness of the Welfare Aspect of Human Rights from the Perspective of Judicial Protection' (2014) 16(3) *Human Rights Review* 239.

36 Fernando Atria, 'Social Rights, Social Contract, Socialism' (2015) 24(4) *Social & Legal Studies* 598.

37 See note 17 above.

38 Mandhav Khosla, 'Making Social Rights Conditional: Lessons from India' (2010) 8(4) *International Journal of Constitutional Law* 739.

39 From a UK perspective, the approach Khosla describes may be better described as one of legitimate expectations being respected: ibid.
40 See *Report on the Fifth Session of the Committee on Economic, Social and Cultural Rights,* UN ECOSOC, 5th sess., UN Doc E/1991/23 (14 December 1991); David Bilchitz, *Poverty and Fundamental Rights: The Justification and Enforcement of Socio-Economic Rights* (Oxford University Press, 2007); Katharine G Young, 'The Minimum Core of Economic and Social Rights: A Concept in Search of Content' (2008) 33(1) *Yale Journal of International Law* 113.
41 See A Sajo, 'Social Rights as Middle-Class Entitlements in Hungary: The Role of the Constitutional Court' in R Gargarella, P Domingo and T Roux (eds), *Courts and Social Transformation in New Democracies: An Institutional Voice for the Poor?* (Aldershot: Ashgate Publishing, 2006); K L Scheppele, 'A Realpolitik Defense of Social Rights' (2004) 82 *Texas Law Review* 1921–61
42 Tushnet, above n 17.
43 Katharine G Young, 'A Typology of Economic and Social Rights Adjudication: Exploring the Catalytic Function of Judicial Review' (2010) 8(3) *International Journal of Constitutional Law* 385.
44 Bilchitz, above n 40.
45 Xenephon Contiades and Alkmene Fotiadou, 'Social Rights in an Age of Proportionality: Global Economic Crisis and Constitutional Litigation' (2012) 10 *International Journal of Constitutional Law* 660.
46 Carol Steinberg, 'Can Reasonableness Protect the Poor: A Review of South Africa's Social Rights Jurisprudence' (2006) 123 *South African Law Journal* 264.
47 K Ewing, 'Book Review: E Palmer, Judicial Review, Socio-Economic Rights and the Human Rights Act' (2009) 7(1) *International Journal of Constitutional Law* 155; Tushnet, above n 17.
48 See, e.g., David Bilchitz, 'Socio-Economic Rights, Economic Crisis, and Legal Doctrine' (2014) 12(3) *International Journal of Constitutional Law* 710.
49 See, e.g., Roberto Gargarella, 'Theories of Democracy, the Judiciary and Social Rights' in Roberto Gargarella, Pilar Domingo and Theunis Roux (eds), *Courts and Social Transformation in New Democracies: An Institutional Voice for the Poor?* (Ashgate Publishing, 2006).
50 See, e.g., Jeff King, *Judging Social Rights* (Cambridge University Press, 2012).
51 Ibid.
52 Pillay, above n 16.
53 See, e.g., Dixon, above n 16.
54 See, e.g., Davis, above n 16; Jeff King, 'Two Ironies about American Exceptionalism over Social Rights' (2014) 12(3) *International Journal of Constitutional Law* 572.
55 See, e.g., Matthew M Kavanagh, 'The Right to Health: Institutional Effects of Constitutional Provisions on Health Outcomes' (2016) 51 *Studies in Comparative International Development* 328.
56 Brinks, Gauri and Shen, above n 1.
57 Siri Gloppen, 'Courts and Social Transformation: An Analytical Framework' in Roberto Gargarella, Pilar Domingo and Theunis Roux (eds), *Courts and Social Transformation in New Democracies: An Institutional Voice for the Poor?* (Ashgate Publishing, 2006).
58 Katharine G Young and Julieta Lemaitre, 'The Comparative Fortunes of the Right to Health: Two Tales of Justiciability in Colombia and South Africa' (2013) 26 *Harvard Human Rights Journal* 179.
59 See Jeff King, *Judging Social Rights* (Cambridge University Press, 2012) 18–19 for a helpful discussion of the different forms of social rights.

60 In the context of an uncodified constitution, the legal basis of the challenges to welfare austerity in the UK would be considered to be part of its constitutional law. The fact that the UK does not have a codified constitution does not mean, of course, that it lacks constitutional law. Rather, it simply means that the sources of constitutional law are the common law, parliamentary legislation, the royal prerogative and constitutional convention.
61 See, e.g., O'Cinneide, above n 18.
62 See, e.g., K D Ewing 'The Death of Social Europe' (2015) 26(1) *King's Law Journal* 76.
63 Tony Prosser, 'Constitutionalising Austerity in Europe' (2016) 1 *Public Law* 111.
64 David Garland, 'The Welfare State: A Fundamental Dimension of Modern Government' (2014) 55(3) *European Journal of Sociology* 327.
65 Ibid 360.
66 Ibid.
67 David Garland, *The Welfare State: A Very Short Introduction* (Oxford University Press, 2016).
68 See also Desmond King and Fiona Ross, 'Critics and Beyond' in Francis G Castles *et al.* (eds), *The Oxford Handbook of the Welfare State* (Oxford University Press, 2010).
69 Couso, above n 2, 72.
70 See, e.g., Rodrigo Uprimny Yepes, 'The Enforcement of Social Rights by the Colombian Constitutional Court: Cases and Debate' in Roberto Gargarella, Pilar Domingo and Theunis Roux (eds), *Courts and Social Transformation in New Democracies: An Institutional Voice for the Poor?* (Ashgate Publishing, 2006)
71 E.g., A Sajo, 'Social Rights as Middle-Class Entitlements in Hungary: The Role of the Constitutional Court' in R Gargarella, P Domingo and T Roux (eds), *Courts and Social Transformation in New Democracies: An Institutional Voice for the Poor?* (Aldershot: Ashgate Publishing, 2006); K L Scheppele, 'A Realpolitik Defense of Social Rights' (2004) 82 *Texas Law Review* 1921–61.
72 Tushnet, above n 17.
73 See, e.g., Khosla, above n 38.
74 Young, above n 43.
75 For a more general argument about expecting too much from the courts, see Malcolm Feeley, 'Hollow Hopes, Flypaper and Metaphors' (1992) 17 *Law & Social Inquiry* 745.
76 Roscoe Pound, 'Law in Books and Law in Action' (1910) 44 *American Law Review* 12.
77 Michael Lipsky, *Street-Level Bureaucracy: Dilemmas of the Individual in Public Services* (Russell Sage Foundation, 1980).
78 Jeffrey Prottas, *People-Processing: The Street-Level Bureaucrat in Public Service Bureaucracies* (Lexington Press, 1979).
79 Steven Maynard-Moody and Michael Musheno, *Cops, Teachers, Counselors: Stories from the Frontlines of Public Service* (University of Michigan Press, 2003).
80 See, e.g., Steven Maynard-Moody and Shannon Portillo, 'Street-Level Bureaucratic Theory' in Robert F Durant (ed.), *The Oxford Handbook of American Bureaucracy* (Oxford University Press, 2010).
81 For discussions of this work, see, e.g., Simon Halliday and Colin Scott, 'Administrative Justice' in Peter Cane and Herbert Kritzer (eds), *The Oxford Handbook of Empirical Legal Research* (Oxford University Press, 2010); C Hunter *et al.*, 'Legal Compliance in Street-Level Bureaucracy: A Study of UK Housing Officers' (2016) 38(1) *Law & Policy* 81.
82 See, e.g., Marc Hertogh and Simon Halliday (eds), *Judicial Review and Bureaucratic Impact: International and Interdisciplinary Perspectives* (Cambridge University Press, 2004).

83 See, e.g., Keith Hawkins (ed.), *The Uses of Discretion* (Oxford University Press, 1992) 444.
84 See, e.g., Simon Halliday, *Judicial Review and Compliance with Administrative Law* (Hart Publishing, 2004).
85 John Baldwin, Nick Wikely and Richard Young, *Judging Social Security: The Adjudication of Claims for Benefit in Britain* (Oxford University Press, 1992).
86 Christopher J Jewell, *Agents of the Welfare State: How Caseworkers Respond to Need in the USA, Germany and Sweden* (Palgrave MacMillan, 2007).
87 R Sainsbury, 'Administrative Justice: Discretion and Procedure in Social Security Decision-Making' in Keith Hawkins (ed.), *The Uses of Discretion* (Oxford University Press, 1992).
88 See, e.g., Jewell, above n 86.
89 Maynard-Moody and Musheno, above n 79.
90 Keith Hawkins, *Law as Last Resort: Prosecution Decision-Making in a Regulatory Agency* (Oxford University Press, 2003).
91 See also David Cowan, *Homelessness: The (In)appropriate Applicant* (Ashgate, 1997); Simon Halliday, 'Institutional Racism in Bureaucratic Decision-Making: A Case Study of Administration of Homelessness Law' (2000) 27(3) *Journal of Law & Society* 449.
92 See, e.g., David Cowan and Simon Halliday, *The Appeal of Internal Review: The (Non-)Emergence of Disputes* (Hart Publishing, 2003); Evelyn Z Brodkin and Malay Majmundar, 'Administrative Exclusion: Organisations and the Hidden Costs of Welfare Claiming' (2010) 20 *Journal of Public Administration Research and Theory* 827; James Fossett and Frank J Thompson, 'Administrative Responsiveness to the Disadvantaged: The Case of Children's Health Insurance' (2016) 26 *Journal of Public Administration Research and Theory* 369.
93 See, e.g., Donald Moynihan, Pamela Herd and Hope Harvey, 'Administrative Burden: Learning, Psychological, and Compliance Costs in Citizen-State Interactions' (2015) 25 *Journal of Public Administration Research and Theory* 43.
94 Adler and Terum caution the reader that: their sample size is small; their data refer only to the highest tier of unemployment benefit; their focus is on the development of policy rules and not on the reality and incidence of rule-application; and their time frame is short, ranging from 2011 to 2014.

Part II

European case studies

Chapter 2

France

Diane Roman

> The French financial situation is a cause of deep anxiety not only to Frenchmen but to their neighbours and friends. What, exactly, are the difficulties in which France finds herself? What are their origins? What are the solutions? Everybody knows that the present situation cannot continue indefinitely. But very few have the courage to face the fact that a crisis will inevitably occur unless remedial steps are taken.[1]

This analysis, describing the French economy just before the Second World War, may still apply, unfortunately, almost 80 years later, despite the actual causes being very different: massive unemployment and a huge public deficit[2] are now, with slow growth, the major issues for the economy.

Since the beginning of the crisis and despite a change in the political majority in 2012, France has been characterised by its continuity in economic policy. No fundamental shifts in the political debate emerged after the crisis, and the 2016 'social and economic emergency state', announced by Hollande[3] should not be seen as a sweeping change. Political discourse provides evidence of this continuity. According to the mainstream narrative, there have been no 'austerity policies' in France. The word itself is not even used, either by members of the government[4] or by politicians. In reply to 'anti-austerity' street protests, Laurent Berger (chair of one of the main trade unions), stated in March 2015:

> [W]ords matter; there is rigour, people are having a rough ride, but there is no austerity in France. We have obtained an increase in the basic income allowances, and wages have not gone down.[5]

Successive governments have scarcely used the words 'rigour' or 'budgetary discipline', choosing instead to focus on 'economy saving programs' or 'budgetary virtue'.[6] As former Finance Minister Pierre Moscovici stated in 2013 (prior to his accession to the European Commission (EC)):

> No room for complacency in any effort to cut spending, but no structural overshooting, no austerity plan . . . We are inventing a new way between deficit reduction and growth.[7]

This new path could be described as 'austerity lite', whose effects are tangible but whose guidelines are empty: a decrease in purchasing power due to an increase of taxation and massive unemployment, reductions in public spending, but no reductions in public sector or private sector wages.

In this context, analysing the reforms to French social welfare law as a response to the global financial crisis is challenging. Indeed, the effects of the 'austerity lite' may be indirect, and hard to pinpoint at first glance. Moreover, the economic crisis provides evidence that the French welfare system, grounded in the principle of solidarity, acts as a protective shield vis-à-vis the economic crisis' consequences. Albeit partially, social protection has helped to cushion the impact of the crisis on the poorest.

Keeping these difficulties in mind, this paper will analyse the recent regulatory reforms to the welfare system and explain the major trends that can be found throughout these changes. As necessary, we will focus on 'social welfare rights', defined as the social non-contributory provisions benefiting individuals to ensure their basic welfare – mainly housing and income for the unemployed or those who are unable to work. However, due to the unique features of the French welfare system, we will also include some contributory provisions, such as family allowances, retirement pensions and health assistance. More specifically, Part II will demonstrate how, despite the crisis and budget cuts, reallocation of resources in times of scarcity has placed stress on the poorest sectors of the population. Part I will show how this shift, focusing on the poverty-stricken, is the final outcome of a steady decay in the social welfare system, whose goal is no longer fighting growing inequalities. A particular stress will be put on case law where it exists, as the highest judges (namely the Constitutional Council – for constitutional issues; the Conseil d'État – for administrative implementation review; and the Cour de Cassation – for civil and criminal cases) ruled a small number of cases in recent years relating to social provisions. Hence, this chapter's purpose will be to provide a general overview of recent political and legal changes to the French social welfare on the basis of budgetary constraints and 'austerity lite' policies and to assess, where relevant, the impact of the rule of law and judicial review to protect the social constitutional provisions against infringements.

I. Forsaking inequality: creeping change

French social provisions are explicitly founded on a general principle of 'solidarité'. Since the implementation of the social security system after the Second World War, the law has established that:

> the organisation of social security is to be founded on the basis of national solidarity. It protects workers and their families against all kind of risks that might reduce or remove their earning capacity. It also encompasses maternity, paternity and family responsibilities.[8]

The '1945 Pact', as it is often called, pursued the aim of a universal system, non-means-tested, giving equal rights to all. However, the crisis has challenged these foundations. According to non-governmental organisation (NGO) reports, French society is an increasingly unequal one with two disconnected extremes: the working class, which is growing poorer, and the richest people, who form the only category whose incomes are continually growing. At the same time, sociologists stress the growing precariousness affecting the middle and lower classes.[9] This increasing 'dualisation' of French society is mostly due to massive unemployment and the inadequacy of the tax system, but it is also partly the result of numerous social security reforms that have reduced the system's redistributive effects. In an attempt to lower the social security deficit, access to retirement pensions, healthcare and job-replacement benefits has been made more difficult. As it will be argued, these three long-running reforms, initiated in the early 2000s, have had particular outcomes on a society already weakened by the current economic situation.

A. Example 1: retirement pensions reform: the consequences for gender equality

Major legislative modifications took place in the field of old-age benefits from 2008 to 2011 under Sarkozy's presidency, with the goal of securing financing for the retirement insurance fund.[10] The reform aimed to prolong the duration of working life through the introduction of various measures: raising both the age of entitlement to the pension from 60 to 62 years and the age of eligibility to full pension irrespective of the length of insurance from 65 to 67 years. Without changing the parameters of the 2010 reform, the left-wing government that came to power in May 2012 expanded the terms and conditions, maintaining the right to retirement at 60 years for people justifying long professional careers.[11] However, it has not increased the amount of the retirement pensions, which have been frozen for two years. One justification may be found in the particularity of the French situation, where the poverty rate decreases with age. Without taking into consideration tax increases that may have affected those subject to Income Tax, the situation of adults of 65 years of age and above has been improving through the development of solidarity mechanisms within pension systems (since 2007, the minimum old-age pension has been increased several times).

However, studies have highlighted the gender impact of the retirement reform. Retirement compensation arrangements, targeting working mothers within the public sector, have been removed: for instance, women with three or more children lost their right to take early retirement. As a result, a wave of early retirements occurred prior to the implementation of the new legal framework. Additionally, the retirement pensions reform impacted the level of male and female retirement pensions differently. In this regard, the High Authority for the Fight against Discrimination and for Equality (HALDE) (an anti-discrimination administrative agency that has since been merged with the Défenseur des droits) opposed the bill, arguing that, without any compensatory measures, the reform would lead to massive indirect discrimination against women.[12] Indeed, due to the gender pay gap and shorter earning periods, the level of retirement pensions that women may apply for is usually 26% lower.[13] Some corrective measures have been implemented,[14] but they may not be sufficient to improve the pension situation of women:

> [B]ecause of the economic crisis, inequalities in the labour market between men and women remain and have even increased and this situation will have an impact on the adequacy of women's pensions.[15]

Although this particular outcome of the reform has not been litigated, one may highlight the potential discriminatory effect of this measure, characterising indirect discrimination based on sex. However, this question struggles to find a place in the French legal system, as a formal conception of equality is still prevalent and overshadows more substantive approaches,[16] as is also evidenced by the example of access to health.

B. *Example 2: health insurance reforms: a crawling privatisation increasing social inequalities in access to medical care*

The Preamble to the 1946 French Constitution guarantees the right to healthcare. Art. 11 states that the nation 'shall guarantee to all, notably to children, mothers and elderly workers, protection of their health, material security, rest and leisure'. As a result, the French working population is covered by statutory national health insurance schemes that are part of the social security system implemented in 1945.[17] State healthcare insurance is partly funded out of payroll taxes. All workers' dependants are automatically covered,[18] as are unemployed and retired persons. In 1999, a major reform led to the implementation of the Couverture maladie universelle (CMU)[19] (Universal Health Coverage). Its purpose was to reduce financial obstacles to access to the Health Insurance Fund. Thus, anyone who is residing in France for more than three months and is not already covered by a health insurance scheme is entitled to primary universal sickness coverage (CMU-B).[20] A total contribution exemption is granted to persons with low incomes. This aid scheme is accompanied by a complementary coverage (CMU-C) granted to people whose monthly income is below €720 per person (€1512 for a couple and two children).[21] Those with limited resources (under €972 per month for a single person, €2042 for a four-person family) are entitled to ACS (Aid for the purchase of complementary health coverage). CMU-C and ACS allow people with low incomes to benefit from coverage of the share of healthcare costs usually not paid by social security: the user charge, the hospital in-patient charge and, within limits, certain expenses in excess of social security rates (such as eyeglasses and dental prostheses).

The French healthcare system is often described as generous. But this has a counterpart: the sickness insurance fund has been in deficit for 25 continuous years due to the conjunction of slow economic growth, extended access to universal medical care and the improvement of health technologies. State healthcare insurance ran a deficit of approximately €5.2 billion in 2016. According to a survey, 91% of the French population believes that the way that healthcare is currently financed is now under serious threat.[22] For many years, the traditional way of curbing social security deficits has been to impose low prices on healthcare services and pharmaceuticals, as well as finding new resources devoted to health insurance (such as the Contribution sociale généralisée (CSG), a social ear-marked tax created in 1990).[23] The implementation of reduced reimbursement rates has been a third remedy used to alleviate the burden on health insurance funds. Currently, the legal reimbursement rate of ambulatory care amounts to 70% of the standard *Sécurité sociale* tariff for doctors' consultations. Furthermore, the law requires patients to register with a referring practitioner, whom they must consult before seeing other general practitioners or specialists. Any disregard for this 'coordinated healthcare circuit' reduces the reimbursement by the social security fund (the legal reimbursement drops from 70% to 30% outside the 'coordinated healthcare circuit'). However, the effects of the reduced reimbursement rates have been partly compensated by the rise of optional private health insurance plans as substitutes for *Sécurité sociale* schemes. According to researchers, these successive reforms lead to 'creeping privatization of health risks, as co-payment measures gradually shift the burden of health expenditures to voluntary private insurance and patients'.[24] Thus, in 2014, the government introduced a new measure to attempt to curb this trend, creating the 'responsible contracts'.[25] Those supplementary health insurance contracts, which determine ceilings for payments in respect of certain medical fees, enable the reduction of tax rates and social charges for policy-holders.

As an additional measure, the 2004 and 2008 Social Security financing plans introduced a general co-payment scheme called *franchises médicales*. This additional fee cannot be covered by any voluntary insurance scheme and must be paid by patients. It was upheld by a 2007 Conseil Constitutionnel decision:

> [I]t is perfectly permissible for the legislature, in order to meet the constitutional requirement of a financial balance of social security, to charge insured people with medical fees that are not covered by the health insurance fund (Conseille constitutionnel décision n. 2007–558 DC du 13 décembre 2007).

Nevertheless, the Constitutional Council warned that the amount of this flat-rate contribution should be fixed in order to avoid infringement of Art. 11 of the 1946 Preamble, noted above. As a result, these 'franchises' amount to €1.00 on each medical consultation and to €0.50 for prescription drugs and any paramedical and medical act. The aggregate amount of these fees cannot exceed €50 per person per year. However, this new co-payment measure triggered many protests. As Palier and Davesne have pointed out,

> For patient organizations, *franchises médicales* have indeed become a symbol of an increasingly unequal health system that puts a growing financial burden on patients, especially low income ones.[26]

Although these reforms were implemented before the economic crisis, their effects have harshened the situation of a significant part of the population whose condition has been exacerbated all at once by the crisis, tax increases and rising unemployment. Two specific examples merit our attention.

The first is foregoing healthcare, widely documented as part of a 'non-take-up phenomenon'. The phenomenon of non-take-up concerns people who, for a variety of reasons, do not contact the relevant services to claim the economic and social rights to which they are entitled.[27] In the healthcare field, the *franchises médicales* have led to increased out-of-pocket charges, creating more obstacles to access to healthcare. According to official studies, 15.9% of people have had to forego care for financial reasons. Among the most precarious, more than 40% had to postpone treatments because of financial difficulties.[28] As the European Committee of Social Rights (ECSR) noted in its 2013 report, even if the implementation of the CMU has constituted a major improvement, many people living under the poverty threshold continue to be excluded from the CMU-C because of the income ceiling.

In addition to financial obstacles, NGOs point out administrative barriers that make access to healthcare very difficult; more than 20% of those entitled to the CMU-C and 75% of those entitled to assistance in obtaining complementary health insurance did not apply. The complexity of the administrative procedures, the excessive requirements in terms of documentation and the substantial length of time necessary to deal with cases additionally provide reasons for not making use of the CMU-B and the CMU-C.[29] Unfortunately, no judicial remedies to this non-take-up phenomenon have yet been sought.

The second pitfall is the increasing discrimination in access to healthcare in France. Studies provide evidence of discrimination in access to medical appointments for people with CMU.[30] For several reasons (prejudice against poor people, worries about the possibility that the presence of disadvantaged populations may bother their habitual clientele and concerns for loss of earnings and paperwork), medical practitioners are prone to refusing appointments for CMU recipients. Despite the law specifically forbidding this kind of discrimination,[31] refusals widely occur[32] and fail to be subjected to criminal sanctions.[33] Additionally, the situation of migrants, especially Roma people, is another area of discrimination in access to healthcare. Act n° 99-641 of 27 July 1999 established the State Medical Assistance (AME), a health coverage system for foreigners without legal immigration status.[34] This system, pursuing a dual humanitarian and public health objective, has been upheld by the Conseil Constitutionnel.[35] However, access to AME is extremely complex, both for patients and health professionals, due to the amount of red tape required, resulting in obstacles to healthcare access. The situation was criticised by the ECSR in a 2012 collective complaint: it found a violation of Article E in combination with Article 11§1 of the Social Charter on the grounds that France had failed to meet its positive obligation to ensure that migrant Roma, including children, whatever their residence status, enjoy an adequate access to healthcare. It also found that there had been a violation of Article E in combination with Article 11§2 of the Charter on the grounds of insufficient opportunities for pregnant Roma women and children to access free and regular consultations and screening.[36]

The higher share of private health expenditures affecting primarily the poor leads to an increase in health inequalities. These also have general consequences on the country's state of health, due to territorial inequalities.[37] Since 1982, *départements* (regional authorities) have played an important role in the social field. They are responsible for the management of social services as well as social aid to children or to the dependent elderly; they also play a major role in providing healthcare, by funding medical centres such as child and maternal protection centres and family-planning centres. However, the financial crisis has had major repercussions for local and regional authorities in France. It has impacted primarily on their resources, which have been stagnant at best and, in some cases, have decreased. Moreover, local authorities must deal with the credit crisis and are struggling to finance their investments. As a result, local authorities have had to postpone or even cancel some of their investments.[38] Financial cuts in local budgets, due to austerity measures, have led local authorities to close some local agencies and to halving support for NGOs. Although there has not yet been any general study, or judicial claims,[39] articles in regional newspapers show evidence of a current trend of greater inequalities in access to healthcare.[40]

More generally speaking, some inequalities may arise from the French health insurance system's structure, as two different layers contribute to covering the same healthcare expenditures (the Sécurité sociale and a vast number of complementary insurance companies). As the French Council of Economic Analysis (Conseil D'Analyse Économique) noticed,

> Such an organisation entails high management costs and encourages an increase in healthcare costs. The current regulation of the complementary insurance market also encourages risk selection, which results in inequalities in access to insurance and healthcare.[41]

The different reforms on healthcare policies lead to a major finding: equal access to healthcare, enshrined in the constitutional provisions, is no longer strongly guaranteed. The empty nature of constitutional social rights can be highlighted in another field, related to access to job-replacement benefits and basic income.

C. Example 3: access to unemployment benefits and basic income

Under Sarkozy's presidency from 2007 to 2012 unemployment regulation was dramatically targeted. At that time, in a notable shift in political discourse, it was increasingly argued that welfare policies were wasteful and that only the 'deserving poor' should be entitled to social benefits. Above all, a strong emphasis was given to the need to tackle social security fraud. Hence, recent social welfare reform policies have focused on activation and incentive programmes as a sustainable way to distinguish between 'deserving' and 'undeserving' poor.[42] This introduction of activation policies took place within an old and controversial debate about the articulation of 'rights and duties' in the Welfare State.

As a matter of fact, the constitutional framework grants job-replacement income as a social right. Art. 11 of the 1946 Preamble states:

> All people who, by virtue of their age, physical or mental condition, or economic situation, are incapable of working, shall have the right to receive suitable means of existence from society.

This constitutional obligation to provide financial assistance to the most vulnerable was implemented through the social security system and the establishment of unemployment insurance in subsequent years.[43] However, despite there being more than six million jobseekers, only in the region of 2.2 million currently receive benefits provided by unemployment insurance. Entitlement to these unemployment benefits requires past contributions to the social security system, and the rules relating to this contributory requirement are complex.

Along with the unemployment benefit system, minimum wage policies have for decades been implemented. The latest one, and probably the most significant in the field of activation policies, is the *Revenu de solidarité active* (RSA), which is an earned income supplement, created in 2008.[44] The RSA allowance replaces some former statutory minimum wages. It aims to secure a minimum income to people, regardless of whether they work. In 2016, the amount of the RSA is €524 for a single person and €1100 per month for a couple with two children (household allowance excluded). These incomes are far below the poverty line. Furthermore, the minimum age for entitlement to minimum income benefits is 25 years old, unless the claimant has a dependent family. The justification for this is that the system encourages family solidarity to combat poverty. However, since 2000, the ECSR has always held that, in the absence of subsistence aid, the existence of other forms of supplementary or conditional assistance for young people would be insufficient to comply with the Social Charter. In September 2010, the RSA was extended to young active people, provided they have been engaged in a professional activity for at least the equivalent of two out of the previous three years. However, this reform, upheld by the Conseil Constitutionnel,[45] has had very limited impact; there have been very few beneficiaries due to some very strict legal conditions. In this vein, while noting the progress made by extending the RSA to some young people under 25, the ECSR has reiterated that under Article 13§1 of the Social Charter, the right to assistance presupposes that the person is unable to obtain resources 'either by his/her own efforts or from other sources'. Furthermore, family solidarity cannot be considered a sufficiently specific 'other source' of income for a person without resources, but rather takes the form of 'a moral value not legally defined'. Family solidarity does not provide persons in need with a clear and precise basis of social support, and, in addition, many families may not be in a position to supply the necessary minimum level of assistance.[46]

In this regard, some ambiguity remains at the core of the French social system. While the protection of the needy is conceived as a human right, other texts define social assistance differently: the general idea is that assistance is at the confluence of a twofold duty. For instance, the French Constitution claims, 'Each person has the duty to work and the right to employment' (Art. 5, Preamble of 1946). The two ideas expressed in the Preamble have been interpreted differently: whereas the constitutional right to work has been interpreted as a poorly consistent right, the duty to work has been significantly implemented by law.

The right to work is weakly monitored by the Conseil Constitutionnel: as a matter of fact, it neither implies the right to keep one's job nor the prohibition of lay-off plans on economic grounds.[47] Admittedly, the Conseil Constitutionnel's case law recognises its constitutional value; as the Council stated in 2006, the right to work imposes on the legislature the commitment to:

> lay down rules to ensure the right of everyone to get a job while ensuring the largest possible exercise of this right and, where applicable, endeavouring to remedy the precariousness of employment.[48]

However, the legislator's obligations are undermined by the Conseil Constitutionnel, which insists on the legislative margin of appreciation. As it stated,

> [T]he constitutional requirement deriving from the provisions referred to above implies implementing a policy of national solidarity in favour of retired workers. Parliament is, however, free to choose such concrete means of implementation as it shall see fit in order to comply with this requirement.[49]

In other words, the Conseil Constitutionnel does not consider itself to have jurisdiction to review the substantive content of legislative enactments in the fight against unemployment, and it has refused to decide whether the Constitution requires a liberal, non-interventionist policy or a social-interventionist one. Such jurisdictional self-restraint can also be found in the administrative law case law.[50]

On the other hand, unlike the constitutional right to work, the constitutional duty to work receives strong implementation. After Sarkozy's election, different reforms tightened the obligations of jobseekers for the receipt of social benefits. It should be noted that these were not strictly correlated to the crisis (the three bills introducing the activation policies were adopted right before the crisis),[51] but their implementation went alongside the growing effects of the economic crisis.[52]

Concerning jobseekers, unemployment benefits and minimum-income schemes cover people of working age but generally require that the person actively seek work. According to Article L5421-3 of the Labour Code, criteria for monitoring the job search imply 'positive acts and repeated genuine and serious job seeking', and a reasonable job offer cannot be refused without good reason (*see infra*). In this regard, the Constitutional Council stated that the right to unemployment benefits cannot be eliminated because it is subsidiary to the right to work. However, legal conditions making these benefits dependent on jobseekers' acceptance of a job or training offer[53] have been enforced by Law n° 2008-758 on the rights and duties of the unemployed.

Labour Code Art. L5411-6 details jobseekers' obligations. Henceforth, to be considered unemployed under French law, one must: i) be available for work as soon as the occasion presents itself and ii) participate and cooperate in the development and maintenance of one's individual job-search plan. Under the contract signed with the Pôle Emploi,[54] the jobseeker commits to iii) being actively and repeatedly searching for work and to iv) accepting a 'reasonable offer of employment'. This Act has restricted the number of job offers that unemployed people may refuse and has introduced penalties for refusals based on geographic mobility or wage levels.[55] Benefits are cancelled or suspended if the jobseeker refuses two reasonable offers of employment that are compatible with their skills and located within a 30 km radius of their home. Sanctions become more severe with the duration of unemployment. The general idea is that the more time passes, the more the pressure grows on jobseekers.

Meanwhile, the more severe the law, the tougher the administrative practices become. Sanctioning by job counsellors has become more coercive; a 2005 decree has made the sanctions easier to hand down and amenable to triggering after a shorter period.[56] The most severe include removal of the person from the unemployment list and suspension of unemployment benefits. Situations leading to these penalties are strictly defined by statute. Being struck off the unemployment list is an administrative sanction and must (in theory) be legally pronounced. Under the statute, jobseekers risk such sanctions if they fail to sign the Personalized Project of Access to Employment (PPAE), or if they refuse a reasonable job offer. In addition, Labour Code Art. L5412-1 provides that the penalty can be imposed on a jobseeker who 'refuses, without any good reason, to appear after being summoned by the *Pôle Emploi*'. However, in practice, the mere non-appearance following a notice or a simple unanswered phone call from the Pôle Emploi have been interpreted as an unjustified refusal. Thus, a report by the Pôle Emploi's Ombudsman has noted that unanswered phone calls, summonses that were never received due to an address change, and emails by the Pôle Emploi that ended up in the spam mailbox have led to removal from the unemployment list.[57] The severity of the legally established sanction and its effects (loss of benefits) stands in stark contrast with such arbitrary and disproportionate practices.

Similarly, the law of 1 December 2008 has framed an identical path for access to basic income. The government's aim was to simplify existing programmes and to fight poverty. The new system, replacing several existing programmes (including the former revenu minimum d'insertion (RMI)), is also available to the 'working poor' with very low incomes. The goal was to prevent situations where the jobseeker earns a certain amount of money by finding a job but then loses a social benefit of the same amount. In other words, the RSA was designed to guarantee higher incomes and to provide a financial incentive so that people who 'work more, earn more', according to Sarkozy's motto during the 2007 presidential campaign. At this time, one of the key features of the RSA is that it is conditioned on and requires some kind of counterpart: beneficiaries have enhanced obligations to seek employment. A recipient's RSA will be suspended after the refusal of reasonable job offers, except in cases of certain personal obstacles (especially child care). Welfare and Family Code (CASF) Art. L262–28 provides that RSA beneficiaries have the obligation to take the necessary steps to create their own activity or actions needed for better social and professional inclusion. People earning less than €500 per month are in a specific situation, according to Art. D262-65 of the Welfare and Family Code. After a social and professional review, they enter in the scope of a 'rights and duties' scheme under which poor people are required to follow a 'pathway to integration' by signing a contract. This contract can be a PPAE with Pôle Emploi. For people furthest removed from the labour market, a specific 'social and professional integration contract', called a 'mutual commitment contract', can be signed.[58] Recipients can be penalised for failing to abide by their 'integration contract' or refusing 'reasonable job offers' that match their profile.[59] Enforcement procedures and penalties that can be imposed by the local authorities (loss of the RSA) were recently amended in order to be more fair and equitable; this proceeding is supposed to respect the adversarial principle and to be gradual and proportionate.[60]

Moreover, regardless of the subsidies provided by Pôle Emploi or the RSA allowances, optional assistance may be available from local authorities. Some of these also require proactive and positive behaviour from the unemployed. Pursuant to administrative case law, a city hall is entitled to impose hours of community service for people to benefit from this optional assistance.[61]

These recent changes concerning increased control on jobseekers and the implementation of the RSA lead us to a main conclusion: the introduction of a kind of workfare policies,[62] albeit not referred to in such terms, has somehow changed the nature of French social welfare – setting out individual duties where before there were rights. This general shift of activation policies occurred during the earlier stages of the economic crisis. Its outcome, aggravated by the crisis, has led to numerous human tragedies. Indeed, the emphasis on scroungers' stigma has had some severe consequences: studies have demonstrated that the 'climate of fear' whipped up by official and media stories on benefits fraud either delay or prevent people in need from obtaining help. Hardening attitudes towards people suspected of being scroungers and cheats discourage poor people from applying for essential benefits. This non-take-up phenomenon is highlighted, especially with regard to the RSA.[63] Reports have also pointed to the burnout among social services' employees caused by lack of funding and staff shortages.[64]

Some alternatives have been experimented with in order to cushion the blow of these provisions. Offering social support to long-term unemployed people is one of them: one aim of these emerging policies is to improve assistance for jobseekers, in the framework of strengthened follow-up. Generally speaking, social support for long-term unemployed people has a twofold objective. First, it aims to facilitate the return to work of people without jobs, in a context of social crisis, unemployment and insecurity. Second, it seeks to enable people experiencing social exclusion to regain or maintain their independence. Many statutes refer to the idea of '*accompagnement*'. For instance, the *Projet Personnalisé d'Accès à l'Emploi* allows 'individually tailored employment support measures'.[65] One may also refer to Labour Code Art. L5131-3, which provides that people 'between ages 16-25 who are in difficulty and face a risk of professional exclusion are entitled to state support for the purpose of access to professional life', or Welfare and Family Code (CASF) Art. L262-27, which provides that 'the beneficiary of the RSA is entitled to social and professional support according to his/her needs provided by one single advisor'.

Covering a wider category of the population, the idea of social support (or professional coaching) tends to be ubiquitous, without being clearly outlined.[66] It is based on two main themes: information and training. On the one hand, statutes emphasize information: social services shall ensure that information on job opportunities is of sufficiently high quality to allow jobseekers to search and make informed decisions about applying for suitable jobs, and that employers receive applications from the most qualified applicants. Case law has recently made clear that this is a legal commitment. Whether from the Pôle Emploi[67] or from the Family Allowances Fund,[68] insufficient information on social benefits can risk legal liability. On the other hand, support through training is another form of activation policy. Specific employment contracts referred to as '*contrats aidés*' are intended to integrate jobseekers through economic activity and, in the long term, to help them find traditional, steady jobs. The '*contrats aidés*' have simultaneously a social and professional vocation.[69] They can be permanent or fixed-term contracts, are subsidized by the State and allow employers to be exempt from social contributions. However, these policies did not meet with their anticipated success: they are still a timid achievement and the number of these contracts remains very low.

These discouraging outcomes did not prevent politicians from attempting to justify and promote these types of programmes. For instance, Hollande's 'generation contract' matches a promise of the elected candidate. Created by the 2013-185 Act,[70] the *contrat de génération* helps to reduce social charges for companies who hire young people on open-ended long-term contracts and at the same time keep a senior worker employed until retirement. Furthermore, another difficulty of these 'social support' policies remains the lack of funding in social services: some official studies show that only 50% of the RSA's beneficiaries have a single advisor and less than half of them have signed an integration contract, although they are legal obligations.[71] And 75% of jobseekers have had a maximum of four interactions, including phone calls or emails, with their Pôle Emploi counsellor in a period of six months.[72] This finding obviously shows a gap between the law in the books, where constitutional and positive law provisions seem to be firmly guaranteed, and the law in action, where implementation programmes are failing mainly due to inadequate resources.[73]

Since the early 2000s, the goal of the different reforms – healthcare, retirement pension and job-replacement income – has been to reduce the social security budget's deficit. Their major outcome has been a slow decay of social welfare: 'responsibilisation' of the insured has put the blame on to those who are seen as opportunists taking advantage of the system rather than as people claiming the rights to which they are entitled. Nowadays, social security is seen less as a 'common good', as the '1945 Pact' intended, and more as a subsidiary system, focused on those deserving it. This change goes along with the increase of 'means-tested' benefits, aiming to assess poverty.

II. Assessing poverty: minimising the effects of the crisis on the poorest

Poverty continues in France: in 2012, in the region of 8.5 million people were living below the poverty line,[74] there were about two million people who lived on less than €645 per month, about 3.6 million were poorly housed, in the region of 690,000 had no personal home and approximately 3.5 million were recipients of food aid. Meanwhile, the intensity of poverty has clearly increased: overall, poor people are now further below the poverty line.[75] Single-parent families are particularly at risk of poverty: their proportion increased from 20.6% of the poor in 2011 to 22.3% in 2012. Similarly, one in five French children (about three million in total) lives in poverty, according to a UNICEF report, underlining that the number of minors facing hardship has grown consistently in recent years due to the economic crisis.[76]

Even though these odds are deplorable, they are evidence that the French Welfare State has cushioned the effects of the economic crisis:

> [W]ithout the redistributive effects of social transfers, the decline in living standards of 20 per cent of the poorest households [in France] would have been four times higher, which would have caused an explosion of inequality.[77]

Indeed, since the election of President Hollande, a political input on those living in greatest poverty has been made, increasing the State social transfers. But, since France is living in a time of financial constraints on public spending, a political choice has been made to reduce other social expenses: while targeted measures are increasing in order to secure a safety net to the most disadvantaged people, services and provisions provided under the principle of universality are dwindling. These changes to the Welfare State call for three comments: first, it is altering the general architecture of the French social system, which used to be grounded in the principle of universality; second, the social rights of the poorest often lack effectiveness because of funding shortfalls or ineffective implementation;

third, very few legal attempts to challenge these 'austerity lite' policies have been made yet, as litigation is not a tool commonly used by legal campaigners or NGOs.[78] To illustrate these three comments, two main examples will be given: the first deals with family policies; the second focuses on the right to housing.

A. Example 1: family policy: reducing the social security deficit or tackling child poverty?

French family policy has traditionally sought to narrow the gap in living standards between families with and without children. Beginning in the early 20th century, family policy has asserted that society has a duty to protect the family unit and to provide all families, especially large ones, with material assistance in the interests of children. From this point of view, the aim was to support families from a so-called 'universalistic' perspective, taking the form of social benefits designed to offset expenses related to having children.[79] This idea is reflected in Art. 10 of the 1946 Constitution Preamble, stating: 'The Nation shall provide the individual and the family with the conditions necessary to their development.' From the 1930s on, all kinds of two-children families have been progressively granted benefits without regard to household income or the parents' marital status. Among different allowances, the major family benefit is family allowance, which used to be a 'non-means-tested' income provided to families with two or more children.[80] Alongside this universal support, other more specific benefits supported single mothers and other vulnerable families. Notably, the former single-parent allowance guarantees a basic income to single-parent families.[81]

This strong family policy has raised many comments. On the one hand, the universalistic perspective of the family welfare system has been credited with producing one of the highest birth rates in Europe. On the other hand, it has also been severely criticised by studies showing a reversed redistribution effect: the higher their income, the more assistance families receive. This situation is due to the existence of various mechanisms supporting families, including tax measures such as the 'quotient familial' system: this method of Income Tax relief takes into account the number of dependent children. It mainly benefits higher-income families though it also enables middle-income families to fall below the threshold for tax liability.

After the crisis, in the early 2010s, family policy has refocused support to low-income families and child-care services.[82] Changes in France occurred in three stages. First, measures were implemented to cushion the effects of the crisis by offering tax breaks to low-income families[83] and by increasing the back to school allowance.[84] This family subsidy is a form of financial aid available to children aged 6 to 18, paid annually at the beginning of each school year. Its amount, which has been increased regularly, varies according to the child's age and the number of children in the household.

The second stage was the decision to put family allowances under a means-test while aiming to absorb the deficit of the social security family branch by 2017.

This has been a recurring political debate since the end of the 1990s: should social policies focus on formal equality, or should they focus on those who really need them?[85] The first brief attempt to put family benefits under means-tested conditions was made by the Jospin Government in 1997, several years before the crisis. The bill was then referred to the Conseil Constitutionnel by applicants pleading that there was a constitutional principle (PFLR) granting families a right to allowances irrespective of the household's financial situation, founded on its responsibility for bringing up and maintaining children. The Conseil Constitutionnel stated that:

> the entitlement of all families to family allowances irrespective of their financial situation cannot be regarded as one of the fundamental principles recognized by the laws of the Republic.[86]

Despite the validation of the Constitutional Court, the law, for political reasons, was repealed a few months after its entry into force. However, in 2014, the left-wing parliamentary majority decided to sustain the 'means-tested conditions' for family allowances.[87] Once again, the Conseil Constitutionnel upheld the bill.[88] The court's decision underlined the legislature's margin of appreciation in social policy-making, and considered that family policy is a whole, including family allowances, administered by social administrative bodies, and tax breaks. As long as the implementing decrees do not set thresholds that would breach the constitutional provisions of Art. 10 of the 1946 Preamble, the bill does not violate the Constitution.

The third step was marked mainly by the 2014 reform on gender equality.[89] In order to tackle gender discrimination, the Bill for Real Equality between Women and Men[90] has created a new kind of shared parental leave, introducing an extra 'use it or lose it' six months for fathers to encourage them to take time off with their children under three years.[91] Unfortunately, as the road to hell is paved with good intentions, this reform has led to the reduction of early childhood benefits. However, the decrease in cash support is allegedly counterbalanced by a major programme to develop child-care/preschool services, with the creation of 275,000 new places by 2018. This programme is accompanied by a plan to combat poverty and foster social inclusion with the aim of extending access to child care for disadvantaged families; 10% of places are reserved for children from families living under the poverty line.[92]

These different reforms have been interpreted as signalling a new political will to refocus support towards low-income families, and to strengthen the role of family support as a pillar of social policy.[93] However, as the French National Council against Exclusion stated,

> Clearly, the first objective of this reform is to reduce the family division's [of the social security system] deficit. Even though it gives a particular attention to poor families, it will have limited impact on the living conditions of poor

> children. Comprehensive reforms to social and family policies remain to be undertaken.[94]

The same finding could apply to housing policy.

B. Example 2: housing policy: proclaiming human rights, rather than implementing them

According to unofficial reports,[95] at least 3.5 million people are poorly housed or homeless in France and about five million people live in a precarious housing situation. This is due to real-estate prices doubling since 2000, while the average annual rent has increased by 3.6%. These evolutions take place in a context of a growing demand for housing, due to an ageing population and an increasing weakening of traditional family ties. The crisis has exacerbated this situation even more: rental evictions have dramatically increased while the economic crisis has encouraged the growth of migration flows. Families with children coming from Eastern Europe (most of them belonging to the Roma people) or African migrants are left without any shelter.[96] Slums, which had disappeared in the 1960s, have come back in French urban centres. According to a National Institute of Statistics and Economic Studies (INSEE) study, in 2012 in the region of 30,000 children in France were sleeping on the streets.[97]

This worrisome situation has appeared despite the existence of numerous social housing networks, various subsidised rent programmes (HLM) and a significant national effort relying on solidarity. Several housing allowances are paid by the Family Allowances Fund (CAF) to nearly six million households, under the provisions of Building and Housing Code Art. L301-1 II, which provides that:

> every person or family having particular difficulties, notably due to the inadequacy of one's resources or living condition, is entitled to aid from the community to access a decent and independent housing or to continue living in it.[98]

The *Allocation Personnalisée au Logement* (APL) is the key piece of the puzzle. This housing allowance is a 'mean-tested' benefit, whose amount may vary according to household income and rental rates.[99]

The French housing crisis has also been exacerbated despite numerous bills purporting to guarantee the right to housing. The 2007–290 DALO Act,[100] which established an enforceable right to decent housing, is one of the most famous abroad. Prior to the DALO Act, several housing laws already established the right to housing, including the Quilliot Act of 22 June 1982, the Mermaz Act of 6 July 1989 and the Besson Act of 31 May 1990. At about the same time, the Constitutional Council stated that housing for disadvantaged people was a response to a demand of 'national interest', and defined the possibility for everyone to have decent housing as an objective of constitutional value, based on the 1946 Constitutional Preamble and the principle of human dignity.[101] In this framework, one of the main provisions of the DALO Act is the creation of a legal cause of action for a broad range of individuals, including people who are homeless and those who are living in uninhabitable locations (for example, people who are threatened with eviction, housed in premises unfit for habitation or otherwise unhealthy or dangerous or who are housed in overcrowded places). It also encompasses people who have been waiting for an 'abnormally long' amount of time after applying for social housing. The DALO Act declares that the right to decent and independent housing is guaranteed by the State. The State is bound by an obligation of result and not merely of best efforts. To that end, the Act introduced a procedure for the effective allocation of housing, involving initial recourse to a *département* level mediation commission and then, if necessary, administrative court proceedings. Remedies at the administrative level include requiring the prefect to house the petitioner in a certain location or imposing a fine on the government, paid to a regional urban development fund.

Theoretically, the DALO Act provides an enforceable right to housing. However, there is 'still a long way to go from intention to implementation'.[102] Two main pitfalls can be underlined. The first is the difficulty of providing enough social housing to meet the need. Prior to the DALO, the Solidarity and Urban Renovation Act aimed to make the construction of social housing compulsory; it required 20% of all primary residential properties in every city to be social housing.[103] In 2013, these quotas have reached 25% in some specific areas.[104] Furthermore, via urban development funds created in each region, the DALO penalties paid by the State are intended to help finance social housing construction. However, the law may be doomed to fail due to the reluctance of the richest towns to comply with the law and the lack of resources of the poorest ones, aggravated by the effects of the financial crisis on local budgets. The DALO enforcement reports show important differences in terms of tensions regarding access to housing, the Île-de-France region being particularly affected. The argument of 'pressure' related to the DALO is not really relayed by State services to local partners to push them to develop the offer. According to some authors, the system of the enforceable right to housing may even widen the existing gap between municipalities that choose to comply with the legal obligations and those that do not.[105]

However, the reason behind the DALO's failure is not only the poor housing supply. A second cause is structural, due to the legal scheme itself and French judges' lack of power to enforce the law. This was clearly demonstrated by a 2015 ECHR decision[106] in a situation where the applicant had not been re-housed after a case under the DALO provision and the judgment had not yet been fully executed. While the fine ordered in that judgment had been paid by the State, it had no compensatory function and was paid to a State-run fund rather than to the applicant. The court took the view that the French Government could not rely on a lack of resources to explain why the applicant, despite the order that the matter be dealt with urgently, had still not been re-housed more than three and a half years later. Consequently, by failing for several years to take the necessary measures to comply with the decision, the French authorities had deprived Article 6§1 ECHR of all useful effect. The court thus found that there had been a violation of this provision.

Due to the recurring difficulties implementing the right to housing, which remains weakly enforceable despite the law, the question of housing has been recently transformed into the right to shelter. As described above, increasing homelessness has created a growing need for emergency shelters. This has led to the foundation of the Urgent Medical Aid Service (Service d'Aide Médicale Urgente) (SAMU) social, first in Paris, and then in all major French cities. This emergency service was established in 1993 to provide temporary shelter and medical care to homeless people. It runs a 24-hour emergency telephone number alert for homeless people (115, which is toll-free). Subsequently, the 2009-323 Act granted an enforceable right to shelter,[107] providing that 'every homeless person facing situations of medical, psychological or social distress shall have access to an emergency shelter assistance anytime', protecting human dignity. This right is widely recognised, whereas the DALO placed restrictions based on immigration status.

However, the lack of funding for the emergency shelter budget has jeopardised the ability to provide effective assistance.[108] For example, during the winter of 2013–14, only in the region of 138,000 nights were granted out of the approximately 355,000 requests made to the SAMU social. A Fédération nationale des associations d'accueil et de réinsertion sociale (FNARS) study[109] showed that in 2011, two out of three calls (65%) to the emergency number 115 were unsuccessful and 75% of families with children received a negative answer. In this alarming context, a new policy was launched by M. Valls' government on 21 January 2013. A multi-annual plan for emergency shelter has allocated in the region of €1.3 billion. However, in spite of this governmental effort, the plan has limits. The first, and perhaps the most important, is a lack of available shelters. The Conseil d'Etat (the highest administrative jurisdiction) stated that the state has a 'best efforts obligation', rather than an obligation of result. Consequently, the judge stated that 'it belongs to the *département* prefect to take over the requests and to determine, through all available means, the types of arrangements required, considering the person's age, health status, and family situation'.[110] Yet, the 'available means' may be scarce. For example, since 2009, the State has focused on housing rather than on shelter:[111] the programme 'Housing First' places financial priority on access to housing, instead of on emergency shelters.[112] As a result, shelter programmes remain underfunded, and the accommodation and social integration centres (CHRS) tighten their eligibility criteria, leading to the spectacle of what has been described as a 'Thénardier syndrome' (in Paris and its suburbs, 22% of temporary shelter is provided by shabby private hotel rooms, as compared to 9% in 2001).[113]

Another worrying consequence is the emergence of slums ('bidonvilles') at the margins of some French cities: makeshift camps of Roma people, refugees or homeless people are regularly dismantled by the police, with the approval of the judges.[114] In this context, the most remarkable change in case law may be a recent decision stated by the Conseil d'Etat, on the situation of the refugees' camp in Calais, known as 'the Jungle'. The situation there has been appalling for years, as refugees seeking asylum in the UK have been gathering in slums near the city. It has further degenerated due to the massacres committed in Syria and the exodus towards Europe of its population. In November 2015, the French administrative supreme court ordered the Pas-de-Calais préfecture to begin rubbish collection, install clean water points and identify and protect unaccompanied minors within the slum, acknowledging that the vulnerable population had been left with no protection from the State, amid living conditions that exposed them to inhuman and degrading treatment, in violation of the State's obligation to protect human dignity.[115]

The case has brought to life the worrisome issue of unaccompanied migrant minors.[116] Under the child welfare provisions (*Aide sociale à l'enfance*), local authorities (*départements*) are legally obligated to help foreign unaccompanied minors and provide them with housing, food, education and care.[117] However, only 40% of foreign youths needing to be taken into care are actually accepted. Bureaucracy, limited resources and lack of political will lead local authorities to use different legal loopholes to turn minors away. These include the use of bone tests to (falsely) determine the age of the migrant and detention in facilities at borders.[118] Several *départements* illegally adopted administrative orders rejecting any new applications from isolated young migrants. A new national policy, framed to protect, evaluate and orientate unaccompanied minors was launched on 31 May 2013, but is not yet fully implemented.[119] As a general conclusion, the French system still lacks sufficient government funding to meet the requirements of guardianship laid out by French law, European law or the United Nations Convention on the Rights of the Child (UNCRC).[120] The situation has been severely criticised by the Défenseur des droits (French Ombudsman): while aware of the impact on local finances of the arrival of numerous unaccompanied minors, the Défenseur des droits reminds *départements* of their legal obligation, under Welfare and Family Code Art. L221-1, to place children at risk into care, regardless of their migrant status.[121]

The issue of the right to housing and to shelter is a perfect illustration of the French situation: despite legal provisions granting a theoretically enforceable right, strong difficulties in their implementation remain. Due to lack of funding in public services and the decision to allocate resources to some needs, rather than to others that are politically controversial (such as migrants), the right has been rendered meaningless.

As a conclusion, two main lessons can be drawn from the examples of French family and housing policies: despite the crisis, or perhaps because of it, and in an attempt to cushion its effects, the laws granting social rights to protect families and access to housing have not been tightened. Quite the opposite, some specific measures have been implemented to focus on the situation of those most vulnerable. Family allowances have been put under means-tested conditions, and access to housing, water and basic resources has been granted by the law. However, these remedies may be ineffective, due to the lack of funding for local authorities charged with their implementation, and the lack of information among beneficiaries ('non-take-up phenomenon').

Sometimes, this non-implementation may be explicitly claimed and justified by the crisis.[122] However, most of the time, non-implementation of these rights is simply not addressed and is ignored by the authorities. This finding leads to another comment: by focusing on the poorest, recent laws have been criticised for somehow changing the traditional approach of the French solidarity system that used to rely on equality: equal rights granted to each and every person.

III. Conclusion

French social reforms, in a context of economic crisis, can be read in two different ways. The first, which is optimistic, focuses on the fight against poverty and social exclusion. It depicts a generous French welfare system, granting social rights as true human rights. As the 1998 Social Exclusion Act stated:[123]

> [M]easures to combat exclusion are a national necessity based on respect for the equal dignity of all human beings and must be accorded priority in every sphere of national policy. Efforts to combat exclusion are aimed at guaranteeing throughout the territory effective access to all fundamental rights in the areas of employment, housing, health protection, justice, education, training and culture, family and child protection.[124]

This logic of social rights as human rights has led to a new approach by welfare programmes, allowing the building of a 'welfare state by the rule of law'.[125] In this respect, the focus on the poorest has helped to cushion the impact of the crisis, which has been less devastating in France than in some other European countries. The French welfare system, grounded on solidarity, has somehow functioned as a shock absorber, protecting the weakest.

The second, more pessimistic view, highlights two major pitfalls of these reforms. First, a rendering of rights as meaningless: while theoretically granted, the rights remain hollow and lack implementation, mainly due to lack of funding. Second, the focus on poverty leads to an increasing reluctance of taxpayers to contribute to a social security system from which they often feel excluded. Stigmatisation towards people living on welfare and migrants, imagined to be profiteers or scammers, is publicly expressed in political discourse. In this respect, the French welfare system, which used to be founded on equality, is showing cracks and the economic crisis is compounding the issue. An official report from the former Médiateur de la République, published at the beginning of the economic crisis, pointed out the distress among a growing number of citizens whose life is characterised by disruptions and, simultaneously, the declining efficiency of social responses in terms of solidarity policies. Far from alleviating citizens' problems, the social security net, meant to reduce shocks, at times inflicts more harm on those it is supposed to help. The report also highlights how,

> finally, our system as a whole is weakening from year to year. Those days when 'community life' was based on the existence of common rules, local authorities who enforced them, and citizens who knew and adhered to them seem to be over. Collective hope has given way to collective concerns and media-induced emotions . . . The main factors of consensus in our society seem to have become obsolete: a diploma no longer guarantees a job; State intervention no longer guarantees the correction or elimination of injustice. Our society, in search of a *raison d'être*, is today more exhausted psychologically than physically.[126]

Notes

1 Charles Rist, 'The Financial Situation of France' (1938) 16(4) *Foreign Affairs*.

2 See generally, Cour des Comptes, *Certification of the French General Social Security System, Financial Statements for 2014* (22 June 2015) <www.ccomptes.fr/en/Publications/Jurisdictions/(filters)/publications-parent_juridiction_s:Cour%20des%20comptes/(sort)/attr_date_filter_dt;desc>.

3 This programme, due for 2016, involves the creation of 500,000 vocational training schemes, additional subsidies for small companies hiring youths or long-term unemployed people and a programme to boost apprenticeships.

4 See, e.g., 'Our Saving Program is No Austerity Plan', *Le Monde* (Paris), 16 April 2014; 'There is No Austerity Policy in France', *Le Point* (Paris), 7 April 2015.

5 Cited in Leila de Comarmod, Marie Bellan and Etienne Lefebvre, 'Laurent Berger: Arrêtons de nourrier la désespérance sociale', *Les Echos* (online), 15 March 2015: 'Les mots ont un sens. Il y a de la rigueur, des gens en bavent mais il n'y a pas d'austérité en France. Nous avons obtenu une hausse des minima sociaux, les salaires n'ont pas baissé.'

6 Former Prime Minister François Fillon, Declaration on General Policy at the Assemblée Nationale on 24 November 2010.

7 'Deficits: No Loosening or Austerity, According to Moscovici', *AFP* (online) 4 March 2013.

8 *Social Security Code* (Fr) Art. L111-1.

9 See Robert Castel, 'Au-delà du salariat ou en deçà de l'emploi? L'institutionnalisation du précariat?' in Serge Paugam (ed.), *Repenser la solidarité: l'apport des sciences socialism* (PUF, 2007) 416.

10 *Loi n° 2010-1330 du 9 novembre 2010* (Fr).

11 *Loi n° 2014-40 du 20 janvier 2014* (Fr). For the long-career retirement pensions, see *Social Security Code* (Fr) Art. L351-1-1.

12 Haut Autorité de Lutte Contre les Discriminations et Pour L'équalité (HALDE), *Deliberation n° 2010-202*, 13 September 2010.

13 Christel Collin, 'Retraites: les femmes perçoivent une pension inférieure de 26 % à celle des hommes en 2012' (2015) 904 *Etudes et résultats*.

14 *Décret n° 2014-566 du 30 mai 2014* (Fr) relatif à la prise en compte des périodes de perception des indemnités journalières d'assurance maternité pour la détermination des périodes d'assurance vieillesse.

15 Sylvaine Laulom, 'Legal Effects of the Economic Crisis on Gender Equality Issue' (2012) 2 *European Gender Equality Law Review* 70.
16 See O Bui Xuan, *Le droit français entre universalisme et différencialisme* (Economica, 2004).
17 National health insurance funds are organised into national and local funds, all of which are private organisations charged with the provision of a public service.
18 This protection has been strengthened by the recent Social Security Financing Act for 2016: see *Loi n° 2015-1702 de 2016* (Fr) Art. 59, which creates a universal health cover ('protection universelle maladie').
19 *Loi n° 99-641 du 27 julliet 1999* (Fr).
20 *Social Security Code* (Fr) Arts L380-1–L380-4.
21 *Social Security Code* (Fr) Arts L861-1–L861-10.
22 Oxfam, *The True Cost of Austerity and Inequality: France Case Study* (September 2013)<www.oxfam.org/sites/www.oxfam.org/files/cs-true-cost-austerity-inequality-france-120913-en.pdf>.
23 For a comprehensive analysis, see B Palier and A Davesne, 'France: Squaring the Health Spending Circle?' in E Pavolini and A Guillén (eds), *Healthcare Systems in Europe under Austerity: Institutional Reforms and Performance* (Palgrave Macmillan, 2013).
24 Ibid 115.
25 *Social Security Financing Act for 2014 2013* (Fr) Art. 56; *Décret n° 2014-1374 du 18 novembre 2014* (Fr).
26 Palier and Davesne, above n 23, 115.
27 P Warin, *What is the Non Take-Up of Social Benefits* (9 June 2014), Books and Ideas <www.booksandideas.net/What-is-the-Non-Take-up-of-Social.html>; P Warin, 'Non-demand for Social Rights: A New Challenge for Social Action in France' (2012) 20(1) *Journal of Poverty and Social Justice* 41.
28 Franck von Lennep (ed.), 'Renoncement aux soins: actes du colloque' (Report, French Ministère du Travail, de l'Emploi et de la Santé, 2012); Héléna Revil, 'Le non-recours aux soins de santé', *La Vie des idées* (13 May 2014) <www.laviedesidees.fr/Le-non-recours-aux-soins-de-sante.html>.
29 European Committee on Social Rights, *Conclusion 2013: France, Art. 11-1* (2013) 2013/def/FRA/11/1/EN, Decision date 6 December 2013, Session no. 264, date of publication 7 January 2014.
30 CMU, 'Fonds de financement de la protection complémentaire de la couverture universelle du risque maladie: Evaluation de la loi CMU' (Report No 4, CMU, July 2009) 82.
31 *Public Health Code* (Fr) Art. L1110-3.
32 Cécile Prieur, 'A Paris, 25% des médecins refusent des patients bénéficiant de la CMU', *Le Monde* (online) 1 July 2009.
33 Stéphane Brissy, Anne Laude and Didier Tabuteau, *Refus de soins et actualités sur les droits des maladies* (Presses EHESP, 2012).
34 *Welfare and Family Code* (Fr) Arts L251-1–L251-3.
35 According to whom, 'in restoring the rule that State medical assistance is to be free of charge for foreign nationals illegally resident in France, Parliament did not breach the requirements stipulated in the eleventh recital to the 1946 Preamble': Constitutional Council, Decision No 2012-654 DC, 9 August 2012, Supplementary Law on finances for 2012.
36 *Médecins du Monde–International v. France* (European Committee on Social Rights, C-67/2011, 11 September 2012).
37 See also Palier and Davesne, above n 23, 122, according to whom, in addition to social inequalities, territorial inequalities have become a major issue.

38 See P Le Gand, 'Crise financière et ressources des collectivités territoriales' (2012) 144(2) *Revue française d'administration publique* 943.
39 In one decision, the Administrative Supreme Court repealed the closing of a hospital ward, due to financial constraint. The Conseil d'Etat stated that the hospital had made a manifestly incorrect appraisal of the measures to be taken in order to reduce costs, based on the needs of the population (Conseil d'Etat, Decision No 73788, 20 February 1990). However, the decision has never been renewed or repeated, despite a persistent spread of closing in the health sector.
40 Cyril Doumergue and Pierrick Merlet, 'Le planning familial en danger de disparition' *La Dépêche du midi* (online), 16 January 2015; Le planning familial, *Non aux baisses de subventions! Planning Familial en danger!* <http://isere.planning-familial.org/pages/non-aux-baisses-de-subventions-planning-familial-en-danger-00237>; Esther Griffe, 'Avenir fragile au Planning familial', *Marsactu* (online) 6 June 2014.
41 Brigitte Dormont, Pierre-Yves Geoffard and Jean Tirole, 'Rebuilding the Health Insurance System' (Les Notes du Conseil d'Analyse Économique No 12, Conseil D'Analyse Économique, April 2014).
42 For a more detailed analysis, see D Roman, 'Activation Policies for the Unemployed in France: "Social Debt" or "Poor Laws"?' in E Dermine and D Dumont (eds), *Activation Policies for the Unemployed, the Right to Work and the Duty to Work* (2014) 79 *Work & Society* 77.
43 Unemployment insurance in France was first established in December 1958 by an agreement concluded by Trade Unions and Employer associations.
44 The *Family and Welfare Code* (Fr) L115-2 establishes that 'the social and professional insertion of the people living in a vulnerable situation contributes to the national necessity of combating poverty and social exclusion. The RSA provides households that lack any form of resources with a minimum income and supplements the earned income of recipients whose income is insufficient to enable them to escape poverty or who are at the bottom of the wage ladder. The beneficiary has a right to a social and professional support in order to facilitate his/her sustainable insertion in employment.'
45 Conseil Constitutionnel, Decision No 2009-599 DC, 29 December 2009 [97].
46 European Committee on Social Rights, *Conclusion 2013: France, Art. 13-1* (2013) 2013/def/FRA/13/1/EN.
47 Conseil Constitutionnel, Decision No 2006-545 DC, 28 December 2006.
48 Conseil Constitutionnel, Decision No 2006-535 DC, 30 March 2006 [19].
49 Conseil Constitutionnel, Decision No 2010-617 DC, 9 November 2010.
50 Administrative Court of Appeal Nancy, Decision No 06NT00644, 30 June 2006.
51 *Loi n° 2006-339 du 23 Mars 2006* (Fr); *Loi n° 2008-758 du 1 août 2008* (Fr); *Loi n° 2008-1249 du 1 decembre 2008* (Fr).
52 It should also be taken into account that there have been no global French activation policies, unlike the 'Work First' programme in the Netherlands or the German '*Fordern und Fördern*'. Only specific and non-coordinated policies were launched, especially in the field of migration, school attendance and access to care. Despite this fragmentation, some overall strategy can be noticed: Their common goal is both to rely on individual responsibility and flexibility to fit into the labour market and to act on individual variables (compensation, behaviour, occupational and geographical mobility) to suit its needs.
53 Conseil Constitutionnel, Decision No 94-657 DC, 25 January 1995.
54 According to *Labour Code* (Fr) art L5411-6-1.
55 *Labour Code* (Fr) arts L5411-6 – L5411-6-4.
56 *Décret n° 2005-915 du 2 août 2005* (Fr).

57 Médiateur National de Pole Emploi, La *Gestion de la Liste des Demandeurs dEemploi: Les Radiations* (Special Report, Pole d'Emploi, January 2013).
58 *Welfare and Family Code* (Fr) art L262-29.
59 *Welfare and Family Code* (Fr) art L262-37.
60 *Décret n° 2012-294 du 1 mars 2012* (Fr); *Welfare and Family Code* (Fr) arts R262-40, R262-68.
61 Conseil d'État, Decision No 193716, 29 June 2001.
62 E Dermine and D Dumont (ed.), *Activation Policies for the Unemployed, the Right to Work and the Duty to Work* (2014) 79 *Work & Society* 77.
63 P Warin, 'Non-demand for Social Rights: A New Challenge for Social Action in France' (2012) 20(1) *Journal of Poverty and Social Justice* 41.
64 Rémi Barroux, 'La souffrance au travail des salariés de Pôle emploi' *Le Monde* (online) 19 October 2009; M Daniel Jamme, 'Pôle emploi et la réforme du service public de l'emploi: bilan et recommandations' (Report, Economic, Social and Environmental Council, June 2011).
65 *Labour Code* (Fr) art L5411-6-1.
66 A Fretel, 'La notion d'accompagnement dans les dispositifs de la politique d'emploi: entre centralité et indetermination' (2013) 11(1) *Revue française de socio-économie* 55.
67 Cour de Cassation, Sociale, Decision No 10-30892, 8 February 2012.
68 Cour de Cassation, Sociale, Decision No 269, 12 October 1995, 195; Cour de Cassation, Civile, Decision No 02-30997, 25 May 2004.
69 D Baugard, 'L'accompagnement dans l'emploi' (2012) 6 *Revue de Droit sanitaire et social* 994.
70 *Loi n° 2013-185 du 1 mars 2003* (Fr).
71 Ministère du Travail, de L'Emploi de la Formation Professionelle et du Dialogue Social, 'L'accompagnement des bénéficiaires du revenu de solidarité active (RSA)' 2013(8) *Dares Analyses* 1.
72 Cour des Comptes, *Pole Emploi à l'épreuve du chômage de masse* (7 July 2015) <www.ccomptes.fr/Accueil/Publications/Publications/Pole-emploi-a-l-epreuve-du-chomage-de-masse>.
73 This idea will be substantially developed in part. II.
74 The most often used poverty threshold is equivalent to 60% of the median standard of living (half earns more, the others earn less). It amounts to €993 per month in 2015.
75 Insee, *Online Statistics* (20 December 2017) <www.insee.fr/fr/themes/document.asp?reg_id=0&ref_id=T15F055>.
76 UNICEF, 'Chaque Enfant Compte. Partout, tout le temps' (Report, UNICEF, 2015).
77 Oxfam, above n 22.
78 With the notable exception of trade unions, in the field of labour work, or NGO's dedicated interest in migrants' rights. For an analysis of this general finding, see L Israel, *L'arme du droit* (Presses de Sciences Po, 2009).
79 Michel Legros, 'Tackling Child Poverty and Promoting the Social Inclusion of Children: A Study on National Policy' (Report, European Commission DG Employment, Social Affairs and Equal Opportunities, May 2007).
80 *Social Security Code* (Fr) art L521-1.
81 *Welfare and Family Code* (Fr) art L262-9. The additional income to RSA grants monthly €879,84 for a single parent with one child, €1099 for a single parent with two children and €219,96 for every supplementary child.
82 O Thévenon, W Adema and N Ali, 'Family Policy in France and Europe: Recent Changes and Effects of the Crisis' (2014) 512 *Population & Societies* 1.
83 *Loi n° 2013-1278 du 29 décembre 2013* (Fr) art 3.

84 *Social Security Code* (Fr) arts L543-1 to L543-2.
85 See B Fragonard, 'Les aides aux familles' (Report, Haut Conseil de la Famille, 9 April 2013).
86 Conseil Constitutionnel, Decision No 97-393 DC, 18 December 1997, [26]–[41].
87 *Loi n°2014-1554 du 22 décembre 2014* (Fr) art 85.
88 Conseil Constitutionnel, Decision No 2014-706, 18 December 2014, [27]–[36].
89 *Welfare and Family Code* (Fr) art L262-9. The maximum monthly amount is €879,84 for a single parent with one child, €1099,8 for a single parent with two children and €659,88 for a single pregnant woman.
90 *Loi n° 2014-873 du 4 août 2014* (Fr).
91 *Social Security Code* (Fr) art L531-4. In 2015, the maximum monthly amount is €390,52.
92 *Welfare and Family Code* (Fr) art L214-7.
93 Thévenon, Adema and Ali, above n 82.
94 Conseil National de Lutte Contre l'Exclusion, *Avis sur la pauvreté des enfants en France* (8 July 2013) <www.cnle.gouv.fr/8-juillet-2013-Avis-du-CNLE-sur-la.html>: 'il est clair que le premier objectif de cette réforme est de réduire le déficit de la branche famille : même si elle accorde une certaine attention aux familles démunies, son impact restera limité sur les conditions de vie des enfants en situation de pauvreté. Une réforme approfondie des politiques familiales et sociales reste à entreprendre'.
95 Abbé Pierre Foundation, *State of Bad Housing* (Report, Abbé Pierre Foundation, 12 August 2013).
96 E Le Méner and N Oppenchaim, 'The Temporary Accommodation of Homeless Families in Ile-de-France: Between Social Emergency and Immigration Management' (2012) 6(1) *European Journal of Homelessness* 83; O Trostiansky, 'Migration and Homeless People in Paris' (2010) *FEANTSA Homeless in Europe Magazine* 7.
97 Françoise Yaouancq *et al.*, 'L'hébergement des sans-domicile en 2012' (2013) 1455 *Insee Première* 1.
98 For a general overview, see Blanche Guillemot and Olivier Veber, 'Evaluation des aides personnelles au logement' (Report, IGAS, May 2012).
99 *Building and Housing Code* (Fr) art L351-1.
100 *Loi n° 2007-290 du 5 mars 2007* (Fr).
101 Conseil Constitutionnel, Decision No 90-274-DC, 29 May 1990; Conseil Constitutionnel, Decision No 94-359-DC, 19 January 1995.
102 C Lévy-Vroelant, 'The Right to Housing in France: Still a Long Way to Go from Intention to Implementation' (2015) 24 *Journal of Law and Social Policy* 88.
103 *Loi n° 2000-1208 du 13 décembre 2000* (Fr) art 55. The Conseil Constitutionnel stated that the obligation for municipalities to comply with a minimum quota of 20% of social housing on their territory, as set down by law, did not breach the constitutional principle of free administration of local authorities: Conseil Constitutionnel, Decision No 2000-436-DC, 7 December 2000.
104 *Loi n° 2013-61 du 18 janvier 2013* (Fr) art 10; *Décret n° 2013-671 du 24 julliet 2013* (Fr); *Décret n°2013-670 du 24 julliet 2013* (Fr).
105 Jean-Philippe Brouant, 'Implementation of the Enforceable Right to Housing (DALO) Confronted by the French Regions' in N Houard (ed.), *Housing Europe – Social Housing in all its States* (La Documentation Française, 2011) 289–90.
106 *Tchokontio Happi v. France* (European Court of Human Rights, C- 65829/12, 9 April 2015).
107 *Welfare and Family Code* (Fr) art L345-2-2.

108 Danièle Hoffman-Rispal and Arnaud Richard, *Comité D'évaluation et de Contrôle des Politiques Publiques sur L'évaluation de la Politique de l'hébergement d'urgence* (Report No 4221, Assemblée Nationale, 26 January 2012).
109 FNARS, *Quelles sont les reponses apportées aux personnes sans abri pendant l'été?* (20 July 2011) <www.fnars.org/images/stories/positions/enquete/enquete_115_fnars_juillet.pdf>.
110 Conseil d'Etat, Decision No 356456, 10 February 2012: 'Il appartient aux services chargés, sous l'autorité du préfet, de prendre en charge les demandes qu'ils reçoivent et de déterminer, parmi les différents moyens d'intervention dont ils disposent, les modalités de prise en charge adaptées à chaque cas, compte tenu notamment de l'âge, de l'état de la santé et de la situation de famille de la personne intéressé'.
111 The French Minister for Housing, S. Pinel, declared: 'Notre objectif est de dépasser la seule réponse à l'urgence et d'aider les personnes les plus démunies à sortir définitivement de la rue, en les accompagnant dans un parcours d'insertion vers le logement.': see Préfet de la Région d'Ile de France, 'Sylvia Pinel entend faire de 2015 une année pour l'hébergement et l'accès au lodgement des plus démunis' (Press Release, 15 January 2015).
112 N Houard, 'The French Homelessness Strategy Reforming Temporary Accommodation and Access to Housing to Deliver "Housing First": Continuum or Clean Break?' (2011) 5(2) *European Journal of Homelessness* 83.
113 Abbé Pierre Foundation, above n 95, 15.
114 See, e.g., Cour de Cassation, Appeal No 14-220953, 17 December 2015. The European case law has contributed to increase the judiciary review on these evictions: see: *Winterstein v. France* (European Court of Human Rights, C-27013/07, 17 October 2013); *ATD Fourth World v. France* (European Court of Social Rights, Collective Complaint No 33/2006, 5 December 2007).
115 Conseil d'Etat, Decision No 394540, 394568, 26 November 2015.
116 For a general overview, see GISTI (ed.), 'Mineurs isolés, l'enfance déniée' (2014) 102(3) *Plein Droit*. According to studies, there would be 6 000 unaccompanied migrant minors in France.
117 *Welfare and Family Code* (Fr) art L221-1, defining the general missions of the child welfare services (Aide sociale à l'enfance).
118 An unaccompanied child may be held in a waiting zone, as confirmed by a decision of the Court of Cassation of 2 May 2001, which ruled that the law does not give any indication of the age of the persons who can be held in a waiting zone. As a result, there is nothing to prevent children from being held there: Court of Cassation, Civile, Appeal No 99-50008, 2 May 2001) However, the inability of the French system to properly protect the children's right to liberty has been condemned by the ECHR: see *Popov v. France* (European Court of Human Rights, C- 39472/07, 19 January 2012).
119 The policy has been partially upheld by the Conseil d'État: see Conseil d'État, Decision No 371415, 371730, 373356, 30 January 2015.
120 See, e.g., the European Parliament report, recalling 'that an unaccompanied minor is above all a child who is potentially in danger and that child protection, rather than immigration policies, must be the leading principle for Member States and the European Union when dealing with them, thus respecting the core principle of the child's best interests': European Parliament, *Report on the situation of unaccompanied minors in the EU* (Report 2012/2263(INI), 26 August 2013).
121 Défenseur des droits, Decision No MDE-2014-127, 29 August 2014.
122 For instance, a general principle of accessibility for all disabled persons was enacted ten years ago by *Loi n° 2005-102 du 11 février 2005* (Fr) on 'Equal rights and

opportunities, participation and citizenship of persons with disabilities'. Thus, buildings open to the general public, public transport, municipalities and public communication services were given ten years (by 2015) to become accessible. Due to financial constraints, implementation has been postponed for another three to nine years: *Loi n° 2014-1090 du 26 septèmbre 2014* (Fr).

123 *Loi n° 98-657 du 29 julliet 1998* (Fr). This bill was adopted by the left-wing majority under L. Jospin's government.

124 *Welfare and Family Code* (Fr) art L115-1.

125 D Roman, 'La Justiciabilité des Droits Sociaux ou les Enjeux de l'édification d'un État de Droit Social' (2012) 1 *Revue des droits de l'Homme*.

126 Law Médiateur de la République, *Annual Report* (2009) <www.defenseurdesdroits.fr/sites/default/files/atoms/files/mr_ra_2009_eng.pdf>.

Chapter 3

Germany

Ulrike Lembke

In 2003, Gerhard Schröder, Germany's social-democratic chancellor, announced 'Agenda 2010'. These reforms, by cutting both wage costs and welfare benefits, aimed to tackle the German recession, reduce the level of unemployment and improve the economy's competitiveness. Reforms of the statutory health insurance system and the centrepiece of the agenda, the so-called Hartz labour market reforms, were set in motion from 2003 to 2005. When the financial crisis hit in 2007, Germany was surprisingly unaffected. Despite analyses indicating otherwise,[1] successive German Governments have explained this in terms of their pre-emptive social cutbacks, urging other European countries to replicate Agenda 2010 as part of successful austerity policies.

The recent history of the German Welfare State can thus be characterised by radical reforms, conflicting concepts and rapid changes. National courts have played an important role in critically evaluating these reforms but have faced the difficulty that the German constitution does not cover explicit social rights and that the implementation of the fundamental principle of the social state is left mainly to political dispute and legislative discretion.

This chapter begins with an outline of the traditional place of social welfare within the German constitution, offering some details of key policy areas. It then goes on to describe the radical Hartz reforms to Germany's system of social welfare that, as noted already, predate the global financial crisis of 2007. Thereafter, the chapter examines significant constitutional litigation challenging aspects of the Hartz reforms. This litigation produced, for the first time in Germany, an articulation of a fundamental right to a guarantee of a dignified minimum existence. The significance of this jurisprudence is considered before the chapter concludes with a consideration of a potential future for social rights in German constitutional law.

I. Social security, the social state and social rights

A. Social state and social rights

Germany was a pioneer of modern state welfare. In the 1880s, imperial Chancellor Otto von Bismarck introduced the first health, injury and pension insurance schemes with the double aim to protect the workforce and to weaken the socialist movement whose leaders he insistently persecuted at the same time (a politics of carrot and stick).[2] During the short period of the Weimar Republic, social rights were covered by the constitution, trade unions gained influence, unemployment insurance was introduced and local social democratic politics dealt with public health, families and housing. But the financial crisis invalidated all efforts. The National Socialist Party promised and offered a nationalist–racist Welfare State based upon exclusion, exploitation and mass murder, and working for many Germans.

The history of the German Welfare State has to be taken into account when dealing with the fact that the 1949 German constitution did not cover social rights[3]. The parliamentary assembly shied away from introducing them, uncomfortable with binding the legislature in this way[4] and determining social order.[5] Even the suggestion of guaranteeing a subsistence minimum by prohibiting the improper refusal of minimum food, clothing and accommodation was rejected due to the fact that it would necessitate at least some public management of food, clothing and housing.

The introduction of the principle of the social state instead was intended to fill this gap. Despite the fact that its shape, meaning and limitations were never identified by the constitutional legislator,[6] the mainstream of legal discourse and jurisprudence took a pragmatic approach, framing the social state as a principle to shape society by legal means with the aim of a just social order, all within broad legislative discretion.[7]

The Federal Administrative Court, in one of its first decisions, emphasised that human dignity would prohibit treating citizens in need of subsistence as an object of state action.[8] Equally, the Federal Constitutional Court, although initially reluctant,[9] eventually acknowledged a public obligation to guarantee the minimum subsistence for a dignified existence.[10] It derived this position from the enshrinement of human dignity, in conjunction with the principle of the social Welfare State covered by basic German law.[11]

However, it must be noted that, at this stage in the development of German social welfare jurisprudence, the Federal Constitutional Court was not identifying a *right* to minimum subsistence. Rather, it was speaking of a state *obligation*. The fundamental rights laid down in the German constitution were generally understood, not as positive guarantees, but only as defensive mechanisms against the state, with few exceptions of institutional guarantees (e.g. marriage). Legal scholars, as well as lawyers, argued that the identification of a state obligation by the Constitutional Court implied corresponding entitlements of the potential benefit recipients. But notwithstanding individual rights covered by the respective statutes, *constitutional* social rights did not result from the principle of the social state.[12] Moreover, although human dignity enshrined in Article 1(1) of the German basic law has always been a very special part of the constitution – its foundation, the state's primary obligation, an objective basic value, inalienable and unlimited – it is not primarily understood as an individual right.

Conceptions of social security and welfare thus remained susceptible to the hierarchical relationship of a granting state and the recipient objects of welfare.

Legislation passed in order to realise the constitutional principle of the social state adhered to the traditional model of social security through social insurance. The conservative German Welfare State model was thus focused on insurance systems and not on the redistribution of wealth.

B. An outline of the German social security system

Generally speaking, Germany's social welfare system[13] was and is based on a current-disbursement principle, meaning that employees pay a certain percentage of their monthly income into the statutory health, care, unemployment and pension insurance funds by which they are insured under the respective laws.[14] Their employers, in turn, pay the same amount.[15]

Health

The health insurance system covers a broad range of treatments and services. Despite the privatisation of hospitals and medical services, access to these treatments and services was funded by the contributions of employees and employers and state subsidies. Unemployed persons are normally covered by the statutory health insurance system. The contributions are paid by the state. Every person, insured or not, is entitled to emergency medical aid regardless of the question of financing.

Housing

Public and legal debates in Germany do not centre on an explicit right to housing (although international human rights' treaties covering the individual social right to housing have force of law in Germany). Nonetheless, preventing and ending homelessness is an important state obligation that also flows from the principle of human dignity and the concept of the social state.

Unemployment

Prior to the Hartz reforms, social benefits for people unemployed or not able to work were paid in three categories: unemployment benefits, unemployment assistance and social assistance. Unemployment benefits were paid to persons who were insured under statutory unemployment insurance. The amount and the duration of pay depended upon the income and the duration of the former employment(s). Employable persons who were not entitled to unemployment benefits could receive state-financed unemployment assistance under the condition of annual means-testing. The amount of the unemployment assistance depended upon a hypothetical income of the respective profession with a view to securing a standard of living on a lower level. Unemployable persons without any other income or assets were entitled to municipality-financed social assistance covering the minimum subsistence level.

II. German welfare reforms after 2003: social cutbacks, conditionality, sanctions, activation and privatisation

A. From a conservative Welfare State to neoliberalism?

From the 1970s onwards, the Western German Welfare State, based as it was upon contributions from a strong workforce, faced severe problems. Industrial employment began to erode, unemployment rates started to increase, while, simultaneously, the labour-market-participation rates of women of all ages and of older and younger male workers remained especially low.[16] In the 1990s, Germany's reunification drove the economy into a full-blown labour market crisis. Mass unemployment and social deprivation hit Eastern Germany, leading to increasing social security deficits.[17]

The Agenda 2010 reforms were totally contrary to custom and people's expectations.[18] From an Anglo-American perspective, the policy move towards 'activation', co-payment for social services and marketisation may seem familiar, modest or even insufficient. But from the viewpoint of the traditional Bismarckian conservative Welfare State, the Western German wealthy ordoliberal Welfare State and the Eastern German socialist all-inclusive model of social security and social services, these reforms were radical[19] and disturbing.[20] Among several consequences, they led to the success of the newly founded party The Left and the loss of social-democratic chancellery in the 2005 federal elections.

B. Hartz IV: unemployment assistance cutbacks, 'activation' policies and pay discrimination

The key elements of the Hartz IV[21] reforms meant fundamental changes for many of the long-term unemployed and their families. Before 2005, tax-funded unemployment assistance followed the general idea of the wage-centered German 'social insurance state'[22] by generating a social entitlement deriving from employment and referring to the level of the recipient's hypothetical or previous income. Thus, the unemployment assistance secured a certain standard of living while the social assistance secured the minimum subsistence level. The key element of the Hartz IV laws was the integration of the unemployment assistance and the social assistance into one benefit scheme on the lower level and the introduction of 'activation policies'.

Merging unemployment and social assistance

An unemployed person who has previously contributed to unemployment insurance now receives earnings-based unemployment benefits, subject to an upper limit of 12 months. However, thereafter (or for employable persons who never contributed), he/she receives means-tested unemployment assistance, less generous than social assistance. Unemployment assistance covers basic subsistence ('Grundsicherung') as well as the reimbursement of accommodation and heating costs. Applying international definitions of poverty, recipients of unemployment assistance after the Hartz reforms are poor.[23] Further, any assets the recipient may own are offset against his or her entitlement to unemployment assistance, subject to an exemption of €200 for each year of a person's life – clearly insufficient to prevent poverty in old age.

The merging of unemployment and social assistance[24] was contradictory to the general consideration that unemployment benefits were previously paid for and therefore owed to the insured as a matter of right.[25] Many unemployed people felt bereft and expropriated, especially older people who became unemployed after many years of working and contribution payments.

The introduction of the 'needs unit'

The unemployed person, their partners and children now constitute a 'needs unit' ('Bedarfsgemeinschaft'). Means-testing is based upon the needs and income of this unit, rather than the constituent individuals. Thus, the assets and incomes of partners living in the same household are reviewed for possible deduction from unemployment assistance.[26] The offset of assets includes the property of children as well. Unmarried recipients of unemployment assistance under the age of 25 are considered to be part of the needs unit of their parents, thus cutting back the amount of their benefits and preventing them from setting up their own households. Moreover, the introduction of needs units has strengthened the financial dependence of women on a male breadwinner, husband or partner by ignoring the gender-hierarchical division of labour between paid employment and unpaid care work.[27]

Pay discrimination suffered by recipients of unemployment assistance

Jobseekers are obliged to accept any offer of 'suitable work'.[28] This includes having to accept precarious, marginal or very low paid work. This policy was accompanied by a deregulation of the temporary work sector and the introduction of exemptions for employers from restrictions on fixed-term working contracts and dismissals.[29] As early as 2003, so called 'mini-jobs' (monthly pay below €450 without any statutory social security) were established. Fifteen per cent of all unemployment assistance recipients perform mini-jobs, and are allowed to keep up to €160 of the additional monthly income.

Despite having higher qualifications, mini-jobbers receiving unemployment assistance are paid significantly lower hourly and monthly wages than mini-jobbers outside Hartz IV regulations, and contrary to expectations, mini-jobs have not worked as a bridge to the normal labour market.[30] Irrespective of astonishing differences concerning the data on persons living below the poverty-risk threshold (60% of average income for the total population) presented by the federal government,[31] the percentage of women and men concerned has not been decreasing since 2005 and children and youth, single parent households, migrants and Eastern Germans are still particularly affected.[32]

'Activating' and welfare conditionality

The centrepiece of the Hartz reforms was the introduction of 'activation policies', with the aim of pressuring the unemployed to re-integrate into the labour market as soon as possible.[33] Public employment agencies were restructured,[34] every jobseeker is now assigned a fixed caseworker, and the newly established jobcentres must now meet quantitative targets.[35] Activation policies are based upon welfare conditionality.[36] Entitlement to unemployment assistance depends upon applicants' availability for work and programme participation. Absence from their places of residence (e.g. for a vacation; to attend a conference or political action; to visit friends or relatives) has to be applied for and approved by the respective jobcentre and must not exceed 21 days per year.

The Hartz laws also introduced financial sanctions in the form of benefits deductions. For example, sanctions will be applied for: unauthorised absence; not attending programmes; failing to comply with individual integration agreements; missing a job interview, or declining a job offer. Since 2007, the first violation entails a 30% reduction in benefits for three months, the second a 60% reduction and, after the third violation within one year, all payments are cancelled, including accommodation and heating costs.[37]

However, German welfare reforms have not gone the 'whole nine yards' towards Anglo-American neoliberalism. Those who are not capable of working due to sickness, disability or care responsibilities, receive means-tested social assistance[38] and will be mostly spared from further activating measures.[39] Since 2012, there have been additional activation measures that do not focus solely on quick labour-market integration but on qualification and employability.[40] Equally, in 2015, statutory minimum wages were introduced because the working poor became a major problem in Germany.[41]

Hartz reforms and social justice

The annual costs and the deficits of the Federal Employment Agency have, however, reached enormous sums, while the social assistance costs reflect an expansion of poverty.[42] Time and again, the Agency had to tamper with the unemployment statistics to be able to announce any achievements. Especially in regions with high unemployment rates, activation policies are at risk of becoming arbitrary, creating, illegitimate pressure and humiliation. Further, the infrastructure privatisations of the 1990s (such as public transportation and postal services) have resulted in higher costs each year for these services, causing special hardship for jobseekers and further redistributing wealth from the poor to the rich.[43] While more and more households, especially single parents and their children, fall under the poverty or poverty-at-risk threshold,[44] the last decade was also an era when a generation of middle-aged West Germans increased their wealth through inheriting their parents' fortunes accumulated in better times. Social justice is in a downward spiral.

C. The reforms of the statutory health insurance system

The statutory health insurance system in Germany covers the prevention of illness, early diagnosis and treatment, medical rehabilitation, sickness benefits and pregnancy/maternity measures. In 2003, the contributions to the statutory health system exceeded 14% of individuals' gross income. Reforms from 2004 to 2009 were targeted at reducing working costs and a shifting of costs from health insurers to insured individuals.

Insurance contributions

Important health insurance contributions (dental prostheses and sickness benefits) have to be paid by employees alone since 2005. Social contribution rates were reduced and the VAT rate raised. Since 2009, the federal government has defined an equal contribution rate for all statutory health insurances but insurers are allowed to raise additional contributions to cover the real costs. Recipients of occupational pensions have had to pay full contributions to the statutory health insurance system for them since 2004.

Co-payment duties

Since 2004, there have been co-payment duties for many pharmaceuticals (although not for especially cheap drugs), medical products and special treatments, as well as for hospital stays. The total co-payment, however, must not exceed 2% of the insured's gross yearly income (1% when chronically ill). The exemptions from this system that social and unemployment assistance recipients had previously enjoyed were terminated. All insured have to pay for glasses and for travel expenses to doctors' premises. The insured are also wholly financially responsible for treatment of secondary diseases of 'self-inflicted' illness, such as the removal of piercings or tattoos. Doctors have to report these treatments to health insurers.[45]

Consultation fee

The 2004 health-insurance reforms introduced the obligation to pay a consultation fee of €10 per quarter with the aim of reducing the total number of consultations. A separate consultation fee was to be paid to dentists. Regular preventive check-ups as well as prenatal care were exempted from this pay duty. Patients who were referred by one doctor to another, for example, by a GP to a specialist, were not obliged to pay a consultation fee for the referred visit if the referral fell into the same quarter. The Federal Social Court held the obligation to pay a quarterly consultation fee to be in conformity with the constitution in 2009.[46] But with effect from 1 January 2013, the obligation to pay a consultation fee was cancelled as a result of the recognition that this obligation did not reduce the total number of consultations but hindered low-income earners and unemployed from seeking necessary medical assistance.

D. Costs of accommodation and privatisation of the housing market

In Germany, the majority (57%) of the population live in rented accommodation. An explicit right to housing was covered by the 1919 German constitution but not included in the German basic law in 1949. But everybody who cannot tackle special difficulties on his or her own is entitled to state support under sections 67 and 68 of the Social Code No. 12 for the finding and keeping of suitable housing. In cases of eviction or when a person finally fails to conclude a tenancy contract, the authorities are legally obliged[47] to provide temporary accommodation for the homeless in hostels, rented rooms or even confiscated apartments.

Unemployment assistance and social assistance include the costs of accommodation and heating. While the basic provision for jobseekers is financed at the federal level, accommodation and heating costs are provided by local authorities. However, these latter costs will only be borne when the accommodation is appropriate both in size and price. Otherwise assistance recipients are forced to terminate their tenancy contracts.

Despite affordable accommodation being hard to find, especially in metropolitan areas, since 2004, federal, regional and local authorities have been selling some hundred thousand apartments that had previously been owned, maintained and rented out by public housing agencies or associations. This public sellout was accompanied by severe cutbacks of social housing, causing an explosion of rents in many urban areas (with peaks in Berlin, which saw a 45% increase in rents from 2004 to 2014).[48] The unemployed will now, generally speaking, only succeed in concluding a tenancy contract in areas where landlords prefer the regular, albeit restricted, payments of the local authority.

Unemployment-assistance recipients may not only face homelessness due to rising rents or the fact that their apartment's size is two square metres beyond the benchmark. As already noted above, their provision of heating and accommodation costs can also be subject to a 100% penalty deduction.

E. Agenda 2010 and the global financial crisis

Were the above reforms the reason why the German economy remained surprisingly unaffected when the global financial crisis hit Europe? This is rather unlikely. It is true that, in contrast to most of its European neighbours, Germany experienced almost no increase in unemployment during the global financial crisis and its exports reached record amounts. However, this was not due to German austerity politics at home, such as welfare reforms, privatization, social cutbacks or taxation (the other important aspects of austerity politics)[49]. Instead, we must look to the following measures.

Decentralization of wage bargaining

Despite the high number and standards of labour-market regulations in Germany, wages and other working conditions are mainly set by the three labour-market parties: trade unions, employers' associations and works councils. The strong decentralisation of the respective negotiation processes from industry or regional level to the level of the single firm or even worker helped to bring down wages at the lower end of the wage distribution.[50] Germany had no statutory minimum wage before 2015 but focused on consensus-based negotiations under the principle of autonomy of wage bargaining. Under the pressure of the enormous costs of German reunification and the opening of Central and Eastern European economies with far lower wages and more flexible working regulations, the trade unions and works councils agreed to local wage settings and opening clauses. The Hartz reforms may have contributed to the increase in low wage inequality,[51] but they neither saved the German economy during the global financial crisis, nor even caused the decrease in the unemployment rate.

Beggar-thy-neighbour policy

Instead, the well-being of the German economy depended on strong export demand from its European neighbours[52] – the increase in wage inequality had caused a significant decrease in domestic consumption. Thus, when the German chancellor advises other European countries to replicate the Hartz reforms – meaning cutbacks in wages and labour costs – we must note that such a policy could only be successful if German wages increased simultaneously, producing a strong export market for its European neighbours.

High flexibility in working hours

Moreover, the behaviour of the German Government as well as employers during the crisis did not entirely follow the main ideas of the Agenda 2010. The government opted for economic-stimulus programmes and the support of short-time work. Instead of policies of hiring (during the boom) and firing (during recession), the social partners agreed on flexible working hours, including working-time accounts, overtime and short-time work down to 'zero hours'.[53] Governmental policy change and high flexibility concerning working hours were important factors for Germany being surprisingly unaffected by the crisis.[54]

Redistribution of low-paid work

The decrease in the unemployment rate was not matched by a corresponding increase of the total amount of working hours across Germany as a whole.

In 2012, the volume of work in Germany was equal to that of 1994. The decrease in the unemployment rate in Germany has been achieved through an increase in irregular and low-paid employment.[55] In 2013, more than 1.3 million employees were entitled to unemployment assistance despite doing paid work ('topping up'): 44% working in jobs that were subject to social security, 36% performing mini-jobs and 10% being self-employed.[56] At a very late stage, in 2015, the German government decided to introduce modest statutory minimum wages. Until then (and for many, until this very day) the saying 'making work pay' meant only that social benefit should stay beyond the lowest wages.[57]

III. The Federal Constitutional Court defining the minimum subsistence level: between human dignity and methods of calculation

In a significant judgment in February 2010, the Federal Constitutional Court decided that the provisions of the SGB II, covering the standard benefits rates for adults and children, were not in compliance with constitutional law.[58] The court stated a fundamental right to a guarantee of a dignified minimum existence following from human dignity enshrined in Article 1(1) of the German basic law in conjunction with the principle of the social Welfare State covered by Article 20(1) of the German basic law.[59]

A. Access to the Federal Constitutional Court

In 2007, a constitutional complaint questioning the constitutionality of the Hartz IV reforms was brought before the Federal Constitutional Court by benefit recipient. He argued that the Hartz legislation breached the rule of law (by lack of transparency and reliable data) and violated the principle of the social state, equality and his property rights. The Federal Constitutional Court rejected his complaint as inadmissible.[60]

In 2009, the Federal Social Court and the Higher Social Court of Hessen submitted three cases to the Federal Constitutional Court, focusing on the problem that children under the age of 14 were entitled to only 60% of the basic provisions, without any definition or ascertainment of children's needs, or any provisions for further age groups. The Federal Constitutional Court used the opportunity to make a landmark decision, though did not discuss the issue of child poverty, nor the deeper root of poverty and benefit-dependency in the life course of youths with poor parents.

B. Highlights of the decision and the scope of judicial review

The decision aroused mixed feelings among the community of social law scholars and lawyers, welfare associations and benefit-recipient organisations.[61] The identification of a human right to a guarantee of a dignified minimum existence constituted a landmark decision. But, at the same time, the court insisted that, in a democratic society, the realisation of this right was the duty of parliament and was a matter for legislative discretion. Thus, the court held that the scope of judicial review was limited[62] to the issue of arbitrariness in the formal method of calculating the minimum subsistence level.

Human dignity – a highest value becomes an individual right

Human dignity is enshrined in the first and most important article of the German constitution, binding all public authorities. It is the highest value of the constitution, inspiring the interpretation and implementation of all other fundamental rights and constitutional norms. Together with personal autonomy, it is the basis for personality rights whose requirements and restrictions derive from Article 2 of the constitution. The sole invocation of human dignity is very rare. It rules out the death penalty, torture and cruel punishment, and prohibits the objectification of human beings. Prior to the decision under examination here, the Federal Constitutional Court had explicitly employed human dignity in conjunction with the principle of the social Welfare State only to articulate a right to social rehabilitation after having served one's sentence.[63]

The social state – a gap in the court's decision

While human dignity as the foundation of the right to minimum subsistence promises the strongest constitutional protection, references to the social state offer very weak individual protection and entitlement. Locating the material realisation of the right within the discretion of the legislature creates a paradox, in that the reality of a right that flows from the highest value of the German constitution is left to parliament, which is bound by this very constitution. This problem is intensified by the lack of elaboration of the principle of the social state – the court has stuck to the tradition of vagueness and non-definition.[64] Thus, a right to minimum subsistence was outlined without going on to deal with questions of inclusion, distribution, autonomy or state–citizen relationships.

Outlining the right to a minimum subsistence level

Despite this gap, the court clearly stated that the right to a guarantee of a dignified minimum existence is not subject to the legislature's disposal. It must be honoured, irrespective of how it is lent concrete shape. More substantively, the right encompasses both the physical existence of an individual and his or her participation in social, cultural and political life, to be secured comprehensively. This identification of a socio-cultural minimum as an integral part of the dignified minimum subsistence level was one of the main innovations of the decision.

The court further held that the legislature must realistically and comprehensively assess all expenditure that is necessary for one's existence. Such assessment must use a transparent, expedient procedure, and be based on reliable figures and plausible methods of calculation.[65] The legislature may identify typical needs by means of a fixed monthly amount, but must grant additional benefits where there are special needs beyond the typical (albeit that such special needs must be irrefutable and recurrent).

Application of the new right to the benefits in question

The Constitutional Court noted that it could not consider the basic provisions of €345, €311 and €207 introduced by the Hartz legislation to be manifestly insufficient. Yet, at the same time, these levels of assistance had not been determined in a constitutional manner by using a suitable method, relying on all necessary facts, sticking to the chosen method in all stages and dealing with plausible figures. Accordingly, the court held that the standard benefits would remain applicable until legislative amendments took place, but not beyond 2010.

C. The calculation of the minimum subsistence level

The Statute on the Calculation of Standard Benefits entered into force from 1 January 2011, its draft having been the subject of heated political discussions due to the fact that the proposed method of calculation only led to a minimal increase in benefits levels.[66] The Statute provides for the method and procedure of benefits calculations, with provisions for adjustment each year in light of price and wage developments. The standard benefits for children and youths are further differentiated. Single parents, pregnant women and persons with disability are entitled to additional payments. Education benefits for children are non-cash benefits, that is, vouchers that are often not redeemed.

In 2012, the Social Court of Berlin initiated a preliminary ruling procedure before the Federal Constitutional Court, querying the constitutionality of the calculation methods on several bases: a change of method within the calculation process; a lack of justification for the exemption of several needs;[67] and the idea that the standard benefits had to stay beyond the lowest income, which the court felt could contribute nothing to the question of the minimum-subsistence level.[68] In July 2014, the Federal Constitutional Court held that the calculation methods were indeed constitutional when regularly adjusted to avoid structural underfunding.[69] Nonetheless, the standard benefits were not increased significantly until 2015: to €399 per month for single adults; €360 for spouses, civil partners and live-in partners; €302 for youth from 14 to 17 years of age; €267 for children under the age of 14 years; and €234 for children under the age of 6 years.

D. Beyond calculation: positive impact and embedded restrictions of the decision

The articulation of a constitutional right to minimum subsistence, will, it is suggested, have an impact beyond the question of benefit calculation methods.

Human rights and social citizenship

First, a constitutional right to minimum subsistence resulting from human dignity is a *human right*. Under the German basic law covering fundamental rights for German and EU citizens and human rights for everybody, this makes a considerable difference concerning the personal scope of application, which must mean something for benefit recipients who are not German citizens. (The significance of the decision for asylum seekers' benefits is discussed further below.) Second, in light of the principle of human dignity meaning that human beings must not be treated as objects of the state, questions can be raised about so-called 'activation policies', given that they involve the hassling and pressuring of benefit recipients to reach state-defined goals concerning social security and the labour market. Although advocates of 'activation policies' emphasise the autonomy and responsibility of benefit recipients, it is questionable how these ideas actually connect with practices of 'activation' in the current German Welfare State. For example, penalty deductions raise severe doubts about the treatment of benefit recipients as subjects as well as the interesting question of whether a minimum-subsistence level can be further minimised without violating human dignity.

Procedural rights

Third, the announcement of an individual social right may strengthen the access to court to exercise this right. While the Federal Employment Agency spends huge amounts of its funds to lose court cases concerning incorrect calculations of individual benefits and other failures, the defamation of benefit recipients who claim their rights in court – and of the lawyers representing them – has reached a new dimension.[70] Time and again, restrictions in the access to social courts were suggested, especially a minimum amount in dispute – lacking explanation why a loss in the statutory minimum subsistence could be excluded from judicial review. It is established case law that constitutional rights include a procedural dimension and that the ability to invoke them effectively before a court is inseparable from the constitutional rights themselves.

Requirements and restrictions

Reaching out to social citizenship is queried by restrictions. In its broad *obiter dicta*, the court values benefits in kind, social services and benefits in cash as equal fulfilments of the state's obligations here. It also emphasises an emergency of need as the requirement for the entitlement to minimum subsistence, thus giving space for varying degrees of welfare conditionality. In a future decision on penalty deductions, the court will be forced to substantiate the balance between fundamental right and legislative discretion in more detail and to decide whether to follow the path to social citizenship or to make further adjustments to the right to minimum subsistence.

IV. Keeping on track: the application of the right to minimum existence

A. Asylum seekers' benefits

In July 2012, the Federal Constitutional Court held that the provisions of the Asylum Seekers Benefits Act governing basic cash benefits were incompatible with the fundamental right to a minimum existence, protected as human dignity in Article 1(1) in conjunction with Article 20(1) of the German basic law.[71] The court decided that these benefits were manifestly insufficient because they had not been changed since 1993 despite considerable price increases in Germany. Furthermore, the benefit levels had not been calculated intelligibly in the first place.

Background

In 1992, the governing and opposing parties agreed on a severe reduction of social benefits for asylum seekers to reduce their numbers in Germany. The 1993 Asylum Seekers Benefits Act excluded asylum seekers from entitlements to social assistance and introduced special benefits below the minimum-subsistence level. Asylum seekers' benefits were generally non-cash benefits and included food, accommodation, heating, clothing, toiletries and consumer goods for the household, plus so-called 'pocket money' at a level of €41 per month for personal needs, such as communication and transport. Under the new law, in contrast to prior entitlement, there was no right to additional payments for pregnant women and single parents, for children's school supplies or for Christmas holidays.

The benefits-in-kind, however, often failed to meet the needs of the asylum seekers and to comply with their religious or cultural norms (especially regarding food). The 'pocket money' was not enough to buy food. Asylum seekers were not allowed to work for at least nine months and, thus, they could not earn any money. Faced with these problems, many local authorities changed to cash payments, while some stick to non-cash benefits, especially vouchers, to discourage 'poverty refugees'. Several civil society organizations collected money to buy these vouchers and supply refugees with cash.

The right to healthcare was also restricted to treatment in the case of painful diseases and acute illness. Chronically ill or disabled asylum seekers 'might' be treated when this was absolutely necessary to safeguard their health. The full protection of the healthcare system could only be enjoyed in the cases of pregnancy or childbirth or after 15 months of asylum seeking. These restrictions were heavily criticised as violations of the principle of human dignity as well as European and international law.[72]

The declaration of unconstitutionality of the Asylum Seekers Benefits Act

In 2010 and 2011, Higher Social Courts initiated a preliminary ruling procedure before the Federal Constitutional Court questioning the conformity of parts of the Asylum Seekers Benefits Act with the constitution. The courts pointed out that the amounts of asylum-seekers' benefits were not based on a constitutionally acceptable method to assess basic needs, up to 31% less than the social benefits that are designed to ensure the minimum subsistence level under the Social Codes and thus evidently insufficient.

The Federal Constitutional Court declared the unconstitutionality of parts of the Asylum Seekers Benefits Act by applying its former ruling on the minimum subsistence level. It emphasised that the right to the guarantee of a dignified minimum existence established by human dignity is a human right that applies to German and foreign nationals who have their residence in Germany alike. It pointed out that adequate benefits have to be ascertained in light of the circumstances in Germany and surely not by referring to the existence level in other countries or the recipient's residence status. Although the methodical calculation of benefits generally falls into the legislature's margin of appreciation, different methods for different groups of persons must be justifiable by facts, and any calculation must consider real needs and actual life circumstances.

The Federal Constitutional Court obliged the legislature to immediately enact new provisions that would secure a dignified minimum existence and ordered, as a transitional arrangement, that asylum-seekers' benefits be calculated according to the general provisions of the Social Codes covering the minimum subsistence level.

Consequences of the constitutional court ruling

As late as 2015, several amendments to the Asylum Seekers Benefits Act entered into force. But the adjustment of asylum-seekers' benefits to the minimum-subsistence level is still incomplete. Although the use of non-cash benefits was terminated, asylum seekers, war refugees and tolerated foreigners are still not entitled to additional payments, and their healthcare remains far below the standards of the statutory health-insurance system. Within legal scholarship, it is doubted whether the reduction of minimum healthcare, maintained by the amended Asylum Seekers Benefits Act, is compatible with the constitutional right to minimum subsistence, thus calling for Constitutional Court activity.[73]

In 2013, the Higher Social Court of North Rhine-Westfalia decided that deductions of asylum-seekers' benefits could not be justified by an assertion that the benefits did not fall short of a *physical* subsistence level or by a claim that the benefit recipients moved to Germany with the sole aim[74] of obtaining these benefits.[75] The court referred to judgments of the Constitutional Court, pointing out that the right to a dignified minimum existence includes *both* the physical existence of an individual *and* the ability to maintain interpersonal relationships and a minimum of participation in social, cultural and political life.

With these court decisions, the German approach to welfare for refugees and migrants differs considerably from the politics of other European countries where the maintenance of national welfare is used to justify restrictions and discriminations.[76] In the face of the arrival of about one million refugees and migrants in 2015, further calls for restrictions, especially returning to benefits in kind, will be heard, but the landmark decision that the right to minimum subsistence is a human right is not to be revised. Meanwhile, adequate housing is the most pressing need.

B. The minimum subsistence level and decisions about one's own diet

In March 2015, the Social Court of Berlin had to consider the issue of deductions from basic subsistence benefits in light of the provision of meals by an employer.[77] The claimant was a recipient of basic subsistence benefits who topped up her income by working for a butcher. Her employer provided daily meals to his employees, consisting of his own meat products. The claimant, a vegetarian, refused to eat these products. As a result, the authority, applying the regulations on unemployment assistance, cut the claimant's subsistence benefits due to being offered daily lunch. The court held that the regulations were not compatible with the constitution. The decision about how to spend subsistence benefits must be left to recipients. The court recalled the legislature's intention to promote individual responsibility and independence. It concluded that autonomous decisions[78] on which food to spend benefits must be respected – a decision for fostering social citizenship.

C. The minimum subsistence level and penalty deductions

Litigation about the constitutionality of penalty deductions from subsistence benefits has produced mixed and, to a certain extent, unclear results. Before exploring these, however, it may be helpful to offer some background.

Background

Before the Hartz IV reforms, penalty deductions could amount to 25%. Such sanctions, however, were not to affect any other person living in the same household. The Federal Administrative Court supported sanctioning under condition of their effectiveness – that is, there had to be a real possibility for the benefit recipient to earn a living.[79]

The Hartz IV reforms thoroughly amended these regulations. As already noted above, under Sections 31ff of the Social Code No. 2, unemployment assistance was made vulnerable to penalty deductions of 30%, and then 60% and ultimately 100%. Penalty deductions can remain in force for at least three months. The law, by not conferring sanctioning discretion on jobcentres, has created 'deduction automatism'. The number of penalty deductions per annum has been increasing and reached 104,470 in April 2015, affecting more than 420,000 benefit recipients.[80]

Where a benefit recipient has suffered a 100% penalty deduction, he or she may apply for benefits in kind. But if that application is rejected by the authority, or not made, the contributions to the benefit recipient's health and long-term care insurance will be stopped. After two months of non-payment, the former benefit recipient's entitlement is reduced to emergency healthcare.

As the reimbursement of accommodation and heating costs is cut as well, penalty deductions bear a high risk of causing homelessness and unbearable debt and exclude the (former) benefit recipient from social security systems.[81]

Contesting penalty deductions in court

In both 2010 and 2015, the Federal Social Court stated that, in general terms, it does not doubt the constitutionality of the new regulations.[82] The Higher Social Court of Thuringia has also held that it has no doubt about the compatibility of penalty deductions with the constitution.[83] The only constitutional restrictions on the penalty regulations thus far has come from the Federal Social Court in 2013, when it qualified its position slightly by holding that the reimbursement of accommodation and heating costs could not be subject to penalty deductions if the sanctioned benefit recipient lived together with two other persons.[84]

However, in May 2015, the Social Court of Gotha initiated a preliminary ruling procedure before the Federal Constitutional Court.[85] The Social Court suggested that the Hartz laws covering penalty deductions from unemployment assistance violated fundamental rights enshrined in the constitution, especially human dignity, the right to physical integrity and the freedom to choose an occupation. The speaker of the Social Court of Gotha pointed out that every person is entitled to a dignified minimum existence and that the legislature's discretion is restricted to the concrete amount of the respective benefits. Given that the legislature defined the benefits in question as precisely covering the minimum existence level, every deduction violates the fundamental right to a guarantee of a dignified minimum existence following from human dignity enshrined in Article 1(1) of the German basic law.

Discussion

Despite the fundamental change from the idea of urging a benefit recipient to work by reducing unemployment assistance to the absolute minimum of three-quarters of the benefits to the idea of suspending all payments including accommodation costs and healthcare insurance contributions, the majority of courts and legal authors adhere to the view that penalty deductions against benefit recipients are justified in order to prevent abuse of the social security system.[86] The legal argument made is that one has to distinguish between the inviolable basis of the entitlement (human dignity) and the amount of the entitlement to be determined (social state) and that, consequently, penalty deductions are not a violation of human dignity or the right to minimum subsistence but rather a legitimately decreased award of benefits within legislative discretion.[87] This suggestion is supported by a second argument: as long as the pure physical existence of the benefit recipient is secured by benefits in kind, penalty deductions are justified.[88] The corollary of these views is that any debate should be restricted to the duration of the deductions and the lack of hardship clauses.[89] The main argument is very seldom employed explicitly: without penalty deductions, minimum subsistence benefits would become an unconditional basic income.[90]

A response to the above arguments may be, first, that a crucial question is not being adequately addressed: how can deductions from a statutorily ***defined minimum*** fail to constitute a violation of the fundamental right to minimum subsistence?[91] Second, the above viewpoint contradicts the social citizenship approach that demands benefits in cash to enable the recipient to identify and prioritise individual needs as an expression of the fundamental right to the free development of one's personality.[92] It also contradicts the idea of a dignified existence minimum including the ability to maintain interpersonal relationships and a minimum of participation in social, cultural and political life as highlighted by the landmark decision of the Constitutional Court. When taking into account the serious doubts that must be had about the effectiveness, proportionality and non-discrimination of penalty deductions, the better view is, surely, that they be abolished.[93] Penalty deductions negate the very idea of a fundamental right to (dignified socio-economic) minimum subsistence and the paradigmatic shift from paternalist welfare to social citizenship.

In May 2016, the Federal Constitutional Court decided not to decide on the compatibility of penalty deductions with the constitution by rejecting preliminary proceedings as inadmissible with very sophisticated reasons.[94] This shows the court's reluctance to stay to the core of its decision by introducing a kind of unconditional basic income as well as its reluctance to overrule itself. The outcome of a future admissible preliminary ruling is open. It should be borne in mind that, in its landmark decision, the Federal Constitutional Court had emphasized the *socio-economic* minimum on the one hand but spoke about benefits in kind on the other.

D. Struggling for a right to housing

The merging of unemployment assistance and social assistance, the cutback of appropriate accommodation costs, the introduction of penalty deductions, accompanied by the privatisation of housing and rising rents have, in combination, caused severe accommodation problems for many unemployed people. The courts and public authorities have followed various approaches. While the entitlement to state support for finding and keeping suitable housing and the state's obligation to provide for emergency accommodation were never questioned, the consideration of 'adequate' or 'suitable' housing varies considerably.

The situation is especially difficult for young adults under the age of 25 who wish to move out of their parents' household. They need the explicit permission of the local authority that finances the reimbursement of accommodation and heating costs. Granting permission lies within the discretion of the local authority and is limited to cases where there are serious social reasons for not living with one's parents or where living in the parents' household is otherwise intolerable.

The courts have rejected the wishes of young adults to live with their partners,[95] even after years of absence from the parental household.[96] Likewise, claims have been rejected where there are family arguments involving bodily conflicts but no attempt to seek external help.[97] However, public authorities have been required to grant permission in cases where a young adult had to travel to his or her training place for more than two hours daily;[98] where a grown-up had no room of her or his own or had broken all contact with his or her parents;[99] or where the situation of the young adult in the household was characterized by social isolation, lack of emotional ties and inadequate housing conditions.[100]

In 2014, the Administrative Court of Neustadt decided that a single room of 25 square metres did not constitute dignified housing for a homeless couple with an eight-year-old child due to the lack of privacy.[101] The court did not employ the term 'right to housing' but emphasised that the state's discretion in assigning accommodation to the homeless is limited by the principle of human dignity enshrined in the constitution, which requires a minimum amount of space and privacy. The Higher Social Court of Saxony-Anhalt has also stated that accommodation without privacy, central heating and a useable bathroom is generally not adequate or suitable.[102]

Although claimants may refer to a fundamental right to housing,[103] only one court decision has employed the term 'right to housing' as part of the right to a dignified minimum subsistence, although without further explanations or special consequences.[104] Welfare organisations, human rights institutions and other civil society actors increasingly try to establish the term and concept of a 'right to housing' in public debates. But with the arrival of about one million refugees and migrants in Germany in 2015, authorities and civil society are experiencing some empirical limits of a right to adequate accommodation and the consequences of two decades of mistaken housing policies.

V. Conclusion: Is Germany becoming a Welfare State with social rights?

The fundamental Hartz reforms encouraged the Federal Constitutional Court to identify the first explicit social right in the German constitution – the right to a guarantee of a dignified minimum existence following from human dignity enshrined in Article 1(1) in conjunction with the principle of the social Welfare State covered by Article 20(1) of the German basic law. The realisation of this right, however, is largely left to political discourse and legislative discretion. The social state remains a blank constitutional principle and there is no referral to social rights enshrined in international human rights treaties. But the amounts of minimum subsistence *were* reconfigured and substantially increased in 2015. And in declaring the unconstitutionality of the Asylum Seekers Benefits Act, the Federal Constitutional Court adhered to its decision of identifying a fundamental – and thus, human – right to minimum subsistence despite facing hard times.

The decision on penalty deductions will be the litmus test for the Constitutional Court's understanding of the German Welfare State. For the time being, the court avoided a substantial decision by rejecting the preliminary ruling procedure due to formal reasons, but this is a mere postponement. When obliged to decide, it cannot be expected that the court will rule contrary to the vast majority of jurisprudence and legal opinion, especially with their stress on legislative discretion. But to rule in compliance with majority opinion, the court would be forced to either withdraw the concept of the socio-cultural minimum by reducing the dignified minimum subsistence back to maintaining physical existence by benefits in kind, or to perform the nearly impossible task of making the dignified minimum subsistence dependent upon the good conduct of the person constitutionally entitled to it without violating human dignity. And the court will not be eager to devalue its recent announcement of a right to minimum subsistence resulting from the highest principle of the German constitution. Whichever compromise the court ultimately develops, neither abandoning the newly identified fundamental right, nor violating the system of checks and balances in parliamentary Germany, its legal reasoning cannot fail to shape the German Welfare State. The Federal Constitutional Court will have to consider inalienable dignity, personal autonomy, legitimate requirements for benefit receiving and the meaning and limits of welfare conditionality.

Despite the long history of the German Welfare State, there is nearly no – or at least no fortunate – history of social rights in German law. Many courts struggle with different welfare models: maintaining inclusion, or human dignity, or rights and duties, or paternalist largesse. In its 2010 landmark decision, the Federal Constitutional Court already included requirements and restrictions such as the adequacy of benefits in kind and a certain understanding of means-testing and subsidiarity of benefits. And yet, the court introduced a socio-cultural minimum and, in its judgment on asylum-seekers' benefits, emphasised the inalienable right to minimum subsistence. Perhaps we can look forward to a new understanding of welfare conditionality and thus to a truly inspiring Sonderweg of Welfare State and social rights thought.

Notes

1 E.g. Brigitte Young, 'The battle of ideas in the Eurozone crisis management. German ordoliberalism versus post-Keynesianism' in Sebastiano Fadda & Pasquale Tridico (eds), *The Economic Crisis in Social and Institutional Context. Theories, Policies, and Exit Strategies* (Routledge 2015) 78-90; and Henning Meyer & Andrew Watt (eds.) *Die 10 Mythen der Eurokrise ... und warum sie falsch sind* (Institut für Makroökonomie und Konjunkturforschung, 2014).
2 Until today, the German Welfare State was shaped by conservative corporatism and some paternalism rather than social citizenship; see Susanne Baer, 'Das Soziale und die Grundrechte' (2014) *Neue Zeitschrift für Sozialrecht* 1: 1–5 (2).
3 But the constitutions of several of the German states, enacted in 1946 and 1947, cover social rights such as the right to work and a working place, to holidays and recreation, to social minimum protection concerning health and old age as well as special protection for working youth.
4 The parliamentary assembly discussed the introduction of fundamental social rights in the light of the Universal Declaration of Human Rights (UDHR) but dissenting votes pointed out that the Declaration was not binding while the fundamental rights of the German constitution were destined to bind the legislation.
5 Christoph Enders, 'Sozialstaatlichkeit im Spannungsfeld von Eigenverantwortung und Fürsorge' (2005) *Veröffentlichungen der Vereinigung der Deutschen Staatsrechtslehrer* 64: 7-52 (9ff).
6 Ibid 13.
7 See Eberhard Eichenhofer, 'Der soziale Rechtsstaat – ein Staat sozialer Rechte?' in Ulrike Haerendel (ed.), *Gerechtigkeit im Sozialstaat* (Nomos, 2012) 140.
8 Federal Administrative Court, judgment of 24 June 1954, V C 78.54, BVerwGE 1: 159–163.
9 Federal Constitutional Court, judgment of 19 December 1951, 1 BvR 220/51, BVerfGE 1: 97–108.
10 Federal Constitutional Court, judgment of 18 June 1975, 1 BvL 4/74, BVerfGE 40: 121–140.
11 Federal Constitutional Court, judgment of 29 May 1990, 1 BvL 20, 26, 184 und 4/86, BVerfGE 82: 60–105.
12 See Eichenhofer, above n 7, 146f, who correctly observes that international social rights are part of binding German law (148ff).
13 It is well known that the Welfare State is constituted by many other means and social services as well, but for the purpose of this chapter we will focus on unemployment assistance, healthcare and housing.
14 Horst Küsters, *Social Partnership: Basic Aspects of Labour Relations in Germany* (Friedrich Ebert Foundation, 2007).
15 Having said that, major groups are not included in this system. Wage-earners with higher incomes may choose private health insurance. Civil servants' healthcare and pensions are co-financed by taxes and state subsidies. And many self-employed people, freelancers and artists are organized in special systems with professional pension funds. The general social security is financed, then, by employees with average or lower incomes and their employers.
16 Gerhard Bosch, 'The German Welfare State: From an Inclusive to an Exclusive Bismarckian model' in Daniel Vaughan-Whitehead (ed.), *The European Social Model in Crisis. Is Europe Losing its Soul?* (Edward Elgar Publishing, 2015) 178.

17 Mark I Vail, *Recasting Welfare Capitalism. Economic Adjustment in Contemporary France and Germany* (Temple University Press, 2010), 85, 103.
18 And until this day, there is no proof that their core objective – improvement of the job-placement service – has been achieved, see Bosch, above n 16.
19 Matthias Knuth, 'Broken Hierarchies, Quasi-Markets and Supported Networks – A Governance Experiment in the Second Tier of Germany's Public Employment Service' in Mark Considine and Siobhan O'Sullivan (eds), *Contracting-Out Welfare Services: Comparing National Policy Designs for Unemployment Assistance* (Wiley Blackwell, 2015) 129f: The Hartz reforms were exceptionally radical in international comparison.
20 Brigitte Young above n 1, 78: start of turning to neoliberalism.
21 The naming of the laws derives from the head of the expert commission that developed the major concepts of the reforms. The commission was appointed by Chancellor Schröder with the aim to by-pass sectoral corporatism as well as the ministry of labour and to present much more far-reaching suggestions, see Reimut Zohlnhöfer and Nicole Herweg, 'Explaining Paradigmatic Change in German Labour Market Policy: A Multiple Streams Perspective' (Paper presented at ECPR Joint Sessions of Workshops, Antwerp, 11–13 April 2012).
22 Timo Fleckenstein 'Restructuring welfare for the unemployed' (2008) *Journal of European Social Policy*, 18(2), 177–188.
23 Küsters, above n 14. Basic subsistence was paid in the amount of €345 per month, plus €311 for spouses/partners; €207 for children under the age of 14 years; and €276 for youths up to the age of 25.
24 See Knuth, above n 19, 131.
25 Vail, above n 17, 106. For similarities with French welfare reforms see Diane Roman, 'Activation Policies for the Unemployed in France: "Social Debt" or "Poor Laws"?' in Elise Dermine and Daniel Dumont (eds), *Activation Policies for the Unemployed, the Right to Work and the Duty to Work* (Peter Lang, 2014) 90ff.
26 Küsters, above n 14.
27 Alliance of German Women's Organizations, Alternative Report in response to the 6th Periodical Report of the Federal German Government on the Convention on the Elimination of All Forms of Discrimination against Women (Submission to the Committee, Berlin 2008).
28 The Committee on Economic, Social and Cultural Rights, *Concluding observations: Germany.* UN-Doc E/C.12/DEU/CO/5, § 19 (2011), warned that this obligation may lead to violations of articles 6 and 7 of the Covenant.
29 Lena Jacobi and Jochen Kluve, Before and After the Hartz Reforms: The Performance of Active Labour Market Policy in Germany (Discussion Paper Series IZA DP No. 2100, Forschungsinstitut zur Zukunft der Arbeit, 2006).
30 Irene Dingeldey, Peter Sopp, Alexandra Wagner, 'Governance des Einkommensmix: Geringfügige Beschäftigung im ALG-II-Bezug' (2012) *WSI-Mitteilungen 1*: 32–40.
31 E.g., while the 3rd Poverty and Wealth Report presented by the Federal Government in 2008, p. 306, states that 16% of men, 21% of women and 26% of minors were living below the poverty risk threshold in 2005, the 4th Poverty and Wealth Report presented by the Federal Government in 2013, p. 461, offers figures of 14% of men, 16% of women and 19.5% of minors for the same year (both reports are available under www.armuts-und-reichtumsbericht.de/DE/Startseite/start.html).
32 Bosch, above n 16, 190ff.
33 Pleading for more sophisticated goals: Jean-Michel Bovin and Eric Moachon, 'Right to Work and Individual Responsibility in Contemporary Welfare States:

A Capability Approach to Activation Policies for the Unemployed' in Elise Dermine and Daniel Dumont (eds), *Activation Policies for the Unemployed, the Right to Work and the Duty to Work* (Peter Lang, 2014) 191ff.

34 Details by Knuth, above n 19, 132ff, and Sebastian Künzel, *Implementing Activation Policies. An Analysis of Social and Labour Market Policy Reforms in Continental Europe with a Focus on Local Case Studies in France and Germany* (Peter Lang, 2015) 154ff.

35 Jacobi and Kluve, above n 29.

36 See Renaat Hoop, 'Political-Philosophical Perspectives on the Duty to Work in Activation Policies for the Unemployed' in Elise Dermine and Daniel Dumont (eds), *Activation Policies for the Unemployed, the Right to Work and the Duty to Work* (Peter Lang, 2014) 47ff.

37 Küsters, above n 14.

38 Jacobi and Kluve, above n 29.

39 This seems to be some advantage compared to the 'activation policies' employed in the United Kingdom where the government has adopted the social model of disability approach to re-define disability with the aim of cutbacks of an out-of-work benefit for sick and disabled persons: see Charlotte O'Brien, 'From Safety Nets and Carrots to Trampolines and Sticks: National Use of the EU as both Menace and Model to Help Neoliberalize Welfare Policy' in Dagmar Schiek (ed.), *The EU Economic and Social Model in the Global Crisis. Interdisciplinary Perspectives* (Ashgate, 2013) 102f.

40 Katharina Zimmermann *et al.*, 'Local Worlds of Marketization – Employment Policies in Germany, Italy and the UK Compared' in Mark Considine and Siobhan O'Sullivan (eds), *Contracting-Out Welfare Services: Comparing National Policy Designs for Unemployment Assistance* (Wiley Blackwell, 2015) 19.

41 See Bosch, above n 16, 190ff.

42 Vail, above n 17, 107, 156.

43 One of the most significant bottom-up redistributions in German history was closely connected to the privatisation of public communication – the successful marketing of the Telekom shares as 'people's shares' before their total loss in value.

44 Bosch, above n 16, 217ff.

45 This payment duty is new and totally alien to the German system, which, until recently, did not consider fault when financing health treatments of persons insured under the statutory health insurance. One may be anxious to find out which further payment duties will follow this paradigmatic shift.

46 Federal Social Court, judgment of 25 June 2009, B 3 KR 3/08 R, BSGE 103: 275–284.

47 It may be interesting to know that this obligation is mainly not followed from social rights regulations but from the statutory regulations on public order that cover police and authority measures against self-endangerment: see Karl-Heinz Ruder, 'Die polizei- und ordnungsrechtliche Unterbringung von Obdachlosen' (2012) *Neue Zeitschrift für Verwaltungsrecht* 20: 1283–1288.

48 The severe problems in offering accommodation for about one million refugees last year highlighted the fatal consequences of a sellout of public and social housing. Now the state is forced to re-purchase.

49 See Andreas Fischer-Lescano, *Human Rights in Times of Austerity Policy* (Nomos, 2014) 11ff.

50 Christian Dustman *et al.*, 'From Sick Man of Europe to Economic Superstar: Germany's Resurgent Economy' (Discussion Paper CDP No 06/2014, Centre for Research and Analysis of Migration, 2014).

51 Ibid.
52 Peter Bofinger, 'Deutschland ist ein Vorbild für Europa' in Henning Meyer and Andrew Watt (eds), *Die 10 Mythen der Eurokrise . . . und warum sie falsch sind* (Report, Institut für Makroökonomie und Konjunkturforschung, 2014), 47–58.
53 Bosch, above n 16, 209ff.
54 Gustav Horn and Alexander Herzog-Stein, 'Erwerbstätigenrekord dank guter Konjunktur und hoher interner Flexibilität' (2013) *Wirtschaftsdienst* 3: 151–155.
55 Ibid.
56 Institut Arbeit und Qualifikation, 'Jeder dritte ALG II-Empfänger stockt auf' (Press Release, 15 April 2013) <www.iaq.uni-due.de/aktuell/presse/2013/130415.php>.
57 See Yannick Vanderborght, 'The Tensions of Welfare State Reform and the Potential of a Universal Basic Income' in Dermine & Dumont (eds) (2014) (n 25) 209–222 (213ff), on the problem of 'activation policies' penalizing people who succeed in finding a low paid job and the solution by introducing a basic income.
58 Federal Constitutional Court, judgment of 9 February 2010, BvL 1/09, 1 BvL 3/09, 1 BvL 4/09.
59 However, this constitutional social right was developed purely from principles of the Basic Law with no reference to international human rights; for their importance see Baer, above n 2, 3f.
60 Federal Constitutional Court, judgment of 7 November 2007, 1 BvR 1840/07.
61 Matthias Schnath, 'Das neue Grundrecht auf Gewährleistung eines menschenwürdigen Existenzminimums – Ein rechtspolitischer Ausblick nach dem Urteil des Bundesverfassungsgerichts' (2010) *Neue Zeitschrift für Sozialrecht* 297–310.
62 In the opinion of many commentators, the limitation of the judicial review was inevitable to compensate for the invocation of the 'absolute' human dignity and to maintain the balance of powers in the parliamentary system: see, e.g. Ferdinand Kirchhof, 'Die Entwicklung des Sozialverfassungsrecht' (2015) *Neue Zeitschrift für Sozialrecht* 1: 1–8 (4f).
63 Federal Constitutional Court, judgment of 5 June 1973, 1 BvR 536/72, BVerfGE 35: 202–245 (235f), judgment of 21 June 1977, 1 BvL 14/76, BVerfGE 45: 187–271.
64 And because the social state is just a principle and a constitutional value to be taken into consideration, the announcement of a constitutional right to minimum subsistence is revolutionary: see Baer, above n 2, 3.
65 A constitutional obligation for the legislator to state its reasons in a transparent procedure was thoroughly rejected: see Timo Hebeler, 'Ist der Gesetzgeber verfassungsrechtlich verpflichtet, Gesetze zu begründen?' (2010) *Die Öffentliche Verwaltung* 18: 745–762. See also Anne Sanders and Damian Preisnerk, 'Begründungspflicht des Gesetzgebers und Sachverhaltsaufklärung im Verfassungsprozess' (2015) *Die Öffentliche Verwaltung* 18: 761–771.
66 This was the definite aim of the legislation, incompatible with the constitution; see Anne Lenze, 'Sind die neuen Hartz-IV-Sätze verfassungskonform?' (2011) *Neue Zeitschrift für Verwaltungsrecht* 18: 1104–1108. For significant higher amounts when using calculation methods in compliance with the constitutional court ruling see Irene Becker and Reinhard Schüssler, Das Grundsicherungsniveau: Ergebnis der Verteilungsentwicklung und normativer Setzungen (Working paper 298 of the Böckler Foundation, 2014); Irene Becker, Der Einfluss verdeckter Armut auf das Grundsicherungsniveau (Working paper 309 of the Böckler Foundation, 2015).

67 E.g. the exemption of financing contraceptives for persons over the age of 25 years, which causes severe detriment to their right to reproductive health.
68 Social Court of Berlin, judgment of 25 April 2012, S 55 AS 29349/11.
69 Federal Constitutional Court, judgment of 23 July 2014, 1 BvL 10/12, 1 BvL 12/12, 1 BvR 1691/13.
70 Concerned: Helga Spindler, 'Polemik gegen "Hartz IV-Anwälte" diskreditiert die Durchsetzung sozialer Rechte' (2014) *info also 4:* 154–161.
71 Federal Constitutional Court, judgment of 18 July 2012, 1 BvL 10/10, 1 BvL 2/11, BVerfGE 132: 134–179.
72 See, e.g. Eberhard Eichenhofer, 'Gesundheitsleistungen für Flüchtlinge' (2013) *Zeitschrift für Ausländerrecht und Ausländerpolitik 5/6:* 169–175.
73 See, e.g. Stephan Rixen, 'Zwischen Hilfe, Abschreckung und Pragmatismus: Gesundheitsrecht der Flüchtlingskrise' (2015) *Neue Zeitschrift für Verwaltungsrecht 23:* 1640–1644 (1642ff), who has no doubt that the reductions in question are incompatible with European and International Human Rights Law (1643).
74 Kirchhof, above n 62, 4 points out that it doesn't matter whether the minimum subsistence creates incentives for migration because the right to minimum subsistence results from human dignity and, thus, is cogent constitutional law.
75 Higher Social Court of North Rhine-Westfalia, judgment of 24 April 2013, L 20 AY 153/12 B ER; Social Court of Frankfurt, judgment of 10 September 2013, S 20 AY 11/13 ER.
76 E.g. in the United Kingdom, see O'Brien, above n 39.
77 Social Court of Berlin, judgment of 23 March 2015, S 175 AS 15482/14.
78 The court emphasised that the decision about one's own diet is often based upon religious or moral reasons to be respected by authorities. However, it considered the decision for a healthy diet based upon personal autonomy sufficient.
79 Federal Administrative Court, judgment of 31 January 1968, V C 22.67; judgment of 10 February 1983, 5 C 115/81.
80 See http://statistik.arbeitsagentur.de.
81 Uwe Berlit, 'Sanktionen im SGB II – nur problematisch oder verfassungswidrig?' (2013) *info also 5:* 195–205, suggests to grant benefits in kind without application and to introduce direct payments by the jobcentre to the accommodation proprietor in case of severe penalty deductions.
82 Federal Social Court, judgment of 9 November 2010, B 4 AS 27/10 R; judgment of 29 April 2015, B 14 AS 19/14 R.
83 Higher Social Court of Thuringia, judgment of 19 October 2015, l 4 AS 878/15 NZB.
84 Federal Social Court, judgment of 23 May 2013, B 4 AS 67/12 R, BSGE 113: 270–277.
85 Social Court of Gotha, judgment of 26 May 2015, S 15 AS 5157/14.
86 Maybe many years of public discourse about the treacherous and lazy benefit recipients happily spending their days in the 'social hammock' are paying off.
87 Most detailed Berlit, above n 81, with extensive further references.
88 E.g. Federal Social Court, judgment of 29 April 2015, B 14 AS 19/14 R; Higher Social Court of Bavaria, judgment of 8 July 2015, L 16 AS 381/15 B ER; Berlit, above n 81, 202f.
89 See Federal Social Court, judgment of 29 April 2015, B 14 AS 19/14 R.
90 See Vanderborght, above n 57, 209–222.
91 See Wolfgang Neskovic and Isabel Erdem, 'Zur Verfassungswidrigkeit von Sanktionen bei Hartz IV' (2012) *Die Sozialgerichtsbarkeit* 134–140, on the incompatibility of penalty deductions with the constitution.
92 Schnath, above n 61, 299.

93 Franziska Drohsel, 'Sanktionen nach dem SGB II und das Grundrecht auf ein menschenwürdiges Existenzminimum' (2014) *Neue Zeitschrift für Sozialrecht* 96–103. Drohsel takes a contrary position to that of Berlit, see above n 81, 204, who offers detailed suggestions for necessary (but in his opinion not constitutionally required) amendments to the current regulations on penalty deductions.
94 Federal Constitutional Court, judgment of 6 May 2016, 1 BvL 7/15.
95 Higher Social Court of Saxony-Anhalt, judgment of 19 September 2012, L 5 AS 613/12 B ER.
96 Higher Social Court of Berlin and Brandenburg, judgment of 19 September 2012, L 5 AS 613/12 B ER.
97 Social Court of Duesseldorf, judgment of 18 October 2010, S 7 (28) AS 224/08.
98 Higher Social Court of Saxonia-Anhalt, judgment of 11 September 2012, L 5 AS 461/11 B.
99 Higher Social Court of North Rhine-Westfalia, judgment of 15 April 2011, L 19 AS 495/11 B ER.
100 Social Court of Duisburg, judgment of 10 February 2011, S 5 AS 252/09.
101 Administrative Court of Neustadt, judgment of 3 June 2014, 5 L 469/14.NW.
102 Higher Social Court of Saxony-Anhalt, judgment of 31 March 2011, L 5 AS 359/10 B ER.
103 E.g. Higher Social Court of Saxonia-Anhalt, judgment of 14 September 2010, L 5 AS 224/10 B ER
104 Social Court of Dresden, judgment of 10 September 2013, S 49 AS 8234/10.

Chapter 4

Italy

Alessandra Albanese

I. Introduction

The aim of this chapter is to investigate the interaction in a time of economic austerity between the legal protection of social welfare rights, ensured in Italy by national courts, and welfare policies enacted by the Italian institutions (government, Parliament, Regions, and local authorities). To fulfil this task, I will start by giving a brief overview of the constitutional principles upon which the Italian welfare model lies, especially by discussing the meaning of the inclusion of social rights in the Constitution. I shall examine the issues that the actual protection of such a category of rights has raised relating to the impact of the recent restrictive financial legal measures and the consequent economic constraints on their enforcement. Then I shall elaborate on the role that the courts – especially the Constitutional Court – play for the protection of such a category of rights in Italy. Remaining on constitutional grounds, I will briefly examine how the model of devolution of powers to regional authorities affects the model of the Welfare State. As we shall see, the economic crisis has affected the distribution of competences between central administration and local authorities in the area of social welfare policies. Finally, I shall outline the main contemporary trends of the evolution of Italian legislation about social rights, with special regard both to the impact of the financial crisis and the role of European Union (EU) law.

II. The welfare model according to the Italian Constitution

Although there is no specific claim about welfare as a mission of the State in the Italian Constitution and eminent scholars have cast doubts on the utility of such a notion,[1] from a legal point of view it is beyond question that Italy can be regarded as a social state and not as a mere liberal state.[2] We can reach such a conclusion by a systematic interpretation of article 3 § 2 and a number of clauses referring to different types of social rights.

The first establishes:

> It is the duty of the Republic to remove all economic and social obstacles that, by limiting the freedom and equality of citizens, de facto prevent full individual development and the participation of all workers in the political, economic, and social organization of the country.

This goal is specified by the provisions that oblige the State to implement various social policies and tasks. We find in the Constitution a graduation in the level of protection depending on a sort of categorisation of rights, so that each social right enjoys multiple dimensions of implementation and enforcement.[3] Suffice it to say that the guarantee of labour rights, on the one hand, and the right to education, on the other, are disciplined in detail by pointing out the specific obligations that both public authorities and private persons are subjected to. Education is the only case for which the Constitution even establishes organisational patterns, compelling the State to create schools for all branches and grades.[4] Something similar is provided for healthcare (although not in such detail), the right to which is the only one expressly named as 'fundamental'.[5] Conversely, the protection awarded to social assistance seems weaker, as it is not worded as a universal human right, but as a right of impaired-disabled or indigent people.[6] Only a progressive interpretation of the basic constitutional principles has, in the last thirty years, been capable of partially widening the meaning of social assistance.

Case law and the doctrinal mainstream suggest that provisions about social rights should directly guarantee a personal interest of the bearer so that such rights can be considered as proper subjective rights that the State and local authorities are obliged to satisfy (as opposed to being only generic goals assigned to the public authorities). However, such a subjective dimension of social rights – despite, in my view, its being easily deducible from the constitutional text – has encountered many hurdles in terms of their enforcement.

We can find hints of such a struggle in the doctrinal discussion that took place immediately after the entry into force of the Constitution of 1948 regarding the relationship between social rights and the conflicting principles of liberty and equality. The link between article 2 of the Constitution (namely, where it recognises and protects liberty rights,[7] including economic freedom) and the said article 3, par. 2 was, for a long time, barely acknowledged by scholars.[8] The idea of substantive equality as intrinsically aiming at redistributive outcomes was seen as unavoidably limiting the rights of somebody in favour of someone else. Using the words of a distinguished Italian scholar, rather than casting light on the 'path of human emancipation' set up by article 3.2,[9] its function of being 'only' a directive to politics was especially stressed: all constitutional provisions that provide for social rights were considered mere directives addressed to the legislature.[10] Therefore, without a statutory law that embodied such rights, there was no way of thinking of them as having any direct effect. Today, however, mainstream constitutional scholarship purports that our constitutional model draws a synergistic relationship between equality and liberty.[11] Gaetano Silvestri,[12] a former

President of the Italian Constitutional Court (the ICC), has described them as having a 'sympathetic relationship', whereby the development of society under the principle of substantive equality can never be disjointed from individual emancipation. Thus, social rights are undoubtedly an important means of social progress and equality, but are primarily individual human rights. This notion has been acknowledged through the introduction into the Constitution of the provision that the delivery of services is necessary to comply with the State's obligation to satisfy social needs, at least to some degree.[13] The new version of article 117 II par. let. (m), in particular, by obliging the State 'to determine the essential level of services that must be guaranteed throughout the territory of the Republic in order to ensure the protection of civil and social rights', clearly establishes that the entitlement to social rights, at least to a certain extent, is irreducible. Such a claim is bolstered by article 120 C. by conferring a subsidiary (substitutive) competence to intervene in relation to non-compliant regional and local authorities, whenever it is necessary 'to guarantee the basic level of benefits relating to civil and social entitlements, regardless of the geographic borders of local authorities'.

It goes without saying, however, that this normative picture about the constitutional foundation of social rights is not always reconcilable with the more practical question of their actual guarantee, which has to take into account the significance of political choices about money allocation. As we shall see in section V, in only a few cases and only for the 'stronger' protected social rights, is it possible to obtain judicial enforcement on constitutional grounds. Indeed, social rights entail positive intervention and a financial commitment and therefore must be balanced with other rights or interests receiving constitutional protection too.

This contention lies at the heart of a theory, elaborated at the beginning of the 1990s, according to which social rights are 'conditional on finance'.[14] In contrast to liberty and civil rights, such conditionality, it is argued, is a structural feature of social rights. This theory has been persuasively criticised both by stressing the political discretion that underpins resource allocation[15] and noting that the issue of 'the cost of rights' is not confined to the field of social rights. It affects a broader range of policies, including the judiciary, national security and even the protection of property – all of which have concurring interests to balance. Suffice it to recall the recent debates in Italy regarding the scarcity of fuel to supply police cars in order to ensure personal security to individuals and the wider public, or regarding the lack of resources to evict people illegally occupying private property. To claim that financial limits are an essential feature of social rights is to show a political preference about how social needs and financial and economic issues should be balanced that, by placing the value of economic efficiency at the same level of human rights, contrasts with the overarching constitutional design mentioned above.[16] However, one has to take into account that in 2012 a constitutional provision establishing the duty to balance revenue and expenditure in the State budget was introduced.[17] Thus, the issue of an absolute limit to social spending is still momentous, even if it negatively affects fundamental social rights such as the basic minimum mentioned above.

III. Decentralisation and the welfare model

The Italian social welfare model is strongly affected by the 'decentralisation' of the Republic, especially because the financial crisis has had its greatest impact on local authorities' activities, reducing their effectiveness in responding to social needs. The paramount question is who establishes social policies and how this is done, for the distribution of law-making between the central State and the Regions, as outlined by article 117 C. regarding the subject matters that affect social policies, strongly conditions the efficiency of social welfare as a whole. Regions possess a range of autonomous law-making powers relating to the different subject matters within social policies. This brings about deficiencies in the definition and coordination of objectives, resource allocation and organisational patterns. For example, as regards social care, the Regions enjoy exclusive law-making competence. In relation to healthcare, however, their competences concur with the State, which establishes the general policy framework. The task of social care–health integration is constantly impaired by the lack of efficiency and coordination that such a disharmony brings about. This situation makes it barely possible to think of an organic intervention at the national level that would ensure a uniform provision of social services throughout the nation.

A way to face this problem would be that the State, pursuant to article 117. 2 let. (m) of the Italian Constitution, sets up the basic levels of benefits relating to civil and social entitlements to be guaranteed throughout the national territory.[18] However, the basic level of social care services – unlike healthcare and education services – has never been determined by the State, which has left Regions adrift, both about what interventions to make and how to fund them.

In addition, the same interpretation of what such basic levels are has become disputed. A textual interpretation would purport that the Constitution wants to guarantee a uniform enjoyment of social rights throughout the territory of the Republic, with the option of Regions improving upon the minimum by, for example, spending more money in a certain area of social care. The 'case law of the crisis' (explored further in section V), however, is leading the ICC to reverse the prima facie meaning of such a provision by declaring unlawful regional provisions that established higher levels of healthcare than the national ones.[19] In these cases, governmental interventions, pursuant to article 120 of the Constitution, to replace regional decisions, have been deemed lawful as instrumental, not only to the economic unity of the State, but also to the guarantee of the same basic levels of social benefits. In this way, however, the provision on the basic levels ends up not ensuring a fundamental non-negotiable standard of protection but rather expressing the maximum level of benefits that the Regions can deliver. This clamps down the regional decision-making regarding the allocation of resources within their budgets for social policies. In fact, it is pretty clear that the court, especially by using the constitutional provision that reserves to the Parliament the power to pass legislation on the 'coordination of public finance', is restructuring Italian devolution in light of the financial crisis.

IV. Trends in welfare policy

A. Up to 2008

In the last ten years, the tension between social rights and financial and economic issues has strongly re-emerged. This tension is a consequence both of the financial crisis and the influence of EU law, which tends to let the market provide social services with as little intervention as possible of the State. Regarding the question as to whether and to what extent the impact of the crisis has brought about significant change in welfare policy, I would suggest that the different intensity of constitutional protections as sketched above directly affects how specific groups of rights have been less or more protected. In other words, rights relating to areas of social policy more prominently enshrined in the Constitution benefited from the stronger position gained thanks to the legislative implementation of the Constitution itself over the years by hindering regressive measures. This pattern, in turn, can be partly seen in the case law as well (see section V).

In fact, it is in relation to education, labour law and healthcare that a sizeable bulk of legislation directly implementing the Constitution was put in place in the 1960s, and continued into the 1970s (up to the foundation of the National Health Service (NHS) in 1978). By way of contrast, the only 'organic statute law' regarding social assistance – weakly guaranteed in the Constitution – was promulgated as late as 2000 and has never been fully implemented. Likewise, the only recent government reforms ostensibly aimed at promoting economic and social development (rather than merely reducing expenses) concerned schools[20] and the labour market (see infra).

Two main trends can be easily detected to outline the basic features of the Italian welfare legislation over the period from the end of the 1970s (the years of the implementation of the regional administration) and the beginning of the 21st century.

The first trend regards the gradual shift from the monetisation of needs (benefits in cash) to the supply of benefits 'in kind' by specifically created public institutions. This can be seen as a way of 'putting the person at the centre' as the recipient of a bespoke care package. This was the political choice that determined, for example, the shift from a mutualistic healthcare system to the national healthcare system and the provision of a national 'integrated' social assistance system. Equally, the implementation of specific policies to make staff available to deal with problems such as children's and teenagers' distress and drug addiction can be reconciled with such a trend. It is important to stress this aspect of welfare provision because it represents a distinct feature of the Italian Welfare State model, whereas in many European countries benefits in cash prevail. Another conspicuous, albeit negative, feature of the Italian welfare system can be somehow traced back to this pattern, which is that unlike other States who provide all citizens in need with a 'guaranteed minimum income' on the grounds of means-tested benefits, Italy does not provide in a general universalistic way any benefit in cash aimed at combatting poverty.

The second trend regards the gradual pursuing of universality in access to services, also boosted by the said progressive interpretation of constitutional provisions, where the backdrop idea is that social rights are human rights belonging to any person and not only to those included in some disadvantaged categories, as it used to be until the 1960s.

These two trends were synergistic: the choice of direct intervention to alleviate needs appeared to best fit the main tenets of the Italian Constitution, inspired by egalitarianism and solidarity and based upon a redistributive function via public expenditure. Such a conception, in turn, underpinned the universality of services – not necessarily free, but provided to all those in need. Such an organisational effort to provide social protection was connected to a strong planning of the delivery of social services, which exempted such services from competition in the market. The overarching tenet was that the market would not be able to guarantee social equity and access to services for the most disadvantaged people. The widest implementation of the universality principle in the Italian welfare system can be found in the Law No 833/1978, setting up the NHS, accessible to anybody in need (for every citizen and also for some categories of immigrants), although not free of charge to everybody. Conversely, the kind of universality implemented by the Law No 328/2000 regarding social assistance was more limited. It was inspired by a sort of 'selective universalism', setting up a system accessible to everybody but giving priority to particularly vulnerable subjects.

From the beginning of the century the considerable cost of direct service delivery – together with inefficiency that has often characterised Welfare State bureaucracy – raised the question of their sustainability in a period of strong reduction of financial resources,[21] with three orders of consequences in terms of change of welfare organisation:

i) social policies are going back to the original pattern of cash benefits. Examples are the introduction in some Regions of vouchers to replace certain services of social assistance or the introduction of a 'social-card' providing free purchases for parents with children under three years of age and indigent people over 60 years of age;
ii) many services have been simply cut out, strongly reducing the services supplied on a universal basis. A good example here is the virtual end of any policy regarding social housing;
iii) boosted by the influence of EU law regarding freedom of services, quasi-market systems for the delivery of social services have been progressively introduced in areas such as healthcare, social assistance and social housing. In such a way, public authorities tend to carry out the role of market regulators and purchasers of services, leaving the production and delivery of services to private providers. Even though in principle such a trend does not put into question either the role of the State in guaranteeing that social needs are addressed or the definition of the standards of such a guarantee, it has opened up this sector to a certain amount of competition. In fact, European

institutions have definitely given up the idea that social services are 'ontologically' extraneous to the market and lacking in economic relevance. They have instead pushed forward the idea that organisational and management forms of social services delivery constitute an area that is not totally reserved to the member states and in principle subjected to the EU rules on market competition.[22]

B. The crisis years

These characteristics of the welfare system were present at the outset of the 2008 financial crisis, which has somehow determined a further acceleration in the said direction of change. The main point to make is that since then there has not been any organic programme of legislative measures to reform the welfare system, despite the fact that expenditure on welfare benefits is frequently mentioned as the area having the biggest impact on the public deficit.

Except for a very controversial reform approved on emergency grounds in 2011 under the Monti Government, aimed at re-regulating the whole area of pensions in order to make savings,[23] in the other areas of welfare policy (healthcare, social assistance and social housing), reforms have not fundamentally modified the organisation of welfare and its legal structure.[24] Nonetheless, we can observe a number of measures aimed at (often dramatically) cutting back costs by decreasing the amount of financial resources devoted to supply social benefits.[25]

The chart below (see Figure 4.1) gives us a clear sense of the scale of reductions in public expenditure in the crucial area of social assistance for disabled persons, immigrants, children, families and so on. The figures in the top line denote the global amount (in millions of euros) transferred from 2008 to 2016 from the State to Regions for the implementation of social assistance policies. The lines below show the same figures broken down according to their different goals (funds to support the benefits for immigrant children without parents, funds for gender policies, funds for youth policies, funds to support the benefits for non-self-sufficient old people and a general fund for all the other social-assistance policies).[26]

In recent welfare legislation, there are other examples of a tentative approach concerning the impact of social transfer on poverty and social inclusion.

A benefit to support the poorest families, named SIA (sostegno per l'inclusione attiva: support for an active inclusion) was introduced for the first time in 2013 as an experimental measure, provided for only one year and limited to the twelve largest cities of the country with more than 250,000 inhabitants. The supplying of such a benefit had to be accompanied by a bespoke plan of social inclusion of each recipient and in addition the measure was particularly oriented to help families with young children. Only very recently, after an intense debate, the so-called 'stability law 2016' has provided for a fund – allocating 600 million euros for the first year – aimed at fighting poverty and exclusion on the grounds of a triennial plan set up by a Decree of the Prime Minster in agreement with the national

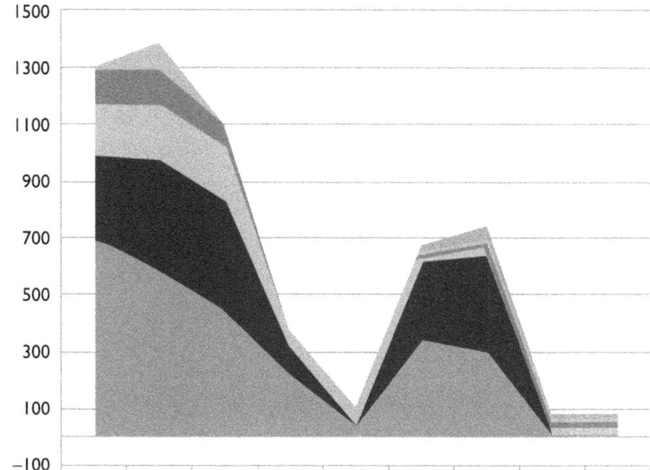

	2008	2009	2010	2011	2012	2013	2014	2015	2016
totale fondi	1.300,7	1.391,6	1.101,6	368,08	115,04	677,18	746,51	82,44	82,59
f. minori stranieri non accomp.	0	0	0	0	5	25	40	20	20
f.pari opp.	0	96	0	0	10	11	21	21	21
f.pol.giovanili	130	130	81	0	0	5	17	6	6
f.famiglia	173	187	185	50	56	17	21	20	20
fna	300	400	400	100	0	275	350	0	0
fnps	698	579	435	218	44	344	297	14	15

Figure 4.1 Chart 1 – State balance-sheet item on social funds (millions).

Source: L. Pelliccia, Il punto sui fondi sociali statali: evoluzione e prospettive per la *Lombardia* (14 May 2014) www.lombardiasociale.it/2014/05/14/il-punto-sui-fondi-sociali-statali-evoluzione-e-prospettive-per-la-lombardia/.

Conference of the Regions and Local Authorities. The law states that, for the ensuing years, the government will implement a new regulation by rationalising existing provisions and introducing a unique type of income support that is means tested and dependent on a poverty threshold. The new measures would partially change the existing system of benefits in cash not relating to the participation in the labour market, possibly moving towards a form of 'guaranteed minimum income'. The real challenge concerns how to implement the general provision just described, which in turn demands coping with a sensible policy of resource reallocation.

A more ambitious reform has regarded the labour market, the consequences of which are still difficult to assess due to its being very recent (May 2015). An act of delegated legislation,[27] the so-called 'Job's Act', provides for a new unemployment benefit – NASPI (*Nuova prestazione di assicurazione sociale per l'impiego*: New Social Insurance for Employment), which seems more perspicuous than the one provided for by so-called Fornero reform,[28] at least with regard to the range of beneficiaries, as non-fixed-term workers have been included within the scheme.

Indeed, all unemployed people who have been working at least 13 weeks in the last four years are entitled to receive assistance. Such benefits can be delivered for a maximum of 24 months, but the actual duration and amount depends on how much contribution the employee has already paid prior to the reform. Once the NASPI expires the unemployed person in need can still get a lower amount for six months (called ASDI: unemployment cheque). Nevertheless, the amount of money that can be delivered to unemployed workers has been reduced and, furthermore, the decree provides for a very harsh set of sanctions for those who do not accept new job opportunities, even if the latter are much worse than one's previous job.[29]

Other recent measures introduced by the Renzi Government show that the strategy of resource reductions in healthcare and social assistance is still ongoing. For example, in August 2015, with the alleged goal of reducing the misuse of medical prescriptions, Parliament passed a new law cutting about 2.5 billion euros of the budget devoted to support Regions' expenses in the healthcare area.[30] These measures affect the benefits relating to specialist medical consultations, diagnostic tests and other services. As with many other decisions regarding budgetary reductions, the law was passed thanks to a confidence vote for the government without any actual parliamentary debate.

V. The protection of social rights in court

A. The guarantee of social rights in the ICC case law

Except for pensions and labour law, the most important and copious decisions made over the years both by the ICC and ordinary courts dealing with social rights regard the areas of healthcare and education. It is about such policies, for example, that the ICC, especially in the 1990s, abandoned its previous notion that norms on social rights were merely directives to the legislature. It began to employ the technique of issuing a decision to create a new principle of law (so-called principle adding decisions) addressed to the legislature in order to declare unlawful statutory laws that did not provide for certain measures necessary to guarantee a social right. As regards education, the ICC came up with 'manipulative' decisions whereby a piece of legislation incompatible with constitutional norms on social rights was directly integrated or changed, without any remand to the legislature. Such techniques were strongly disputed. These 'creative' decisions represent the furthest limit ever reached by the ICC as regards the relationship between the court and the Parliament. And they permitted scholars to speak about a strand of case law amounting to a 'stubborn defence' of social rights.[31]

There are other significant decisions encompassing this orientation. Decision No 251/1987, for example, regarding the school attendance of disabled pupils, stated that the statutory provision that 'it shall be made easier' rather than 'it shall be assured' was contrary to the correct interpretation of article 34 C. in conjunction with articles 2 and 3. A very important statutory law about the full protection of disabled people, Law No 104/1992, then followed as a direct consequence of that decision.

As for the right to health, we can cite Decision No 509/2000 whereby the ICC – endorsing pre-existing case law by ordinary courts – quashed a regional piece of legislation for being too rigid since it did not provide for exceptions to the rule that healthcare expenses for treatment abroad have to be previously authorised. The law in fact did not permit the reimbursing of a patient for the cost borne for treatments necessary to avoid an imminent and serious threat to health. In the view of the ICC, this regional law did not guarantee such an 'intangible core of healthcare rights as the one that the Constitution protects as an inviolable part of human dignity'.[32]

However, these creative decisions of the Constitutional Court have, for some time now, been considerably diminishing in number. In fact, the ICC is by and large sympathetic with the theory of social rights as being conditional on finance to which it first adhered in the 1990s (Decision No 155/1990) and that, after a period of uncertainty, from 2005 onwards became firmly rooted in its case law under the pressure of the financial crisis and the more stringent EU fiscal rules.[33]

The ICC, thus, has become wary of the consequences of its decisions on the public purse[34] and the lack of concrete provisions to protect social needs as well as choices to reduce social services receive less criticism from the ICC than in the past. Ultimately, the theory of social rights as being conditional on finance has recently been textually and emphatically re-confirmed in a ground-breaking decision of 2011 relating to healthcare. Here, the ICC framed a principle first expressed in 2005[35] as an 'indisputable conclusion':

> [T]he necessity to secure universality and fullness of social assistance in our Country in present times clashes with the scarcity of financial resources available for a general plan of measures for assisting people in need.[36]

There is, however, a sort of 'last-resort' safeguard constituted by the notion of a 'minimum content' of at least those social rights that appear to be more accurately disciplined in the Constitution. This minimum content is not something that refers to an actual social minimum (as a bundle of resources to give substance to the right at stake) but rather a sort of argumentative device traceable to reasonableness to capture the non-negotiable core of a right. This is a stance that closely reminds us of such decisions of the German Constitutional Tribunal as the ones that have dealt with the *Wesengehalt*, the essential core, as a stronghold of fundamental rights (*Grundrechte*). The ICC by applying the criterion of 'minimum content' (or 'essential core') has repeatedly declared the unreasonableness of legislative dispositions whose implementation could have impeded a certain right to a great extent.[37]

A paradigmatic example of this strand of case law is Decision No 80/2010 dealing with the rights of disabled students to have a special teacher long enough to address the seriousness of their disability. The ICC quashed a provision that provided for a legislative cap on the number of such special teachers in any school based on the teacher–student ratio. Such a provision had replaced a previous one that made it possible to overcome this cap by using fixed-term contracts if necessary to support students with very serious disabilities. The repeal of such a measure was held to be unlawful by the ICC in the light of the constitutional right to education and assistance.

The literature has rightly emphasised how attentively the court linked the abstract acknowledgement of a right with the specific need of an individual.[38] The unreasonableness of the impugned law lay upon its abstractness, that is to say the lack of a means-tested or bespoke service for particularly disadvantaged people. Another aspect worthy of a mention regarding this decision is where the court, censuring the inflexibility of the law, underlines the importance of the organisational dimension of the delivery of services that embodies any specific social right. In other words, a discretionary space should be granted to the public administration to tailor the service to the needs of a person. Normally such a conferral of discretionary power is meant to be a hurdle to the full enjoyment of social rights, for it is perceived as antithetical to the same definition of a legal right as a state of affairs in which a person is entitled to obtain something without being subject to any evaluation or choice of his/her counterpart. The case at hand shows, instead, that here a conferral of discretionary power is necessary to set aside the obstacles that in fact impede the full enjoyment of a social right.

Another important instance of such a position of the ICC can be seen in a recent highly disputed judgment for its impact on public expenditures, where the court has come to rule the unconstitutionality of statutory provisions that had quashed the mechanisms safeguarding the purchasing power of pensions.[39] The law had been passed to give a quick and concrete answer to financial imbalances, under the pressure of EU Authorities.[40] The argument of the Constitutional Court was that, because such provisions also affected the lowest pensions, they infringed the principle of proportionality and the fundamental right to receive an economic treatment adequate to ensure a sufficient quality of life.[41]

B. The ordinary (civil) courts' and administrative courts' case law

Along with the ICC case law, which is played inevitably within the dialectics of the relationship with the legislature, there has historically been considerable room for ordinary courts to protect social rights. Ordinary (civil) courts have been especially proactive in cases where the granting of benefits, in cash or directly supplied in kind to individuals, was at stake. A number of cases revolve around immigration, healthcare, education and the labour market and the bulk of case law has not been significantly impaired by the crisis. Also regarding this litigation, one can note that the more a certain claim is based on the intimation of a right with a stronger protection in the Constitution, the more the claimant is successful.

Dealing, of course, with individual cases, and given the fundamental principle that a decision of a court has effects between the parties only, it is very difficult to assess the overall impact of this case law. Nonetheless, certain strands of decisions can bring about noteworthy general consequences and budgetary effects.

The most relevant conceptual aspect of the attitude of ordinary courts is the direct application of constitutional norms when legal provisions to implement such rights are either absent or inadequate. Among many decisions – prevalently relating to the healthcare area – we have to confine ourselves to picking just a few to flesh out the arguments offered. The decisions dealing with the reimbursement of healthcare expenses incurred abroad are a very good example. This strand of case law lets us note how the courts, and especially the Court of Cassation (SC), have progressively fine-tuned the concept of an 'irrepressible core' of certain rights in a way that, in spite of recalling the analogue concept carved out by the ICC, relies to a greater extent upon the concrete content of a service.

Hence, the Supreme Court has recently included 'palliative treatments' in such a core, despite their being neither urgent nor indispensable for the recovery of a patient, by arguing that such treatments contribute to giving shape to the principle of personal dignity.[42] In several other cases the Supreme Court has disregarded (dis-applied) administrative decisions that affected this irrepressible core of a social right. In fact, ordinary courts do not possess the power to quash administrative decisions – only administrative courts may do so – but the Supreme Court in such cases often rules that an administrative decision is null and void and as such it is incapable of determining any legal effect on a right. This is why an ordinary court can merely disregard the administrative decision instead of leaving the case to the same administrative court. This strand of case law has been very important for making the proclamation of a social right entitlement more effective and for widening its content, even beyond the issue of the scarcity of funds in times of austerity. Moreover, it has foisted new models of balancing on the legislature and administrative authorities, which have to be made *ex post*, that is, after the guarantee that the non-amendable core has been secured.

When this pattern does not operate, it can be troublesome to establish whether a civil or administrative court is competent to hear a case revolving around social rights claims. It is not uncommon that the Supreme Court deals with social rights issues only to work out a conflict of competence between administrative courts and civil courts. In such cases the SC has indeed limited access to the merits of the litigation, but still its rulings can be relevant as *obiter dicta*.

For example, a fresh decision of the Supreme Court, sitting as united chambers (the apex of the judicial system),[43] in spite of the rule that establishes that any litigation in the area of public service is reserved to administrative courts, has brought back into the civil court's jurisdiction the competence to assess school decisions to disallow the measures provided for the so-called individual education plan granting disabled students a conspicuous amount of assisted teaching. In this case the SC has argued that the rule that reserves to administrative courts the competence to deal with public-service litigation is to be interpreted in the sense that it stands on condition that the exercise of discretionary administrative power is at stake. The result of this ruling of the SC is that a claimant often needs to sue the school twice, before two different courts: first by lodging a recourse with the administrative court if he or she wants to challenge how the education plan has been made (which implies the exercise of unfettered powers); second, by lodging another recourse before a civil court if he or she wants to contend that the plan has not been correctly implemented. Paradoxically, then, the notion of an irrepressible core of a social right can have adverse consequences for the effectiveness and fairness of the system of redress when in order to obtain the protection needed a person wants to challenge both the plan and its implementation.

However, in recent years the role of administrative courts has increasingly gained in importance, partly due to the mentioned change in the law that brought all litigation on 'public services' within their jurisdiction. More important, however, is the fact that administrative courts have seen the range of remedies to hold administrative authorities to account increased after the entry into force in 2010 of the Administrative Court Procedure Act[44] and ever since have acquired a certain expertise and attitude to reinforce the substantive content of individual social rights, surmounting the notion of a review only focused on a revision of individual administrative decisions aimed at their possible annulment.[45] From this perspective the inconveniences deriving from the said conflicts of competences – which in the end revolve around the question as to who is the ultimate judge of human rights – are even less justifiable.

A recent survey of the administrative court case law regarding the right to education[46] shows that in an increasing number of cases both regional administrative courts and the Council of State have come to the point of ordering administrative authorities to act in a specific way to protect specific individual rights, even using interim relief and compensatory measures.

VI. Conclusions

We can now offer some final remarks. A first point regards the policies enacted by the government and the Parliament in the area of welfare rights to combat the financial crisis. It must be stressed again that welfare reforms approved in recent years have been made essentially under an emergency pattern, as they consist mostly of measures included in financial legislation aimed to reduce public expenditure. Consequently, they have not been integrated into a coherent programme of reforms. Statutory laws (most of the time anticipated by law decrees) have often been drafted in a very short time, without proper parliamentary debate. The only somewhat coherent pieces of legislation regard the labour market and pensions, on the one hand, and education, on the other. As to the latter, however, the so-called 'good school' reform[47] seems to be devoted more to regulating teaching recruitment (so, once again, addressing labour issues) than to implementing the right to education. One has to take heed, however, that the setting up of a coherent programme of welfare reforms is objectively hampered by the allocation of legislative competences between the State and the Regions.

A second point regards what areas of social welfare policy have been protected from the blows of the economic crisis. Healthcare and education (especially relating to benefits for disabled students) have been protected from the cuts (also in court) to a greater extent than other welfare areas. This, in my opinion, is a result of the fact that in the Italian Constitution health and education find a stronger entrenchment than other social rights. Consequently, State and public authorities have in the past made extensive investment in these areas, supplying services that have become structural components of the Italian polity despite the asymmetries between the different parts of the country.

The third point is derived from the analysis of the case law. We have seen that both the Constitutional Court and ordinary (civil) courts have been engaged in protecting the social rights enshrined in the Italian Constitution well before the recent economic crisis and, in fact, have played an important historical role in the implementation of constitutional provisions. As far as the ICC is concerned, for many years it has been applying a balancing test between the guarantee of social rights and other constitutional protected interests: on the one hand, by applying the principles of equality and solidarity, it has been capable of centring the Italian welfare model around the protection of rights; on the other, taking into account the need for economic and financial efficiency, it has embraced the theory of social rights as conditional on finance. Such an approach tries to harmonise the guarantee of social rights with the respect due to legislative discretion in allocating the available financial resources. The result is a quite cautious and not always predictable case law. After 2008, the worsening of the conditions imposed by the financial curb has deepened this trend. It must be recalled, however, that the balancing test is not the unique criterion used by the ICC at the point of judging the constitutionality of laws affecting social rights. It goes hand in hand with the notion of an 'essential core' of social rights as a firm barrier against the reduction of their protection. The content and the extension of the 'essential core' must be defined, according to the ICC case law, by applying the principles of reasonableness and respect of human dignity. As to 'ordinary' (civil) courts, they have more steadily kept granting protection to social rights, especially in certain welfare areas such as healthcare and disability, by interpreting the relevant constitutional provisions as giving place to 'strong rights'. The same criterion of an 'essential core' of social rights has been in some cases widened to the maximum possible extent, especially by using an anti-regressive concept according to which in principle politics is not allowed to reduce the levels of protection already guaranteed.

As paradoxical as it may appear, it seems to me that in times of crisis the guarantee that courts have managed to secure to some social rights is even more efficacious and significant than that that they normally give to 'negative' rights. To take a simple example, we may compare the actual protection obtained by disabled students under the 'positive' right to have full teaching assistance at school with the fundamental 'negative' right to the reasonable length of a trial/proceeding, which is continuously violated in Italy but for which the only remedy is compensation in cash,[48] a remedy, hence, which is far from effective.

Notes

1 See Massimo Severo Giannini, 'Stato sociale: una nozione inutile' (1977) 1 *Scritti in onore di C. Mortati* 141, one of the leading public law scholars of the past century, for whom it was a superfluous legal notion because of its pure political and 'morphological' value.

2 S Fois, 'Analisi delle problematiche fondamentali dello "Stato sociale"' (1999) 2 *Diritto e Società* 163; F Rimoli, 'Stato sociale' in *Enciclopedia Giuridica Treccani* 4 (2004) 9.

3 G Corso, 'I diritti sociali nella Costituzione italiana' (1981) *Rivista Trimestrale di Diritto Pubblico* 755, 759.

4 *Constitution of the Italian Republic 1947* (Italy) art 33.2: 'The Republic lays down general rules for education and establishes state schools for all branches and grades.'; *Constitution of the Italian Republic 1947* (Italy) art 34: 'Schools are open to everyone. Primary education, which is imparted for at least eight years, is compulsory and free. Capable and deserving pupils, including those without adequate finances, have the right to attain the highest levels of education. The Republic renders this right effective through scholarships, allowances to families and other benefits, which shall be assigned through competitive examinations.'

5 *Constitution of the Italian Republic 1947* (Italy) art 32: 'The Republic safeguards health as a fundamental right of the individual and as a collective interest, and guarantees free medical care to the indigent.'

6 *Constitution of the Italian Republic 1947* (Italy) art 38: 'Every citizen unable to work and without the necessary means of subsistence has a right to welfare support. Workers have the right to be assured adequate means for their needs and necessities in the case of accidents, illness, disability, old age and *involuntary unemployment*' (emphasis added).

7 *Constitution of the Italian Republic 1947* (Italy) art 2: 'The Republic recognizes and guarantees the inviolable rights of the person, both as an individual and in the social groups where human personality is expressed. The Republic expects that the fundamental duties of political, economic and social solidarity be fulfilled.'

8 On the arguments spent by the different scholars in the above-mentioned debate, see A Baldassarre, 'Diritti Sociali' in *Enciclopedia Giuridica Treccani* 4 (1991) 7.

9 M Luciani, 'Costituzione, bilancio, diritti e doveri dei cittadini' in *Dalla crisi economica al pareggio di bilancio: prospettive, percorsi e responsabilità* (Giuffrè, 2013) 685.

10 See Vezio Crisafulli, *La Costituzione e le sue disposizioni di principio* (Giuffrè, 1952) 135. Vezio Crisafulli was a leading scholar of constitutional law of the last century, who was also judge of the Italian Constitutional Court from 1968 to 1979.

11 M Mazziotti Di Celso, 'Diritti sociali' in *Enciclopedia del Diritto* 7 (1963) 802; M Luciani, 'Sui diritti sociali' in Pace (ed.), *Studi in onore di M. Mazziotti di Celso* (Cedam, 1995) 103; A Giorgis, *La costituzionalizzazione dei diritti all'uguaglianza sostanziale* (Jovene, 1999); B Pezzini, *La decisione sui diritti sociali* (Giuffrè, 2001); A Pioggia, *Diritto sanitario e dei servizi sociali* (Giappichelli, 2014).

12 Gaetano Silvestri, *Dal potere ai principi. Libertà ed uguaglianza nel costituzionalismo contemporaneo* (Laterza, 2009). Gaetano Silvestri was a judge of the Italian Constitutional Court from 2005 to 2013 and was its president from 2013 to 2014.

13 *Constitutional Law No 3/2001* (Italy).
14 F Merusi, 'I servizi pubblici negli anni Ottanta' (1985) 1 *Quaderni regionali* 39, 52; Baldassarre, above n 8, 28.
15 B Pezzini, 'Principi costituzionali e politica della sanità: il contributo della costituzionale alla definizione del diritto sociale alla salute' in E Gallo and B Pezzini (eds), *Profili attuali del diritto alla salute* (Giuffré, 1998) 27.
16 M Luciani, 'Economia nel diritto costituzionale' (1990) 4 *Digesto delle Discipline Pubblicistiche* 377; M Luciani, above n 9, 126.
17 This measure has been introduced mainly in art 81 C., which now reads: 'The State ensures the balance between the revenue and expenditure of its budget, taking into account the adverse and favourable phases of the economic cycle'; but also arts 97, 117 and 119 C. have been modified to enforce it: *Constitution of the Italian Republic 1947* (Italy).
18 For an analytical investigation about the many problems that have arisen from the mentioned provision, see C Tubertini, *Pubblica amministrazione e garanzia dei livelli essenziali delle prestazioni* (Bononia University Press, 2008).
19 Italian Constitutional Court, Decision No 28/2013; Italian Constitutional Court, Decision No 104/2013.
20 *Law 107/2015* (Italy), called 'the good school' (la buona scuola), provides new rules for teacher recruitment, attributes more competences to school managers and gives a stronger autonomy to schools in organising their teaching programmes. To be fair the law is mainly devoted to abolishing the misuse of successive fixed-term contracts allowed by Italian legislation to recruit teachers for the public schools. The European Court of Justice (ECJ) in its preliminary ruling on 25 November 2014, concerning Italian legislation on teacher recruitment, declared that 'the framework agreement on fixed-term work concluded on 18 March 1999, which is set out in the annex to Council Directive 1999/70/EC of 28 June 1999 concerning the framework agreement on fixed-term work . . ., must be interpreted as precluding national legislation . . . . which, pending the completion of competitive selection procedures for the recruitment of tenured staff of schools administered by the State, authorises the renewal of fixed-term employment contracts to fill posts of teachers and administrative, technical and auxiliary staff that are vacant and unfilled without stating a definite period for the completion of those procedures': *Rafaella Mascolo and Others v Ministero dell'Instuzione, dell'Universitá e della Ricerca and Comune di Napoli* (European Court of Justice, Joined Cases C-22/13, C-61/13 to C-63/13 and C-418/13, 26 November 2014).
21 The period of expansion of the Welfare State had begun to shrink already in the mid-nineties, especially with a momentous reform of the pension system, which was shifted from a pay-as-you-go scheme, where the rate of substitution between pensions and salaries was up to 80%, to another where such a rate was destined to gradually decrease until it reached almost one-third.
22 It is not sufficient to prove the contrary to point out certain contradictory stances detectable in the ECJ case law, such as the very recent decision whereby it came back – after many years of an opposite ruling – to the position that there is indeed an exclusive State power in the organisation and handling of social services and pensions: *Azienda sanitaria locale n 5 <Spenzzino> and Others v San Lorenzo Soc. coop. sociale and Croce Verde Cogema cooperativa sociale Onlus* (European Court of Justice, C-113/13, 11 December 2014).
23 The reform, known as 'legge Fornero' from the name of the Labour Minister, was approved by Decree Law (*Law 20/2011* (Italy)) and converted by the Parliament into the *Law 214/ 2011* (Italy). The Decree had been prepared in twenty days and named 'Salva Italia', i.e., 'Save Italy', to make clear the economic emergency it had to tackle.

24 For a detailed description of crisis measures taken by Italian legislature see D Tega, 'Welfare rights and economic crisis before the Italian Constitutional Court' (2014) 172 *European Journal of Science Law* 63.
25 D Tega, 'Welfare rights in Italy, in social rights in times of crisis in the Eurozone: the role of fundamental right's challenges' (Working Paper No 15, European University Institute Working Papers, 2014) 50.
26 The decline of the fund for social policies started long before the beginning of the global financial crisis of 2008, even if after this year its amount has been dramatically cut, as we have seen before in the figures shown in section IV.B. According to the official report published by the Region Conference the national fund for social policies was reduced from €1.884.346.940 of 2004 to €317.000.000 of budget forecast for 2014; during 2014 the fund was further reduced to 262.618.000: Conferenza delle Regioni e delle Province Autonome, *Dossier politiche sociali 2004-2012* (25 March 2014) <www.regioni.it/newsletter/n-2465/del-25-03-2014/dossier-politiche-sociali-2004-2014-12333/>.
27 Decree 22/2015 (Italy).
28 See note 23.
29 About this reform see the commentary of G Bronzini, 'Il reddito minimo garantito e la riforma degli ammortizzatori sociali' (Working Paper No 270, Centre for the Study of European Labour Law 'Massimo D'Antona', 2015).
30 *Law 78/2015* (Italy).
31 C Panzera, 'Legislatore, giudici e Corte costituzionale di fronte al diritto alla salute (verso un inedito "circuito" di produzione normativa?)' in P Bianchi (ed.), *La garanzia dei diritti sociali nel dialogo tra legislatore e Corte* (Plus, 2006).
32 Italian Constitutional Court, Decision No 509/2000.
33 Very illustrative of this trend is the decision *Aktiebolaget NN v Skatteverket* (European Court of Justice, C-111/05, 29 March 2007). For a more detailed analysis of the evolution of the ICC decision about social rights protection and financial limitations see: B Pezzini, above n 11. See also C Salazar, 'Crisi economica e diritti fondamentali' (Paper presented at 28th Convegno annuale dell'Associazione Italiana Costituzionalisti, Rivista, 2013) for the idea of a truly 'constitutional case law of the crisis', which has led the ICC to increasingly take into account the consequences of its own decisions on economic figures.
34 C Salazar, above n 33.
35 Italian Constitutional Court, Decision No 511/2005.
36 Italian Constitutional Court, Decision No 248/2011.
37 This approach has been endorsed by the ECJ in 2012 in a preliminary ruling concerning an Italian case in the field of social housing benefits, stating that a member state may limit the application of the principle of equal treatment to citizens of third countries, save the obligation to grant the 'core benefits' in respect of the commitment to social assistance and social protection enshrined in art 34 of the Charter of Fundamental Rights of the European Union: *Servet Kamberaj v Istituto per l'Edilizia sociale della Provincia autonoma di Bolzano (IPES) and Other* (European Court of Justice, C-571/10, 24 April 2010).
38 A Pioggia, 'Giudice amministrativo e applicazione diretta della Costituzione: qualcosa sta cambiando?' in Vittoria Barsotti, *La Costituzione come fonte direttamente applicabile dal giudice* (Maggioli Editore, 2012); E Boscolo, 'Istruzione e inclusione: un percorso giurisprudenziale attorno all'effettività dei diritti prestazionali' (2014) 2 *Munus, Rivista giuridica dei servizi pubblici* 165 .
39 Italian Constitutional Court, Decision No 70/2015. For a commentary on the decision, see Stefano Giubboni, 'Le pensioni nello Stato costituzionale' (2015) 23 *Menabo de Etica ed Economia*.
40 Provided for by the emergency law (Salva Italia) passed by the Monti Government in 2011.

41 For a slightly different account of the ICC stance see S Civitarese, 'Austerity and social rights in Italy: A long standing story', UK Constitutional Law Association Blog (17 December 2015) <https://ukconstitutionallaw.org/>.
42 Italian Supreme Court, Labour Law Section, Decision No 9969/2012.
43 Italian Supreme Court, Decision No 25011/2014. See also E Scoditti, 'I diritti fondamentali fra giudice ordinario e giudice amministrativo' (2015) 140 *Il Foro Italiano* 962.
44 Code of Administrative Court Procedure, Delegated Decree No 104, 2 July 2010.
45 E Boscolo, above n 38.
46 Ibid.
47 D Tega, above n 24.
48 *Law 89/2001* (Italy).

Chapter 5

Spain

Dolores Utrilla

I. Introduction

Article 1(1) of the 1978 Spanish Constitution (hereinafter SC) defines Spain as a social and democratic State subject to the rule of law. The constitutional enshrinement of the social State clause and of certain social rights, together with the strong economic growth experienced during the three decades following the passing of the SC, led to the development of quite an advanced[1] welfare State.[2] Yet, since 2008, social welfare policies have been intensely affected as a result of the economic and financial crisis.

The seriousness of the Spanish economy's deterioration since 2008 is well known: it suffices to note the unemployment rate (26.9% during the first quarter of 2013), the risk of poverty and social exclusion rate (28% in 2013), the percentage of public deficit (5.8% in 2014) or the amount of public debt (97.70% of GDP at the end of 2014).[3] In 2009, the European Commission started a (still ongoing) excessive deficit procedure against Spain. In June 2012, the deepening of the banking crisis led Spain to ask the European Union for financial assistance in order to complete the process of restructuring and recapitalisation of its banking sector. A total amount of €41,000 million was granted to Spain under the condition of meeting obligations arising from the excessive deficit procedure and of following recommendations to address macroeconomic imbalances within the framework of the European Semester. Consequently, Spanish authorities have adopted a series of austerity measures aimed at cutting back public expenditure,[4] deeply affecting the legal regime of virtually all social welfare rights, including both contributory and non-contributory social benefits. No social welfare policy area has been shielded from austerity measures during this period.

This chapter provides an overview of these welfare rights cutbacks, as well as of their constitutional context and judicial reception. The analysis will focus on those reforms relating to three of the main social non-contributory benefits: health protection, housing, and benefits for the unemployed and those in situations of dependency due to disability, illness, or age. Given the impossibility of addressing all the austerity measures taken throughout this period, the analysis will be limited in general terms to the measures adopted by the central State, although some of the most relevant measures taken by the regions or Autonomous Communities will also be highlighted.

With respect to the social rights examined, the following elements will be tackled: their constitutional basis, the cutback measures adopted and the judicial response thereto. Such an analysis will allow for the formulation of some concluding remarks about the impact of austerity measures on the Spanish constitutional and social welfare system.

II. Constitutional basis

A. General principles

The legal regime of social welfare rights is strongly conditioned by the four structural principles of the SC: (a) the Social state clause, (b) the democratic State clause, (c) the rule of law clause and (d) the autonomic State clause.

a) ***The social State clause*** (Article 1(1) SC) requires public powers to foster the effective equality and freedom of citizens. Legal scholarship usually distinguishes two dimensions within this clause. On the one hand, there is an *instrumental dimension* that is usually identified with the constitutional principle of efficacy (Article 103(1) SC).[5] This principle imposes on all public powers the duty to act in such a way that the pursued general or public interests are satisfied in an effective manner.[6]

   More significant for the purposes of this chapter, however, is the *material or substantive dimension*, resulting in a duty of public authorities to promote freedom and equality of individuals and groups (Article 9(2) SC). This general duty, which must guide the interpretation and the enforcement of the whole SC, is further specified in other constitutional provisions. Some of the most noteworthy are Article 10(1) (principle of human dignity), Article 14 (principle of equality) and Articles 39 to 52 (principles governing the economic and social policy).[7] Articles 39 to 52 identify certain social goals that are closely related to the idea of the welfare State. They include both guidelines for the action of public powers and rights of citizens, such as the right to health protection (Article 43), right to housing (Article 47) and the protection of disabled people (Article 49).[8]

   However, these principles are not the only mechanism through which the SC protects social welfare. There are certain social rights that, due to their systematic location within the constitutional text, are endowed with a reinforced level of protection in the same way as (classic) fundamental rights – for example, the right to education (Article 27) and the right to strike (Article 28(2)). Equally, in some areas a social content has been inferred from the objective legal dimension of (classic) fundamental rights. For instance, from the principle of human dignity (Article 10(1)) an obligation has been derived for the State to aid those who lack a minimum standard of living.[9]

These different kinds of social rights are subjected to diverse regimes of constitutional protection. Rights enshrined in Articles 14 to 38 SC (fundamental rights in the broad sense) are binding on all public authorities and may only be regulated by law. Their core content must be preserved in any case (Article 53(1) SC). Rights contained in Articles 14 to 30 (fundamental rights in the strict sense) are additionally granted a preferential judicial protection regime before ordinary courts and before the Spanish Constitutional Court (hereinafter referred to as SCC) through the individual appeal for constitutional protection (*recurso de amparo*) (Article 53(2) SC).

Rights covered by Articles 39 to 52 SC (principles governing the economic and social policy), however, are provided with a far lower standard of constitutional protection: their recognition, respect and protection, 'shall guide legislation, judicial practice and actions by the public authorities', while 'they may only be invoked before ordinary courts according to the legal provisions by which they are developed' (Article 53(3) SC). This has a twofold meaning. On the one hand, it results in extensive legislative autonomy concerning the scope and the efficacy of Articles 39 to 52, so that in the absence of legislative provision a citizen cannot claim an individualised benefit before the courts.[10] On the other hand, however, it turns into a set of limits on public authorities, whose actions are constrained by the need to meet certain objectives and goals, the observance of which can ultimately be controlled by the SCC.[11] Furthermore, the constitutional enshrinement of these principles results in an entitlement for the legislature to restrict other opposing constitutional principles or rights. This happens, for example, when the right to housing (Article 47 SC) is linked to the social function as a limit on property rights (Article 33(2) SC).

This regime of constitutional protection applicable to social rights is further examined below from the point of view of the other structural principles of the Constitution.

b) ***The democratic State clause*** (Article 1(1) SC), within this context, confers a central role to the democratic legislature when it comes to defining, within the limits set by the SC, the scope of social rights and the legal regime of public benefits relating to them. This, in turn, has two consequences.

First, the open-ended wording of the constitutional provisions aimed at protecting social rights, together with their configuration – in most cases – as mere principles governing economic and social policy, enables the democratic legislature to shape them in many different ways and to adapt their scope in light of the socio-economic circumstances at any given time.[12] The legislative scope of manoeuvre is not unrestricted, however. The SC sets certain limits on the restriction or reversibility of social policies.[13] Such limits include the figure of the core content of rights (Article 53(1)), the minimal conditions for the development of a dignified human life (Article 10(1)), the principle of non-retroactivity of provisions restricting rights (Article 9(3)) and the principles of reasonableness (Article 9(3)) and proportionality.

Second, the abstract definition of the content of social rights and of the corresponding social policies is incumbent only on those public authorities endowed with democratic legitimacy: that is, the legislature and, to the extent allowed by the law, the government and the public administration. Notably, judges (as well as the administration when it acts as a mere enforcement body) are *not* allowed to take redistributive social policy decisions based on criteria of their own. This prohibition, which has been referred to as the 'fear-clause' (*Angstklausel*),[14] stems from Article 53(3) SC in connection with the principles governing economic and social policy. The SCC has endorsed this interpretation by stating that the establishment of a right to public benefits rests solely with the legislature, which cannot be replaced in this task by the judge.[15]

c) ***The rule of law clause*** (Article 1(1) SC) is expressed in this context through the binding character of the social rights enshrined in the SC, notwithstanding the fact that their legal regime and normative weight differ depending on their systematic location within the constitutional text. Especially in the case of rights covered by Articles 39 to 52, their binding character manifests itself primarily in the possibility of their observance being monitored by the SCC. This issue will be separately addressed later (section IV below).
d) ***The autonomic State clause*** (Article 2 SC) guarantees the right of autonomy to nationalities and regions with the limits of the solidarity and the unity of Spain, and has given rise to the so-called Autonomic State (*Estado Autonómico*). For present purposes, it suffices to note that most competences relating to public social policies have been assumed by the regions or Autonomous Communities for example, the competences with regard to housing, health and social services, among others (Article 148 SC). Yet the State still has the power to participate in the design of these kinds of policies under different transversal competences listed in Article 149(1) SC. Furthermore, Article 137 also recognises the principle of autonomy for the self-government of municipalities, provinces and islands, which is of significance since a large part of social welfare benefits are provided at the local level.

B. Specific areas of social welfare policy

Healthcare

Article 43(1) SC recognises the right to health protection, while Article 43(2) SC states that it is incumbent upon public authorities to organise and safeguard public health by means of preventive measures and necessary benefits and services. Furthermore, other constitutional provisions refer to the health protection of certain groups: the elderly (Article 50), consumers (Article 51(1)), disabled people (Article 49), and workers (Article 40(2)).

Notwithstanding the broad formulation of Article 43 SC, a positive and a negative content of the right to health protection can be identified. In its negative dimension, it imposes on public powers a duty to refrain from any action that may damage people's health. In its positive dimension, the right to health protection results in a duty of public authorities to safeguard the health of people through preventive measures, benefits and services, although it does not impose the establishment of a universal and free public health service.[16]

To date, the SCC has never defined the constitutionally protected content of the right to healthcare. Indeed, its scarce case law on health protection refers almost exclusively to the distribution of healthcare competences between the central State and the Autonomous Communities. As for the substantive scope of Article 43 SC, the Court has said only that this provision imposes on public authorities a twofold duty: (1) to deploy the corresponding administrative activity of provision of benefits and (2) to develop the necessary action to safeguard people's health.[17] On some occasions, the SCC has linked the right to health protection with other (classic) fundamental rights: the right to personal integrity (Article 15) has been held to include the right to health protection in its negative dimension,[18] although for the infringement to be substantiated, there must be a serious and genuine risk to personal integrity.[19]

In this respect, it must be taken into account that Article 10(2) SC foresees that the constitutional provisions recognising rights and freedoms shall be interpreted in conformity with the international treaties and agreements on human rights ratified by Spain.[20] From the point of view of the right to healthcare, the International Covenant on Economic, Social and Cultural Rights (ICESCR) is of major importance. Article 12 ICESCR enshrines the right of everyone to the enjoyment of the highest attainable standard of physical and mental health, and it imposes on States the obligation to create the conditions that would assure to everyone medical service and medical attention in the event of sickness. The Committee on Economic, Social and Cultural Rights (ESCR Committee) has interpreted this provision in the sense that it imposes, as a minimum, the core and unescapable obligations of providing essential medicines and of ensuring access to health facilities, goods and services on a non-discriminatory basis, especially for vulnerable or marginalised groups. The ESCR Committee has also interpreted that Article 12 ICESCR forbids the adoption of any retrogressive measures concerning the right to health, in particular when they are incompatible with the above-mentioned core obligations arising from such a right.[21] The SCC has, however, shown reluctance thus far to use the ICESCR and the General Comments of the ESCR Committee as interpretative parameters of constitutional rights, in contrast to what appears to be becoming usual in other jurisdictions.[22]

Housing

Article 47 SC reads as follows:

> All Spaniards are entitled to enjoy decent and adequate housing. Public authorities shall promote the necessary conditions and shall establish appropriate standards in order to make this right effective, regulating land use in

> accordance with the general interest in order to prevent speculation. The community shall participate in the benefits accruing from the urban policies of the public bodies.

The wording of Article 47 SC is quite broad and undetermined. Apart from declaring the binding nature of this provision,[23] the SCC has not defined its scope. In particular, it has not clarified what 'decent and adequate housing' means, nor has it outlined the boundaries of this right vis-à-vis the legislature. Nonetheless, it is undisputed that the 'enjoyment' of a home can take place through various means (ownership, leasing and so forth).[24] It is also apparent that the 'decent' nature of a home is closely related to the principle of human dignity (Article 10(1) SC), which in turn has been linked by the SCC to the existence of an invulnerable vital minimum that any legal status must ensure.[25]

As for international human rights law, the interpretative value of which in accordance with Article 10(2) SC should not be disregarded, Article 11 ICESCR contains the right of everyone to adequate housing. According to the ESCR Committee, the concept of 'adequacy' relates to different indicators, among which are the following: availability of services, materials, facilities and infrastructures; affordability; habitability, in terms of hygiene, healthiness and safety; legal security of tenure; and accessibility, particularly with regard to disadvantaged groups.[26] Furthermore, the ESCR Committee has stated that the right to housing includes the prohibition of forced evictions in the absence of adequate procedural guarantees and legal remedies for those affected.[27]

Unemployment and dependency

The right to social protection of people who are unemployed or in situations of dependency (due to disability, illness or age) does not have a specific constitutional foundation. Yet, both social rights can be inferred from different constitutional provisions.

First, Article 49 SC imposes upon public authorities a duty to carry out a policy of preventive care, treatment, rehabilitation, and integration of those with physical and mental disabilities, as well as a duty to provide them with special protection so that they can enjoy the rest of their constitutional rights. Second, Article 50 SC requires public authorities to guarantee a sufficient income for citizens in old age and to promote their welfare through a system of social services that provides for their specific problems, including health problems. Third, Article 41 SC begins by stating that public authorities:

> shall maintain a public Social Security system for all citizens which will guarantee adequate social assistance and benefits in situations of hardship, especially in cases of unemployment.

The SCC has declared that Article 41 implies that, although no citizen in an objective situation of need can be unprotected by the Social Security system,

> in determining situations of need to be addressed, the legislature enjoys a wide scope of discretion when it comes to regulating and modifying public benefits in order to adapt them to needs at any given time, taking into account the general context in which these situations arise.[28]

Moreover, the protection of both dependent and unemployed people can easily be inferred from the right to health protection (Article 43 SC), the right to personal integrity (Article 15 SC), the principle of human dignity (Article 10(1) SC) and, more generally, from the substantive dimension of the social State clause (Article 9(2) SC). The SCC has held that,

> it is a requirement of the social State subject to the rule of law that those people whose basic needs are not covered by the non-contributory scheme of the Social Security system may have access to other social aids or benefits.[29]

Likewise, the Court has linked the principle of human dignity to the existence of a minimum amount of resources sufficient to cover the basic human needs.[30] Of major interest, also from the point of view of the right to housing, is the Court's case law according to which human dignity imposes on public powers the duty not only to develop the relevant provision of benefits, but also to take appropriate measures of protection for which purpose 'it is reasonable and consistent to create a patrimonial sphere intangible to the executive action of creditors'.[31]

Finally, it must be recalled that the European Social Charter of 1961, the original version of which was ratified by Spain, includes the right to social and medical assistance, particularly for those without adequate resources (Article 13), while Article 11(1) ICESCR enshrines the right of everyone to an adequate standard of living.

III. Policy reforms

This section explores the main sector-based reforms affecting the social rights discussed above. However, before doing so, we must first examine a more general and recent constitutional reform: namely, the amendment of Article 135 SC.

A. General – Article 135 SC

The amendment to Article 135 has profoundly transformed the constitutional framework within which social welfare policies are developed. The amendment incorporates into the Constitution a set of economic and financial principles and rules that seriously restrict the possibilities of deploying the social State clause, and that also affect the democracy and the autonomic State clauses. The context in which this constitutional reform took place was the negotiations that led to the adoption of the Treaty of Stability, Coordination and Governance in the Economic and Monetary Union (EMU) in March 2012.

This Treaty contains an obligation on the Contracting States to incorporate the principle of budgetary stability into their domestic legal order through provisions of binding force and permanent character (preferably with a constitutional rank) or otherwise guaranteed to be fully respected and adhered to throughout national budgetary processes. A few months before the conclusion of the Treaty, Spain stepped forward and endowed the principle of budgetary stability with constitutional rank by amending Article 135 SC.[32] The way in which this reform was carried out is emblematic of a more general phenomenon: the economic crisis' depletion of representative institutions, such as parliaments, and the colonisation of public decision-making mechanisms by financial and economic interests that are distanced from the general interest.[33]

On 5 August 2011, Prime Minister Zapatero received a letter from the President of the European Central Bank (ECB) and the Governor of the Bank of Spain, in which the adoption of several steps of structural adjustment was suggested, including the introduction of strict standards of budgetary control and the reduction of public expenditure. On 26 August 2011, the parliamentary groups of the two major political parties in the national parliament (the left-wing Socialist Party and the right-wing People's Party) presented a proposal to amend Article 135 SC. Despite the impact the reform would have on some of the main structural features of the SC, it was not carried out through the reinforced reform procedure enshrined in Article 168 SC. Instead, it was effected through the general – and more flexible – reform procedure of Article 167 SC, which requires neither the highest parliamentary majorities nor the holding of a referendum.[34] Moreover, the reform was carried out through the urgency procedure and was passed at a single reading, resulting in a restriction on parliamentary debate and on submission of amendments.[35] No referendum was called. The combination of all these factors led to the reform being passed on 8 September 2011, just over a month after its submission.[36]

Article 135 SC currently enshrines budgetary stability as a principle governing the activity of all public administrations; it prohibits the State and the Autonomous Communities from exceeding a certain percentage of structural deficit, which must be determined through a State's act within the margins established by EU law, and it foresees the absolute priority of debt services payments. This provision seriously restricts the capacity of public authorities to develop the social State clause by resorting to public indebtedness. The subversion of the constitutional framework that it involves,[37] as well as the (in substance rather) anti-democratic procedure through which it was approved,[38] have been strongly criticised.

From September 2011 on, Article 135 has been the constitutional foundation invoked by the different policy reforms aimed at cutting back public expenditure. This provision has been developed by means of Organic Act 2/2012, which provides for strict budgetary and financial control mechanisms of the State over the Autonomous Communities including the possibility of suspending the autonomy in situations of extreme non-compliance.[39] Likewise, Article 135 has been adduced as the constitutional foundation for the restriction of local entities' financial autonomy through Act 27/2013.

The sections that follow tackle some of the most relevant austerity measures taken by the State regarding the specific social welfare rights under examination.[40]

B. Healthcare

Prior to the crisis, Spain had one of the most advanced public healthcare systems in the world. In 1986 the groundwork for a universal public healthcare service was laid down,[41] and in 2003 free and universal public healthcare was established.[42] However, austerity measures taken in the course of the economic crisis have deeply affected this model, and in particular its (a) *universality*, (b) *status as a free service,* and (c) *quality.*

a) The *personal scope of the right to healthcare*, that is, the circle of right holders, has been restricted from 2012. First, access to service benefits of the *Sistema Nacional de Salud* (National Health System, NHS) is no longer universal. Instead, it is linked to the contribution of the user.[43] Only those having the status of an insured or a beneficiary of an insured are entitled to public healthcare.[44] Other residents must either take out private medical insurance or access the NHS by joining a 'special agreement', a health-insurance scheme that involves the payment of a monthly fee.[45] This means that certain groups are now excluded from the NHS: illegal immigrants and, in certain circumstances, unemployed non-resident Spaniards with no right to an unemployment benefit or aid.[46] Only three types of service benefits remain universal regardless of the patient's legal status: emergency care due to serious illness or accident, pregnancy care and healthcare for the under-aged.
b) Some service benefits of the NHS that were provided for free until 2012 are now subject to *financial contributions by users.* The portfolio of services common to the whole State is divided into three categories or packages. Only the first one, referring to basic or essential services, is completely financed with public funds. The other two packages, relating to supplementary and ancillary services, are linked to user contributions or co-payments. This includes, inter alia, drugs, orthoprosthetic services and dietetic products provided on an ambulatory basis, as well as non-emergency medical transport and non-essential or supporting services for chronic pathologies.[47] On the other hand, the scope of the public pharmaceutical service benefit has been restricted.[48] Until 2012, access to a broad list of medicines was free for pensioners and subject to an average contribution of 40% for other users. Nowadays, most drugs are no longer part-financed by the NHS,[49] and those that remain within the NHS are subjected to a greater contribution by the user. The amount of such contribution is periodically fixed by the Spanish Government in proportion to the income level of citizens,[50] although there are contribution

ceilings for chronically ill patients and pensioners in long-term treatments. Exemptions to the co-payment regime are provided for certain particularly vulnerable groups, such as people receiving treatment for a work accident or occupational disease or recipients of non-contributory pensions. Apart from these measures, from 2012 some Autonomous Communities have established an additional fee for the provision of administrative services related to pharmaceutical benefits (the so-called '€1 per prescription surcharge'), which has recently been declared unconstitutional, as will be shown later.[51]

c) The *organization and conditions* for the provision of the public healthcare service have also been modified in different Autonomous Communities in order to reduce public expenditure. Such administrative self-organisation steps have included the closure of health centres in certain time bands, the reorganisation of service times and places, the outsourcing of certain health services and the reduction of medical staff, among others. For example, in Madrid a procedure for outsourcing the management of the public health service corresponding to various public hospitals was launched in 2013. Nevertheless, this led to a strong social response and to several judicial challenges, and the regional government withdrew the project in January 2014. In Castilla-La Mancha, the regional government approved a regulation in 2012 by which the public service of continuous and urgent healthcare was reorganised, involving the night closure of certain health centres in some rural areas.[52] This step led to several challenges before ordinary courts and was finally abandoned by the Autonomous Community.[53]

C. Housing

Contrary to the healthcare scenario, by the onset of the crisis Spain still lacked an adequate and comprehensive system of protection of the right to housing,[54] even though different public policies had been designed and implemented in this field. Indeed, in the years preceding the crisis both the State and the Autonomous Communities had passed plans for subsidised housing as well as different forms of aid in order to facilitate access to housing by disadvantaged social groups. However, since 2009 a sharp worsening in the level of protection of this right has taken place. This has occurred through two routes: (a) the adoption of restrictive measures and (b) the omission of sufficient measures of protection against the growing number of evictions stemming from the crisis.

a) *Restrictive measures* have included the removal of public aid and the decrease of protection of the right to housing in private law relationships. First, Royal Decree 1713/2010 removed direct aid for the purchase of subsidised housing and reduced the amount of other aid for the promotion and access to subsidised housing. Second, the so-called 'basic emancipation income for young people' was removed through Royal

Decree- Law No. 20/2011, and for those already enjoying it, its amount was reduced by more than 25% through Royal Decree-Law No. 20/2012. Third, the legal regime of urban leases, which, prior to the crisis, was quite favourable for tenants, was also amended. Among other steps, an express procedure for the eviction of tenants was introduced by Act 19/2009, and their right to the compulsory extension of urban leasing agreements was reduced from five to three years through Act 4/2013.

b) The right to housing has also been dramatically affected by the *sharp increase in the number of evictions* as a result of foreclosure proceedings provoked by the growing interest rates of mortgages, the worsening of working conditions, the rise of unemployment, and the cut of social subsidies.[55] From 2008 to 2012, a total number of 244,278 evictions took place, while 415,117 foreclosure proceedings were initiated.[56] This situation has led to the adoption of several steps aimed at protecting mortgage debtors. Nevertheless, they have proven to be clearly insufficient for two reasons. First, these measures apply only to mortgage debt incurring in a situation of very extreme economic precariousness. Second, reforms have only partially contributed to overcoming the two main deficiencies of Spanish legislation in this domain: the impossibility for mortgage debtors to be released from the part of debt remaining after the foreclosure of their properties, and the lack of effective defensive mechanisms in the course of judicial foreclosure proceedings.

The first relevant steps for the protection of mortgage debtors were taken in 2012. Firstly, Royal Decree-Law No. 6/2012 introduced a Code of Good Banking Practice based on the voluntary adherence of banks, which intended to promote mortgage debt restructuring as well as property transfer in lieu of payments for extremely low income debtors. Soon afterwards, Royal Decree-Law No. 27/2012 established a two-year suspension of foreclosure proceedings related to the main residences of particularly vulnerable families.

From 2013 new steps were taken in response to recent case law of the Court of Justice of the European Union (CJEU)[57] to which reference will be made later (section IV below). Act 1/2013 introduced different measures reinforcing the protection of mortgage debtors. For example, judges in foreclosure proceedings were granted the power to construe clauses in the enforceable mortgage contract as unfair; limits were set on late-payment interests related to mortgages on main residences; a partial release of debts remaining after foreclosure proceedings was provided for under certain conditions; and payment of mortgage debts through the transfer of property to the creditor was introduced for very exceptional cases. It should be emphasised that Act 1/2013 was passed disregarding the proposals contained in a popular legislative initiative signed by about a million and a half citizens, which provided for a general introduction of property transfer in lieu of payment.[58] Subsequently, and as a consequence of a new CJEU ruling,[59] Royal Decree-Law No. 11/2014 amended once again the legal regime of judicial foreclosure proceedings, enabling debtors to appeal against judicial resolutions that rejected their opposition to mortgage enforcement.

Finally, some Autonomous Communities have adopted their own measures to protect the right to housing of mortgage debtors. The most significant example is that of rules enabling the temporary expropriation of the use of houses in imminent eviction where either their former owners/tenants are at risk of social exclusion or their physical or mental health is threatened – for example, Andalusia's Decree Law 6/2013. Nevertheless, the Spanish Constitutional Court has recently declared this measure unconstitutional, as will be shown later (section IV below).

D. Unemployment and dependency

Although the social protection of dependent people has been addressed in a fragmented fashion since the 1980s,[60] its general legal regime was consolidated through Act 39/2006, which foresaw the creation of a System for Autonomy and Care for Dependency (hereinafter the Dependency System). This system was conceived as a universal and comprehensive protection mechanism to be developed, financed, and implemented by all levels of public administration (national, regional, and local). It would consist of a diversified catalogue of social benefits, including financial aid and service benefits, and it was to be gradually deployed pursuant to the timetable provided for by Act 39/2006. However, some of the basic features of the Dependency System have been deeply affected by austerity measures undertaken during the economic crisis. Reforms in this field may be classified into three groups.[61]

a) First, *financial aid for the provision of non-professional care* (that is, care provided to dependent people at their homes by relatives or friends) has been restricted. The amount of such aid has been reduced by more than 15% by the State, and the Autonomous Communities are allowed to set further reductions.[62] Moreover, the State has stopped paying social security contributions corresponding to non-professional caregivers.[63]
b) Second, the *mechanisms for financing the Dependency System* have been amended. The minimum funding to be provided by the State has been reduced by more than 13%.[64] Further, since 2012 the joint contribution to be made by the central State and the Autonomous Communities through collaboration agreements has been suspended,[65] so that the funding of the system shifts largely to the Autonomous Regions, whose budgetary and financial autonomy, as already noted, has been greatly reduced through the amendment of Article 135 SC. Moreover, the legal regime of co-payment by the users has also been modified.[66] Due to this reform, beneficiaries' contributions have increased each year since 2012, so that nowadays individuals assume more than 50% of the cost of the services they receive.
c) Third, the *timetable for the progressive deployment* of Act 39/2006 has undergone successive reforms in order to postpone the implementation of the Dependency System for those people suffering from a less severe situation.[67] These reforms have included the removal of the backdating of entitlement:

administrative decisions granting such rights are now effective only from the moment of decision, and no longer from the date of application.[68]

Apart from measures aimed at the social protection of dependent people (some of whom are in a precarious economic situation due to the impossibility of entering the labour market), in the years preceding the crisis both State and Autonomous Communities had taken several steps to protect unemployed people who lacked the necessary resources to live.[69] The most significant ones were unemployment non-contributory allowances[70] and minimum-income schemes (known as 'active insertion income' at a State level,[71] and as 'integration minimum income' or the like at a regional level[72]). Some of these benefits have been restricted in recent years, as has happened, for example, with the minimum-integration income in Catalonia[73] or with the national active insertion income.[74] No significant new protection measures have been adopted in this area at the State level, except for several temporary programmes for unemployment protection and professional integration, designed for long-term unemployed people who meet a series of strict requirements.[75]

IV. Judicial response

A. General

The above-mentioned restrictive measures concerning social welfare rights have led to several appeals before courts. Most of these appeals are still pending at the time of writing. Nonetheless, it can still be noted that the framing of many social rights as *principles* of the economic and social policy intensely conditions the mechanisms for their judicial protection.

Although administrative regulations and decisions implementing cutback measures may be challenged before ordinary (administrative) courts, social rights may only be invoked in accordance with the legal provisions by which they are developed. Pursuant to the fear-clause (*Angstklausel*) contained in Article 53(3) SC, although ordinary courts are bound by governing principles in Articles 39 to 52 SC when interpreting and applying legal norms, they cannot make redistributive decisions basing on criteria of their own. For this reason, Spanish judges are bound by the law even if it leads to 'antisocial' results in a particular case.[76] This makes it difficult for ordinary courts to take an activist approach towards measures constraining social welfare rights.

Having said that, it will be shown how administrative judges have still overturned some administrative measures restricting social rights through mechanisms related to the notion of good administration. Moreover, ordinary civil courts, which are the ones who must apply rules concerning foreclosures and evictions, have lately shown a trend towards interpreting such norms in a very favourable way for mortgage debtors, for which they have occasionally used the mechanism of the preliminary ruling before the CJEU.

As regards legislative measures, they may only be challenged before the SCC, and Spanish law does not permit an individual citizen to challenge directly the constitutionality of legislative measures that touch on the rights tackled in this chapter. Direct individual appeal for constitutional protection is designed only for those rights enshrined in Articles 14 to 30 SC. Measures restricting the social rights examined herein can only be subject to SCC review by way of a judge-referred constitutional question, or through the appeal of unconstitutionality (which may only be lodged by the President of the Spanish Government, fifty Members of the Spanish Parliament, fifty Senators, a regional government, a regional parliament or the Ombudsman). The SCC can control the constitutionality of measures affecting these rights through other mechanisms, but, again, only certain constitutional bodies may lodge such questions.

Equally, in Spain there is no procedural mechanism for challenging the inactivity of the legislator. This is controlled through political means.[77] Moreover, the SCC has stated that the constitutional configuration of principles governing the social and economic policy make it highly unlikely that an individually considered piece of legislation will be deemed unconstitutional by omission, that is, due to the fact that such specific law does not satisfy the goals imposed by those principles.[78]

B. *Healthcare*

Some of the NHS reform measures discussed above have been challenged before the SCC. Various appeals of unconstitutionality against Royal Decree 16/2012 have been lodged by the Autonomous Communities. The cases are still pending. The President of the Spanish Government has in turn challenged different laws enacted by some Autonomous Communities in contradiction to the healthcare reforms adopted by the State. One prominent example is the appeal lodged against a Decree passed by the Basque Country[79] through which public healthcare services are granted to illegal immigrants within the Autonomous Community. The case is still pending, but the SCC has already refused to order the interim suspension of the contested Decree. The Court has explicitly taken into account the special nature of the public interests at stake, which are linked to the right to health protection and even with the right to life and personal integrity (Article 15 SC), and has stated that such interests 'cannot get impaired by the mere consideration of an eventual economic saving' that, moreover, 'is not sufficiently determined'.[80]

To date, the SCC has already ruled on some legislative reforms undertaken by certain Autonomous Communities. The SCC has upheld the constitutionality of legal provisions empowering the Autonomous Community of Madrid to outsource the management of several public hospitals.[81] According to the SCC, the mere legal possibility of awarding contracts for the management of the public health service is not by itself inconsistent with Article 43 SC because it neither affects the legal framework governing citizens' access to the service, nor alters the public financing or content of such service. The Court did not go into the assessment of the material impact that the effective implementation of the challenged rule may have on the right to health protection or on the right to equality, but it understood that such an assessment cannot be performed within a process of abstract constitutionality review.[82] Conversely, the so-called '€1 per prescription surcharge' of Madrid and Catalonia was declared unconstitutional on the ground that it amounted to an encroachment of the competences of the State.[83]

As for ordinary administrative courts, some relevant interim and final rulings must be highlighted. In a challenge brought by several municipalities, the High Court of Justice of Castilla-La Mancha ordered the interim suspension of the Regions' administrative regulation rearranging the autonomic health service and foreseeing the night closure of some health centres.[84] The court granted the suspension on the basis that the implementation of the contested provision could result in a health risk that is inconsistent with the constitutional duty of health protection. In its decision, it highlighted that the economic reasons invoked for the adoption of the measure offered insufficient justification. As a result, the challenged regulation was withdrawn by the regional government. Soon afterwards, the same court overturned the Autonomic plan of human resources in the health sector, which foresaw the refusal to extensions in active service of doctors who had reached retirement age. According to the court's reasoning, the challenged measure lacked a specific and objective justification, as well as involving an important modification of the medical staff without adequate planning or an appropriate assessment of the demand of healthcare services.[85]

The High Court of Justice of Madrid ordered the interim suspension of an administrative procedure that contracted out the management of the health services of several hospitals in Madrid.[86] The court based its interim decision on the need to preserve the efficacy of an eventual final ruling that would annul the contested administrative decisions, since the effects of the contracting-out process may be quite difficult to reverse. Likewise, the court took into account the fact that the damages resulting from suspension were of a strictly economic nature, as well as the fact that the economic savings on which the contested measure was founded were not sufficiently justified.

C. Housing

The Spanish legal framework on foreclosures and evictions has been challenged before both Spanish and European courts in recent years. A different attitude can be detected in this respect between the SCC, on the one hand, and European and Spanish lower courts, on the other.

In 2011 the SCC rejected a question of unconstitutionality about the compatibility of the legislation discussed above with the right to an effective legal remedy (Article 24(1) SC) and the right to housing (Article 47 SC). At that time, Spanish law stated that the assessment of the unfair character of a clause in a mortgage contract should be performed in a separate judicial proceeding, so that the judge of the foreclosure proceeding could not take interim measures – such as suspension of the eviction – based on the alleged unfair character of a mortgage clause.

Quite surprisingly, the SCC considered the question unfounded, even declaring that it had been lodged with the improper purpose of:

> challenging in an abstract way the constitutionality of a legal scheme as contrasted with a hypothetical alternative model, the setting of which is reserved for the legislator.[87]

Later on, the SCC declared the unconstitutionality of the Andalusian legislation that allowed the temporary expropriation of the use of foreclosed homes in favour of their former owners.[88] In a judgment that confirms a clearly recentralising trend in its case law,[89] the Court maintained that the contested autonomic legislation encroached upon the State's competence in general economic planning, even though housing is an exclusive competence of the Autonomous Communities.

The CJEU has taken a quite different approach when examining the compatibility of Spanish foreclosure and evictions law with EU law, within the context of several preliminary rulings raised by Spanish ordinary civil courts. In *Aziz*,[90] the CJEU ruled that the regime of consumer protection contained in Directive 93/13/EC applies to mortgage contracts, and that the Directive is incompatible with any legislation that does not allow the judge of the foreclosure proceeding to assess the unfairness of a mortgage clause and to grant interim relief. This interpretation would subsequently be consolidated in *Banco Popular Español*[91] and in *Sánchez Morcillo*.[92] These CJEU rulings have had a considerable impact in Spain. They led to the introduction of some measures for the protection of mortgage debtors through Act 1/2013 and Royal Decree-Law No. 11/2014 (see section 3 above). Having regard to the CJEU's case law, the Spanish Supreme Court started to declare void those mortgage clauses that established a minimum-interest rate regardless of the Euribor ('floor clauses') in the absence of any transparency,[93] and lower courts began to order interim suspension of evictions where the unfairness of a mortgage clause was questionable.[94]

The European Court of Human Rights (ECtHR) has also ruled on two cases regarding evictions under Spanish law. Although both applications were finally rejected by the Court,[95] interim relief was granted during their pendency based on the existence of children and the lack of an alternative housing for the affected families.[96] Following this, some Spanish courts have relied on this precedent to suspend evictions relating to families with children.[97]

D. Dependency and unemployment

To date, there have been no relevant judicial challenges of measures restricting social protection of unemployed people. In contrast, some reforms regarding the social protection of dependent people have been contested before the SCC and before ordinary courts.

In 2008, the Ombudsman lodged an unconstitutionality appeal before the SCC against a Valencian Budget Act according to which a lack of administrative response in procedures for granting benefits to dependent people would amount to a rejection of their applications.[98] In a ruling that is of great interest for other cases pending before the court, the contested Act was declared unconstitutional and void on the basis that it exceeded the material scope of Budget legislation. According to the SCC,

> the mere fact that a measure may lead to savings of public expenditure is insufficient to establish that it has enough connection with the inherent content of Budget Acts.[99]

Currently, other dependency-related cases are pending before the court, such as the appeal lodged by the Valencian socialist parliamentary group against the regional legislation establishing the co-payment regime for dependency benefits.[100]

As for ordinary administrative courts, some judgments already exist, overturning certain administrative measures restricting dependency protection. The National High Court annulled an Agreement of the Territorial Council of the Dependency System establishing the co-payment regime for dependency benefits,[101] due to the fact that it had not been approved according to the procedure established for the enactment of administrative regulations.[102] Similarly, the High Court of Castilla-La Mancha declared void a regional administrative regulation restricting dependency benefits,[103] due to the existence of serious irregularities in the procedure for the adoption thereof.[104] Finally, the High Court of the Autonomous Region of Valencia overturned a regional Decree establishing the co-payment regime of certain dependency benefits.[105] According to the court, since the contested measure imposed a financial contribution in connection with a service that is objectively necessary to meet basic users' needs, it should have been shaped as a fee, and therefore its establishment should have been done through a norm having the force of a law.[106]

V. Conclusion

Cutbacks of social welfare rights during the economic crisis portray a phenomenon of 'deconstitutionalisation', understood as the dissolution of the constitutional order through serious and continuous violations of its letter and spirit.[107]

From the point of view of the social State clause, the most significant reform has been the amendment of Article 135 SC and the resulting constitutional enshrinement of the principle of budgetary stability and the rule of absolute priority of public debt payments. Indeed, virtually all austerity measures adopted since September 2011 have been based on Article 135 and on the subsequent need to reduce public spending. Notwithstanding this, it seems apparent that Article 135 alone may not justify all restrictive measures on constitutional rights, including those of a social character. This conclusion is based on a twofold reasoning.

First, budgetary stability is shaped in Article 135 SC as a principle, that is, as a legal norm that can be met to different extents. From this it follows that public decisions intended to safeguard budgetary stability at the expense of other constitutional principles must conform to the requirements arising from weighting,[108] and in particular they must be proportionate (reasonable) and must respect the core content of the affected constitutional principles. Even the absolute priority of public debt payments, which is shaped as a rule in Article 135, could justify a restriction of other constitutional principles only in a scenario of impossibility for public authorities to obtain further financial resources. In other words: as long as it is legally possible to adopt public policies that allow for reconciliation of Article 135 with other constitutional principles, the binding force of these other principles impose on the democratic legislator a duty to adopt such policies, at least to the extent necessary to respect the core content of the threatened constitutional principles.

Second, the principle of budgetary stability in no way dictates which mechanisms should be used to meet its requirements. This, in turn, results in three consequences. First, budgetary stability does not actually entail *per se* the reduction of public expenditure, since it can also be met by increasing public revenues. Second, the need to reduce public expenditure does not prejudice how cutbacks should be distributed. Obviously, the decision to devote more or less public resources to national security or to education is political in nature, but it must be taken within the limits set out by the SC and hence requires the performance of the appropriate weighing among the legal principles at stake. Third, even in a scenario of public-expenditure constraint in social policies, public authorities remain responsible for the protection of social welfare rights. To that end, the available resources must be managed with efficacy and efficiency (Articles 103(1) and 31(1) SC). Moreover, it must be recalled that social rights impose on public authorities not only the duty to develop the corresponding service provision activity, but also the duty to adopt protection measures. Particularly striking from this latter perspective is the adoption of restrictive measures that are aimed not at reducing public expenditure, but at boosting the functioning of a specific market. This is the case of measures weakening the legal status of tenants in private urban lease contracts.

The afore-mentioned arguments, as well as the general constitutional mechanisms restricting the reversibility of social policies, make it possible to state that Spanish constitutionalism has the capacity to counter welfare cutbacks even after the amendment of Article 135. In spite of this, such mechanisms have not yet been used in a consistent manner – quite the opposite, in fact. Hitherto, social reforms restricting social rights have been set aside almost exclusively on procedural rather than on substantive grounds: the SCC has overturned austerity measures based on the infringement of constitutional rules of distribution of competences among State and the Autonomous Communities: ordinary courts have set aside administrative cutback reforms on the grounds that procedural rules were disregarded. In contrast, legal challenges to cutbacks based on substantive legal rules tend to be unsuccessful.

Besides the principle of social State, the democracy clause has also been severely affected by social welfare reforms. The avoidance of Parliament through the generalised use of emergency legislation and budget acts portrays an alarming deterioration of the democratic quality of decision-making mechanisms.[109] This trend is corroborated by two ancillary phenomena: the reluctance to take into consideration the demands of the affected social groups, on the one hand, and the restriction of the freedoms of expression and assembly, on the other. This latter circumstance, in turn, brings to the fore how a scenario of economic crisis can have an impact not only on social welfare rights, but also on classic or civil rights.[110]

In close connection with the erosion of the social and democratic State clauses, austerity measures have also affected the decentralised structure of political power-sharing derived from the SC. Rules on budgetary stability and on local government reform have heavily constrained the capacity of Autonomous Communities and of local authorities to shape social welfare policies. Indeed, although a large part of the legislative and regulatory competences regarding social rights remain in the hands of regional and/or local authorities, the growing financial and budgetary control exerted by the central State over these other levels of government is leading to a progressive emptying of the decentralised social policies. Moreover, the State's legislation and the SCC's case law in recent years show an undisguised recentralising bias, so that the scope of the decentralised competences is being progressively reduced. This has allowed the State to take certain measures restricting social welfare rights, as well as (succesfully) challenging some regional welfare-related measures. From this latter standpoint, it is important to note that most legal challenges against social cutbacks, those lodged before the SCC in particular, have confronted different levels of government and/or different political groups. This phenomenon is not new, but it may be assumed that it has grown over the crisis. Apart from being a natural consequence of the limitations faced by individual citizens in getting access to the SCC when it comes to challenging legislative measures affecting social rights, this situation makes it apparent that social welfare reforms have been placed at the forefront of the political struggle in Spain over these years.

Finally, and as a corollary of the foregoing, social welfare restrictions bring to the fore the loss of effectiveness of the SC as an instrument of social direction. A clear proof thereof is the formalistic approach of the SCC to social welfare reforms. In most of the cases, the Court has also shown an extreme deference to the principle of the democratic State and the resulting freedom of configuration of the legislature, to the clear detriment of the rule of law, which requires such freedom to be exercised within the limits set by the Constitution, and the outline of which rests – precisely – with the SCC.

Notes

1 Albeit that by 2007 the percentage of public expenditure on social policies in Spain (20% GDP) ranked below the average of the Eurozone countries (27% GDP). Flores Anarte, 'El ataque constitucional al Estado social: Un análisis crítico de la reforma del artículo 135 de la Constitución Española' (2014) 9 *Revista Internacional de Pensamiento Político* 321, 337.

2 Even when they are usually used interchangeably, the notions of 'social State' and 'welfare State' are not synonymous, but the latter refers to one of the many possible configurations of the former. See Rodriguez de Santiago and Medina Alcoz, 'Social Rights in Spain' (National Rapport presented at the International Congress of Comparative Law 2014, Vienna, 2015).
3 European Commission, Stability Program Update Kingdom of Spain 2015–2018, p. 21 [available at: http://ec.europa.eu/europe2020/pdf/csr2015/sp2015_spain_en.pdf, last visited 12 March 2017].
4 The first reaction to the economic crisis involved the adoption of public expenditure measures aimed at reactivating the economy. However, in 2010 this approach changed and austerity measures began to be taken. See Rodriguez Fernandez, 'Labour Rights in Crisis in the Eurozone: The Spanish Case' in Kilpatrick and De Witte (eds), *Social Rights in Times of Crisis in the Eurozone: The Role of Fundamental Rights' Challenges* (Working Paper No 5, European University Institute, 2014) 104.
5 Parejo Alfonso, 'La eficacia como principio jurídico de la actuación de la Administración pública' (1989) 218–19 *Documentación Administrativa* 15; Parejo Alfonso, *Eficacia y Administración: Tres Estudios* (Ministerio de Administraciones Públicas, 1995) 107; Arroyo Jimenez, *Libre empresa y títulos habilitantes* (Centro de Estudios Políticos y Constitucionales, 2004) 86; Santamaria Pastor, *Principios de Derecho Administrativo General I* (Iustel, 2009) 66.
6 Arroyo Jimenez, above n 6, 86.
7 As well as, in general, all the constitutional provisions that subordinate market-economy mechanisms to the general interest. See, for example, articles 33(2), 38 and 128(1) of the Constitution.
8 In addition, principles governing the economic and social policy include the protection of family and children (article 39), certain workers' rights within an employment relationship (article 40(2)), assistance and benefits from a public social security system (article 41), protection of Spanish workers abroad (article 42), right of access to culture (article 44(1)), promotion of science and scientific research (article 44(2)), right to enjoy an environment suitable for the development of the person (article 45), youth protection (article 48), special protection of old age (article 50) and protection of consumers and users (article 51).
9 Rodriguez de Santiago and Medina Alcoz, above n 2.
10 Spanish Constitutional Court, Judgment 36/1991, 14 February 1991 [5].
11 Lopez Pina, 'Capítulo III: De los principios rectores de la política social y económica' in Alzaga Villaamil (ed.), *Comentarios a la Constitución Española* (Cortes Generales, 1997) 24.
12 Spanish Constitutional Court, Judgment 65/1987, 21 May 1987 [17]; Spanish Constitutional Court, Judgment 37/1994, 10 February 1994 [4]; Spanish Constitutional Court, Judgment 128/2009, 1 June 2009 [4].
13 This issue has been widely covered by the Spanish scholarly literature. See, e.g., Ponce Sole, *El Derecho y la (ir)reversibilidad limitada de los derechos sociales de los ciudadanos. Las líneas rojas constitucionales a los recortes y la sostenibilidad social* (Instituto Nacional de Administración Pública, 2013).
14 Rodriguez de Santiago and Medina Alcoz, above n 2.
15 Spanish Constitutional Court, 36/1991, Judgment 14 February 1991 [5].
16 Borrajo Dacruz, 'Artículo 43' in Alzaga Villaamil (ed.), *Comentarios a la Constitución Española* (Cortes Generales, 1997) 196.
17 Spanish Constitutional Court, Judgment 113/1989, 22 June 1989 [3].
18 This connection between health and personal integrity has recently been reinforced by the SCC's use of the case law of the European Court of Human Rights: Spanish Constitutional Court, Order 239/2012, 12 December 2012 [5].

19 Spanish Constitutional Court, Judgment 35/1996, 11 March 1996 [3]; Spanish Constitutional Court, Judgment 119/2001, 24 May 2011 [6].

20 Moreover, Article 96(1) SC states that 'once officially published in Spain, validly concluded international treaties shall form part of the internal legal order'.

21 Committee on Economic, Social and Cultural Rights, *General Comment No 14: The Right to the Highest Attainable Standard of Health (Art. 12)*, 22nd sess., UN Doc E/C.12/2000/4 (11 August 2004).

22 Pissarello, 'El derecho a la vivienda: constitucionalización débil y resistencias garantistas' (2013) 14 (3) *Espaço Jurídico* 135, 149.

23 Spanish Constitutional Court, Judgment 152/1988, 20 July 1988 [2]; Spanish Constitutional Court, Judgment 7/2010, 27 April 2010 [7].

24 Pisarello, above n 23, 142.

25 Spanish Constitutional Court, Judgment 120/1990, 27 June 1990 [4]; Spanish Constitutional Court, Judgment 57/1994, 28 February 1994 [3].

26 Committee on Economic, Social and Cultural Rights, *General Comment No. 4: The Right to Adequate Housing (Art 11(1) of the Covenant)*, 6th sess., UN Doc E/1992/23 (13 December 1991).

27 Committee on Economic, Social and Cultural Rights, *General Comment No 7: The right to adequate hosing (Art 11.1): forced evictions*, 16th sess., UN Doc E/1998/22 (20 May 1997), annex 4.

28 Spanish Constitutional Court, Judgment 184/1990, 15 November 1990 [5].

29 Spanish Constitutional Court, Judgment 239/2002, 22 December 2002 [7].

30 Spanish Constitutional Court, Judgment 113/1989, 22 June 1989 [3].

31 Ibid.

32 In Spain, the principle of budgetary stability was already contained in Act 18/2001. Within EU law, it was reflected in Article 104 of the Treaty establishing the European Community, and it is nowadays enshrined in Article 126 of the Treaty on the Function of the European Union.

33 Pisarello, 'Los derechos sociales en tiempos de crisis: resistencia y reconstrucción' (Paper, Observatori DESC, 2011) <http://observatoridesc.org/sites/default/files/gerardo_desc_y_crisis.pdf>.

34 On the different procedures of reform and the way in which Article 35 SC was amended, see Flores Anarte, above n 1, 325.

35 Indeed, two members of a minority parliamentary group brought the constitutional reform before the Spanish Constitutional Court based on an alleged breach of their right to political participation (article 23), but the Court held the appeal inadmissible. See Spanish Constitutional Court, Order 9/2012, 13 January 2012.

36 It was officially published on 27 September 2011.

37 Alvarez Conde, 'La reforma del artículo 135 CE' (2011) 93 *Revista Española de Derecho Constitucional* 160, 161; Baylos Grau, 'Lealtad constitucional, Estado social y límite al déficit público' (Paper presented at Cuadernos de la Fundación: Reforma del articulo 135 de la Constitucion, Madrid, 25 September 2011) 5; Vaquer Caballeria, 'Derechos sociales, crisis económica y principio de igualdad' in *Informe Comunidades Autónomas 2011* (Working Paper, Instituto de Derecho Público, 2012); Flores Anarte, above n 1. The preamble of the constitutional reform explicitly refers to this change by stating that 'budgetary stability acquires a genuine structural meaning and conditions the action of public powers, the maintenance and the development of the social State clause of article 1(1) of the Constitution, as well as the present and future prosperity of citizens. A value the constitutional enshrinement of which is justified in order to limit and to guide the action of public authorities.'

38 Baylos Grau above n 38.

39 About its impact on the Autonomous Communities' political autonomy, see De la Quadra Salcedo Janini, '¿Se ha transformado la autonomía política y financiera

de las Comunidades Autónomas tras la reforma constitucional del artículo 135 y la adopción de la Ley Orgánica 2/2012, de 27 de abril, de Estabilidad Presupuestaria y Sostenibilidad Financiera?' (2013) 6 *Cuadernos Manuel Jiménez Abad* 59.

40 Nevertheless, the vast majority of social welfare policies (if not all of them) have been negatively affected by restrictive measures during the crisis. E.g., concerning education, the number of students in each classroom and university fees were raised through Royal Decree-law 14/2012 (Spain). As regards pensions, their revaluation was suspended by Royal Decree-law 28/2012 (Spain). Likewise, contributory unemployment benefits were reduced through Royal Decree-law 20/2012 (Spain).

41 Act 14/1986 (Spain).

42 Act 16/2003 (Spain).

43 Royal Decree-law 16/2012 (Spain) art 1.

44 The concepts of 'insured' and 'beneficiary' in article 1 of Royal Decree-law 16/2012 (Spain) have been developed through Royal Decree 1192/2012 (Spain).

45 Royal Decree 573/2013 (Spain).

46 Act 22/2013 (Spain) art 11.

47 Royal Decree-law 16/2012 (Spain) art 2.

48 Royal Decree-law 16/2012 (Spain) art 4.

49 Medicines excluded from public funding are those necessary for the treatment of minor syndromes and symptoms, as well as more than 400 drugs listed in Decision of 2 August 2012 of the General Directorate of Basic Services Package of the NHS.

50 See Decision of 10 September 2013 of the General Directorate of Basic Services Package of the NHS, modifying the conditions for the contribution of users to the funding of medicines included in the National Health System.

51 See, e.g., Act 8/2012 (Madrid) art 2; Act 5/2012 (Catalonia) art 41.

52 Decision of 20 November 2012 of the Department of Health and Social Services of the Government of Castilla-La Mancha.

53 Decision of 25 March 2013 of the Department of Health and Social Services of the Government of Castilla-La Mancha.

54 Pisarello, above n 23.

55 The United Nations Special Rapporteur on adequate housing reported in 2009 and in 2012 how the alarming figures of evictions were leading to a situation of housing emergency in Spain. See Special Rapportuer, *Report of the Special Rapporteur on adequate housing as a component of the right to an adequate standard of living, and on the right to non-discrimination in this context*, UN Doc A/HRC/10/7 (17 February 2009); Special Rapporteur, *Special Rapporteur on adequate housing as a component of the right to an adequate standard of living*, UN Doc A/67/286 (10 August 2012).

56 Directorate General for Internal Policies of the European Parliament, 'The impact of the crisis on fundamental rights across member states of the EU: comparative analysis' (2015) <www.europarl.europa.eu/RegData/etudes/STUD/2015/510021/IPOL_STU(2015)510021_EN.pdf>.

57 *Mohamed Aziz v Ctalunyacaixa* (European Court of Justice, C-415/11, 14 March 2013).

58 Aguero Ortiz, 'Medidas introducidas por la Ley 1/2013, comparativa con el RDL 6/2012, y el soterramiento de la ILP' (2013) 6 *Revista CESCO de Derecho de Consumo* 66.

59 *Sánchez Morcillo and Abril García v. Banco Bilbao Vizcaya Argentaria* (European Court of Justice, C-169/14, 17 July 2014).

60 See, e.g., Act 13/1982 (Spain) and Act 51/2003 (Spain).

61 In this section, we follow the classification proposed by Durán Bernardino, 'La incidencia de las últimas reformas en materia de dependencia, ¿sostenibilidad o destrucción del sistema?' (2015) 5 *Revista de Información Laboral*.
62 Royal Decree-law 20/2012 (Spain) transitional provision 10.
63 Ibid additional provision 8.
64 Ibid transitional provision 11. On this reform, see Gonzalez de Patto, 'La reforma de la protección social de los cuidadores no profesionales de las personas en situación de dependencia. Retrocesos e incertidumbres' (2014) 11 *Revista Doctrinal Aranzadi Social* 253.
65 Act 2/2012 (Spain) additional provision 40; Act 17/2012 (Spain), additional provision 84; Act 36/2014 (Spain), additional provision 73.
66 Territorial Council of the System for the Autonomy and Care for Dependency, *Agreement of 10 July 2012 on the improvement of the dependency system* (3 August 2012)<www.boe.es/diario_boe/txt.php?id=BOE-A-2012-10468>.
67 Royal Decree-law 20/2011 (Spain) final provision 14; Act 2/2012 (Spain) final provision 8; Royal Decree-law 20/2012 (Spain) art. 22.
68 Royal Decree-Law 8/2010 (Spain) art. 5.
69 An overview of these measures in Blasco Rasero, 'La protección social del Estado: ayudas asistenciales a favor de los ciudadanos sin recursos suficientes para vivir' (2012) 154 *Civitas. Revista Española de Derecho del Trabajo* 165.
70 Contained in Chapter Three of the Codified Text of the General Social Security Act, approved through Royal Legislative Decree 1/1994 (Spain).
71 Royal Decree 1369/2006 (Spain).
72 See, e.g., Act 10/1997 (Catalonia); Act 1/2007 (Canary Islands); Act 15/2001 (Madrid); Act 9/2007 (Valencia). A general overview of these measures can be found in European Commission, '*Informe sobre los sistemas de rentas mínimas en España*' (2014) <www.eapn.es/ARCHIVO/documentos/recursos/1/1410503349_emin_informe_septiembre_2014.pdf>.
73 As such, Act 7/2011 (Catalonia) and Act 5/2012 (Catalonia) have removed the universal character of the right to an integration minimum income, making it dependent on budgetary availability; they have tightened the eligibility requirements for accessing such benefit; and they have suppressed the retroactive effect of its granting.
74 Royal Decree-law 20/2012 (Spain); Royal Decree-law 16/2014 (Spain).
75 See Royal Decree-law 10/2009 (Spain), Royal Decree-law 1/2011 (Spain) and Royal Decree-law 16/2014 (Spain).
76 Rodriguez de Santiago, *La Administración del Estado social* (Marcial Pons, 2007).
77 Rodriguez de Santiago and Medina Alcoz, above n 2.
78 For many, see Spanish Constitutional Court, Judgment 45/1989, 20 February 1989 [4].
79 Decree 114/2012 (Basque Country).
80 Spanish Constitutional Court, Order 239/2012, 12 December 2012.
81 Act 8/2012 (Madrid) art 62.
82 Spanish Constitutional Court, Judgment 84/2015, 30 April 2015.
83 Spanish Constitutional Court, Judgment 71/2014, 6 May 2014; Spanish Constitutional Court, Judgment 85/2014, 29 May 2014.
84 High Court of Castilla-La Mancha (Administrative Division), Orders of 17 January 2013 and 29 January 2013.
85 High Court of Castilla-La Mancha (Administrative Division), Judgment of 26 June 2013.
86 High Court of Madrid (Administrative Division), Orders of 2 September 2013 and 27 January 2014.
87 Spanish Constitutional Court, Order 113/2011, 19 July 2011.

88 Spanish Constitutional Court, Judgment 93/2015, 14 May 2015.
89 In this respect, see the dissenting opinion of Justice Xiol Rios to Spanish Constitutional Court, Judgment 93/2015, 14 May 2015.
90 *Mohamed Aziz v Ctalunyacaixa* (European Court of Justice, C-415/11, 14 March 2013).
91 *Banco Popular Español SA v Rivas Quichimbo and Cun Pérez* (European Court of Justice, C-547/12, 14 November 2013).
92 *Sánchez Morcillo and Abril García v. Banco Bilbao Vizcaya Argentaria* (European Court of Justice, C-169/14, 17 July 2014).
93 This case-law was initiated by the Spanish Supreme Court (Civil Chamber), Judgment 485/2012, 9 May 2013.
94 Some lower Courts have even reached agreements concerning the way in which ECJ case-law will be applied; see, e.g., Court of First Instance No 1 of Alicante, Agreement of 23 April 2013.
95 *A.M.B. and Others v Spain* (European Court of Human Rights, C-77842/12, 28 January 2014); *Mohamed RAJI and Others v Spain* (European Court of Human Rights, C-3537/13, 16 December 2014).
96 *A.M.B. and Others v Spain* (European Court of Human Rights, Order re C-77842/12, 6 June 2012); *Mohamed RAJI and Others v Spain* (European Court of Human Rights, Order re C-3537/13, 15 January 2013).
97 For many, see Court of First Instance No 39 of Madrid, Order 1649/2012, 6 March 2013.
98 Act 15/2007 (Valencia) additional provision 11.
99 Spanish Constitutional Court, Judgment 86/2013, 11 April 2013.
100 Act 7/2014 (Valencia) arts 35, 44.
101 Agreement of 27 November 2008 of the Territorial Council of the System for the Autonomy and Care for Dependency, on the ascertainment of the economic capacity of the beneficiaries and the criteria for their contribution to the dependency system.
102 National High Court (Administrative Division), Judgment 90/2009, 25 February 2011.
103 Regulation of 29 July 2013 of the Health and Social Services Department of the Government of Castilla-La Mancha.
104 High Court of Castilla-La Mancha (Administrative Division), 9 March 2015.
105 Decree 113/2013 (Valencia).
106 High Court of Valencia (Administrative Division), 20 November 2014.
107 Baylos Grau, 'La deconstitucionalización del trabajo en la reforma laboral del 2012' (2013) 61 *Revista de Derecho Social* 19; Diez Sanchez, 'Deconstitutionalisation of social rights and the quest for efficiency' in Kilpatrick and De Witte (eds), *Social Rights in Times of Crisis in the Eurozone: The Role of Fundamental Rights' Challenges* (Working Paper No 5, European University Institute, 2014).
108 Alexy, *Teoría de los derechos fundamentales* (E. Garzón Valdés trans, Centro de Estudios Políticos y Constitucionales, 1993).
109 Rodriguez Fernandez, 'Labour Rights in Crisis in the Eurozone: The Spanish Case' in Claire Kilpatrick and Bruno De Witte (eds), *Social Rights in Times of Crisis in the Eurozone: The Role of Fundamental Rights' Challenges* (Working Paper No 5, European University Institute, 2014).
110 Cutting-back measures have led to a strong reaction on the part of civil society, which in turn has resulted in the increase of social protest movements. Faced with this situation, the State has recently passed a new Citizen Security Act (Organic Act 4/2015) that imposes significant limits on the freedoms of expression, assembly, and demonstration.

Chapter 6

The United Kingdom

Jed Meers

In assessing the aims behind one of the most controversial planks of the UK Coalition Government's welfare reform agenda – a housing benefit penalty for under-occupation, commonly known as the 'bedroom tax' – Laws LJ stated that in addition to the perceived imperative of saving public funds, the change was also seeking to 'shift the place of social security support in society'.[1] There was no elaboration by the court on what was meant by this 'shift': whether it was from the national to the local,[2] of responsibility and risk to the individual and household level,[3] in the perceived meaning of 'fairness'[4] or to a smaller state.[5] It was merely an indication that there was something more to the 'core augmentation'[6] of the 'mantra of austerity'[7] than simply saving money.

This chapter is focused on how the courts have engaged with this 'shift' in the UK. What emerges demonstrates the complexity and inherent limitations in the UK constitutional context. The courts have struggled to delineate their role in the wake of this austerity-induced shift, with the intensity of proportionality review proving an almost insurmountable bar to many claimants' challenges. The twin-gears of a 'cut-and-devolve' approach, where central budgets are reduced and responsibility for provision pushed downwards to local government, introduces complicated multi-level considerations as the welfare reform agenda becomes fragmented across institutions. Deficiencies elsewhere lead to an over-reliance on limited procedural obligations, which prove ineffective for dealing with the complicated cumulative effect of large-scale welfare reform programmes. The legal challenges to reforms in the Welfare Reform Act 2012, which provide the focus of the discussion that follows, demonstrate how these issues, among others, render many of the public law tools available to claimants challenging such policies largely blunt.

Given the space available, the discussion here is far from comprehensive. Instead, this chapter focuses on some of the key issues that have arisen in legal challenges to the Welfare Reform Act 2012. It is in two sections. The first provides a concise overview of the UK constitutional context, the motivations for reform and the importance of (and associated problems with) 'localism'. The second outlines themes that emerge from the case law: (i) the reliance on procedural challenges under equality obligations – particularly the Public Sector

Equality Duty (PSED) – in the appeals, (ii) the increasing importance of discretionary mitigation mechanisms as opposed to statutory exemptions, and how their role in a number of flagship reforms raises questions about the ability of discretion at the local authority level to sit alongside austerity at the central level and (iii) the over-reliance and inherent limitations of discrimination challenges to assert social rights.

I. Preliminary issues – the UK constitution and the welfare reform agenda

Before turning to an overview of the welfare reform agenda and its accompanying legal challenges, it is important to first provide some constitutional context. To attempt to capture the UK constitution is a 'treacherous affair'[8] and many efforts begin by outlining the ongoing disagreements over even its basic components.[9] As it is uncodified and comprised of conventions, statutes and principles stretching from the thirteenth century to the modern day, it does not easily lend itself to summary. The focus of this section is far more modest. It seeks to outline the two elements of the UK constitutional settlement that are of particular importance when looking at challenges to welfare reform measures: the incorporation of the ECHR into domestic law under the Human Rights Act 1998,[10] and the tribunal system of redress and its relationship with judicial review.

Most of the discussion in this chapter focuses on challenges brought via judicial review, and consequently it is worth briefly setting these cases within the broader appeals framework in the UK. There are separate tiers of courts within the UK system, and the nature of each of their 'constitutional functions'[11] has become increasingly fragmented as the workload has been shared between them. At the lower end of the system are the statutorily created tribunal courts (the First Tier Tribunal (FTT) and Upper Tier Tribunal (UTT)), [12] and at the higher end the High Court, Court of Appeal, and finally the Supreme Court. The bulk of judicial oversight in social security cases is serviced by the lower end tribunals. Social security payments have their own chamber – the Social Entitlement Chamber – where first-instance appeals can be heard by (relatively) specialist judges, and the workload tends to be sizeable, with 507,131 cases lodged in 2012–13 following the introduction of the Welfare Reform Act 2012.[13] This right to appeal exists for *most* decisions made by the two administering government departments – the Department for Work and Pensions (DWP) and Her Majesty's Revenue and Customs (HMRC) – and by local authorities in their administrative social security functions, but this right is a statutory creation[14] and some 'benefits' (notably Discretionary Housing Payments (DHPs) discussed elsewhere) fall outside of its scope.

The FTT considers issues of both law and fact,[15] and its decisions can be appealed only on an 'error of law'[16] to the UTT. In some limited circumstances, the UTT can exercise judicial review functions akin to that of the High Court, but this is principally limited to immigration cases. There is a right to appeal from UTT decisions up to the Court of Appeal. For cases without a route for appeal, challenges can be made to decisions by public bodies, and secondary legislation itself, in the High Court under judicial review. This is a route mandated by common-law, with some imposed procedural requirements under the Civil Procedure Rules.

Judicial review challenges form the bulk of cases under consideration here. There are numerous grounds under which a claimant can bring a challenge: illegality, irrationality, procedural impropriety and legitimate expectation. The bulk of the cases below – and in challenges to welfare reforms more generally – are focused on the 'illegality' ground, particularly with reference to the procedural duties on public sector decision makers under Equality Act 2010 and on the compatibility of administrative action and/or secondary legislation with the ECHR articles as domesticated under the Human Rights Act 1998. As a relatively tight statutory duty, the former is outlined with reference to specific cases below, but the latter warrants some discussion here – particularly with reference to the exercise of proportionality.

Human Rights Act 1998: proportionality and judicial humility

A fundamental element of the UK constitutional position, particularly in the context of challenging welfare reforms, is the incorporation of the ECHR articles into domestic law under the Human Rights Act 1998. Its introduction allowed for positive rights-based challenges against public authorities under judicial review for the first time. This development, however, raises complications. In the UK, there is not an 'ex-ante'[17] framework for assessing unconstitutional behaviour by constitutional actors, and the incorporation of a statute that encroaches into this territory has the potential to clash with the great weight ascribed to the principle of 'parliamentary sovereignty' – particularly the importance of avoiding the (unelected) judiciary striking down legislation put forward by a democratically elected legislature.[18]

As a consequence of this, the desire to champion the ECHR rights domestically has been 'tempered by an equally forceful desire not to overstep the proper boundaries of judicial power'. In other words, in not wishing to overstep their constitutional role, courts should be 'properly humble about [their] own capacities'.[19] This is explicit for qualified rights under the convention, with Articles 8–11 allowing for their breach if it can be justified as 'necessary in a democratic society', and other articles – for our purposes, particularly the Article 14 Prohibition of Discrimination – are subject to a 'proportionality' assessment, which determines whether the interference with a convention right is justified. The principle is well-established and its logic 'impeccable'[20] and largely uncontroversial – the problems arise when the courts come to apply its constitutive stages.

Proportionality review is a 'structured mechanism'[21] that asks the court to consider four key questions: (i) whether the measure adopted pursues a legitimate aim, (ii) whether there is a rational connection between the aim pursued and policy adopted, (iii) whether the aim could have been achieved using a less intrusive measure and (iv) whether, on balance, the benefits of achieving the aim by the measure outweigh the dis-benefits resulting from the restriction of the relevant protected right.[22]

Importantly, the severity of the test applied can differ depending on the issue at hand and the institution(s) involved, for perfectly valid reasons of 'institutional competence and democratic legitimacy'.[23] In the context of social security benefits, this has led to the application of the deferential 'manifestly without reasonable foundation' test to the first three elements of the proportionality exercise outlined above; namely, the aim pursued and its connection to the measure, and the intrusiveness of the policy relative to alternative options must not be 'manifestly without reasonable foundation'. The final question, which calls on the court to balance the interests of the community against any interference with protected rights, does not lend itself to a varying intensity of review – instead 'all relevant interests fall to be weighed and balanced'.[24]

As will become apparent in the discussion below, despite the clarity of the test and its supporting case law, proportionality review has been poorly applied throughout successive judicial review challenges to welfare reforms. This is for two key reasons. The test has often been applied without the institutional sensitivity required to adequately assess multi-level decision making:[25] for instance, assessing the legitimacy of a policy aim is more problematic in (the very common) cases where local authorities are acting under a statutory obligation. The aim of the policy ((i) above) is with the government, but the means of implementing it ((ii) and (iii) above) is with the local authority. Second, following this first point, difficulties in undertaking the review often result in the court simply asking whether the policy itself is 'manifestly without reasonable foundation'. This is a different test, far more akin to a *Wednesbury* unreasonableness articulation of irrationality,[26] which fundamentally avoids the reasoning demanded by proportionality review. As a central plank of judicial review challenges, these issues are revisited below.

II. The welfare reform programme: motivations and key policies

Having provided a primer on the relevant constitutional elements, this section now turns to the 2010 Coalition Government's welfare reform programme. It does not intend to give a complete account of the 2010 UK Coalition Government's welfare reform agenda. To do so would leave room for little else. Instead, it highlights some of the key reforms within the Welfare Reform Act 2012 that underpin the discussion that follows, and briefly assesses the government's stated motivations for reform. Even the objectives articulated by the ministers responsible for the policies, however, can lack clarity or appear contradictory, with the Act adhering to what Vieira and Pinto call the 'new politics of welfare reform'[27] – a complicated, intricate and often self-contradicting set of ideological assumptions and political motivations that have provided the context for changes in welfare policy.

Despite difficulties in teasing out a 'shared rhetorical position' on welfare policy, [28] the Coalition Government was clear that the 'core argumentation'[29] behind the reforms in the Welfare Reform Act 2012 was 'austerity' in response to the global financial crisis. Its measures were designed to reduce expenditure on welfare payments by about £19 billion a year across the 2010–15 Parliamentary term, with – excluding changes to the state pension – 'few stones left unturned'.[30] There were multiple changes to housing benefit, both by tenants claiming in the private rented sector (under Local Housing Allowance (LHA)) and the social rented sector, with new caps, penalties and changes to uprating introduced affecting hundreds of thousands of households. Disability benefits were also subject to sizeable retrenchment,[31] with the replacement of the UK's principle disability benefit, Disability Living Allowance (DLA), with a 'more rigorously tested' Personal Independence Payment (PIP).[32] A 'benefit cap' was introduced for all claimants receiving working-age benefits (excluding disability benefits), set at £500 per week for couples and families, and £350 for single people[33] – although this has since been reduced in the Welfare Reform and Work Bill 2015. This has been coupled with a heavily increased sanctions programme (of up to three years of social security support withdrawal) for those claiming unemployment benefits who do not meet the requirements of their personalised 'claimant commitments', such as non-attendance at interviews.[34]

Some of these reforms are still ongoing – chiefly the fundamental re-packaging of multiple in-work and out-of-work benefits (Housing Benefit, income-based Jobseeker's Allowance and Employment and Support Allowance, Income Support, Working Tax Credits, and Child Tax Credits) and other payments, such as child-care subsidies, into one, 'simplified' payment under Universal Credit.[35] The policy is the 'centrepiece' of the government's 'make work pay' agenda,[36] and is designed to simplify the benefits system,[37] increase the financial incentives to work and save money – estimated at £2.7 billion per year due to reduced administration costs and lower unemployment.[38] The new benefit is currently being rolled out in pathfinder areas using a 'lobster-pot' principle, where simple cases (principally, single unemployed individuals) are taken on to the scheme, and remain on it as their circumstances change.[39] The scheme has been rolling out for availability at all Jobcentres since Spring 2016 and the transition process should complete by September 2018.[40]

Before turning to some of the issues that have arisen in the challenges to these reforms, it is worth noting three key things about the motivations behind the Welfare Reform Act 2012. First, 'austerity' is not the only explicit factor behind its implementation; the economic principles behind austerity are invariably accompanied by the political promotion of individual responsibility for welfare provision.[41] The reforms follow the green paper '21st Century Welfare'[42] and the white paper 'Universal Credit: Welfare that Works'[43] that both underscore ideological motivations distinct from simply furthering austerity with welfare reforms. Instead they seek to dis-incentivise what is perceived as a national problem of 'benefit dependency'[44] and facilitate an 'activation turn' in welfare policy.[45]

Second, many of the welfare reforms, or mechanisms designed to mitigate them, are administered or implemented at the local authority level.[46] This has led to austerity being tied with 'localism', or the more short-lived idea of the 'Big Society',[47] which prioritise local authority and community decision-making over that of central government. In the context of welfare reform, however, this can prove problematic – especially at a time when new responsibilities are given alongside tighter budgets. Some argue that this renders any premise of real local decision-making 'hollow',[48] and it raises some particular problems in legal appeals, as discussed below.

Finally, it is worth noting that the package of policy changes in the Welfare Reform Act 2012 overlap and intersect in complicated ways – both in how they function, and their overall impact on those affected by them. By way of illustration, there were 20 individual equality impact assessments for the Welfare Reform Act 2012 alone – each of which detailing potential issues for protected groups connected to their own constituent provision, but neglecting completely to assess how they may link together in the patchwork of reforms as a whole.[49] This cumulative impact problem is discussed in more detail with reference to procedural challenges below.

Interrogating localism: an extension of 'austerity localism'

As outlined above, the welfare reform agenda in the UK has been characterised by a 'cut-and-devolve' approach, namely, reducing centrally administered budgets for programmes or individual social security payments, and then placing the onus on local authorities or other decentralised bodies to manage or mitigate the impact.[50] This approach has a clear rationale embedded in the 'localism' discourse.[51] The principle is a simple one: if savings to welfare programmes have to be made, those closest to the impact are better placed to implement, mitigate or target them than a central government department. This approach, however, warrants examination, particularly when 'localism' becomes tied to an 'austerity' programme – described elsewhere as 'sink or swim localism'[52] or 'austerity-localism'.[53] There are many implications of this hybrid approach, but within the focus of this chapter there are four key problems of this 'fetishisation'[54] of localism that have manifested themselves in the second section.

First, there is an assumption that because many of the most pertinent impacts of reducing social security expenditure are discernible at the local level, solutions to them are best served at that level as well. This fails to recognise the problematic political asymmetry between the two: by reducing central expenditure and pushing decisions downwards, governments can 'externalise responsibility'[55] for the impacts of spending reductions, while local authorities find themselves in a 'political cul-de-sac',[56] unable to change their fundamental basis. The contradiction between these two political scales can serve to distance the 'electoral connection' between the voters and those with responsibility for policy[57] – in other words, it places responsibility for controversial policies on local authorities who are not politically responsible for their implementation or design.

Second, in shifting this responsibility to the local level, it may be that this guise of 'localism' is not 'politically innocent'[58] – rather, it is seeking to avoid explicitly delineating the boundaries of who will, and importantly will not, be affected by individual policies. Devolving these problematic issues down to local authority levels can serve as a form of political sleight of hand, moving the legislative focus away from arguments over who should bear the burden of reductions in social security expenditure, and towards the discussion of local authority provision for these decisions. In other words, conflicts are 'deliberately fudged'.[59] This process has had explicit attention elsewhere, particularly in the 'blame avoidance' literature, which argues that in the exercise of welfare retrenchment, governments will attempt to 'minimise' the visibility of reform in its legislative design.[60]

Third, and linked to this second issue, this view of how discretion fits into the delivery of the austerity agenda requires an approach different to that offered by the 'conventional view'[61] of public law approaches, which often regard discretion through the (in)famous Dworkin analogy of the 'hole in the doughnut',[62] or as a 'black box' through which public law rights are 'refracted'.[63] Both of these perspectives understand discretion through the structural position it occupies in the delivery of determined policy aims. Either discretion is *pari passu* with rules with both negatively correlated with each other, or discretion distorts the intention behind the rules that bring it into being. The first two points above highlight how this structural view of discretion becomes unsettled in this 'localism-austerity' context, where discretion's role is not relative to its legislative purpose, but instead avoids the articulation of that purpose altogether.

Fourth, these issues pose particular problems for the courts when assessing proportionality in human-rights-based challenges. The proportionality exercise demands, inter alia, that 'weighing all relevant factors, the measure adopted achieves a fair or proportionate balance between the public interest being promoted and the other interests involved'.[64] Within this 'austerity localism' context, however, this balancing exercise cannot operate on a common scale; namely, it shifts the focus away from the justification of the policy, and towards a justification of localism. Put another way, the government is granted deference for its own decision-making, even when this decision is to push responsibility downwards to local authorities. This leads to the deferential tests discussed elsewhere in this chapter – principally the 'manifestly without reasonable foundation' bar – being applied *not* to the potential discrimination by the policy itself, but instead the mechanism of pushing the decision downwards.

This results in judgments that are dominated by the consideration of 'imaginary administrative decisions'[65] which, by virtue of the availability of judicial review to challenge them, can be presumed to be convention compliant. This has arisen particularly with reference to DHPs, where their availability – and the assumption that they will be awarded lawfully – justifies the supporting legislation, as opposed to the courts directing their attention to the questions at the heart of the proportionality appeal.[66] This approach at best abates the intensity of the proportionality review and, at worst, renders the bar so high as to be almost unassailable.

These four issues do not mean that 'localism' is always problematic or misguided. Instead, it simply highlights that the current constitutional protections within the UK are ill-equipped to deal with the coupling of an austerity agenda mitigated or implemented at the local level. This allocation of resource and responsibility among tiers of government is a significant change to the 'administrative constitution',[67] rather than simply being a dry issue of policy implementation. In other words, 'localism' must be some sort of *end* in its own right, as opposed to simply a *means* of delivering or alleviating the hardship caused by policies determined at the central level. In the context of assessing government motivations for the welfare reform agenda, this *end* is not articulated well, or often, at all.

III. Assessing themes in the legal challenges

A. Procedural challenges and the importance of cumulative impact

Given the clear focus of the reforms on those in receipt of certain benefits – especially housing and disability benefits – they overlap with each other within certain constituencies of claimants to create a complicated cumulative impact. This has the potential to exacerbate the severity of the reforms for certain populations – particularly those with disabilities who live in social housing, who are both disproportionately affected by social security and housing benefit reforms,[68] and also less likely to be able to effect a change in their circumstances by, for instance, finding work or moving property.[69]

This cumulative impact causes problems for the courts, particularly when assessing procedural obligations on the government, such as the Public Sector Equality Duty (PSED).[70] The picture is complicated by two further factors.

First, overlapping reforms can cause problems in the utilisation of discretionary mitigation mechanisms (principally in the form of DHPs, discussed in more detail below). The 'cut-and-devolve' approach prioritises localised discretionary pots of financial assistance over centrally determined exemptions; however, the cumulative impact of reforms can lead to difficulties in both determining the severity and case of a claimant's need, and also the sufficiency of budgets allocated for such mitigation.

This complexity is worsened as a result of the austerity agenda stretching across multiple Government departments. As outlined in the first section of this chapter, cuts made elsewhere in government can spill into the same households affected by welfare reforms. A good example can be seen in the scrapping of the Educational Maintenance Allowance (EMA) – a payment of up to £30 per week for students aged 16–18 in full-time education from low-income families. O'Hara highlights how this measure disproportionately affects the same constituency of claimants as the Social Sector Size Criteria (SSSC), adding a further annual loss to the household of £1,260.[71] Moreover, this effect can be seen in the operation of mitigation mechanisms as well. Ongoing research by Lupton has identified that teachers at schools in areas with particularly low socio-economic indicators are utilising Pupil Premium[72] funds to provide support to families affected by welfare reform measures, which has included buying food and providing clothing.[73] This demonstrates how the changes induced by welfare reform measures can alter the context in which other reforms – many with aims not connected to welfare reform at all, like the Pupil Premium – operate.

The Public Sector Equality Duty

Before turning to the inability of the procedural obligations to deal with the problem of compound impact, it is worth first outlining the nature, and limits, of the duty in two key cases appealing high-profile welfare reforms. Under the PSED, set out in s.149 Equality Act 2010, all public bodies must in the exercise of their functions 'have due regard to the need to': (i) eliminate discrimination to those with protected characteristics (such as gender, race and having a disability),[74] (ii) advance equality of opportunity and (iii) foster good relations between those with a protected characteristic, and those without.

There is a sizeable body of case law, described in *Bracking* as 'two lever arch files'[75] worth, which has built up around the interpretation of this duty. These do not warrant detailed consideration here. It is important, however, to note the emphasis given by the courts on the existence of an 'important evidential element'[76] that can demonstrate the 'recording of steps taken by the decision maker to meet their statutory requirements', and that the minister must 'assess the risk and extent of any adverse impact'.[77] This does not have to be in the form of a formal equality impact assessment, but the courts will assess whether there has been compliance as matters of fact, with close scrutiny of evidence put before them.[78]

The duty has been described as being of 'incredible importance in preventing the full burden of austerity being carried by the most vulnerable in society',[79] and a 'heavy burden upon public authorities'[80] – however, it still suffers from severe limitations in the context of challenging welfare reform packages.

Although it is regularly bolted-on to other challenges, the judicial review appeals that followed the closure of the Independent Living Fund (ILF) provide a particularly notable example of the problem at hand. Before its closure, and despite a complex history, the ILF worked with local authorities to provide care packages for people with disabilities amounting to about £360 million per annum.[81] In *R. (on the application of Bracking)* v *Secretary of State for Work and Pensions*[82] the decision to dissolve the fund, cut the budget and transfer the remaining money to local authorities to administer (although not in a ring-fenced way) was challenged under the PSED. The court considered that the 'true message'[83] of a prior consultation on the impact of this decision had not been communicated to the minister, the impact had consequently not been properly considered and the PSED not met.

This judgment is often heralded as an example of the high bar that the PSED places on decision-makers.[84] In his judgment, McCombe LJ underscored that the duty 'is a heavy burden upon public authorities',[85] and there was a duty to provide 'hard evidence'[86] that it had been sufficiently discharged. Indeed, he went as far as to suggest that issues of equality should be 'placed at the centre of formulation of policy' if and when they arise.[87]

The closure of the fund provides an ideal case study to examine the PSED as, following the judgment of the court, a new minister was appointed and the same decision was taken again. Many of the same claimants and mostly the same lawyers, brought a challenge on this second decision to close the fund in *R (on the application of Aspinall, Pepper and others)* v *Secretary of State for Work and Pensions*.[88] Effectively, the same legal argument was re-run as the 'Minister was no better informed about those matters this time round than his predecessor was'.[89]

The issue before the court was a fairly routine application of a narrow PSED consideration: did the minister 'have sufficient material before him to be able to truly appreciate the implications of closing the ILF for those most likely to be affected by its closure'.[90] The court was satisfied that 'it was certainly not a "tick-box exercise" conducted in a legal or factual vacuum'[91] and the criticisms that were levied at the use of this material in *Bracking* were not held to be applicable here, and the particular focus on the narrower ground of the minister requiring more information to adequately discharge his duty – particularly on the numbers who would be affected – was dismissed categorically by the court.[92] Indeed, Andrews J suggested that 'short of going down the pilot scheme route . . . there was nothing that he could have done that would have left him any better informed than the results of the consultation did'.[93] On the specific point raised by the claimants of knowing the numbers of people affected in more detail, it was held that '[the minister] did not need to know precisely how many of them were likely to be affected or to carry out a quantitative assessment of the impact. It sufficed that he knew, as he did, that the impact would be substantial and significant.'[94]

The unsuccessful challenges in *Aspinal*[95] – and in cases dealing with other reforms, such as *Zacchaeus 2000 Trust*[96] – demonstrate the heavy limitations on a procedural duty to challenge welfare reforms. In *Aspinal*,[97] the same decision was taken by the minister as in *Bracking*, with broadly the same evidence, but with the supporting documentation re-drafted to meet the requirements of the PSED. As highlighted by the court, the minister did not need to know how many people would be affected – simply that a lot of people would be affected badly. [98]

Consequently, these procedural duties are a sizeable administrative burden, but are often relegated to a test of administrative competence rather than whether issues of equality were 'placed at the centre of formulation of policy'.[99] This is perhaps to be expected of what is, by its very nature, a *procedural* duty. However, in light of the issue of the cumulative nature of welfare reform programmes, there are further problems with a reliance on procedural challenges.

First, as has been the case in all of the PSED challenges following the Welfare Reform Act 2012, any potential adverse impact is assessed on the policy's own terms. No attempt has been made by the government to undertake a cumulative impact assessment for those with protected characteristics – such as those with disabilities – for the reforms dealt with in this chapter.[100] Despite undertaking analysis on the distributional effects of multiple policies across household income distributions,[101] even if one is able to focus down on narrow ranges of income, pockets of compound impact can be easily lost given its concentration on a number of relatively small constituencies who may not be easily identified by income alone.[102] Indeed, research by the Equality and Human Rights Commission, which has attempted to address this lacuna, suggests that the cumulative impact of welfare reform is 'substantial and widespread'.[103]

The inability of individual equality impact assessments to sufficiently address risks of adverse impacts has been highlighted elsewhere. Shandu and Stephenson have seen this same problem in their assessment of equality impact assessments at the local government level,[104] and the Social Security Advisory Committee have recommended that some form of cumulative impact assessments are introduced for some populations affected by welfare reforms, so potential adverse impacts can be addressed, 'particularly to the most vulnerable claimants'.[105] The Parliamentary Joint Committee on Human Rights, following submissions made on the UN Convention on the Rights of Persons with Disabilities and the UN Convention on the Rights of the Child, have themselves also called for a unified assessment of the likely cumulative impact of the welfare reforms,[106] following the Equality and Human Rights Commission describing a single department being responsible for monitoring and assessing the cumulative impact of spending review and budget decisions as 'vital'.[107]

The appeals for impact to be addressed more adequately resulted in a petition calling for a cumulative impact assessment for welfare reforms on people with disabilities being debated in Parliament.[108] The government position is that a 'cumulative impact assessment would be so complex and subject to so many variables that it would be meaningless'.[109] It is suggested here that there are two problems with this assertion. First, the argument here is not that the cumulative effect of *all* government welfare reforms on those with protected characteristics should be considered in detail. Instead, it is suggested that the inter-dependency of certain aspects of the welfare reform package is so great that at least some consideration of their interaction must be warranted in order to assess the potential for adverse impact. For example, in separate judicial review challenges to the SSSC, Benefit Cap, and changes to Local Housing Allowance, when assessing justification of the regulations, the existence of DHPs were considered alongside that of the benefit reductions – in other words, the issue of justification was assessed on the 'scheme as a whole'.[110] When satellite schemes are integral to the functioning of the policy consideration, limiting assessments to the impact of one policy simply on its own terms is clearly insufficient.

Second, it would simply be necessary for the government to *consider* the cumulative impact, by exploring potential overlaps between policies and the consequent risk for those with protected characteristics, not to 'produce the perfect study'.[111] Other organisations have already produced cumulative impact reports of their own, for example: the Equality and Human Rights Commission,[112] the Children's Commissioner,[113] Contact a Family[114] and the Scottish Parliament's Welfare Reform Committee.[115] As suggested by the Social Security Advisory Committee, 'such methodological problems [are not] insurmountable to the extent that headline findings cannot be produced'.[116]

B. The importance of discretion: the rise of Discretionary Housing Payments

One of the most notable features of the current welfare reform programme has been its dependence on discretionary forms of mitigation as opposed to statutory exemptions. This has been principally in the form of Discretionary Housing Payments (DHPs) – a previously 'very small[-]'[117] scale form of discretionary relief distinct from the benefits system introduced in 2001. The growing expectations of these payments to mitigate the impact of changes to social security,[118] and the associated burden they have shouldered in legal appeals,[119] has led to their use growing dramatically from approximately 2,000 awards annually in 2002/3,[120] to more than 390,000 in 2013/14.[121]

In the Coalition Government's effort to avoid 'standing back and imposing something',[122] this 'DHP strategy'[123] has introduced a layer of administrative discretion. DHPs have become the only viable mitigating mechanism for many of those affected by the Coalition Government's flagship welfare reforms, particularly the SSSC, the Benefit Cap and changes to Local Housing Allowance. Following the Conservative Government's budget on 8 July 2015, their use is set to grow further, with about £800 million earmarked for DHPs across the course of the next Parliament.[124]

The payments have proven to be essential for the continued legality of the SSSC and the Benefit Cap, but the case law itself produces an inherent irony. The underpinning regulations grant few statutory exemptions, seemingly in a bid to avoid enforceable legal rights and consequent 'juridification of welfare'.[125] However, the courts have carved a function for DHPs that attempts to re-create the effect of such statutory exemptions in certain circumstances.

The section details the role of these payments in three sections. The first looks at the underpinning DHP regulations and how the scheme has evolved since its inception in 2001. The second looks at the way in which the courts have treated the payments, particularly as a source of justification for otherwise unlawful discrimination. The final section makes some conclusions about their future judicial scrutiny, drawing on recent case law.

The evolution of the scheme: the introduction of DHPs

In common with most of the social security system, the DHP scheme does not lend itself easily to a clear and concise description. Mummery LJ remarked of its underpinning regulations that 'I would not award it the top prize in a competition for plain English'.[126] Most of the relevant statutory provisions, however, can be found within the Discretionary Financial Assistance Regulations 2001,[127] which outlines the features of and eligibility requirements for the payments, and the Discretionary Housing Payments (Grants) Order 2001,[128] which details how local authorities can claim the cost of DHPs back from central government. In summary, the DWP provides an initial allocation of funds to local authorities based on a series of welfare reform impact measures and data on previous baseline DHP expenditure,[129] which the local authority can then award to claimants who are in receipt of housing benefit and apply for support with their rent.

There are two areas of statutory control on this process. First, there are limits on the amount of money that can be spent by the local authority on awarding DHPs. Aside from their initial allocation by the DWP, [130] local authorities can top-up the DHP funds available using their own finances, but only to 2.5 times the original allocation. Second, awards can only be made to those receiving housing benefit to assist with rent or 'housing costs'.[131] They cannot exceed the eligible rent for the property[132] or cover certain statutorily exempted areas, such as benefit sanctions or service charges.[133] Aside from this, local authorities are left largely to their own devices to decide how to make DHP awards, bound only by the general principles of public law. The payment of DHPs is distinct from the payment of housing benefit. Although there is a right to a written decision with stated reasons[134] and to seek review,[135] the payments fall outside of para. 6 of schedule 7 to the Child Support, Pensions and Social Security Act 2000 and are therefore outside of the jurisdiction of a First-tier Tribunal.[136]

Panacean payments: the treatment of DHPs in case-law

Despite being introduced in 2001, there have been a number of legal challenges to DHPs that have attempted to clarify their function, especially regarding their role in the assessment of proportionality and adherence to equality duties.[137] This section focuses more tightly on their role in response to reforms in the Welfare Reform Act 2012, and particularly the SSSC, where cases have been dominated with the consideration of these payments. Indeed, Dyson MR in *R. (On the Application of MA)* v *Secretary of State for Work and Pensions*[138] indicates that 'if read in isolation and without regard to the DHP scheme [the SSSC] plainly discriminates'[139] against the disabled, so it is necessary to analyse 'the scheme as a whole'.[140]

The cases have turned principally on familiar arguments around discrimination using Article 1 of the First Protocol (right to property), which is now well established as including housing benefit,[141] or Article 8 (right to respect for the home), to leverage Article 14 (prohibition of discrimination). There are four key elements that unite the cases on how indirect discrimination can be 'justified' through the presence of DHPs.

First, there is a common recognition that the adoption of DHPs as opposed to a statutory exemption is about more than simply servicing 'austerity'; the courts instead accept that there is an ideological undercurrent that informs the changes. This is reflected in the title to this chapter, which echoes the assertion by LJ Laws that the intention of the SSSC is, in part, to 'shift the place of social security in society'.[142] This is important, as discriminatory treatment is difficult to justify solely for the purposes of saving money,[143] so aligning the policy scheme with other more loosely defined aims – such as localism[144] and the 'social and political' aspects of the austerity agenda[145] – helps to provide further supplementary aims.

This bleeds into the second key issue of the welfare reform agenda being 'unquestionably'[146] sited within the rubric of 'high policy',[147] which leads to the application of the deferential 'manifestly without reasonable foundation' test.[148] This 'strong deferential tenor'[149] sets an incredibly high bar for the claimants to pass, as the court has to be satisfied that there is a 'serious flaw' in the scheme that produces a discriminatory effect.[150]

Third, DHPs are considered to align with these high policy aims by demonstrating characteristics that advance the vague notions of 'localism'[151] and 'austerity'[152] tied to the reforms, being described as exhibiting an element of 'local accountability',[153] flexibility in responding to changing needs (such as variability in severity of disability),[154] and being responsive to ongoing evaluation in their ability to be 'topped up'[155] as required by the DWP.

These beneficial characteristics articulated by the DWP and in the latter case law sit at odds with the disparaging treatment given to them in the earlier case of *Burnip v Birmingham City Council*,[156] where the payments' temporary nature and consequent lack of reliability were given as reasons why they could not 'come anywhere near providing an adequate justification for the discrimination' in cases involving children with disabilities being unable to share a room.[157] The *Burnip* treatment has been distinguished from the present policy environment on the basis that the overall DHP pot has been kept under review and has been increased, alongside the Welfare Reform Act reforms taking place in the 'shadow of the financial crisis'.[158]

Finally, following the interpretation in the later cases of *Rutherford*,[159] *Cotton*[160] and *A*,[161] it is clear that the justification of discrimination caused by the SSSC's current formation is dependent not only on the existence of the DHP scheme itself, but *also* on adequate assurances of the stability of the mitigation it provides in cases where there would otherwise be unlawful discrimination. Despite the 'understandable anxiety [and] stress'[162] of making applications, or periods where the shortfall is not covered, 'the use of DHPs as the conduit for payment may be justifiable, [but] it will not be justified if it fails to provide suitable assurance of present and future payment in appropriate circumstances'.[163] This requirement sits awkwardly alongside the widespread recognition of local authorities that DHPs are 'not intended as a long term solution',[164] particularly for those affected by the so-called 'bedroom tax'.

Future directions in the judicial treatment of DHPs

In most of the case law following the Welfare Reform Act 2012, DHPs have been considered as part of the justification for other regulations – particularly the

SSSC. However, the High Court has heard a judicial review of the application of DHPs themselves in *R. (on the application of Hardy)* v *Sandwell MBC*,[165] which dealt with the assessment of Disability Living Allowance/Personal Independence Payments (the principle disability benefits within the UK, with the former transitioning over to the latter) as income when applying for DHP applications.

This judgment is significant, as it highlights the potential for the United Nations Convention on the Rights of Persons with Disabilities (UNCRPD) to act as an interpretive guide to the application of Article 14 in cases involving DHPs. This is a significant development, particularly given the prevalence of disability among those affected by the measures that DHPs seek to mitigate,[166] and the propensity of the UNCRPD to create a 'heightened standard of scrutiny'[167] when considering discrimination against those with disabilities. With this in mind, there are three key points worth considering here.

First, *Hardy* held that DHPs engage the first part of the first protocol (right to property). Although it is clearly established that Housing Benefit falls under Article 1/1, DHPs have generally fallen outside of this definition as they are not a prescribed form of benefit.[168] The court, however, highlighted the necessity of DHPs to ensure the legality of the SSSC, and as such they formed 'an integral part of HB entitlements for disabled applicants', and they have 'at least a legitimate expectation that they will be used to supplement a shortfall'.[169] This demonstrates the sizeable difference travelled from the *discretionary* scheme outlined above.

The second key issue is how the United Nations Convention on the Rights of Persons with Disabilities, or the UN Convention on the Rights of the Child, can assist with the interpretation of discrimination and justification in the context of these discretionary payments. When assessing the justification of the 'benefit cap' in *R. (on the application of JS)* v *Secretary of State for Work and Pensions*,[170] the Justices disagreed on the applicability of the United Nations Convention on the Rights of the Child as an interpretive guide to Article 14. The issue was the drawing of a conduit between the type of discrimination alleged and the party affected (a problem below in section four) – with a majority of the court deciding that the claimants could not justify using a treaty concerning one group (children) to assist in the interpretation of discrimination against another (women).[171]

However, it is clear that there is a link between any tenants with disabilities and the UNCRPD. This is underscored in *Burnip* with reference to the overall legislative scheme for Local Housing Allowance, where although the case turned on other grounds, Maurice J indicated that he would have been willing to use the UNCRPD as a guide for his interpretation of Article 14 and find in favour of the claimants on that basis.[172]

This could be significant in future appeals to the welfare measures contained within the Welfare Reform Act 2012 and the lowering of the Benefit Cap in the Welfare Reform and Work Bill 2015. Article 19 UNCRPD in particular offers the potential to 'illuminate our approach to both discrimination and justification'[173] in cases involving housing benefit, given its focus on the right of those with disabilities to live independently and choose their place of residence on an equal basis to others.[174] Broderick goes as far as to suggest an eventual 'fusion' between ECHR's treatment of disability discrimination and the norms of the UNCRPD,[175] and the majority position of the Supreme Court in *JS* demonstrates the important interpretative role the convention could play in future appeals to housing benefit changes.

In the wake of the Welfare Reform and Work Bill 2015, DHPs look set to continue to play a central role in the delivery of ongoing reforms to welfare and, consequently, their lawfulness. The 2015 July Budget identified a total allocation of approximately £800 million across the next parliament for DHPs, to 'help ensure Local Authorities are able to protect the most vulnerable housing benefit claimants',[176] and the flagship Universal Credit – gradually rolling out across the country – utilises DHPs as a form of discretionary mitigation. Their use as a means of mitigating the effects of the policy has broad support in the House; the argument has been more focused on the funding provided for them. Indeed, the Labour Party put forward an amendment to the bill to require the Social Security Advisory Committee to review the DHP funding levels each year.[177] To what extent they can provide mitigation from reforms for vulnerable populations in the face of increasing expectations remains to be seen, but DHPs are set to stay.

C. Drawing conduits: protected groups and the reliance on discrimination

As is clear from the discussion above, most of the challenges following the Welfare Reform Act 2012 have been facilitated by arguments based on equality and discrimination, either through procedural obligations such as those imposed by the Equality Act 2010, or through human rights protections under Article 14 (prohibition of discrimination). This approach can only assert the social rights of those who are in protected categories – either those with 'protected characteristics' under the Equality Act 2010,[178] or those that fall within Human Rights Act 1998 Article 14's predetermined statuses or the broader category of those with 'other status'.[179]

Although this is of particular assistance when dealing with many of those who are affected by welfare reform programmes, especially claimants with disabilities, the necessity to draw a conduit between a protected group and those facing adverse impact in order to facilitate a challenge presents some problems. As is well established, the categories themselves are social constructs, and membership of them may be difficult to universally define by physical and societal parameters,[180] and those within it may not have a base of shared experience.[181] Others have criticised the homogenisation of certain groups, such as those with disabilities, into single groups with an associated single identity and set of problems.[182] Referred to by Vellani as the 'tyranny of the category',[183] pre-determined classifications like these struggle to deal with the complexity and intersectionality between these constructed groups.[184]

This problem can be seen in some of the cases discussed above. For instance, in *Zacchaeus 2000 Trust*[185] and *JS*[186] both judgments turned on the drawing of a conduit between the groups protected under the PSED or Article 14, and the negative impact complained of – the former concerned the protected characteristic of age and the impact of schoolchildren being forced to move schools, and the latter concerned a link between gender discrimination under Article 14 and the UNCRC. In both cases, the link could not be adequately drawn so both cases consequently failed.

The dependence on these procedural equality duties and anti-discrimination obligations runs the risk of giving 'priority to groups who can congregate under a "status" label to the detriment of those living in poverty more generally'.[187] The Coalition Government decided not to implement the softer requirement for public bodies to have 'due regard' to socio-economic disadvantage contained within the original formulation of the Equality Act 2010 due to concerns that it would be unnecessary 'red tape',[188] which follows the trend for legal protection from inequality for pre-determined statuses, but for socio-economic inequality to be 'left to the welfare state'.[189] Although it is clearly not for the courts to determine Welfare State policy, this overreliance on limited statuses can prove particularly problematic as functions are decentralised as the potential for unequal impact is heightened.

IV. Conclusions

The discussion above has attempted to summarise some of the key findings of the more detailed report that underpins it.[190] There are four key points worth emphasising in this concluding section.

First, it is clear that the package of measures introduced in the Welfare Reform Act 2012, and those that have followed in the Welfare Reform and Work Bill 2015, are not justified solely by the demands of 'austerity'. Instead, throughout successive appeals, they are tied to other vehicular concepts,[191] such as 'fairness' and 'localism', which work to both ensure their ongoing legality and draw the decision making further into the 'sphere of social policy'.[192] These justifications can often be problematic and at times contradictory – particularly when budgets are cut at the same time that responsibility is decentralised. This is not to say that these aims are not valid, or could not be nobly pursued by government. Indeed, the merits (or lack thereof) of austerity are well beyond the author's remit. Instead it is suggested that this lack of clarity contributes to social rights being unable to play a heavier role in this 'tricky debate'[193] than they do at present.

Second, the dramatically increased role played by DHPs has been a central feature of the 2010 welfare reform programme, and the discretionary payments are set to continue to be the key mitigation mechanism for further reforms, such as the lowering of the Benefit Cap.[194] This extra layer of administrative discretion has been granted largely as an alternative to offering statutory exemptions to reforms and, as a consequence, political debate about those who should bear the weight of the welfare reform agenda has been blurred at the edges.[195] Their treatment by the courts has been problematic, with a series of arguably misguided assumptions about their efficacy leading to an assessment that they justify otherwise unlawfully discriminatory welfare reforms.

Third, the heavy emphasis on procedural or discrimination-based challenges has led to a series of limitations, particularly in the assessment of cumulative impacts of welfare reforms, and problems associated with the categorisation of the disadvantaged. This approach comes at the expense of those who fall outside of protected categories, but nevertheless suffer unjust treatment. As the case-law continues to develop, more problems of this over-reliance are exposing themselves – particularly ongoing debates with treating eligibility requirements for discretionary assistance schemes (such as the council tax reduction scheme) as engaging Article 1 Protocol 1 of the ECHR.[196] More broadly, the difficulties of attempting to use human rights instruments as a means of offering proxy protection are increasingly being questioned.[197]

Finally, it is worth noting the direction of the 'shift' this chapter has attempted to deal with. Many areas of potential reforms are conspicuous by their absence; for example, the welfare reform programme deals almost exclusively with working-age benefits – pension credit and related passported benefits for those in retirement have been exempted from the 'austerity' reforms. Instead, the direction of the 'shift' is focused on 'responsibilising'[198] those out of work or in low-paid work, and introducing layers of further conditionality to enforce adherence. It is a shift that has proven difficult to challenge using current public law tools, and one that is still ongoing.

Notes

1 R (MA & others) v The Secretary of State for Work and Pensions [2013] EWHC 2213 [58] (per Laws LJ).
2 Patricia Kennett *et al.*, 'Recession, Austerity and the "Great Risk Shift": Local Government and Household Impacts and Responses in Bristol and Liverpool' (2015) 41 *Local Government Studies* 622, 623.
3 Ibid 640.
4 Helen Carr and Dave Cowan, 'The Social Tenant, the Law and the UK's Politics of Austerity' (2015) 5 *Oñati Socio-legal Series* 83.
5 Martin Smith and Rhonda Jones, 'From Big Society to Small State: Conservatism and the Privatisation of Government' (2015) 10 *British Politics* 226, 227.
6 United Kingdom, *Parliamentary Debates*, House of Lords, 14 February 2012, col 705.
7 Paul O'Connell, 'Let Them Eat Cake: Socio-Economic Rights in an Age of Austerity' in Aoife Nolan, Rory O'Connell and Colin Harvey (eds), *Human Rights and Public Finance: Budgets and the Promotion of Economic and Social Rights* (Bloomsbury Publishing, 2014) 60.
8 Grégoire Webber, 'Eulogy for the Constitution that Was' (2014) 12 *International Journal of Constitutional Law* 468, 470.
9 Douglas Vick, 'The Human Rights Act and the British Constitution' (2002) 37 *Texas International Law Journal* 477.
10 See *Human Rights Act 1998* (UK) s 3, which requires the Courts to read primary and subordinate legislation in a way that is compatible with convention rights.

11 Sarah Nason, 'The Administrative Court, the Upper Tribunal and Permission to Seek Judicial Review' (2012) 21 *Nottingham Law Journal* 13.
12 See *Tribunals, Courts and Enforcement Act 2007* (UK).
13 Jeremy Sullivan, *Senior President of Tribunals' Annual Report* (2015) <www.judiciary.gov.uk/wp-content/uploads/2015/02/senior_president_of_tribunals_annual_report_2015_final.pdf>.
14 See, e.g., *Child Support, Pensions and Social Security Act 2000* (UK) sch 7 [6]; *Social Security Act 1998* (UK) sch 2; Universal Credit, Personal Independence Payment, Jobseeker's Allowance and Employment and Support Allowance (Decisions and Appeals) Regulations 2013/381 (UK).
15 *Social Security Act 1998* (UK) s 12(8)(a).
16 *Tribunals, Courts and Enforcement Act 2007* (UK) s 11.
17 Mark Elliott, 'The Principle of Parliamentary Sovereignty in Legal, Constitutional, and Political Perspective' in Jeffrey Jowell, Dawn Oliver and Colm O'Cinneide (eds), *The Changing Constitution* (8th edition, OUP, 2015) 28.
18 Alison Young, *Parliamentary Sovereignty and the Human Rights Act* (Hart, 2009) 19.
19 *R (Lord Carlile of Berriew and others) v Secretary of State for the Home Department* [2014] UKSC 60 (per Lady Hale) [105].
20 The Rt Hon Lady Justice Arden DBE and Lady Justice Arden, 'Proportionality: The Way Ahead?' (2013) *Public Law* 498.
21 Alan Brady, *Proportionality and Deference under the UK Human Rights Act: An Institutionally Sensitive Approach* (Cambridge University Press, 2012) 6.
22 Frankie McCarthy, 'Human Rights, Property and the Recovery of Medical Costs for Asbestos Diseases (Wales) Bill in the Supreme Court' (2015) *Edinburgh Law Review* 373, 375.
23 Brady, above n 21, 246.
24 *Re Recovery of Medical Costs for Asbestos Diseases (Wales) Bill* [2015] UKSC 3 [52] (per Mance LJ).
25 Brady, above n 21, 18.
26 For a detailed assessment of the differences between the two, see Anne Davies and Jack Williams, 'Proportionality in English Law' in Sofia Ranchordás and Boudewijn de Waards (eds), *The Judge and the Proportionate Use of Discretion* (Routledge, 2016) 73.
27 Mónica Brito Vieira and Pedro Ramos Pinto, 'Understanding the New Politics of Welfare Reform' 61 *Political Studies* 474.
28 Richard Hayton and Libby McEnhill, 'Rhetoric and Morality – How the Coalition Justifies Welfare Policy' in Judi Atkins *et al.* (eds), *Rhetoric in British Politics and Society* (Palgrave MacMillian, 2014), 102.
29 HL Deb, 14 February 2012, c705.
30 Ian Cole, 'Is a Little Knowledge about Welfare a Dangerous Thing? A Small Scale Study into Attitudes Towards, and Knowledge About, Welfare Expenditure' (2015) 9 *People, Place & Policy Online* 50.
31 For a more detailed discussion of the impact of *Welfare Reform Act 2012* (UK) reforms to those with disabilities, see Neville Harris, 'Welfare Reform and the Shifting Threshold of Support for Disabled People' (2014) 77 *The Modern Law Review* 888, 926.
32 Kayleigh Garthwaite, 'Fear of the Brown Envelope: Exploring Welfare Reform with Long-Term Sickness Benefits Recipients' (2014) 48 *Social Policy & Administration* 782, 784.
33 See *Welfare Reform Act 2012* (UK) s 96.
34 Ruth Patrick, 'Working on Welfare: Findings from a Qualitative Longitudinal Study into the Lived Experiences of Welfare Reform in the UK' (2014) 43 *Journal of Social Policy* 705.

35 Philip M Larkin, 'The New Puritanism: The Resurgence of Contractarian Citizenship in Common Law Welfare States' (2014) 41 *Journal of Law and Society* 227, 250.
36 Christina Beatty, Steve Fothergill and Donald Houston, 'The Impact of the UK's Disability Benefit Reforms' in Colin Lindsay and Donald Houston (eds), *Disability Benefits, Welfare Reform and Employment Policy* (Palgrave Macmillan UK, 2013) 148.
37 Larkin, above n 34, 250.
38 Helen Kowalewska, 'Diminishing Returns: Lone Mothers' Financial Work Incentives and Incomes under the Coalition' (2015) *FirstView Social Policy and Society* 1.
39 United Kingdom, *Parliamentary Debates*, House of Lords, 14 February 2012, col 907.
40 United Kingdom, *Parliamentary Debates*, House of Commons, 10 June 2015, c1289W.
41 Kevin Farnsworth and Zoë Irving, 'Varieties of Crisis, Varieties of Austerity: Social Policy in Challenging Times' 20 *Journal of Poverty and Social Justice* 133, 134.
42 Department of Work and Pensions, *21st Century Welfare* (2010) <www.gov.uk/government/uploads/system/uploads/attachment_data/file/181139/21st-century-welfare_1_.pdf>.
43 Department of Work and Pensions, *Universal Credit: Welfare that Works* (2010) <www.gov.uk/government/uploads/system/uploads/attachment_data/file/181145/universal-credit-full-document.pdf>.
44 Peter Dwyer and Sharon Wright, 'Universal Credit, Ubiquitous Conditionality and its Implications for Social Citizenship' (2014) 22 *Journal of Poverty and Social Justice* 27, 33.
45 Mark Simpson, '"Designed to Reduce People . . . to Complete Destitution": Human Dignity in the Active Welfare State' (2015) *European Human Rights Law Review* 66, 70.
46 Erika Kispeter and Sue Yeandle, 'Local Welfare Policy in a Centralised Governance System: Childcare and Eldercare Services in a Period of Rapid Change in Leeds' in Dagmar Kutsar and Marjo Kuronen (eds), *Local Welfare Policy Making in European Cities* (Springer, 2015) 107.
47 Smith and Jones, above n 5.
48 Kispeter and Yeandle, above n 45, 104.
49 For access to these documents, see Department for Work and Pensions, *Collection: Welfare Reform Act 2012: equality impact assessments* (23 July 2012) <www.gov.uk/government/collections/welfare-reform-act-2012-equality-impact-assessments>.
50 See the discussion of the Independent Living Fund and the Council Tax Reduction Scheme outlined elsewhere in this chapter.
51 See Elena Vacchelli, 'Localism and Austerity: A Gender Perspective' (2015) 80 *Soundings: A Journal of Politics and Culture* 83; Chris Grover, 'Localism and Poverty in the United Kingdom: The Case of Local Welfare Assistance' (2012) 33 *Policy Studies* 349, 351.
52 Vivien Lowndes and Lawrence Pratchett, 'Local Governance under the Coalition Government: Austerity, Localism and the "Big Society"' (2012) 38 *Local Government Studies* 21.
53 David Featherstone *et al.*, 'Progressive Localism and the Construction of Political Alternatives' (2012) 37 *Transactions of the Institute of British Geographers* 177.
54 Ibid.
55 Lowndes and Pratchett, above n 51.

56 Frank Gaffikin, 'Paradoxes in Local Planning in Contested Societies' in Simin Davoudi and Ali Madanipour (eds), *Reconsidering Localism* (Routledge, 2015).
57 John Huber and Charles Shipan, *Deliberate Discretion?: The Institutional Foundations of Bureaucratic Autonomy* (Cambridge University Press, 2002) 2.
58 Featherstone *et al.*, above n 52, 178.
59 Tony Prosser, 'The Politics of Discretion: Aspects of Discretionary Power in the Supplementary Benefits Scheme' in Michael Adler and Stewart Asquith (eds), *Discretion and Welfare* (Heinemann, 1981) 150.
60 Giuliano Bonoli, 'Blame Avoidance and Credit Claiming Revisited' in Guiliano Bonoli and David Natali (eds), *The Politics of the New Welfare State* (Oxford, 2012) 93.
61 Anna Pratt and Lorne Sossin, 'A Brief Introduction of the Puzzle of Discretion' (2009) 24 *Canadian Journal of Law and Society* 301.
62 Ronald Dworkin, *Taking Rights Seriously* (Bloomsbury Publishing, 2013) 31.
63 Prosser, above n 58, 150.
64 *Re Recovery of Medical Costs for Asbestos Diseases (Wales) Bill* [2015] UKSC 3 [52] (per Mance LJ).
65 Brady, above n 21, 18.
66 See *Rutherford v Secretary of State for Work and Pensions* [2014] EWHC 1631 (Admin) [46] (per Stuart-Smith J); *The Queen on the application of A v The Secretary of State for Work and Pensions [2015] EWHC 159 (Admin)* [65] (per Worcester HHJ); *R (MA & others) v The Secretary of State for Work and Pensions* [2013] EWHC 2213 [82] (per Dyson MR).
67 Tony Prosser, 'Constitutionalising Austerity in Europe' (2015) *Public Law* 111, 112.
68 Simon Duffy, *A Fair Society? How the Cuts Target Disabled People* (2013) <www.centreforwelfarereform.org/uploads/attachment/354/a-fair-society.pdf>.
69 Social Security Advisory Committee, 'The Cumulative Impact of Welfare Reform' (Occasional paper No 12, Social Security Advisory Committee, April 2014).
70 *Equality Act 2010* (UK) s 149.
71 Ibid.
72 A government fund introduced in April 2011 providing approximately £600 million per annum to assist schools at increasing the attainment of disadvantaged pupils. The money can be used at the discretion of the school itself (with some government controls and accounting/reporting measures).
73 Ruth Lupton, *What is the Impact of the 'Bedroom Tax' on Children and Schools?* (15 April 2014) <http://blog.policy.manchester.ac.uk/featured/2014/04/what-is-the-impact-of-the-bedroom-tax-on-children-and-schools/>.
74 *Equality Act 2010* (UK) s 149(7).
75 *R. (on the application of Bracking) v Secretary of State for Work and Pensions* [2013] EWCA Civ 1345 [25] (per LJ McCombe).
76 Ibid.
77 Ibid.
78 Tom Hickman, 'Too Hot, Too Cold or Just Right? The Development of the Public Sector Equality Duties in Administrative Law' (2013) *Public Law* 325, 339.
79 Helen Carr, 'The Public Sector Equality Duty – a Mainstay of Justice in an Age of Austerity' (2014) 36 *Journal of Social Welfare and Family Law* 208, 210.
80 *R. (on the application of Bracking) v Secretary of State for Work and Pensions* [2013] EWCA Civ 1345 [59] (per McCombe LJ).
81 Ibid [5] (per Blake J).
82 Ibid.
83 Ibid [42] (per McCombe LJ).

84 Helen Carr, 'The Public Sector Equality Duty – a Mainstay of Justice in an Age of Austerity' (2014) 36 *Journal of Social Welfare and Family Law* 208, 210.
85 *R. (on the application of Bracking) v Secretary of State for Work and Pensions* [2013] EWCA Civ 1345 [59] (per McCombe LJ).
86 Ibid [64] (per McCombe LJ).
87 Ibid [59] (per McCombe LJ).
88 *Aspinall, Pepper and Ors, R (on the application of) v Secretary of State for Work and Pensions & Anor* [2014] EWHC 4134 (Admin).
89 Ibid [47] (per Andrews J).
90 Ibid [47] (per Andrews J).
91 Ibid [48] (per Andrews J).
92 Ibid [123] (per Andrews J).
93 Ibid [124] (per Andrews J).
94 Ibid [130] (per Andrews J).
95 *Aspinall, Pepper and Ors, R (on the application of) v Secretary of State for Work and Pensions & Anor* [2014] EWHC 4134 (Admin).
96 *R (Zacchaeus 2000 Trust) v Secretary of State for Work and Pensions* [2013] EWCA Civ 1202.
97 Aspinall, above n 94.
98 Apinall, above n 94.
99 *R. (on the application of Bracking) v Secretary of State for Work and Pensions* [2013] EWCA Civ 1345 [59] (per McCombe LJ).
100 Alan Roulstone, 'Personal Independence Payments, Welfare Reform and the Shrinking Disability Category' (2015) 30 *Disability & Society* 673, 683.
101 Social Security Advisory Committee, above n 68.
102 Declan Gaffney, 'Retrenchment, Reform, Continuity: Welfare under the Coalition' (2015) 231 *National Institute Economic Review* 44, 49.
103 Ibid 49.
104 Kalwinder Sandhu and Mary-Ann Stephenson, 'Layers of Inequality: A Human Rights and Equality Impact Assessment of the Public Spending Cuts on Black Asian and Minority Ethnic Women in Coventry' (2015) 109 *Fem Rev* 169, 174.
105 Social Security Advisory Committee, above n 68.
106 Equality and Human Rights Commission, *Briefing to the Joint Committee on Human Rights on the UK's Compliance with the UN Convention on the Rights of the Child* (February, 2015) <www.parliament.uk/documents/joint-committees/human-rights/EHRC_briefing_on_the_CRC_050215.pdf>.
107 Equality and Human Rights Commission, *Future Fair Financial Decision-Making* (1 February 2015) <www.equalityhumanrights.com/en/publication-download/future-fair-financial-decision-making-report >.
108 For more information on the petition, see: Karen Machin, Rosemary O'Neill and Pat Onions, 'Pat's Petition: A New Approach to Online Campaigning' (2014) 24 *Groupwork* 9.
109 United Kingdom, *Parliamentary Debates*, House of Commons, 10 July 2013, col 413.
110 *R (MA & others) v The Secretary of State for Work and Pensions* [2013] EWHC 2213 [40] (per Dyson MR).
111 Social Security Advisory Committee, above n 68.
112 Howard Reed and Jonathan Portes, 'Cumulative Impact Assessment: A Research Report by Landman Economics and the National Institute of Economic and Social Research (NIESR) for the Equality and Human Rights Commission' (Research Report No 94, 2014).

113 Children's Commissioner, *A Child Rights Impact Assessment of Budget Decisions* (27 June 2013) <www.childrenscommissioner.gov.uk/publications/child-rights-impact-assessment-budget-decisions-including-2013-budget-and-cumulative-0>.
114 Contact a Family, 'The Cumulative Effect – The Impact of Welfare Reforms on Families with Disabled Children Now and for Future Generations to Come' (Briefing Paper, Contact a Family, 2012).
115 Welfare Reform Committee, 'The Cumulative Impact of Welfare Reform on Households in Scotland' (Report, SP Paper 657, Scottish Parliament, 2015).
116 Social Security Advisory Committee, above n 68.
117 Peter Kemp, *Housing Allowances in Comparative Perspective* (Policy Press, 2007) 113.
118 Simon Rahilly, 'The Election of a Coalition Government and an Austerity Budget' (2010) 17 *Journal of Social Security Law* 207.
119 Grainne McKeever, 'Social Sector Size Criteria' (2015) 22 *Journal of Social Security Law* 13.
120 Andrew Leicester and Jonathan Shaw, *A Survey of the UK Benefits System* (Briefing Note No 13, The Institute for Fiscal Studies, 2003).
121 David Evans, *Use of Discretionary Housing Payments* (Report, Department for Works & Pensions, 2014).
122 United Kingdom, *Oral Evidence taken before the Work and Pensions Committee*, House of Commons, 13 February 2014, col 720.
123 Ibid.
124 United Kingdom, *Copy of the Summer Budget Report – July 2015 as Laid before the House of Commons by the Chancellor of the Exchequer when Opening the Budget*, House of Commons 264.
125 Suzanne Fitzpatrick, Bo Bengtsson and Beth Watts, 'Rights to Housing: Reviewing the Terrain and Exploring a Way Forward' (2014) 31 *Housing, Theory and Society* 447, 455.
126 *R (Gargett)* v *Lambeth London Borough Council* [2008] EWCA Civ 1450 [16] (per Mummery LJ).
127 Discretionary Financial Assistance Regulations 2001/1167 (UK).
128 Discretionary Housing Payments (Grants) Order 2001/2340 (UK).
129 United Kingdom, *Housing Benefit Circular* (HB Circular S1/2015, Department for Work, 30 January 2015).
130 Discretionary Housing Payments (Grants) Order 2001/2340 (UK) reg 2.
131 *R (Gargett)* v *Lambeth London Borough Council* [2008] EWCA Civ 1450.
132 Housing Benefit Regulations 2006/213 (UK) regs 12-12D.
133 Discretionary Financial Assistance Regulations 2001/1167 (UK) reg 3.
134 Ibid reg 6.
135 Ibid reg 8.
136 This issue was considered as part of an appeal to the Upper Tribunal in *EA v Southampton CC* [2012] UKUT 381 AAC.
137 For instance, see *CPAG v Secretary of State for Work and Pensions* [2011] EWHC 2616 (Admin); *R (Zacchaeus 2000 Trust) v Secretary of State for Work and Pensions* [2013] EWCA Civ 1202.
138 [2014] EWCA Civ 13.
139 *R. (On the Application of MA)* v *Secretary of State for Work and Pensions* [2014] EWCA Civ 13 (per Dyson MR).
140 Ibid [40] (per Dyson MR).
141 See *R (RJM)* v *Secretary of State for Work and Pensions* [2008] UKHL 63.
142 *R (MA & others) v The Secretary of State for Work and Pensions* [2013] EWHC 2213 [58] (per Laws LJ).
143 C Tobler, *Indirect Discrimination: A Case Study Into the Development of the Legal Concept of Indirect Discrimination under EC Law* (Intersentia, 2005), 249.

144 *R (MA & others) v The Secretary of State for Work and Pensions* [2013] EWHC 2213 [66] (per Dyson MR).
145 *Rutherford v Secretary of State for Work and Pensions* [2014] EWHC 1631 (Admin) [61] (per Stuart-Smith J).
146 *R (MA & others) v The Secretary of State for Work and Pensions* [2013] EWHC 2213 [54] (per Dyson MR).
147 Ibid [54] (per Dyson MR).
148 *Rutherford v Secretary of State for Work and Pensions* [2014] EWHC 1631 (Admin) [45] (per Stuart-Smith J).
149 Jonas Christoffersen, *Fair Balance: A Study of Proportionality, Subsidiarity and Primarity in the European Convention on Human Rights* (Martinus Nijhoff Publishers, 2009) 270.
150 *R (MA & others) v The Secretary of State for Work and Pensions* [2013] EWHC 2213 [54] (per Dyson MR).
151 Ibid [66] (per Dyson MR).
152 See ibid [50] (per Dyson MR); *Rutherford v Secretary of State for Work and Pensions* [2014] EWHC 1631 (Admin) [61] (per Stuart-Smith J).
153 *Rutherford v Secretary of State for Work and Pensions* [2014] EWHC 1631 (Admin) [32] (per Stuart-Smith J).
154 *R (MA & others) v The Secretary of State for Work and Pensions* [2013] EWHC 2213 [74] (per Dyson MR).
155 Ibid [72] (per Dyson MR).
156 [2012] EWCA Civ 629.
157 *Burnip v Birmingham City Council* [2012] EWCA Civ 629 [46] (per Henderson J).
158 *R (MA & others) v The Secretary of State for Work and Pensions* [2013] EWHC 2213 [64] (per Dyson MR).
159 *Rutherford v Secretary of State for Work and Pensions* [2014] EWHC 1631 (Admin).
160 *R. (on the application of Cotton)* v *Secretary of State for Work and Pensions* [2014] EWHC 3437 (Admin).
161 *R. (on the application of A)* v *Secretary of State for Work and Pensions* [2015] EWHC 159 (Admin).
162 *R. (on the application of Cotton)* v *Secretary of State for Work and Pensions* [2014] EWHC 3437 (Admin) [30] (per Males J).
163 *Rutherford v Secretary of State for Work and Pensions* [2014] EWHC 1631 (Admin) [48] (per Stuart-Smith J).
164 Department for Work & Pensions, 'Evaluation of Removal of the Spare Room Subsidy '(Research Report No 913, Department for Work & Pensions, 2015) 44.
165 [2015] EWHC 890 (Admin).
166 See Department for Work & Pensions, Evaluation of Removal of the Spare Room Subsidy (Research Report No 882, Department for Work & Pensions, 2014) 39.
167 Andrea Broderick, 'A Reflection on Substantive Equality Jurisprudence: The Standard of Scrutiny at the ECtHR for Differential Treatment of Roma and Persons with Disabilities' (2015) 15 *International Journal of Discrimination and the Law* 101, 115.
168 *Child Support, Pensions and Social Security Act 2000* (UK) sch 7 [6(1)].
169 *R. (on the application of Hardy)* v *Sandwell MBC* [2015] EWHC 890 (Admin) [48] (per Phillip J).
170 [2015] UKSC 16.
171 Ibid [119–30] (per Carnwarth LJ).

172 *Burnip v Birmingham City Council* [2012] EWCA Civ 629 [22] (per Hendersen J).
173 Ibid.
174 *United Nations Convention on the Rights of Persons with Disabilities*, A/RES/61/106 (entered into force 24 January 2007) Article 19.
175 Broderick, above n 166, 116
176 United Kingdom, *Copy of the Summer Budget Report – July 2015 as laid before the House of Commons by the Chancellor of the Exchequer when opening the Budget*, House of Commons 264.
177 United Kingdom, *Parliamentary Debates*, House of Commons, 20 July 2015, c1269.
178 *Equality Act 2010* (UK) s 4.
179 Which has included, for example, prisoners. See *SS v United Kingdom* (2015) 61 EHRR SE3 [38].
180 Beth Omansky Gordon and Karen E Rosenblum, 'Bringing Disability into the Sociological Frame: A Comparison of Disability with Race, Sex, and Sexual Orientation Statuses' (2001) 16 *Disability & Society* 5.
181 Sarah Keenan, *Subversive Property: Law and the Production of Spaces of Belonging* (Routledge, 2014) 18.
182 Nick Watson, 'Well, I Know This Is Going to Sound Very Strange to You, but I Don't See Myself as a Disabled Person: Identity and Disability' (2002) 17 *Disability & Society* 509, 511.
183 Fayyaz Vellani, *Understanding Disability Discrimination Law through Geography* (Ashgate, 2013) 182.
184 Floya Anthias, 'Intersectional What? Social Divisions, Intersectionality and Levels of Analysis' (2013) 13 *Ethnicities* 3, 15.
185 *R (Zacchaeus 2000 Trust) v Secretary of State for Work and Pensions* [2013] EWCA Civ 1202.
186 *R. (on the application of JS)* v *Secretary of State for Work and Pensions* [2015] UKSC 16.
187 Sandra Fredman, 'The Public Sector Equality Duty' (2011) 40 *Industrial Law Journal* 405.
188 James Hand, Bernard Davis and Charles Barker, 'The British Equality Act 2010 and the Foundations of Legal Knowledge' (2015) 41 *Commonwealth Law Bulletin* 3, 14.
189 Becci Burton, 'Neoliberalism and the Equality Act 2010: A Missed Opportunity for Gender Justice?' (2014) 43(2) *Industrial Law Journal* 122, 138.
190 The full report is available at: www.socialrights.co.uk
191 Carr and Cowan, above n 4, 83.
192 Philip Sales and Ben Hooper, 'Proportionality and the Form of Law' (2003) 119 *Law Quarterly Review* 426.
193 Mary Dowell-Jones, 'The Economics of the Austerity Crisis: Unpicking Some Human Rights Arguments' (2015) 15 *Human Rights Law Review* 193, 210.
194 *Welfare Reform and Work Bill 2015* (UK) s 7.
195 Prosser, above n 58, 169.
196 *R. (on the application of Logan) v Havering LBC* [2015] EWHC 3193 (Admin) [34] (per Blake J).
197 For a persuasive account of the problems associated with this, see: Philip Larkin, 'Delineating the Gulf between Human Rights Jurisprudence and Legislative Authority' (2016) 23(1) *Journal of Social Security Law* 42, 63.
198 Stuart Lowe and Jed Meers, 'Responsibilisation of Everyday Life: Housing and Welfare State Change' (2015) 27 *Social Policy Review* 55.

Chapter 7

Austerity, conditionality and litigation in six European countries

*Michael Adler and Lars Inge Terum**

I. Introduction

The aim of this chapter is to examine the relationship between austerity, conditionality and the rule of law. After the financial crisis in 2008, the economies of many countries went into decline and, in response to this situation, governments implemented austerity measures, such as cutting public expenditure and raising taxes. Increased conditionality, which refers both to the imposition of stricter conditions and more severe sanctions, is often regarded as an austerity measure and, in this chapter, we examine whether, in the countries considered in this book, conditions and sanctions were tightened in the years after 2008. We also investigate whether the courts provided a measure of protection to those subject to conditionality and conclude by asking whether, instead of seeing changes in conditionality as a response to economic circumstances, it is more appropriate to see them as the outcome of political choices.

Although the five countries analysed in this book differ in many ways, we have also included Sweden, traditionally regarded as the quintessential social democratic Welfare State, in our analysis in this chapter. By so doing, our analysis of the impact of austerity on conditionality covers a more representative sample of Western European countries.[1]

The chapter is divided into six sections. In section II, we offer a definition of austerity and describe its impact on each of the six countries. We describe the actions that governments took following the financial crisis as they attempted to deal with its consequences by implementing spending cuts and/or tax rises and look at the impact of government policies on the economic and social well-being of individuals. In section III, we analyse the nature and extent of conditionality and the scope and severity of conditions and sanctions in order to evaluate whether it was tightened during the years of austerity. In section IV, we describe the structure of support for the unemployed and the level of protection achieved in each of the six countries since they provide a context for a comparison. In section V, we look at the extent to which conditionality has been challenged in the courts and ask whether the courts have provided a measure of protection to those who have been subject to conditionality. Finally, in section VI, we discuss whether conditionality can be understood as an austerity measure or whether it is better understood in terms of political ideology.

II. Austerity

The recent experience of austerity in Europe and the USA was a response to the financial crisis that began in September 2008 when the investment bank Lehmann Brothers filed for bankruptcy. The initial response of a number of governments, prompted especially by the US Federal Reserve and the Bank of England, was to bail out collapsing financial institutions and stimulate the market by quantitative easing. However, the subsequent response was predominantly to implement what became known as austerity measures. Most countries experienced a decline in Gross Domestic Product (GDP) per capita that they attempted to deal with by cutting public expenditure and/or by raising taxes.

In attempting to trace the economic and social impact of austerity we present time series data for a range of economic and social indicators over the 10-year period 2005–14 (for details, see Tables A1–A8 in the Appendix to this chapter). We consider the impact of the financial crisis on the 'real economy' by tracing changes in GDP per capita, employment levels, unemployment levels and the at-risk-of-poverty (AROP) rate, and its impact on government by tracing changes in direct and indirect taxes, public and social expenditure and the 'generosity' of benefits. We use the level of GDP per capita as our indicator of the 'severity of the crisis';[2] levels of employment, levels of unemployment and the at-risk-of-poverty (AROP) rate as indicators of economic and social well-being, and levels of taxation, levels of public expenditure, levels of social expenditure and benefit generosity as indicators of austerity measures.

Tables A1–A8 reveal the level of each of the indicators at a given point in time as well as changes in the level over time. It is important to bear in mind the level of the indicator before the financial crisis and the fact that the individual indicators are not, of course, independent. Thus, for example, the level of unemployment has implications for social expenditure, and thus for public expenditure and for the at-risk-of-poverty rate. However, taken together, the seven indicators provide a fairly comprehensive picture of the economic and social impact of austerity in each of the six countries.

A. *The severity of the crisis*

All six countries experienced sustained growth in the pre-crisis period. This is illustrated in Figure 7.1, which reveals a steady growth in GDP per capita over this period.

Following the financial crisis, there was an immediate fall in GDP per capita in five of the countries, while Germany's economy started to contract a year later. Thus, in all six countries, GDP per capita was substantially lower (by 3.5–6.0 per cent) in 2009 than it had been in 2008. However, in five of the six countries (the exception was Spain), it began to increase again in 2010. In Germany, the

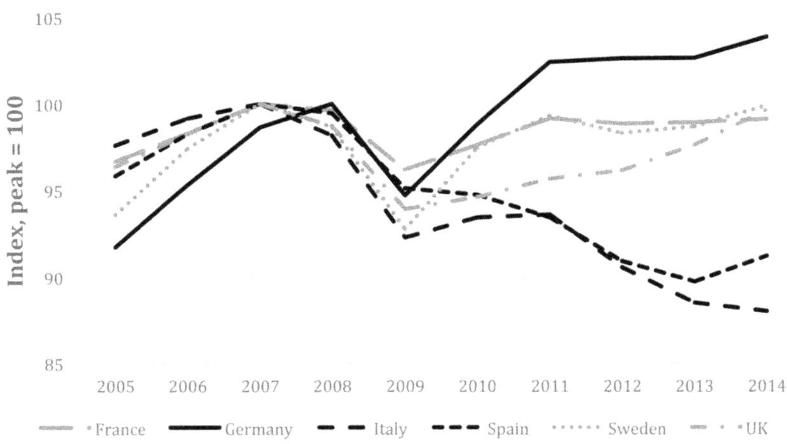

Figure 7.1 Levels of GDP per capita, 2005–14 (measured in US dollar at constant prices, using 2010 public–private partnerships (PPPs)).

increase was quite rapid – GDP per capita passed the 2008 level in 2011 and was 3.9 per cent above it in 2014. In France, Sweden and the UK, it was much more sluggish – in France it was still marginally below (by 0.5 per cent) the 2008 level in 2014 and in Sweden and the UK it was only marginally above it (by 1.28 per cent and 0.94 per cent respectively). However, in Italy and Spain, GDP per capita had still not recovered in 2014, five years after the financial crisis. In 2014, GDP per capita in Italy stood at 10.4 per cent below the 2008 level and in Spain at 8.29 per cent below the 2008 level. We can conclude that austerity had a relatively short impact in Germany, a rather longer one in France, Sweden and the UK and that, in terms of its severity and duration, it had the greatest impact in Italy and Spain.[3] It should, however, be noted that the drops in GDP per capita understate the decline relative to where countries would have expected to be before they were hit by the financial crisis (see Table 7.1).

Table 7.1 Changes in GDP per capita following the financial crisis of 2008

	2009/2008	*Changes from 2008 to 2014*	*2014/2008*
France	–3.4%	Still below 2008 level in 2014.	–0.5%
Germany	–5.3%	Passed 2008 level in 2010; continuous rise after that.	+3.9%
Italy	–6.0%	Passed 2008 level in 2010; declined after that.	–10.4%
Spain	–4.4%	Still below 2008 level in 2014.	–8.3%
Sweden	–6.0%	Passed 2008 level in 2011; static after that.	+1.3%
UK	–4.9%	Passed 2008 level in 2014.	+0.9%

B. Economic and social well-being

In order to understand the impact of the financial crisis on the economic and social well-being of individuals we present data for employment, unemployment and poverty rates.[4] It could be argued that levels of employment and levels of unemployment are not particularly good indicators since the former includes part-time employment, temporary employment and other forms of precarious employment, such as employment on 'zero-hours contracts' while the latter lumps together short-term unemployment, long-term unemployment and youth unemployment. The latter affects people who have never worked before as well as people who were previously in work and can have long-term consequences not only for those concerned but also for the wider community. There is some merit to these arguments but, for the purposes of this discussion, we think that levels of employment and unemployment, together with the at-risk-of-poverty rate, provide an adequate overview of the economic and social effects of the financial crisis and a reasonable basis for comparison. Key changes from 2005–7 to 2010–14 are set out in Table 7.2 below.

Here Italy and Spain, which were hardest hit by the financial crisis, represent the two extremes. Italy faced the financial crisis with a low employment rate of just over 60 per cent and this fell by 1.8 per cent over the period. Although it had an average unemployment rate of about 7 per cent before the financial crisis, this ended up at more than 10 per cent after the crisis. Spain started out with a higher employment rate of just under 69 per cent before the financial crisis but this fell back to 60 per cent over the period. Its unemployment rate of 8.5 per cent before the financial crisis tripled during the period of austerity and ended up at 23.3 per cent. The experiences of Italy and Spain can be contrasted with those of France, Sweden and the UK where there were no significant changes in employment or unemployment, and even more so with Germany. It will be recalled that, of the six countries considered here, Germany was least affected by the financial crisis and, partly as a result of this, employment increased (by almost 6 per cent)

Table 7.2 Changes in levels of employment, unemployment and poverty before and after the financial crisis. Differences between averages (percentage points) for 2005–7 and 2011–14

	Severity of crisis	*Changes in employment rate*	*Changes in unemployment rate*	*Changes in AROP rate*
France	++	–0.1	+1.2	–0.1
Germany	+	+5.9	–4.4	+0.3
Italy	+++	–1.8	+3.7	+2.7
Spain	+++	–8.7	+14.9	+3.6
Sweden	++	+0.8	+1.2	+1.1
UK	++	–0.5	+2.3	+0.1

and unemployment decreased (by more than 4 per cent) over the period. There were very few changes in the at-risk-of-poverty rate – the only two countries in which there were any significant changes were Spain (where it increased by 3.6 per cent) and Italy (where it increased by 2.7 per cent).

We can conclude that the impact of the austerity measures introduced by governments in the wake of the financial crisis on the economic and social well-being of individuals was substantial and enduring in Spain and Italy, but much less so in the other four countries. This is consistent with the findings of a recently published comparison of austerity measures across Europe, which concluded that 'austerity-driven welfare reforms in nine countries considered have been less comprehensive than might have been expected'.[5]

C. *Austerity measures*

Raising taxes and cutting expenditure are the main austerity measures and the six countries differed in their preferences for one or the other.[6] Table 7.3 shows that the clusters France/Italy and Spain/Sweden represent the two extremes.[7] In France and Italy, priority was given to increasing taxation, while in Sweden and the UK priority was given to cutting levels of public and social expenditure. In France and Italy, increases in taxation were associated with increases in public expenditure and, at the same time, increases in expenditure on various forms of protection. At the other extreme, cuts in taxation in Sweden and the UK were associated with cuts in public expenditure although, in both countries, social expenditure was exempted from these cuts and increased by small amounts. Germany and Spain adopted mixed strategies in that, although levels of taxation were cut, public expenditure was increased, in Spain by as much as 7.2 per cent, making it possible for the Spanish Government to increase its expenditure on social protection. Thus, the two countries that were most affected by the financial crisis (Italy and Spain) both increased their expenditure on social protection. This was mainly because more people were in need of protection rather than due to increases in benefit

Table 7.3 Changes in levels of taxation, expenditure and benefit generosity before and after the financial crisis. Differences between averages (percentage points) for 2005–7 and 2011–14

	Severity of crisis	*Changes in taxation*	*Changes in public expenditure*	*Changes in social expenditure*	*Benefit generosity*
France	++	+1.6	+4.3	+2.6	0
Germany	+	–0.7	+1.7	–0.4	–1
Italy	+++	+2.2	+3.4	+3.0	2
Spain	+++	–3.5	+7.2	+5.8	5
Sweden	++	–2.9	–2.9	+0.3	10
UK	++	–1.6	–1.4	+2.3	+2

generosity, which fell in four of the six countries, most noticeably in Sweden. Benefit generosity increased in France and, rather surprisingly, in the UK where it increased by 2.6 per cent over the period in question.[8]

The net replacement rate (NRR) is the most generally used measure of benefit generosity. It shows how taxes and benefits affect the incomes of people in and out of work for different types of families, for example, for single people or for couples with children where the partner is/is not in work.[9] In Sweden, the decline in NRR of 8.5 per cent was particularly striking.[10] In Sweden, the decline in NRR of 10 per cent was particularly striking. There was a marked decline in Spain (of 5 per cent) and smaller declines in Italy (2 per cent) and Germany (1 per cent). There was no change in NRR in France, and in the UK it went up by 2 per cent. In the period 2011–2014, the NRR was highest in France (67 per cent) and Germany (66 per cent) but considerably lower in the UK (55 per cent) and Sweden (53 per cent).

III. Conditions and sanctions

As mentioned above, increased conditionality is often regarded as an austerity measure. Conditionality refers to the attachment of conditions to the receipt of benefits or services and the imposition of sanctions for those who do not meet the conditions. It applies to some areas of social policy but not to others and its application differs between countries. We focus here on conditionality in unemployment benefit schemes, broadly defined to include unemployment insurance (UI), unemployment assistance (UA) and social assistance (SA) schemes for unemployed people. Following Knotz and Nelson,[11] we regard conditionality as the primary or 'first-tier' concept that comprises 'conditions' and 'sanctions', both of which may be regarded as 'second-tier' concepts.

The receipt of unemployment benefit has always been subject to conditions. Traditionally, these referred to the circumstances that gave rise to a claim. People who lost their jobs 'without good cause', for example, by leaving their work voluntarily or as a result of misconduct, and people who were not available for work, for example, because they were on strike or still under a contract of employment, were not entitled to benefit. The punishment was disqualification, usually for a limited period. These eligibility conditions can be referred to as *ex ante* conditions. However, since the 1980s, a new set of conditions have been introduced. With the adoption of active labour market policies (ALMPs) in many countries, recipients of unemployment benefit have increasingly been expected to actively look for work and benefit has only been awarded on the condition that they do so. The punishments for not doing so are known as (benefit) sanctions. These behavioural conditions can be referred to as *ex post* conditions and, in different countries and at different times, they have varied in severity and duration. *Ex-post* conditionality is more controversial than *ex-ante* conditionality and, over time, it has become more prevalent.

In this section, we examine the strictness of the behavioural requirements relating to the receipt of unemployment benefit and the scope and severity of sanctions for non-compliance in 2014 in the five countries considered in the book, with the addition of Sweden, using data taken from a recent Organisation for Economic Co-operation and Development (OECD) report.[12] In addition, by comparing data in this report with data in an earlier OECD report,[13] we can analyse changes in conditionality and sanctions from 2011 to 2014. Thus, we are able not only to analyse variations in conditionality and sanctions between these six countries, but also to consider changes over time during the period of austerity. We can also look at the relationship between conditions and sanctions, which is not as straightforward as may have been expected.

The OECD report is based on a study of conditionality in unemployment benefit schemes in 40 countries in 2014. Six indicators of the strictness of conditions[14] and five indicators of the scope and severity of sanctions[15] were compiled by country experts. Each indicator was measured on a 1–5 scale, where 1 (least strict) was the lowest score and 5 (strictest) the highest score on each variable. It should be noted that the data refer to the highest tier of unemployment benefit, even where more unemployed persons are in receipt of unemployment benefit from a lower-tier scheme. Thus, they refer to unemployment insurance (UI), where a UI scheme exists, rather than to unemployment assistance (UA) or social assistance (SA) for the unemployed, whatever roles these schemes play in providing support for the unemployed. It should also be noted that the data refer to the strictness of the rules outlined in legislation or regulations. Thus, they describe how the schemes ought to work rather than the ways in which they actually work on the ground. This is quite a serious limitation since the strictness of conditions and the severity of the sanctions depend on how the rules are implemented. The report does not include any data on the incidence of sanctions and it appears to be the case that comparative data on incidence are not collected, either by the OECD or by anyone else.[16]

A. The strictness of conditions

Langenbucher, following Venn, distinguishes between, on the one hand, *availability requirements and suitable work criteria* and, on the other, *job-search and job monitoring requirements*. The first category refers to whether a benefit recipient: a) must be available and actively searching for work while participating in active labour market programmes (ALMPs), such as training programmes or work-experience placements; and b) needs to demonstrate that s/he is available for work, and whether s/he can refuse a job offer in a lower-status occupation because it is too far away or for any other reason. The second category refers to how often claimants have to prove that they have been searching for work and what they need to do to document their job-search efforts. In calculating a mean score, each of these two categories is given the same weight.[17] As explained above, each indicator was measured on a 1–5 scale – a score of 1 would mean that very few requirements had to be met, a score of 5 that there were many requirements. The OECD reports make it clear that, although there are differences between countries, the imposition of conditions is widespread and the extent to which they are used considerable. This is supported by the data in Table 7.4, which refers to 2014.

The 'strictness of conditions scores' range from a low of 4.0 for Spain to a high of 7.5 for Sweden. The only country in which there was an increase in the 'strictness of conditions score' from 2011 to 2014 was the UK. In the other five countries, it remained the same.[18]

The scope and severity of sanctions

Sanctions for voluntary unemployment are an example of sanctions for breaching *ex ante* conditions while the other sanctions, that is, for refusing a job offer and failing to attend interviews or take part in job-training activities are examples of sanctions for breaching *ex post* conditions. Langenbucher distinguishes between sanctions for voluntary unemployment, for refusing a job offer and for refusing to take part in activation measures. In calculating a mean score, each of the three categories is given the same weight.[19] As with the severity of conditions, each indicator was measured on a 1–5 scale – a score of 1 would mean that the period of disqualification was very short, for example, less than one month, while a score

Table 7.4 The strictness of conditions in unemployment benefit schemes, 2014

	France	*Germany*	*Italy*	*Spain*	*Sweden*	*UK*
Availability requirements and suitable work criteria						
Need to be available for work during ALMP	4	5	4	1	5	5
Can refuse if job involves change of occupation	3	4	4	2	4	3
Can refuse if job is far away	1.5	3	3	2	3	3
Can refuse for other reasons	5	3	3	5	3	3
Job search/ Monitoring requirements						
Extent of monitoring	4	3	1	1	4	5
Amount of documentation required	3	4	1	2	4	3.5
Strictness of conditions score	**6.9**	**7.3**	**4.5**	**4.0**	**7.5**	**7.3**

Note: Strictness of conditions score = availability score + job search/monitoring score; availability score = average of four components; job search/monitoring score = average of two components.

Table 7.5 Strictness of sanctions in unemployment benefit schemes

	France	*Germany*	*Italy*	*Spain*	*Sweden*	*UK*
For voluntary unemployment	4	3	5	5	3	3
For refusal of job offer						
First refusal	1	1	4	3	1	3
Repeated refusals	3	2.5	4	4.5	3	4.5
For refusing to participate in ALMPs						
First refusal	1	1	4	2	1	1
Repeated refusal	3	2.5	4	4.5	3	3
Scope and severity of sanctions score	**8.0**	**6.5**	**13.0**	**12.0**	**7.0**	**8.8**

Note: Scope and severity of sanctions score = voluntary unemployment score + refusal of job offer score + refusal to participate score; refusal of job offer score = average of two components; job search score = average of two components. The 'scope and severity of sanctions scores' range from a low of 6.5 for Germany to a high of 13.0 for Italy. Again, the only country in which there was an increase in the 'scope and severity of sanctions score' from 2011 to 2014 was the UK. In the other five countries it remained the same.[20]

of 5 would mean that the period of disqualification was much longer, perhaps indefinite. The circumstances that can give rise to sanctions are many and varied and, as Table 7.5 makes clear, the sanctions that are imposed can be pretty severe. Thus, there are quite a lot of 4s and 5s in the table.

B. The relationship between conditions and sanctions

We argued earlier that conditionality is the 'first-tier' concept while conditions and sanctions are 'second-tier' concepts. We now examine the relationship between these two 'second-tier' concepts empirically, that is, we ask whether or not stringent behavioural conditions associated with the receipt of unemployment benefit are associated with severe sanctions for those who fail to meet these conditions.

As can be seen in Figure 7.2, Spain and Italy are least strict in terms of conditions and most severe in terms of sanctions.[21] On the other hand, Germany and Sweden are among the strictest in terms of conditions but are the least severe in terms of sanctions. The UK is rather harsh in terms of both conditions and sanctions, France somewhat less so. In fact, among the 40 countries in the OECD study, only Slovenia, Luxemburg, Portugal, Croatia, Estonia and Malta (all of them very small countries) are harsher overall than the UK.[22] In addition, the UK was the only one of the six countries considered here to increase the strictness of conditions and the severity of sanctions from 2011 to 2014.[23]

Figure 7.2 indicates that conditions and sanctions appear to be alternatives rather than measures that work together. Countries appear *either* to emphasise

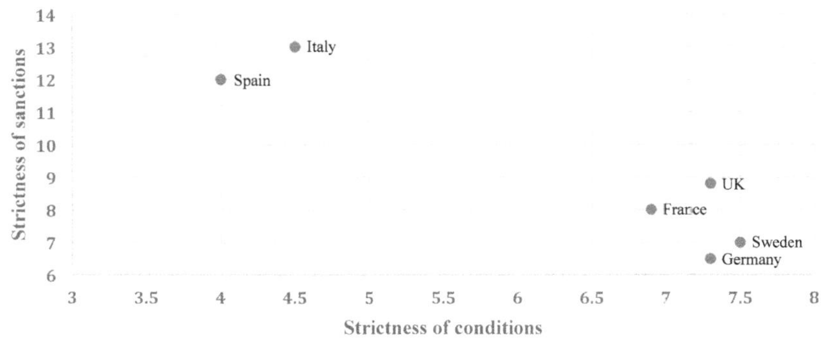

Figure 7.2 The relationship between the strictness of conditions and the severity of sanctions, 2014

conditions *or* to emphasise sanctions. Why Italy and Spain emphasise sanctions while the other four countries emphasise conditions calls for an explanation but we are unable to provide one.

Unemployment protection can be characterised in terms of the mix of benefit schemes that are deployed, the ways in which these schemes are implemented and the level of protection that is achieved, measured in terms of benefit generosity. Data relating to means and ends are available but, unfortunately, no comparative data about process is available.

C. The relationship between conditions and benefit generosity

It is reasonable to suggest that countries with generous benefits will impose the strictest conditions on claimants.[24] However, this is not supported by the OECD data that suggests the opposite: countries with generous benefits appear to impose the least strict conditions on claimants.[25] It is mainly Sweden and the UK, on one side, and Spain and Italy on the other, which produce this trend. To illustrate this, Figure 7.3 is based on the mean NRR for a two-parent family with two children where the unemployed parent previously earned an average wage in 2014.

Among the countries with the highest replacement rates, the correlations are as expected for France and Germany, which impose strict conditions on the receipt of benefit. However, Spain and Italy are rather more lenient. In addition, the two countries with the lowest replacement rates (Sweden and the UK) impose very strict conditions on the receipt of benefits. The patterns are very much the same for different family types. Thus, for single claimants and for couples with children where the spouse does not work, negative correlations between strictness

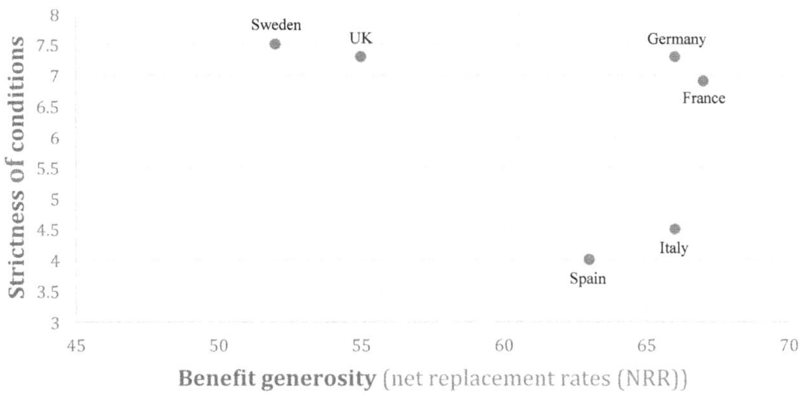

Figure 7.3 The relationship between benefit generosity and the strictness of conditions, 2014[26]

of conditions and benefit generosity are found for Sweden and the UK, on the one hand, and for Spain and Italy, on the other.

IV. The structure of unemployment protection

The impact of sanctions depends on whether people who are sanctioned from a higher-tier scheme can claim support, albeit probably at a lower level, from a lower-tier (safety-net) scheme. It follows that it is important to take into account the structure of unemployment protection in each of the six countries considered here.

A. The structure of unemployment protection in the six countries

Each of the countries considered here has a contribution-based unemployment insurance (UI) scheme and most have means-tested unemployment assistance (UA) schemes as well. Some countries also have means-tested social assistance (SA) schemes run by local authorities. These different schemes can be seen to constitute a hierarchy with UI schemes on the top, in that they are most generous and least stigmatised, and SA schemes on the bottom, in that they are least generous and most stigmatised. UA schemes come in the middle. In what follows, we consider the structure of unemployment protection in each of the six countries. All the information is taken from Clasen and Clegg.[27]

France[28]

In 1990, France had a three-tiered benefit structure comprising unemployment insurance (UI), means-tested unemployment assistance (UA) – with separate schemes for the long-term unemployed and new entrants to labour market – and means-tested social assistance (SA). The structure of benefits did not change over the next 20 years although UI (for good contributors) and SA (for bad contributors) grew while UA was 'squeezed'.

From 2005 onwards, conditionality was promoted, particularly in SA – all SA claimants had to register as jobseekers – and sanctions could be applied to all jobseekers, irrespective of benefit status.

Germany[29]

Prior to implementation of *Hartz* Reforms in 2002, Germany also had a three-tier system of support for the unemployed (UI+UA+SA). As a result of the *Hartz* Reforms, unemployment assistance and social assistance were merged and, since then, Germany has had a two-tier system comprising contributory UBI (UI) and means-tested UBII (UA). UBI lasts for 12 months (24 months for those aged 58+).

Conditionality is stricter and sanctions are more readily applied in UBII than in UBI. This is because insurance-based rights are regarded as stronger than rights to tax-financed benefits. Means-tested social assistance (SA) is still available for those who are unable to work due to sickness, disability or old age but unemployed people who are sanctioned are not eligible and are not provided with any other means of support.[30]

Italy[31]

Until the mid-1990s, the unemployment benefit system was based on a single UI tier, comprising traditional contributory UI and UIR (unemployment insurance with reduced eligibility) paid as a lump sum, which provided meagre protection against unemployment (at the same time, there were quite generous schemes providing compensation for temporary working-time reduction and collective dismissals). Both UI and UIR became more generous and more inclusive over time. A means-tested, tax-financed SA scheme was introduced in 1998 but abolished in 2004. In addition, there are two special schemes, financed by the European Social Fund, providing compensation for workers who are required to work less without being dismissed. These schemes were extended in 2009. Initial enthusiasm for ALMPs went into reverse in 2004. Adoption of stricter conditionality (in 2000 and 2002) was more apparent than real due to 'implementation deficits'.

Spain[32]

A new contributory UI scheme for the self-employed was added to the existing contributory UI scheme in 2010. Those who have exhausted their entitlement may claim means-tested UA. In addition, there are two additional, means-tested, schemes for the long-term unemployed who have exhausted their entitlement to UI or UA – RAI, which was introduced in 2000, and PRODI (Temporary Programme for Unemployment Protection and Integration), which was introduced in 2009. Both are time limited. PRODI was introduced by the Spanish Government as part of a stimulus package. ALMPs have had a low profile across the board.

Sweden[33]

Unemployment insurance consists of two separate parts, a flat-rate basic insurance scheme and an optional earnings-related scheme. To be entitled to either of them, a claimant has to have been in employment for at least six months. To be entitled to earnings-related benefit, the claimant must have been a member of an unemployment insurance fund for at least 12 months. Those who do not qualify for unemployment insurance or exhaust their entitlement to it can claim social assistance provided by municipalities. Thus, there is a three-tier system of support.

United Kingdom[34]

Prior to the introduction of Jobseeker's Allowance (JSA) in 1996, the UK had a two-tier system of support for the unemployed comprising contributory unemployment benefit (UI) and means-tested income support (SA). Since 1996, it has had a single benefit (JSA) for those who are unemployed, comprising contributory-based JSA (UI) and means-tested JSA (UA). Contributory-based JSA lasts for 6 months – until 1996, UI had lasted for 12 months. Many recipients of JSA also receive other means-tested benefits, in particular Housing Benefit.

Conditionality and sanctions apply to both contributory-based JSA (UI) and means-tested JSA (UA). There is a system of discretionary 'hardship payments', paid at 60 per cent of normal entitlement to those who are literally destitute and have no other means of support, but the provision is an extremely residual one and sanctioned claimants are often not told about it.[35] Although 'vulnerable' claimants[36] can apply immediately, most claimants are not allowed to apply for the first two weeks after the sanction is imposed. The system of support can perhaps best be described as one-tier plus.

The structure of unemployment protection in the six countries is summarised in Table 7.6 below.

Other things being equal, it would seem that the same level of sanctions in UI would have most impact in Italy, which has a one-tier system of unemployment protection, followed by the UK, and least impact in France and Sweden (which have three-tier systems). The effect of the structure of unemployment protection on the severity of sanctions is set out in Table 7.7 below: + represents least amplification, +++ represents most. Somewhat perversely, the effect of the structure of unemployment protection is to amplify the effect of sanctions in Italy and Spain, where sanctions are most severe, but not to do so in France and Sweden, where sanctions are least severe.

Table 7.6 The structure of unemployment protection

	France	*Germany*	*Italy*	*Spain*	*Sweden*	*UK*
1st tier	unemployment insurance	unemployment benefit I	unemployment benefit	unemployment insurance	earnings-related	contribution-based JSA & income-based JSA
2nd tier	unemployment assistance	unemployment benefit II		unemployment assistance	flat-rate basic allowance (not means-tested)	
3rd tier	social assistance administered by municipalities		(introduced in 1998; abolished in 2004)		administered by municipalities	residual hardship fund administered by DWP
	3-tier	**2-tier**	**1-tier**	**2-tier**	**3-tier**	**1-tier plus**

Table 7.7 How the structure of unemployment protection amplifies sanctions

	France	*Germany*	*Italy*	*Spain*	*Sweden*	*UK*
Severity of sanctions						
Score	8.9	6.5	13.0	12.0	7.0	8.8
Rank	4	6	1	2	5	3
Structure of benefits						
Number of tiers	3	2	1	2	3	1+
Amplification effect	+	++	+++	++	+	+++

V. Legal challenges to conditionality[37]

There have been three European Court of Human Rights (ECHR) cases in which it has been argued that the attachment of conditions to the payment of unemployment benefit contravened Article 4[38] but they have all failed. Only one of these cases, *Schuitemaker*, can be described as recent and the facts of that case applied to circumstances that arose before the recent financial crisis. There has also been one ECHR case in which the refusal to allow a claimant to appeal against the imposition of a sanction was held to contravene Article 6.[39]

In *X v Netherlands*[40] the applicant was a specialised worker in the building industry. He claimed unemployment benefit and was required as a condition of payment to accept work that he considered to be unsuitable for a person with his qualifications and socially demeaning. He refused the job offer, was denied benefit and brought a complaint that this constituted a violation of Article 4. The Commission declared the complaint inadmissible, observing that it was open to the claimant to refuse the work and that its acceptance was only a condition for the grant of unemployment benefit. There could therefore be no question of forced or compulsory labour within the meaning of Article 4.

In *Talmon v Netherlands*[41] the applicant was a scientist. He claimed unemployment benefit and was required as a condition to accept work that he considered unsuitable. Because of his refusal to do it, his benefit payments were reduced. He complained that by having his benefits reduced he was being forced to do work to which he had a conscientious objection, contrary to Article 4. The application was declared manifestly ill-founded and inadmissible.

In *Schuitemaker v Netherlands*[42] the applicant was a philosopher by profession. She claimed unemployment benefit and was told that her benefits would be reduced unless she was willing to take up a wider range of employment than she considered suitable. She complained under Article 4 that she was being forced to take up labour irrespective of whether it would be suitable for her. The court held that her application was inadmissible. It noted that the obligation that she complained of was in effect a condition for the granting of benefits, and stated as a general principle that a state that has introduced a system of social security is fully entitled to lay down conditions that have to be met for a person to be eligible for benefits under that system.

In *Mendel v Sweden*,[43] the applicant was registered with the Employment Service and its activities included a guarantee scheme designed mainly to give the unemployed greater opportunities to find a job. Each participant was required to attend information meetings, to meet his or her supervisor on a regular basis and to apply for suitable jobs. In 2005 the Employment Service excluded the applicant from the scheme on the grounds that she had failed to comply with these requirements. She unsuccessfully challenged this decision before the National Labour Market Board and their decision indicated that no appeal lay against it. However, the ECHR unanimously held that this constituted a breach of the applicant's right of access to a court under Article 6.1.

In the **United Kingdom**, two cases that reached the superior courts questioned the legality of conditionality in terms of its compatibility with the ECHR.

The first case *(Reilly No. 1)*[44] concerned the legality of the Jobseeker's Allowance (Employment, Skills and Enterprise Scheme) Regulations 2011 (SI 2011/917), which purported to establish 'work experience' and 'training' programmes that claimants had to take part in as a condition of receiving benefit and for which they would be sanctioned if they failed to do so. The legal challenge focused on the legality of the regulations that established the training programme and on their compatibility with Article 4.

In the High Court, the judge found that the regulations were validly made but the decision was over-ruled in the Court of Appeal, which found that they were *ultra vires* because the claimants were not provided with an adequate description of the programmes or the circumstances in which they could be required to participate in them as required by the primary legislation. However, the Court of Appeal rejected the Article 4 part of the claim, arguing that 'to amount to a violation of Article 4, the work had to be not only compulsory and involuntary, but the obligation to work, or its performance, must be "unjust", "oppressive", "an avoidable hardship" [or] "needlessly distressing"'. The Court of Appeal did not consider that the imposition of the work condition in this case, which was intended to support the purpose for which the conditional benefit was provided, met the starting point for a possible contravention of Article 4. The Court of Appeal's decision was subsequently upheld by the UK Supreme Court, which held that the conditions imposed on recipients of Jobseeker's Allowance (JSA) 'come nowhere close to exploitative conduct at which Article 4 is aimed'.

The second case *(Reilly No. 2)*[45] concerned the legality of being required to participate in an unpaid work scheme that had been declared *ultra vires* in the first case, in spite of the fact that the Secretary of State for Work and Pensions had introduced new regulations with retrospective effect. The two claimants submitted that the new legislation was incompatible with their rights to a fair hearing under Article 6 of the ECHR and one of them, who had been sanctioned, also argued that, by withholding his benefit, the Secretary of State had deprived him of a 'possession; to which he had a right under Article 1 of Protocol 1 (A1P1) of the EHCR and that this could not be justified "in the public interest"'.

The Court of Appeal held that 'it is contrary to the rule of law, protected by Article 6, for a State to legislate in the course of ongoing legal proceedings, to decide an issue before the court, when it does so to its own advantage, as a party in the dispute. Such an interference with Article 6 rights can only be justified "by compelling grounds of public interest"'. In their decision, the judges concluded that there were no 'compelling grounds of the general interest' to justify the interference with the Article 6 rights and that there had been a violation of Article 6. However, they asserted that this only applied to the minority of claimants who had pursued claims in the courts or tribunals. On the A1P1 point, the Court of Appeal held that the claimant was not deprived of a possession merely on the basis of not being able to receive the benefit in the future due to the application of the sanction. The claimant did not have a property right to future benefits because he did not meet the required conditions to be able to continue to receive the benefit: 'in order to establish a property right, the applicant must fulfil the requirements for receipt of the benefit at the relevant time' and 'the sanction decisions were effective and lawful unless or until overturned'.

To sum up, although *Reilly No. 1* and *Reilly No. 2* were successful on procedural grounds, the attempts to invoke the ECHR to declare aspects of conditionality and the imposition of sanctions unlawful were unsuccessful in both cases. Two further cases reached the superior courts but neither made any reference to the ECHR and both were unsuccessful.

In **Germany**, it has been argued that aspects of conditionality contravened the Basic Law, that is, the German Constitution. The Federal Social Court had previously stated that, in general terms, it had no doubt about the constitutionality of the new regulations.[46] The Higher Social Court of Thuringia also held that it had no doubt about the compatibility of sanctions with the Constitution.[47] The only constitutional restrictions on the sanctions regulations so far have come from the Federal Social Court that, in 2013, qualified its position slightly by holding that the reimbursement of accommodation and heating costs could not be subject to sanctions if the claimant lives together with two other persons.[48]

However, as pointed out by Lembke in her chapter in this volume, in May 2015 the Social Court of Gotha raised a preliminary reference before the Federal Constitutional Court (FCC),[49] contending that the *Hartz IV* laws, by providing for penalty deductions from unemployment assistance, violated fundamental constitutional rights, such as human dignity, the right to physical integrity and the freedom to choose an occupation.[50] The question has not been dealt with by the Federal Constitutional Court, however. In May 2016 it rejected the preliminary reference as inadmissible in relation to determined legal technicalities.

As far as conditionality is concerned, the Federal Social Security Court (BSG) and the Federal Administrative Court (BVerwG) have held that the instruments of conditionality in unemployment assistance schemes are means of 'help to self-help' in the sense that the work that is offered to the unemployed person helps her or him to get accustomed to a work-based and work-oriented society. Thus it should not be thought of as imposing a burden on them but of helping them to become integrated into the labour market,[51] and that case-management and jobseeker contracts are lawful contracts under public law.[52]

All in all, we can say that the limited amount of litigation in Germany on the constitutionality of conditionality has, at least so far, produced some pretty limited results.

In other countries, although there have been some legal challenges to conditionality, these have all been concerned with whether decisions are made in accordance with the relevant law. In **France**, a 2005 decree made sanctions easier to impose after shorter periods of time. Jobseekers risk sanctions if they fail to sign the Personalised Project of Access to Employment (PPAE) or if they refuse a reasonable job offer and they can be imposed if, without a good reason, they fail to appear after being summoned by the Pôle Emploi (Employment Centre). These practices have now been extended to recipients of basic income. Although activation policies place much greater emphasis on individual duties rather than on individual rights, there do not appear to have been many legal challenges to them. However, case law does make it clear that the obligation to actively look for a job or to make efforts of 'insertion' has to be written into the contract between the unemployed person and the Pôle Emploi, that this has to be 'freely negotiated' by the two parties[53] and that no other obligation can be legally imposed.[54] If these conditions are not met, then sanctions are unlawful.

In **Italy**, the Italian Constitutional Court (ICC) has always been rather deferential, granting the legislature a significant margin of discretion in determining how to implement constitutional provisions regarding social rights.[55] Since the 1990s, the focus of judicial review has moved from ensuring the complete protection of social rights to assessing the reasonableness of policies aimed at reducing social welfare entitlements against the backdrop of massive cuts in public spending on social welfare. The most prominent feature of this new trend has been that social rights are now seen as ontologically conditional (or conceptually dependent) on finance. However, to counterbalance the financial conditionality of social rights, the concept of a minimum or essential core inherent to each social right – which is to be guaranteed regardless of any budgetary constraint – was then elaborated by the ICC.

In a number of cases this stance was instrumental in protecting welfare entitlements. Thus, in 2010, the ICC ruled that the creation by the state of exceptional funds to cope with poor people's needs regarding food, health and energy supply or to assist young couples and one-parent families in buying their home, although infringing regional legislative powers on social assistance, was nonetheless lawful in the face of 'imperious social demands induced by the present grave national and international economic crisis'.[56] At other times, for example in 2013, the same circumstances led the court to strike down regional measures aimed at enhancing the 'basic level of social rights' established under the Italian

Constitution, interpreting 'basic' as a cap and not as a threshold to the benefits to be awarded throughout the country.[57]

Against this background, it is perhaps surprising that there have not been any challenges to the constitutionality of the new legislation that introduces a much stronger conditionality regime in Italy. This may be due to its novelty but there are probably deeper reasons for it, principally the difficulty of finding constitutional grounds for making such a challenge.

In **Spain**, although legislative measures can be challenged before the Spanish Constitutional Court (SCC), Spanish law does not allow an individual citizen to undertake such challenges when they refer to the 'principles governing economic and social policy' that are set out in the Spanish Constitution. Individual appeal for constitutional protection is designed only for the provisions set out in those Articles that deal with 'fundamental rights'. The constitutionality of measures restricting social rights can only be raised by judges (in the ordinary courts) or by the President, 50 members of the Spanish Parliament, 50 Senators, a regional government, a regional parliament or the Ombudsman. Thus, it is perhaps not surprising that, to date, there have been no relevant judicial challenges of measures restricting the social protection of unemployed people and that there have been no challenges to the legality of conditionality.

In **Sweden**, although the activation decision cannot be appealed, the decision to sanction can be appealed to an administrative court. However, a successful appeal does not have much of an impact because, where the courts hold a decision to be unlawful and remit it to the authorities, the authorities frequently make another decision with the same effect in a lawful manner.[58] To date, no appeals over sanctions have involved references to the Swedish Constitution or the ECHR.

When imposing sanctions, decision-makers use wide discretionary powers and individuals may be sanctioned not only for failing to attend when required to do so but also when officials think they are poorly motivated or not active enough in their job-seeking. It is not always clear where responsibility lies – activation workers have no formal powers to impose sanctions but communicate incriminating information to social workers who then make the decision. Claimants may be referred to national or local labour-market training schemes but the former are better and the latter more punitive. Unfortunately, supervision is poor and local authorities, whose powers are very loosely defined in legislation, are largely unaccountable.

Sweden has traditionally adopted a *green light*[59] approach to legal scrutiny but, following a series of reforms to administrative law provoked by the ECHR, it does now seem to be moving towards a *red-light* approach. Advocates of the former place their hopes in the state, which they see as the fundamental guarantor of the freedom of the individual, and emphasise the use of legislation and regulation rather than the role of the judiciary and the use of the courts, arguing that where the courts declare actions to be unlawful, they are usually substituting their own value judgements for those of the democratically elected legislature.

Advocates of the latter, on the other hand, mistrust the state, which is seen as a threat to the freedom of the individual, and favour a strong role for the courts in scrutinising the legality of administrative decisions. Thus, they believe that the main aim of administrative law is (or ought to be) to curb or control the state and the main instruments for achieving this goal are the courts and the judiciary.

All in all, there appear to have been few legal challenges to the introduction of behavioural conditions or the imposition of benefit sanctions in the six countries considered in this chapter. Most of the small number of legal challenges that have been brought have been 'internal' challenges, which have sought to challenge the legality of day-to-day practices in terms of their consistency with statutory requirements. Few of them have been 'external' challenges, which have sought to challenge day-to-day practices in terms of their consistency with higher order principles enshrined in international conventions (in particular the ECHR), national constitutions or (in the case of the UK) the common law, and none of these challenges has been successful.[60] Thus, governments have, in effect, had a free hand and legal challenges to conditions and sanctions have not, so far, provided any significant degree of protection for those who have been subject to them. Although governments are supposedly held to account by standards embodied in the rule of law, legal challenges have failed to limit the right to unemployment benefit from being hedged around by more and more conditions or to protect those who are subject to sanctions for failing to meet these conditions from being deprived, often for substantial periods of time, of their right to minimum subsistence.

VI. The relationship between austerity, conditions and sanctions

A. Austerity and conditionality

In each of the six countries, stricter behavioural conditions and more severe sanctions procedures were introduced some years before the financial crisis of 2008/9 and before the austerity measures that were outlined in the introduction kicked in. In most countries, their promotion was associated with the introduction of active labour market programmes (ALMPs) in the period from 1985 and 2005. Moreover, a comparison of the two OECD reports[61] makes it clear that, in five of the six countries, behavioural conditions and benefit sanctions were not enhanced during the years of austerity, that is, in the period since 2009. It follows that austerity does not account for conditionality.

However, it is possible that austerity affected the enabling and the punitive or sanctioning components of activation policy in different ways. In a recent paper, Eleveld notes that, since enabling measures are costly, austerity may have prompted governments to cut back on them and to rely on punitive sanctions instead.[62] Unfortunately, she does not produce any empirical evidence to support this argument. A reduction in expenditure on enabling measures, if there was one, could have been due to a decline in unemployment or to the fact that enabling measures were not very effective.[63]

European Commission statistics indicate that, compared with 2008/9, expenditure on active labour market policy (ALMP) measures in 2013/14 [64] fell in Germany, Italy and Spain but rose in Sweden and France.[65] The reasons for these differences are not obvious. However, although it is reasonable to think that those governments that cut back on the enabling component of activation policy (Germany, Italy and Spain) would have placed greater emphasis on the punitive component, the only country in which punitive measures were strengthened following the financial crisis was the UK and there is no evidence to suggest that this was to compensate for cuts in enabling measures.[66] In introducing a harsher conditionality regime in 2012,[67] the UK Government's motivations were, in part, instrumental and, in part, expressive. Influenced by supply-side economics, the government believed that stricter behavioural conditions and more severe sanctions would make it less attractive for unemployed people to stay on benefits and encourage them to find employment. If that were the case, it follows that the number of unemployed claimants would fall and this would probably have resulted in expenditure savings.[68] However, as it turns out, there is little evidence in the UK that stricter behavioural conditions and more severe sanctions were effective in getting many claimants back into work. A recent study[69] has shown that, from 2005 to 2014, less than 20 per cent of those who left Jobseeker's Allowance (JSA) moved into employment.[70] However, because the UK Government remains committed to recalibrating the balance between rights and responsibilities, it is most unlikely that, in spite of the absence of evidence of their effectiveness, it will make its conditionality regime less harsh.

Considered as a whole, the evidence presented in this chapter provides substantial support for Civitarese's assumption that '[t]he financial crisis of 2008 did not determine a fracture, a special constitutional law of the crisis, since certain patterns and principles . . . were well in place beforehand'.[71]

B. Economic determinism or political choice

Two general hypotheses can be formulated to explain Welfare State developments. One, which we refer to as the 'economic hypothesis' sees Welfare State developments as driven by economic forces, in particular, by the state of the economy. In its different forms, it attributes Welfare State developments to the 'logic of industrialisation',[72] to the needs of advanced capitalism[73] or to the modernisation process.[74] The other, which we refer to as the 'political hypothesis' sees Welfare State developments in terms of power relations and as the consequence of political decisions. Different variants attribute Welfare State developments to struggles over politics and social class[75] and to the structure and interests of the state or polity.[76]

As shown in Table 7.5 above, sanctions were most severe in Italy and Spain, the countries that were hardest hit by the financial crisis, and least severe in

Germany and Sweden, the countries that were hit least hard. This might be seen as providing some support for the economic hypothesis. However, as shown in Table 7.4, behavioural conditions were least severe in Italy and Spain, where the impact of the financial crisis was greatest, and most severe in the four other countries where the impact of the financial crisis was less severe. This is not at all what the economic hypothesis would have predicted. And, in any case, the behavioural conditions and benefit sanctions were all in place before the onset of the financial crisis and, with the exception of the UK, were not increased following the crisis.

The fact that behavioural conditions and benefit sanctions were introduced and retained, as much by governments of the left as by governments of right, provides little support for the political hypothesis. With the swing of the political pendulum, conditions and sanctions introduced by governments of the left have, by and large, been retained and developed by governments of the right and *vice versa*. Thus, political partisanship does not seem to provide an explanation.

How, then, can the adoption of conditions and sanctions, and variations in their incidence and severity, be explained? The most likely explanation would seem to be in terms of the widespread scepticism towards unconditional rights, the pervasive view that the Welfare State needs to be recalibrated to achieve a better balance between rights and responsibilities, and the extensive adoption of supply-side measures in the delivery of public services. Although this set of beliefs seem to have become the new orthodoxy, the precise forms that it takes and the extent to which it is taken, vary from one country to another. However, there does not seem to be any relationship between the potency of these views and the classification of Welfare States into liberal Welfare States (represented here by the UK), corporatist Welfare States (represented here by France and Germany), social democratic Welfare States (represented here by Sweden),[77] and Southern European (represented here by Spain and Italy).[78] Thus, although there was no way in which we could have known this in advance, the addition of Sweden to the comparison between the five countries analysed in this book does not alter our conclusions. It is, however, reassuring to note that, among the 40 countries included in the recent OECD report, the composite measure of the strictness of conditionality[79] does not appear to be related to the classification of Welfare States into four regime types.

C. Conditions and sanctions

At the beginning of this chapter, following Knotz and Nelson,[80] we characterised conditionality as a primary or 'first-tier' concept that comprises 'conditions' and 'sanctions', both of which may be regarded as 'second-tier' concepts. However, instead of a positive correlation between conditions and sanctions, which is what we may have expected, there appears to be a negative correlation – more severe sanctions are encountered with less strict conditions in Spain and Italy while less severe sanctions are encountered with stricter conditions in France, Germany,

Sweden and the UK.[81] This may indicate that 'conditions' and 'sanctions' refer to two different phenomena that perform different functions and are introduced for different reasons, something that would call for closer examination – both theoretically and empirically.[82]

Somewhat perversely, the effect of the structure of unemployment protection is to amplify the effect of sanctions in Italy and Spain, where sanctions are most severe, but not to do so in France and Sweden, where sanctions are least severe.[83] Of the countries that provide relatively more generous benefits, two (France and Germany) impose strict conditions on the receipt of benefit while the other two (Spain and Italy) are rather more lenient, while the two countries that provide relatively less generous benefits (Sweden and the UK) impose very strict conditions on the receipt of benefits.[84] Legal challenges to conditionality in the courts have provided very little protection for claimants who are required to meet strict behavioural conditions on the receipt of benefit and/or are subjected to sanctions that may leave them destitute. The most likely explanations for the prevalence of conditionality are probably the widespread scepticism towards unconditional rights, the pervasive view that the Welfare State needs to be recalibrated to achieve a better balance between rights and responsibilities and the extensive adoption of supply-side measures in the delivery of public services.

Appendix

Table A1 Level of GDP per head of population 2005–14. USD constant prices, 2010 PPPs.

	2005	*2006*	*2007*	*2008*	*2009*	*2010*	*2011*	*2012*	*2013*	*2014*
France	35,577	36,169	36,796	36,663	35,402	35,921	36,488	36,376	36,412	36,478
Germany	37,483	38,948	40,308	40,859	38,698	40,377	41,859	41,950	41,960	42,454
Italy	35,923	36,495	36,807	36,141	33,966	34,394	34,450	33,333	32,585	32,397
Spain	32,760	33,590	34,182	34,001	32,515	32,383	31,940	31,083	30,677	31,181
Sweden	40,088	41,732	42,834	42,265	39,734	41,756	42,546	42,111	42,274	42,806
UK	36,555	37,272	37,929	37,444	35,623	35,884	36,288	36,474	37,028	37,795

Source: OECD Statistics, *Level of GDP per capita* <https://stats.oecd.org/Index.aspx?DataSetCode=PDB_LV> (accessed 10 October 2016).

Table A2 Employment rates as a percentage of working age population, 2005–14

	2005	*2006*	*2007*	*2008*	*2009*	*2010*	*2011*	*2012*	*2013*	*2014*
France	64	64	64	65	64	64	64	64	64	64
Germany	65	67	69	70	70	71	73	73	74	74
Italy	58	58	59	59	57	57	57	57	56	56
Spain	64	65	66	64	60	59	58	56	55	56
Sweden	72	73	74	74	72	72	74	74	74	75
UK	72	72	71	72	70	69	69	70	71	72

Source: Eurostat, *Employment Statistics* (31 January 2017) <http://ec.europa.eu/eurostat/statistics-explained/index.php/Employment_statistics>.

Table A3 Unemployment rates as percentage of the labour force, 2005–14

	2005	*2006*	*2007*	*2008*	*2009*	*2010*	*2011*	*2012*	*2013*	*2014*
France	8.5	8.5	7.7	7.1	8.7	8.9	8.8	9.4	9.9	10.3
Germany	11.2	10.3	8.7	7.5	7.7	7.0	5.8	5.4	5.2	5.0
Italy	7.7	6.8	6.1	6.7	7.6	8.4	8.4	10.7	12.2	12.7
Spain	9.2	8.5	8.2	11.2	17.9	19.9	21.4	24.8	26.1	24.4
Sweden	7.5	7.1	6.2	6.2	8.4	8.6	7.8	8.0	8.0	8.0
UK	4.8	5.4	5.3	5.6	7.5	7.8	8.0	7.9	7.5	6.1

Source: Eurostat, *Unemployment Statistics* (11 August 2016) <http://ec.europa.eu/eurostat/tgm/table.do?tab=table&init=1&language=en&pcode=tsdec450&plugin=1>.

Table A4 AROP rate – persons at-risk-of-poverty as percentage of total population, 2005–14

	2005	*2006*	*2007*	*2008*	*2009*	*2010*	*2011*	*2012*	*2013*	*2014*
France	18.9	18.8	19.0	18.5	18.5	19.2	19.3	19.1	18.1	18.5
Germany	18.4	20.1	20.6	20.1	20.0	19.7	19.9	19.6	20.3	20.6
Italy	25.6	25.9	26.0	25.5	24.9	25.0	28.1	29.9	28.5	28.3
Spain	24.3	24.0	23.3	23.8	24.7	26.1	26.7	27.2	27.3	29.2
Sweden	14.4	16.3	13.9	14.9	15.9	15.0	16.1	15.6	16.4	16.9
UK	24.8	23.7	22.6	23.2	22.0	23.2	22.7	24.1	24.8	24.1

Source: Eurostat, *Europe 2020 indicators - poverty and social exclusion* (11 August 2016) <http://ec.europa.eu/eurostat/tgm/refreshTableAction.do?tab=table&plugin=1&pcode=t2020_50&language=en>.

Table A5 Direct and indirect taxes plus social security contributions as a percentage of GDP, 2005–14

	2005	*2006*	*2007*	*2008*	*2009*	*2010*	*2011*	*2012*	*2013*	*2014*
France	44.5	44.9	44.3	44.3	43.9	44.1	45.2	46.5	47.4	47.9
Germany	38.5	38.8	38.8	39.2	39.6	38.2	38.7	39.3	39.4	39.5
Italy	39.2	40.3	41.6	41.5	42	41.7	41.7	43.7	43.6	43.7
Spain	35.9	36.7	37.1	32.9	30.6	32.1	32.0	33.0	33.8	34.4
Sweden	47.5	46.8	45.8	44.9	45.1	44.1	45.5	43.5	44.8	43.7
UK	35.9	36.5	36.2	37.7	34.9	35.5	35.9	35.2	34.9	34.4

Source: Eurostat, *Tax Revenue Statistics* (25 November 2016) <http://ec.europa.eu/eurostat/statistics-explained/index.php/tax_revenue_statistics>.

Table A6 General public expenditure a percentage of GDP, 2005–14

	2005	2006	2007	2008	2009	2010	2011	2012	2013	2014
France	52.9	52.5	52.2	53.0	56.8	56.4	55.9	56.8	57	57.3
Germany	46.2	44.7	42.8	43.6	47.6	47.3	44.7	44.5	44.5	44.3
Italy	47.1	47.6	46.8	47.8	51.2	49.9	49.1	50.8	51.0	51.2
Spain	38.3	38.3	38.9	41.1	45.8	45.6	45.8	48.0	45.1	44.1
Sweden	52.7	51.3	49.7	50.3	53.1	51.2	50.5	51.7	52.4	51.7
UK	42.8	42.9	42.8	46.6	49.6	48.8	46.9	46.8	45.0	43.9

Source: OECD, *General Government Spending (SOCX)* (accessed 13 March 2017) <https://data.oecd.org/gga/general-government-spending.htm>.

Table A7 Social expenditure a percentage of GDP, 2005–14

	2005	*2006*	*2007*	*2008*	*2009*	*2010*	*2011*	*2012*	*2013*	*2014*
France	29.6	29.0	28.8	29.1	31.5	31.7	31.4	31.5	31.9	31.9
Germany	27.0	25.8	24.8	25.0	27.6	26.8	25.5	25.4	25.8	25.8
Italy	24.9	25.0	24.8	25.8	27.8	27.8	27.5	28.1	28.6	28.6
Spain	20.9	20.9	21.3	22.8	26.1	26.7	26.8	27.1	26.8	26.8
Sweden	28.7	28.1	27.0	27.2	29.4	27.9	27.2	27.7	28.1	28.1
UK	20.2	20.0	20.1	21.6	23.9	22.8	22.7	23	21.7	21.7

Source: OECD, *Social Expenditure Database (SOCX)* <https://data.oecd.org/socialexp/social-spending.htm> (accessed 13 March 2017).

Table A8 Benefit generosity 2005–14: net replacement rates (NRRs) for the first month of unemployment

	2005	*2006*	*2007*	*2008*	*2009*	*2010*	*2011*	*2012*	*2013*	*2014*
France	68	68	67	67	67	67	67	67	67	67
Germany	68	68	67	66	68	67	67	66	66	66
Italy	66	65	65	64	65	63	62	63	63	66
Spain	69	68	69	68	67	67	66	65	63	63
Sweden	66	65	59	57	56	55	54	54	53	52
UK	53	53	53	54	55	55	56	56	55	55

Source: OECD, *Benefits and Wages Tax: Benefit Calculator* <www.oecd.org/els/soc/benefitsand wagestax-benefitcalculator.htm> (accessed 13 March 2017).

Note: NRRs in this table are the average for two family types (a) single persons with no children and (b) couples with two children where the spouse does not work.

Notes

* The authors wish to record their thanks to the editors for their general advice, and to Aksel Hatland, Bob Kagan and Axel West Pedersen for their extremely helpful comments on earlier drafts of this chapter, which enabled them to avoid some egregious errors and to sharpen up their arguments.

1 Gøsta Esping-Andersen has argued that different types of Welfare State are associated with distinctive sets of economic and social arrangements and identified three types of Welfare State in Western Europe: corporatist Welfare States found in much of continental Europe, liberal Welfare States exemplified by the UK and Ireland and social democratic Welfare States found in the Nordic countries. Of the countries included in this book, France and Germany are examples of corporatist Welfare States while the UK is an example of a liberal Welfare State but there are no examples of social democratic Welfare States. In his 1990 study, Italy was classified as a corporatist Welfare State but Spain was not included. It should be noted that Esping-Andersen's typology has been the subject of a great deal of criticism and it has been suggested that, in light of recent developments, it is outdated. Thus, more recent work, e.g. by Maurizio Ferrera, has proposed a fourth type of Welfare State, namely the Southern European Welfare State, exemplified by Italy and Spain. For a discussion of different types of Welfare State, see Gøsta Esping-Andersen, *The Three Worlds of Welfare Capitalism* (Polity Press, 1990). See, also, Maurizio Ferrera, 'The "Southern Model" of Welfare in Social Europe' (1996) 6(1) *Journal of European Social Policy* 17.

2 In so doing, we follow the general approach of Antoine Bozio and his colleagues. See Antoine Bozio *et al.*, 'European Public Finances and the Great Recession: France, Germany, Ireland, Italy, Spain and the United Kingdom Compared' (2015) 36(4) *Fiscal Studies* 405.

3 Our estimates of the severity of austerity differ somewhat from those of Bozio *et al.*, above n 2. This is because they compare 'troughs' with 'peaks' (which may have occurred before 2008) while we compare 'troughs' with measures of GDP per capita for 2008.

4 Detailed statistics can be found in Tables A2–A4 in the Appendix.

5 Ludvig Norman, Katrin Uba and Luke Temple, 'Austerity Measures across Europe' in Liam Foster *et al.* (eds), *In Defence of Welfare 2* (Policy Press, 2016) 55.

6 See Tables A5–A8 in the Appendix.
7 In order to reduce the impact of year-by-year fluctuations, the comparisons in Tables 7.2 and 7.3 are not between single years but, rather, between the averages for the three years before the financial crisis (2005–2007) and a five-year period after its initial impact had been felt (2011–2014).
8 See Table A8 in the Appendix.
9 Using the 'OECD Tax-benefit Calculator', the net replacement rate (NRR) indicates how much income an unemployed person receives in the first month of unemployment. See OECD, *Benefits and Wages: Tax Benefit Calculator* <www.oecd.org/els/soc/benefitsandwagestax-benefitcalculator.htm>.
10 Although Sweden currently has a low replacement rate, this was not always the case. In 2005, the net replacement rates were at the same level as those in Denmark and Norway. However, over the next 10 years, the net replacement rates for Denmark and Norway remained much the same while that for Sweden declined steadily.
11 Carlo Knotz and Moira Nelson, 'Quantifying Conditionality: A New Database on Conditions and Sanctions for Unemployment Benefit Claimants' (Paper presented at ESPANet Conference, Poznan, 5–7 September 2013).
12 Kristine Langenbucher, 'How Demanding are Eligibility Criteria for Unemployment Benefits – Quantitative Indicators for OECD and EU Countries' (Social, Employment and Migration Papers No 166, OECD, 2015).
13 Danielle Venn, 'Eligibility Criteria for Unemployment Benefits – Quantitative Indicators for OECD and EU Countries' (Social, Employment and Migration Papers No 131, OECD, 2012).
14 Being available for work during ALMPs, being required to change occupation, being required to travel to work, other reasons for refusing a job offer, whether job search activities are monitored and being required to document job-search activities.
15 Sanctions for voluntary unemployment, for refusing a job offer (first refusal and repeated refusal) and for refusing to participate in ALMPs.
16 In a recent paper, one of us has described the spectacular increase in the number of benefit sanctions that took place in the UK in the period from 2002 to 2012. In 2012, the number of benefit sanctions imposed actually exceeded the number of fines imposed in the criminal courts. See Michael Adler, 'A New Leviathan: Benefit Sanctions in the Twenty-first Century' (2016) 43(2) *Journal of Law and Society* 195.
17 See Langenbucher, above n 12, [12]–[17]. Since a different weighting system, and, even more fundamentally, a different set of criteria would produce a different score, too much credence should not be placed on the scores in the bottom line of the table.
18 Ibid annex B.
19 Ibid.
20 Ibid annex B [47]. The increase resulted from a change in legislation.
21 It is important to stress that all the data refers to 'law in the books', rather than 'law in action', i.e. to policies rather than practices, and do not refer to the ways in which those policies are actually implemented. As noted above, this is quite a serious limitation since the strictness of conditions and the severity of the sanctions depend on how the rules are implemented.
22 See Langenbucher, above n 12, figure 5. The comparisons are based on a composite measure of the strictness of conditions and sanctions.
23 Ibid [44]. For a fuller discussion, see Section IV.A below.
24 This is because the there is a greater incentive for people to apply for benefit where the NRR is high than to do so where it is low. Strict behavioural conditions

are a way of making it harder for them to meet the entitlement conditions and to claim the benefit. There is also a greater incentive for the authorities to get people off benefit where the NRR is high than where it is low and failure to meet the strict behavioural conditions is one way of achieving this end.

25 Unlike Immervoll, we have chosen to look at the relationship of benefit generosity with conditions, rather than with sanctions or with conditionality, because access to unemployment benefit seems to be at issue here. See Herwig Immervoll, 'Activation Policies in OECD Countries: An Overview of Current Approaches' (Policy Note No 14, The World Bank, June 2012).

26 See Table 3 (strictness of conditions) and Table A8 (benefit generosity).

27 Jochen Clasen and Daniel Clegg (eds), *Regulating the Risk of Unemployment* (Oxford University Press, 2011). Although it can be assumed that the book gives an accurate account of the structure of unemployment protection in each of the countries that were included, it was published in 2011 and therefore does not take account of changes that may have been introduced since then.

28 Daniel Clegg, 'France: Integration Versus Dualisation' in Jochen Clasen and Daniel Clegg (eds), *Regulating the Risk of Unemployment* (Oxford University Press, 2011).

29 Irene Dingeldey, 'Germany: Moving Towards Integration whilst Maintaining Segmentation' in Jochen Clasen and Daniel Clegg (eds), *Regulating the Risk of Unemployment* (Oxford University Press, 2011).

30 Lembke, Ch. 3 in this volume.

31 M Jessoula and P Vesan, 'Italy: Partial Adaptation of an Atypical Benefit System' in Jochen Clasen and Daniel Clegg (eds), *Regulating the Risk of Unemployment* (Oxford University Press, 2011).

32 F J Mato, 'Spain: Fragmented Unemployment Protection in a Segmented Labour Market' in Jochen Clasen and Daniel Clegg (eds), *Regulating the Risk of Unemployment* (Oxford University Press, 2011).

33 O Sjöberg, 'Sweden: Ambivalent Adjustment' in Jochen Clasen and Daniel Clegg (eds), *Regulating the Risk of Unemployment* (Oxford University Press, 2011).

34 J Clasen, 'The United Kingdom: Towards a Single Working-Age Benefit' in Jochen Clasen and Daniel Clegg (eds), *Regulating the Risk of Unemployment* (Oxford University Press, 2011).

35 A recent survey found that only 23 per cent of sanctioned JSA claimants and 13 per cent of sanctioned ESA claimants had been told about hardship payments. About half of them (13 per cent of sanctioned JSA claimants and 5 per cent of sanctioned ESA claimants) applied for a hardship payment. See Department for Work and Pensions (UK), *The JobCentre Plus Offer: Final Evaluation Report* (28 November 2013) <www.gov.uk/government/organisations/department-for-work-pensions/about/research#research-publications>, 162.

36 Defined as claimants, or their partners who are pregnant or have a chronic health condition, or claimants who are responsible for a child under 16 or a qualifying young person or are caring for a severely disabled person.

37 Section VI is based on a comprehensive survey of legal challenges to conditionality in each of the six countries and the ECHR, which is available from the authors on request. The authors would like to thank the following for their help in the preparation of the survey: Stefano Civitarese (University of Chieti-Pescara), Mel Cousins (Trinity College, Dublin), Eberhard Eichenhofer (University of Jena, Berlin), Thomas Erhag (University of Gothenberg), Neville Harris (The University of Manchester), Philip Larkin (Brunel University, London), Ulrike Lembke (University of Hagen), Frans Pennings (Utrecht University), Diane Roman (François Rabelais University, Tours) and Paul Van Aerschot (University of Helsinki).

38 Article 4 provides: '1. No one shall be held in slavery or servitude. 2. No one shall be required to perform forced or compulsory labour. 3. For the purpose of this Article the term "forced or compulsory labour" shall not include: (a) any work required to be done in the ordinary course of detention imposed according to the provisions of Article 5 of this Convention or during conditional release from such detention; (b) any service of a military character or, in the case of conscientious objectors in countries where they are recognised, service exacted instead of compulsory military service; (c) any service exacted in case of an emergency or calamity threatening the life or well-being of the community; (d) any work or service which forms part of normal civic obligations.'

39 Article 6.1 provides: 'In the determination of his civil rights and obligations . . ., everyone is entitled to a fair and public hearing within a reasonable time by an independent and impartial tribunal established by law. Judgment shall be pronounced publicly but the press and public may be excluded from all or part of the trial in the interests of morals, public order or national security in a democratic society, where the interests of juveniles or the protection of the private life of the parties so require, or to the extent strictly necessary in the opinion of the court in special circumstances where publicity would prejudice the interests of justice.'

40 [1976] 7 DR 161.

41 [1997] EHRLR 448.

42 Application No 15906/08 (unreported), 4 May 2010.

43 (European Court of Human Rights, C-28426/06, 7 April 2009).

44 R (*Reilly and Wilson) v Secretary of State for Work and Pensions* [2013] 1 WLR 1 2239; [2013] EWCA Civ; [2013] UKSC 68 [83], [90] *('Reilly No. 1')*. For a commentary on this case, see Phillip Larkin, 'A Permanent Blow to Workfare in the United Kingdom or a Temporary Obstacle? Reilly and Wilson v Secretary of State for Work and Pensions' (2013) 20(3) *Journal of Social Security Law* 110.

45 *R (on the application of Reilly and Hewstone) v Secretary of State for Work and Pensions* [2016] EWHC Civ 413 (*'Reilly No 2'*). For a commentary on this case, see Phillip Larkin, 'Engaging with the Human Rights Angle: Reilly (No. 2) v Secretary of State for Work and Pensions' (2015) 22(2) *Journal of Social Security Law* 85.

46 Bundessozialgericht [Federal Social Court], B 4 AS 27/10, 9 November 2010; Bundessozialgericht [Federal Social Court], B 14 AS 19/14 R, 29 April 2015. The account of this case is taken from Lembke, Ch. 3 in this volume.

47 Higher Social Court of Thuringia, l 4 AS 878/15 NZB, 19 October 2015.

48 Bundessozialgericht [Federal Social Court], B 4 AS 67/12 R, 23 May 2013.

49 Social Court of Gotha, S 15 AS 5157/14, 26 May 2015. The account of this case is also taken from Lembke, Ch. 3 in this volume.

50 The Higher Social Court of Bavaria, L 16 AS 381/15 B ER, 8 July 2015 decided not to uphold the view of the Social Court of Gotha and held penalty deductions of up to 100 per cent to be compatible with the Constitution as long as the physical existence was secured by benefits in kind.

51 See Bundessozialgericht [Federal Social Court], BSGE 97, 231; Bundesverwaltungsgericht [Federal Administrative Court] BVerwGE 23, 149, 156.27, 58, 63.29, 99.

52 See Bundessozialgericht [Federal Social Court] BSGE 96, 40.112, 241.

53 Conseil d'État, Decision No 194040, 29 November 1999; Conseil d'État, Decision No 282963, 23 April 2007: le refus d'un bénéficiaire de l'ancien RMI de signer un contrat d'insertion a pu légalement justifier la suspension du versement de l'allocation, tout comme le refus de se conformer aux prescriptions du contrat.

54 Conseil d'Etat, Decision No 377138, 15 December 2015: le président du conseil départemental ne peut légalement justifier une décision de suspension par la circonstance que le bénéficiaire n'aurait pas accompli des démarches d'insertion qui ne correspondraient pas aux engagements souscrits dans un contrat en cours d'exécution.

55 This account draws quite heavily on Stefano Civitarese, 'Austerity and Social Rights in Italy: A Long Standing Story' on UK Constitutional Law Association Blog (17 December 2015) <https://ukconstitutionallaw.org/>.

56 Italian Constitution Court, Decision No 121/2010.

57 Italian Constitution Court, Decision No 104/2013.

58 It can have an impact in other cases, for example where unlawful sanctions are quashed or rejected applications for social assistance are remitted to be approved.

59 See Carol Harlow and Richard Rawlings, *Law and Administration* (Cambridge University Press, 3rd edn, 2009) Ch. 2.

60 As Anja Eleveld points out, the International Covenant on Economic, Social and Cultural Rights (ICESR) and the European Social Charter (ESC) do set a number of restrictions on the reduction, suspension or termination of social assistance due to work-related sanctions. However, it needs to be born in mind that the rights enshrined in the ICESR and the ESC are non-justiciable. See Anja Eleveld, 'Work-related Sanctions in European Welfare States: An Incentive to Work or a Violation of Minimum Subsistence Rights?' (SSRN Research Paper No 2016/01, The Amsterdam Centre for Contemporary European Studies, 15 June 2016) 11–12.

61 Langenbucher, above n 12; Venn, above n 13.

62 Eleveld, above n 60.

63 David Card, Jochen Kluve and Andrea Weber, (2010) 'Active Labour Market Policy Evaluations: A Meta-analysis' (2010) 120(548) *The Economic Journal* 452; Jochen Kluve, 'The Effectiveness of European Active Labor Market Programs' (2010) 17(6) *Labour Economics* 904.

64 LMP measurers include: training, job rotation and job sharing, employment incentives, supported employment and rehabilitation, direct job creation, and start-up incentives.

65 See Eurostat, *Public Expenditure on Labour Market Policy Measures, by Type of Action* <http://ec.europa.eu/eurostat/tgm/refreshTableAction.do?tab=table&plugin=1&pcode=tps00077&language=en>.

66 Data on ALMP expenditure for 2013 and 2014 in the UK were not available from Eurostat.

67 The Jobseeker' Allowance Regulations 2012 (UK) that came into force in 2013, tightened up the work-search requirements for Jobseeker's Allowance and Universal Credit, and introduced a much tougher sanctions regime for recipients of these benefits.

68 The reduction in the cost of benefits would have to be greater than the cost of implementing the rather labour-intensive active labour market procedures.

69 Rachel Loopstra *et al.*, 'Do Punitive Approaches to Unemployment Benefit Recipients Increase Welfare Exit and Unemployment: A Cross-area Analysis of UK Sanctioning Reforms' (Working Paper No 2015-01, Department of Sociology, University of Oxford, January 2015). This study found that, for each 100 adverse sanction decisions, about 7.4 claimants moved into work whereas 35.9 claimants moved on to 'unknown destinations', i.e. 'dropped out'.

70 Although the threat of being sanctioned does probably persuade some claimants to step up their job-search activities, the main effect of imposing sanctions is to eject claimants from the benefits system and to distance them from the world of work.

71 Civitarese, above n 55.
72 See Clark Kerr *et al.*, *Industrialism and Industrial Man* (Penguin Books, 1960/1973).
73 See James O'Connor, *The Fiscal Crisis of the State* (St Martin's Press, 1973).
74 See Peter Flora, *Growth to Limits: The Western European Welfare States since World War II* (De Gruyter, 1986).
75 Walter Korpi, *The Democratic Class Struggle* (Routledge & Kegan Paul, 1983) emphasises the role of social democracy while Peter Baldwin, *The Politics of Social Solidarity: Class Bases of the European Welfare State, 1875–1975* (Cambridge University Press, 1990) emphasises the role of the middle classes.
76 Peter B Evans, Dietrich Rueschemeyer and Theda Skocpol (eds), *Bringing the State Back In* (Cambridge University Press, 1985).
77 See Esping-Andersen, above n 1.
78 See Ferrera, above n 1.
79 See Langenbucher, above n 12.
80 See Knotz and Nelson, above n 11.
81 See Figure 7.1.
82 It should be noted that, since the empirical evidence for the negative correlation between conditions and sanctions is based on data from a very small number of countries (six) at one point in time, it should therefore be treated with some caution. Nevertheless, it is surprising and seemingly unprecedented. In the comparative literature on regulatory enforcement, there do not appear to be any findings suggesting that the more stringent or specific the regulatory controls, the less severe are the penalties for violations – or vice versa. However, when a regulated industry is concentrated and very sensitive to reputational considerations, as in the case of banks, pharmaceutical companies and big brand name packaged food producers, regulators can impose strict controls and yet only rarely resort to formal penalties. That said, it is unlikely that analogous reputational concerns apply to individuals who may violate the conditions of unemployment benefit programmes. We are indebted to Bob Kagan for these observations.
83 See Table 7.4.
84 See Figure 7.2.

Part III

Theoretical discussions

Chapter 8

Should a minimum income be unconditional?

Stuart White

It is widely accepted that in a just society, citizens must have access to an income sufficient to meet basic needs, a *minimum income*. However, in most Welfare States, for most citizens of working age, access to a minimum income is typically conditional on employment-related activity such as job search, training or work itself. Moreover, as a number of contributions to this volume show, the policy trend for many years – preceding the financial crash – has been in the direction of increased work conditionality in this sense.[1] Is work conditionality justifiable? Should access to a minimum income be unconditional, at least in this work-related respect? In this paper, I shall explore a case for unconditional minimum income (UMI). The core idea is that while conditionality is justified under appropriate circumstances, there is always a significant risk that the relevant conditions will not hold, rendering conditionality unjust. Moreover, the dangers from unjust conditionality can be severe. How should we respond to this context of risk and danger? I argue for a pluralistic response within which one element is to work to diminish conditionality and to shift towards a UMI.

I begin in section I with a discussion of possible justifications for conditionality. Having first shown that the issue is not settled simply by invoking the concept of 'social rights', I note how paternalist and fairness arguments are offered for conditionality. I elaborate the fairness argument for conditionality that focuses on the principle of reciprocity: that those who choose to share in the benefits created by others' productive efforts should make a reciprocal effort in return. I indicate how this principle, far from being a 'neo-liberal' idea, is deeply rooted in egalitarian traditions of political thought and how making a minimum income conditional on work is also a common-place within this tradition.

Section II then situates the reciprocity principle within a wider discussion of economic fairness. The obligations we have under this principle, which putatively justify conditionality, must be understood in the context of various rights we have to fair treatment in the organisation of our economic system. Under justice as *fair* reciprocity, the obligation to work, as an expression of the reciprocity principle, is conditional on these rights being sufficiently met. When they are not, conditionality is unjust: it enforces an obligation that does not obtain and, in the process, may also threaten to deepen the unjust disadvantage suffered by some. In this important sense, therefore, *the justice of conditionality is conditional.*

What if, as is arguably the case in many Euro-Atlantic nations today, the conditions for just conditionality are not met? Section III discusses three responses. One response, of course, is to redouble our efforts to bring about the economic and social conditions under which conditionality is just. A second response is to think about the political processes through which conditionality is decided and designed and to consider how those subject to conditionality can have greater voice in these processes. A third response is to eschew conditionality in view of the risks and dangers it holds and seek to move towards a UMI. There is something apparently odd in this argument for UMI in that it seems simultaneously to be sceptical of our capacity as democratic citizens (to create the conditions of fair reciprocity) while also optimistic about it (to enact a UMI). However, I argue that this asymmetry is plausible, and so does not undermine this case for UMI. Section IV concludes.

I. Why conditionality?

Getting a minimum income through the Welfare State is 'conditional' when eligibility for the cash payments is linked to the satisfactory performance of behavioural requirements, typically related to employment, for example, job search, training or 'work' itself. A minimum income is unconditional, in the sense I intend here, when eligibility lacks any conditionality of this behavioural kind. If a society ensures all citizens an income on this unconditional basis at a level sufficient to meet basic needs, then it gives its citizens an unconditional minimum income or UMI. Note that as defined here, a UMI is not necessarily a universal cash grant. A UMI could be secured by a system of transfers that tops up income from other sources rather than by a uniform grant. I put that design issue to one side for this paper and focus just on the issue of conditionality related to behaviour, and to employment-related conditionality in particular.

Conditionality of this kind is sometimes said to be necessarily in tension with the idea that a minimum income as the focus of a 'social right' is an element of what T H Marshall termed 'social citizenship'.[2] Rights, so the argument goes, have an intrinsic quality of being unconditional. So, if a minimum income is the focus of a social right, it may seem that receipt of a minimum income must itself be unconditional. To advocate conditionality, on this view, is to imply that minimum income is not the focus of a 'social right' and, thus, implies a rejection of the philosophy of 'social citizenship'.[3] However, as I have argued in earlier work, the issue is not so straightforward.[4] When we say that a minimum income is the focus of a social right, we have to be clear as to what exactly this means. Is the right in question a right to be *given* a minimum income? Or is it a right of *reasonable access to* a minimum income? The social right to a minimum income can be understood, fundamentally, as a right of the citizen to have reasonable access to a minimum income. For some citizens, this may well imply a right to be given a minimum income because they lack the capacity and/or opportunity to acquire an income through their own efforts. But if, say, an individual is able to work, and society offers them a job as a means of earning a minimum income, and this job is not itself in any way degrading or harmful, then this individual arguably has reasonable access to a minimum income even if they are not given this income. The reasonable access consists, precisely, in this job opportunity. By extension, a Welfare State that offers citizens access to a minimum income but subject to forms of conditionality is not necessarily violating their social rights: as in the hypothetical job example, the work-related conditionality of the minimum income may be consistent with the right of reasonable access to a minimum income.

That all said, however, we surely do need a good reason to insist on conditionality. It is not reasonable to make the income conditional on an arbitrary basis. What reason, or reasons, then may we have? Two promising reasons are paternalism and fairness. On the paternalist view, conditionality is justified because it is *good for the 'welfare recipient'*.[5] It is of benefit to receivers of income support that they are subject to behavioural requirements, for example, because, it is alleged, attachment to employment is good for well-being and conditionality helps to maintain this attachment. According to the fairness argument, it is part of a fair scheme of social cooperation that people receive income support conditionally (when it is reasonable to expect them to meet the relevant behavioural requirements); the conditions help promote behaviour that is *fair to others*. I will focus on the fairness argument here.

There are of course many different theories of distributive justice and so potentially many accounts of how conditionality is linked to fairness. One idea one sometimes hears is that citizens have an obligation to be 'self-sufficient'. Conditionality is then defended as a means of encouraging self-sufficiency. Self-sufficiency here means, primarily, that one enjoys an income without the need to draw on state transfers. Thus, self-sufficiency is logically connected to the idea, prominent in many governments' justifications for reforms to the benefits system, that 'benefit dependency' is a bad in itself.[6] One feature of this view, however, is that it seems to assume that the distribution of income generated through the market is presumptively just. 'Transfers' effected through the tax-benefit system then look like intrusions into the underlying, presumptively just market-based distribution, and, *as intrusions*, they look like something that needs to be discouraged. However, from the standpoint of many theories of justice (such as that of John Rawls, for example), we may not regard a market-generated distribution as presumptively just. A just distribution may be one that is produced through a market system that itself operates on the basis of highly 'redistributive' tax-benefit rules. Taxes and transfers are not, on this view, necessarily intrusions into a just distribution. Rather, they help to define what a just distributive scheme really is. On this view, however, there is no reason to think that there is a general duty to achieve 'self-sufficiency' in the original sense. Receiving a high level of transfers through the tax-benefit system may be exactly what justice demands for a given individual, and there is no wrong here that stands in need of correction through extra effort on their part.

The idea of self-sufficiency must be clearly distinguished from another idea that can also feature in fairness arguments for conditionality: the idea of reciprocity. According to what we may term the reciprocity principle, each of us owes our society, as a matter of fairness, a reasonable productive contribution in return for receiving a sufficiently fair share of the economic benefits generated by our fellow citizens. The idea is not the same as self-sufficiency because it does not imply that everyone should ideally have an income entirely independent of state transfers. It does not necessarily imply that people should 'put in' economically goods or services equivalent in value to what they 'take out' (an idea close to the aforementioned idea of self-sufficiency). It may mean, rather, that all citizens, sharing in their society's collective product, 'do their bit', within the bounds of their respective capacities and opportunities, to contribute to this product. Conditionality in the income support system is then presented as a means of ensuring that citizens do not enjoy income support on terms that violate the reciprocity principle.[7]

So understood, the reciprocity principle, and the advocacy of conditionality based on this principle, actually has strong roots in traditions of egalitarian political thought. Unlike the idea of self-sufficiency, it is by no means in itself a 'right-wing' or 'neo-liberal' idea. By way of illustration, consider the writings of the Spanish anarchist-communist, Isaac Puente. Puente's *Libertarian Communism* was adopted as the platform of the anarcho-syndicalist trade union, the CNT, in 1936, just prior to the outbreak of the Spanish Civil War.[8] Puente says here that 'libertarian communism' will '*bring into common ownership* everything that goes to make up the wealth of society' and at the same time '*make it a common obligation* that each contribute to . . . production according to their energies and talents' with the resulting output distributed according to need.[9] Puente clarifies what is involved in making contribution to production a 'common obligation'. In rural areas, he says: 'Whosoever refuses to work for the community (aside from the children, the sick, and the old) will be stripped of their other rights: to deliberate [in the local council] and to consume.'[10] Meanwhile, in the towns, unions will issue each worker with a 'producer's pass-book'. The pass-book will include details about consumption needs ('for instance, size of family') but 'the number of days and hours worked will also be noted in these pass-books'. The pass-book entitles the worker to goods and services: 'The only persons exempted from this requirement will be children, the aged, and the infirm.'[11]

Puente is far from being unusual on the socialist left in insisting on work as a condition of income (with exceptions for children, the aged and for sick and disabled people). Gerrard Winstanley (the seventeenth-century English 'Digger'), Karl Marx, Rosa Luxemburg and R H Tawney all argue that income is properly conditional on work in a non-/post-capitalist society.[12] Underpinning much of this left advocacy of conditionality is commitment to some version of the reciprocity principle.

II. 'Conditionality is conditional'[13]

The reciprocity principle, however, is just one aspect of the broader idea of designing economic structures so that they embody fair terms of social cooperation.[14] This wider notion of fair terms of social cooperation provides crucial context for the reciprocity principle. It both supports it, and points to a range of other considerations that shape and constrain fairness in the application of the reciprocity principle. Let's outline some of these conditions for fair reciprocity.

A. Reciprocity-based work obligations must be applied consistently and equitably

A first set of conditions for fair reciprocity concern consistency and equity in enforcing work-related, reciprocity-based obligations. For example, if work obligations are enforced through the income-support system, fairness requires that these obligations are enforced equally for all receiving income-support payments. Like cases must be treated alike in the administration of the relevant conditionality rules.[15]

Second, if work obligations are enforced through the income-support system, fairness requires that they are also enforced for others in a position to get an income without satisfying the reciprocity principle. In capitalist societies, some people are able to enjoy income without working because of their ownership of assets. In some cases, this may be connected with productive contributions in ways that make the income consistent with the reciprocity principle. But in some cases, this will not be the case. For example, if someone inherits a large fortune and then lives off the return on the inherited assets, this may well mean that they are able to enjoy an income without meeting the reciprocity principle. Large capital gains that accrue to asset-owners without any productive effort on their part also have this 'unearned' quality and enable the owners to get goods and services without satisfying the reciprocity principle. Equity in the enforcement of reciprocity-based work obligations requires that we avoid the asymmetry that consists in targeting those making use of the income-support system while ignoring these kinds of asset-based income. The fact that many of the asset-rich choose to work is not pertinent. The point is that they have the freedom not to that we are denying the asset-poor when we enforce work obligations through the income-support system.[16]

Third, if work obligations are enforced through the income-support system, fairness requires that they are enforced in ways that respect due process and that prevent the imposition of requirements that are unreasonable. Those subject to conditionality must have adequate rights to challenge decisions made about their eligibility and not stand at the mercy of bureaucratic judgement. In addition, the conditions themselves must be reasonable in content. In particular, they must not require activity that is degrading or damaging to the individual.

Thus far, we have spoken about 'work' and 'employment' in more or less interchangeable terms. However, much work in our societies is not done in an employment relationship or, indeed, as self-employment. For example, many citizens, especially women, do unpaid care work for family and friends. A fourth aspect of equity in the application of the reciprocity principle is that as a society we recognise the ways in which this work may also meet citizens' obligations under the reciprocity principle. We should avoid equating reciprocity-satisfying contribution reductively with market-facing work to the exclusion of unpaid care work.[17] This is one reason why if carers are subject to conditionality rules, the obligations defined under these rules must be reasonable in light of their responsibilities as carers.

B. The fairness of enforcing work-related activity in the income-support system depends on the wider fairness of the economic system

Our points above about asset-based incomes and recognising the contribution of unpaid care work begin to show how fairness in the application of the reciprocity principle requires us to look at the wider structure of the economy. This point needs to be expanded. If we have reciprocity-based obligations to work, then we have them in the context of an economy and society that treats us sufficiently fairly in other important respects. Intuitively, it is reasonable to expect us to do our bit for a cooperative scheme that has our interests at heart as much as anyone else's. But if the scheme we belong to evidently denies us fair opportunity and reward, then the obligation to do our bit does not apply. Nobody has an obligation to do their bit in a cooperative venture that is designed in a way that unfairly does them down. As suggested, this has implications both for the structure of opportunity, affecting access to things like education, jobs and finance and for the structure of rewards, including, centrally, the distribution of after-tax income from work. The essential point is made effectively by Tommie Shelby in his discussion of whether work obligations apply to the black ghetto poor in the USA:

> [J]ob opportunities for low-skilled workers are severely limited and the jobs that are available are often menial, dead-end service positions that pay wages too low to provide adequate economic security for a family. Now it might be replied that if the ghetto poor do not want to take these low-wage jobs they should develop their skills . . . As is widely known, however, the quality of education available to ghetto residents is generally so substandard that most cannot get a basic education there, let alone proper preparation for college . . . This lack of equal educational opportunity, which in turn creates an unfair employment opportunity scheme, vitiates any obligation to work.[18]

As Shelby explains, this does not mean that the ghetto poor (or radically unjustly disadvantaged individuals more generally) have no duties. They retain 'natural duties' to one another and to others, as persons, including the duty to help to create just social structures.[19]

But specifically 'civic obligations', such as the obligation to work, which are a matter of reciprocity to one's fellow citizens in the context of a cooperative scheme between equals, do not apply when the cooperative scheme is radically unfair (to those who are disadvantaged by this radical unfairness). Note also that any effort to enforce these supposed, but actually non-existent work obligations may have the effect of consolidating or exacerbating aspects of the underlying unjust disadvantage. For example, conditionality rules may have the effect of weakening the bargaining power of disadvantaged workers thereby consolidating or exacerbating the low rewards that they receive. In themselves, the rules may add stress and suffering to the lives of disadvantaged workers, thereby exacerbating their disadvantage. Here it is also worth noting that when egalitarians such as Isaac Puente or Rosa Luxemburg endorsed conditionality, they did so as a feature of a society that had undergone radical reconstruction in terms of its structure of opportunities and reward. They were not endorsing conditionality as such or under all circumstances, but for a specific kind of society that they aspired to create.

To recap, then, we have argued that conditionality is potentially justified by an appeal to the reciprocity principle as one element of fairness in social cooperation. However, the concern for fair terms of social cooperation also provides an important *critical context* for understanding and applying this principle. It suggests some important conditions that need to be met for reciprocity-based conditionality to be just. Thus, we may sum up the import of this section's argument to this point in the slogan: '(just) conditionality is conditional'.

At the level of policies and institutions, what are the sort of conditions that would have to be met in order for conditionality to be fair (according to the reciprocity-based argument we have been considering)? Based on the foregoing discussion, relevant policies/policy objectives include:

1. *Due process and dignity rights.* Those receiving income support must have sufficient rights within the income-support system to protect them against procedural injustice and against unreasonable (undignified, harmful) demands. A particular area of concern here must be due process and dignity in assessments about the capacity to work in cases of sickness or disability.
2. *Fair taxation of asset income.* To prevent wealthy asset-holders violating the reciprocity principle, there must be sufficient taxation of inheritances and unearned wealth.
3. *Recognition and support for care work.* To ensure that care work is appropriately treated as a form of contribution in satisfaction of the reciprocity principle, there must be sufficient public recognition and material support for care work. Conditionality rules in the income-support system must be calibrated to show recognition of this work.
4. *Fair equality of opportunity.* For all citizens to have obligations under the reciprocity principle, there must be a sufficient degree of equality of

opportunity in education and the labour market, and in access to finance (which is shaped by initial endowments of wealth).
5. *Fair rewards.* For all citizens to have obligations under the reciprocity principle, there must be a sufficient degree of fairness in the structure of rewards for productive efforts.

One possible objection that may be advanced at this point is that citizens are likely to disagree to some extent about what the exact principles in play here look like. For example, what constitutes a fair reward structure? Just when is asset income illegitimate because of its 'unearned' status? When are due process rights strong enough? In response, I do accept that there is indeed a range of reasonable disagreement about what the conditions involve. Even if one were to adopt a specific theoretical perspective, such as John Rawls's conception of justice, it is probable that there will be reasonable disagreement even within this perspective about necessary institutions and policies. It would surely be unreasonable for any of us to insist that conditionality is just only when the very exact conditions we have in mind are met (if, indeed, we have a very exact conception of what these conditions are). Nevertheless, there is a limit on what can count on a reasonable interpretation of any one of these conditions. I assume here that reasonable interpretations must at least be strongly informed by intuitions of the kind that underpin, for example, Rawls's theory of justice.[20] These include the intuition that individuals with similar ability and motivation should have similar chances of occupational success regardless of their family background and the intuition that market-based inequalities in reward reflective of differences in natural ability are 'arbitrary from a moral point of view' and that there is accordingly reason to question them in developing a public conception of fairness in rewards.

The striking implication of the conditions set out above, particularly if one accepts the suggested broadly 'Rawlsian' interpretation of them, is that *a substantial amount of conditionality in the contemporary UK (and in many other advanced capitalist countries) is likely to be unjust.* The policies are almost certainly not in place to meet the five conditions. But conditionality in the income-support system is just only if these conditions are met. Since they are not, it cannot be just.

It is important to add one further thought in light of the theme of this volume. How is the context of 'austerity' likely to affect the likelihood of societies such as the UK meeting the 'conditions for conditionality'? The answer, I think, is that austerity is likely going to make it even harder to meet them. Consider, for example, that the first austerity budget of the Coalition Government in the UK in 2010 included the abolition of the Child Trust Fund (CTF), which aimed at ensuring every young person a modest sum of wealth on reaching adulthood. This cut almost certainly took UK society further away from meeting the fair equality of opportunity condition for fair reciprocity.[21] In the UK, austerity has also involved very concerted efforts to reduce spending on 'welfare' itself.[22] This creates pressures towards cost-cutting in the administration of the income-support system that risks jeopardising the due process and dignity rights of those receiving income support.

Our discussion thus far has been quite general. To get a clearer picture of what is at stake with conditionality policy, and of the dangers that can come with unjust conditionality, let's look at one such policy in the UK that has been widely criticised. Employment Support Allowance (ESA) was introduced in the UK in 2008 (it was therefore originally designed prior to the financial crash and the arrival of austerity). It is a cash benefit intended to provide an income for those unable to get a job due to sickness or disability. A key feature of ESA is the Work Capabilities Assessment (WCA). This is supposed to test 'fitness for work'. All ESA claimants have to go through the WCA. Depending on how many points they score, based on functional impairments for which the test looks, they are then assigned to different groups. Some are denied ESA and immediately moved on to the main, means-tested unemployment benefit, Job Seeker's Allowance, and subject to the rigorous conditionality rules that it involves. Some are granted ESA, but placed in the Work-Related Activity Group (WRAG) where they are subject to work-related activity requirements or are sanctioned. Others are placed in the Support Group, on a higher level of benefit, with no requirements to engage in work-related activity. The WCA has been the subject of widespread criticism for the alleged unfairness and inhumanity of the way it allocates sick and disabled people between these categories.[23] Consequently, it has become the focus of vigorous campaigning by disabled people, with support from influential blog sites such as Sue Marsh's *Diary of a Benefit Scrounger*[24] and 'Bendygirl's' (Kaliya Franklin's) *Benefit Scrounging Scum*.[25] The problems with the WCA are also indicated by the high number of successful appeals against decisions.[26] In 2015, the Department for Work and Pensions (DWP) released figures under a Freedom of Information (FoI) request that show that from December 2011 to February 2014 more than 2,000 people died within two weeks of their ESA claim ending after being found 'fit for work' under the WCA.[27] In terms of the framework presented above, it is very questionable as to whether the WCA respects the due process and dignity rights of sick and disabled people. In addition, the expectation of employment itself is being pressed against the background of a labour market that is far from being justly configured for sick and disabled people in terms of fair equality of opportunity and fair rewards. Moreover, there is evidence that the effects of unjust conditionality in this case are very severe.

We should also note that there is some reason to think that austerity was a contributory factor in the rollout of the policy. Declan Gaffney points out that the policy was originally subject to an annual review for five years, including one before national rollout.[28] The review in November 2010 identified problems with the WCA in the areas it was then being used to reassess existing benefit claimants, and recommended holding off on the national rollout of reassessment until the problems had been addressed. The government pressed ahead anyway. Why? Gaffney comments: 'The context of retrenchment cannot be ignored. In March 2011 (thus, just before the national rollout of reassessment) the DWP

[Department of Work and Pensions] was forecasting that expenditure on incapacity benefits/ESA would fall from £13.2 billion to £10 billion . . . by 2014/15, with a net saving of £1 billion . . . from reassessment: it is all too easy to see why a department which was already tasked with delivering major expenditure cuts would have been unwilling to sacrifice these savings.'[29]

III. Responding to unfair conditionality

So, conditionality is arguably just when it expresses a reciprocity principle. But this reciprocity-based argument must be qualified as indicated above. 'Conditionality is conditional': it is justified by reciprocity only when certain other important conditions of fairness have been satisfied. It seems likely, however, that the relevant conditions are not satisfied in many advanced capitalist countries today and that conditionality is therefore unjust in these countries at this time, given the existing policies and institutional framework. How should we respond to this apparent finding that conditionality is just in principle but likely unjust in practice?

One response is to concede that conditionality is indeed unjust in practice but to recall that there is also a potential paternalist justification for it. Perhaps this may work, but we should note two challenges that any such proposed justification will have to meet. One is the general challenge of justifying paternalism at all. The second, and I think more serious, challenge, consists in showing that a policy that is unfair to a group of people can nevertheless be good for them. Can one make a convincing argument that coercing people receiving income support into work-related activity is good for them even if this coercion is unfair? I do not think unfairness rules out the possibility of (net) benefit to the receiver of income support but, as said, it presents a serious challenge to the paternalist defence of conditionality.

Putting the paternalist argument to one side, then, how may we respond? Three responses suggest themselves: (1) prioritise the conditions of just conditionality, (2) restructure the policy-making process around conditionality so as to increase the voice and influence of those who stand most to be affected and (3) seek to reduce conditionality and move towards some form of UMI.

The first response is to prioritise at the policy level the conditions for just conditionality. If conditionality is unjust because certain policies and institutions are not in place to meet the relevant conditions for just conditionality, then let us introduce the policies and institutions we need. There is clearly something to be said for this response, particularly as an immediate response to problems with existing conditionality rules. For example, if a conditionality rule is set up and/or administered in a way that threatens the due process and dignity rights of citizens, as is arguably the case with the WCA in the UK, then reforming it to reduce or stop this is of course a sensible response.[30] If the political opportunity to do it is there, one would surely wish to do it.

That said, it is worth pausing to reflect on how ambitious this response is, taken by itself, and on the risks and dangers that come with this ambition. Let's recall the five conditions for just conditionality we set out above. Now let's consider what we may have to do in policy terms to meet all of them. What would we need to do? Much more in the way of procedural rights for income-support recipients? New and significant taxes to substantially reduce unearned wealth, for example, inheritance, capital gains and land value taxes? An expansion of public subsidies to support care workers? Restructuring of the education system to foster greater equality of opportunity? Policies to address inequality in initial endowments of wealth and in access to finance (for example, a restored and expanded version of the UK's CTF)? Stronger rights for sick and disabled people to accommodation in the workplace? A new legal regime to foster unionisation so as to compress wage inequalities? More progressive taxation at the top end of the income range to promote greater fairness in rewards? If the list is not endless, it is certainly going to be quite long. Considerations of social justice give us reason to pursue all of these policies, I think, but there is clearly a great deal of ambition wrapped up in setting them as political objectives.

The risk, of course, is that we are not going to achieve them. The risk is that the citizens of polities such as the UK and other advanced capitalist countries are not going to legislate for all of them, certainly not any time soon, and perhaps not ever. In the language of Rawlsian-influenced political theorists, we are at risk of having to live for some considerable time to come under 'non-ideal' conditions, where some important demands of economic fairness are not met. When we ask how we should respond to unjust conditionality our response needs to factor in this risk. It is not enough, I have come to think, to offer a list of prescriptions for public policy without considering the very substantial political risk that they will not get adopted.[31]

This point perhaps suggests a second line of response: to address the political system and the processes through which policy is made. In the context of this paper's topic, we may focus in particular on the policy-making process around income support and conditionality. The general idea is to prioritise reforming the process to increase the voice and influence of those who stand most to be affected by conditionality rules. A related response is to consider how to create more opportunities for legal and constitutional challenges to conditionality rules.[32] Again, this response clearly has much to be said for it. Again, however, it has limitations. One limitation is that while it may work well for things like due process and dignity rights in the design of income-support schemes, it does not directly address wider aspects of social justice on which fair reciprocity, and thus just conditionality, also depends.

The third response is to try to eschew conditionality and seek to move towards a UMI. The basic idea is that since background conditions for fair reciprocity are not satisfied, and there is a serious risk that they will not be satisfied in the future, we should proceed on the assumption that conditionality is likely to be unjust for the foreseeable future and, given the dangers from unjust conditionality, seek to move away from it as much as we can. Introducing a full UMI, set at a level sufficient to meet a standard set of basic needs, with additional benefits to cover the higher living costs of sick and disabled people, is the ideal. However, even a 'partial' UMI, set at a level below this, would arguably go some way towards reducing the stakes of unjust conditionality.[33]

Developing this basic idea more fully, one can present the argument for this in terms of a revisionary conception of social insurance. Conventionally, social insurance refers to Welfare State schemes in which citizens pay tax-like premiums into a collective pot and in return receive benefits in the event of certain events occurring such as sickness, unemployment or old age. One other risk that we always face, however, is that our society may be in some significant way unjust in its economic structure. This risk also gives rise to dangers, particularly and more obviously so for those who are disadvantaged by the background injustice. One danger is that we become subject to unjust conditionality rules, with all the dangers that this in turn can produce in terms of weakened bargaining power, loss of dignity and additional stress and suffering. Now imagine that we take up a variant of the Rawlsian perspective, looking at things from the perspective of the worst-off group, but here understood in the non-ideal context of an unjust society. If we take up this perspective, of those most exposed to the risk and dangers of background injustice, we would surely have reason to seek to minimise the use of conditionality.[34] This way we enhance our bargaining power, protect our dignity and remove one possible source of stress and suffering. (One may put the argument in a form that uses Rawls's notion of the 'veil of ignorance'. If, tomorrow, we were going to be randomly allocated to a place in the economic hierarchy of our society, so that we did not know how exposed to unjust disadvantage and unjust conditionality we would be, what kind of social policy would we recommend? How much conditionality would we propose? Would we not, perhaps, seek to limit its use given the risks and dangers involved?)[35] One may thus refer to this as the *social insurance argument* for a UMI, acknowledging that we are using the term 'social insurance' here in a somewhat revisionary way.

One objection to this argument for UMI as a response to unjust conditionality is that it seems to rest on simultaneously taking both pessimistic and rosily optimistic views about what is politically feasible. On the one hand, the argument is premised on the substantial risk that our society is and will remain economically unjust in significant ways. This reflects a pessimism about what is politically feasible in terms of policies to promote economic justice. On the other, the argument takes as its conclusion that we should seek to introduce a UMI. But obviously a full UMI is itself a highly ambitious political objective. The conclusion therefore demands an optimism about what is politically feasible. Does this not contradict the earlier pessimism? If we are optimistic about the prospects for a UMI, why should we not also be optimistic for creating the conditions of fair reciprocity and just conditionality? And if we are optimistic about the latter, this removes the rationale for considering UMI as a response to a problem of unjust conditionality.

I think this objection is valid insofar as we think that the relative political feasibility of creating the conditions of fair reciprocity and introducing a UMI are more or less the same. However, while both are undoubtedly ambitious, this does not necessarily mean that they are *equal* in terms of political infeasibility. The social insurance argument has bite, so to speak, so long as one thinks that the introduction of a UMI is *more* politically feasible, and so requires less optimism, than creating the conditions for fair reciprocity. The optimism implied by the argument's conclusion does not contradict the pessimistic opening premise if the optimism involved is, so to speak, one notch or two down on the scale from the optimism required to reject this opening premise. The question then is whether we have reason to view the introduction of a UMI as more politically feasible than creating the conditions for fair reciprocity. This is a matter of political judgement, rather than philosophical argument and, moreover, the judgement involved must be very contextual in terms of time and place. My own political judgement is that in, say, the contemporary UK the introduction of at least a partial UMI, set at a level that meets a subset of basic needs, is more politically feasible than creating in full the conditions for fair reciprocity. I think one can reasonably see the argument, therefore, as supporting *a direction of reform* towards UMI as part of a pluralistic response to unjust conditionality.

A second objection to, or at least critical observation about, the UMI response to unjust conditionality is that it seems to allow for some injustice of its own. In the discussion above we focused on the effects of conditionality on the unjustly disadvantaged. But if we make UMI available to all this will also be enjoyed by those who are unjustly advantaged. Roughly speaking, this will include the group that Richard Arneson once referred to as 'nonneedy bohemians' – those who have highly marketable skills but who prefer to pursue more fulfilling activities than paid work.[36] They, too, will get the UMI, and they, too, will therefore have some capacity to withdraw from work and live off the UMI. Since they are not unjustly disadvantaged by the background economic structure, we should perhaps see this behaviour as unjust. It will presumably add to the tax paid by those, advantaged or disadvantaged, who do choose to do paid work. My response to this objection is that a UMI will allow for this kind of injustice, but that at the 'non-ideal', second-best level of analysis we are currently working at, it is better to accept this injustice than the injustices that would occur if we make income support conditional. One may add that the division between the unjustly disadvantaged workers and 'non-needy bohemians' in practice is not necessarily sharp: people in the latter group can easily become sick or disabled and then vulnerable to the dangers of unjust conditionality.

IV. Conclusion: a pluralist response to unfair conditionality

In most Welfare States the provision of income support is typically conditional, for most working-age adults, on work-related activity. If anything, the tendency in recent years has been towards increased, tightened conditionality. The practice of conditionality finds ethical support in the principle of reciprocity: that we should all 'do our bit' in terms of making a productive contribution to society in return for the benefits we share in that others produce. However, if we accept the reciprocity-based rationale for conditionality, we also have to accept the wider concern with fairness in social cooperation of which it is one expression. We have to be consistent and equitable in applying the reciprocity principle itself, and we have to apply it in a policy and institutional context that sufficiently respects other requirements of fairness, such as in relation to the distribution of opportunity and rewards. In this sense, conditionality itself is conditional. In many societies, such as the contemporary UK, we have reason to think that the relevant conditions for just conditionality are not satisfied. How should we respond to this as citizens?

Ideally, of course, we should respond as citizens by legislating to change our policies and institutions so that the relevant conditions are satisfied. However, there is a high risk that this will not happen, certainly not in the near future. A second response, also worthy of support, is to work to improve the political, policy-making process so that the voice and influence of those who stand to be most affected by conditionality policies is increased. Third, in view of the likely limitations of the first two responses, we should also work to reduce conditionality itself and try to create a UMI. At the start of our discussion I made the point that a UMI is not logically entailed by the very concept of a 'social right'. However, our discussion of the justification of conditionality, and the risks and dangers of unjust conditionality, suggests that while a UMI is not logically entailed in this way, there is a strong argument in practice for including a UMI in the system of social rights. As defined here, a UMI is not identical to a basic income (a grant paid to all on a uniform basis with no test of means or willingness to work). But insofar as we create a basic income, this can help create at least a partial UMI. The growing interest in basic income in many countries is therefore a hopeful sign.[37]

Notes

1 This is certainly the case in the UK. Intensification of conditionality under the Labour Governments of 1997–2010 is noted by Baumberg: Ben Baumberg, 'Three Ways to Defend Social Security in Britain' (2012) 20(2) *Journal of Poverty and Social Justice* 149. Further tightening under the Coalition Government of 2010–15 is noted by Gaffney: Declan Gaffney, 'Retrenchment, Reform, Continuity: Welfare under the Coalition' (2015) 231 February *National Institute Economic Review* 44, 47. See, more generally, the discussion in Adler and Terum's chapter in this volume.

2 T H Marshall, 'Citizenship and Social Class' in T H Marshall (ed.), *Citizenship and Social Class* (Cambridge University Press, 1950) 1; Stuart White, 'Social Rights and the Social Contract: Political Theory and the New Welfare Politics' (2000) 30(2) *British Journal of Political Science* 507.

3 See Lembke, Chapter 3 in this volume, for a discussion of this debate within the German context.

4 White, above n 2; Stuart White, *The Civic Minimum: On the Rights and Obligations of Economic Citizenship* (Oxford University Press, 2003).

5 Lawrence Mead, *The New Politics of Poverty: The Nonworking Poor in America* (Basic Books, 1992) 184, emphasis added.

6 Meers, Ch. 6 in this volume; Roman, Ch. 3 in this volume. See also Andrew Duncan, 'Welfare Conditionality, Inequality and Unemployed People with Alternative Values' (2010) 9(4) *Social Policy and Society* 461, 465–6, who reports in his interview study strong majority acceptance of the 'wealth ethic', according to which it is legitimate not to work provided one has independent wealth and so no need to claim state transfers.
7 White, above n 4; Stuart White, 'A Social Democratic Framework for Benefit Conditionality' in Kate Stanley and Liane Lodhe with Stuart White (eds), *Sanctions and Sweeteners: Rights and Responsibilities in the Benefits System* (Institute for Public Policy Research, 2004).
8 Puente, Isaac, *Libertarian Communism* (1932) <http://libcom.org/files/Libertarian%20communism%20-%20Isaac%20Puente.pdf>.
9 Ibid 28, emphasis in the original.
10 Ibid 43.
11 Ibid 44.
12 White, above n 4, 52–9.
13 I owe this phrase to Declan Gaffney.
14 John Rawls, *A Theory of Justice: Revised Edition* (Harvard University Press, 1999); Tommie Shelby, 'Justice, Deviance, and the Dark Ghetto' (2007) 35(2) *Philosophy and Public Affairs* 126.
15 This may be harder than it sounds if there is also an effort to 'personalise' packages of support and obligation for benefit recipients. 'Personalisation' may be desirable in some ways but may also increase the challenge of ensuring consistency and equity of treatment.
16 The early twentieth-century British 'New Liberal', Leonard Hobhouse, puts the point well: 'The moralist . . . is concerned lest we should insist too much on rights and too little on duties . . . The only doubt is whether the stern disciplinarians who insist on self-support fully realise the revolutionary nature of their doctrine. If a system is wrong which maintains an idle man in bare necessaries, a system is much more wrong which maintains an idle man in great superfluity, and any system which allows the inheritance of wealth on the great scale is open to criticism on this score': Leonard T Hobhouse, *The Labour Movement* (Macmillan, 1912) 16–17.
17 Clare Cochrane *et al.*, *Something for Nothing: Challenging Negative Attitudes to People Living in Poverty* (Report, Oxfam, 2010).
18 Shelby, above n 14, 146–7.
19 Ibid 144–59.
20 Rawls, above n 14. This said, I think a number of non-Rawlsian perspectives would also support an approach like that suggested here, and the judgement that contemporary advanced capitalist societies do not meet the conditions of fair reciprocity. Such non-Rawlsian approaches arguably include the pluralistic theory of social justice put forward by David Miller and some versions of left-libertarianism such as that proposed by Michael Otsuka: see David Miller, *Principles of Social Justice* (Harvard University Press, 2000); Michael Otsuka, *Libertarianism without Inequality* (Oxford University Press, 2003).
21 Stuart White, 'Basic Capital: A Policy Whose Time Has Come . . . and Gone?' (2012) 21(1) *The Good Society* 61.
22 Meers, Ch. 6 in this volume.
23 A key problem is that the WCA is a test of functional impairment but it is a mistake to make any direct or general inferences about a person's real-world capacity to do a job simply from a particular level and pattern of functional impairment. See Baumberg B, Warren J, Garthwaite K, Bambra C. *Rethinking the Work Capability Assessment*. London: Demos, 2015.

24 Sue Marsh, *Diary of a Benefit Scrounger* <http://diaryofabenefitscrounger.blogspot.co.uk/>.
25 Bendygirl (Kaliya Franklin), *Benefit Scrounging Scum* <http://benefitscroungingscum.blogspot.co.uk/>.
26 Gaffney, above n 1.
27 Patrick Butler, 'Thousands have died after being found fit for work', *The Guardian* (online), 27 August 2015.
28 Gaffney, above n 1, 46–7.
29 Gaffney adds, 'In the event, expenditure in 2014/15 is now forecast to be £3.7 billion higher than forecast in 2011': ibid 47.
30 Ben Baumberg *et al.*, *Rethinking the Work Capability Assessment* (Demos, 2015).
31 This represents a change from the perspective I set out in White, above n 2.
32 In the UK, this would ultimately require the creation of a written constitution, something of a constitutional revolution. Meers, this volume, discusses the resources in the UK for challenging the legality of reforms to the benefits system. However, as Utrilla notes in her discussion of welfare reforms in Spain, even with a written constitution that includes social rights, courts tend to give legislatures some room for discretion: Utrilla, Chapter 5 in this volume. Albanese's discussion of the Italian case in this volume points out that Italian courts have recently retreated somewhat from judicial activism in support of individual social rights: Albanese, Chapter 4 in this volume. For a discussion of what we ought to expect from courts in the context of austerity, see King, Chapter 10 in this volume.
33 In the UK, many key cash benefits, such as Job Seeker's Allowance, are set below a defensible basic needs standard. What I have in mind by a 'partial' UMI, therefore, would be something like Job Seeker's Allowance minus the conditionality rules that are presently attached to it.
34 A qualification to this would be for any paternalist arguments that can pass the challenge I discussed earlier in this article.
35 I do not want to put too much emphasis on arguing from a 'veil of ignorance'. By itself, this kind of thought-experiment is too dependent on assumptions about attitudes to risk on the part of those behind the veil. The important thing is to think about how conditionality looks from the standpoint of the worst-off and the thought-experiment may have some use in helping us access this perspective.
36 Richard Arneson, 'Is Work Special? Justice and the Distribution of Employment' (1990) 84(4) *American Political Science Review* 1127.
37 See, e.g., Anthony Painter and Chris Thoung, *Creative Citizen, Creative State: The Principled and Pragmatic Case for a Universal Basic Income* (Report, RSA, 16 December 2015).

Chapter 9

The social dimension of fundamental rights in times of crisis

Francesco Ferraro

In what follows, I will challenge the view that the fragility of social rights in times of crisis is determined by their presumptive differences in 'nature' with respect to civil rights. I will try to show that neither their contractualist understanding – which allows for rights conditionality – nor their allegedly different structure exposes them to being emptied of their original meaning and neutralised by crisis-driven policies. The negative impact of such policies is rather on democratic resource allocation and on the social dimension of all fundamental rights, both civil and social. In my view, this is the outcome of a prevailing tacit ideology, favouring an unrestricted free market.

I. Civil vs social rights: could (and should) we tell the species apart?

The debate regarding the differences in 'nature' between so-called civil rights (often also called 'liberty rights') and social rights is long-standing and still ongoing. The questions addressed are whether there are constitutive differences between the two categories and, if so, what those differences are: do they relate to content, structure or other characteristics?

In the philosophical literature on human rights, some 'minimalist' stances have denied that social rights can be seen as genuine human rights. Michael Ignatieff, for instance, has famously held that only 'negative' liberty rights could be seen as expressing the minimal requirements of human dignity that human rights should express as a barrier against intolerable, 'radical' evil. Following Isaiah Berlin, he holds that the basic value of human dignity lies in the protection of human agency, understood as the capacity of each individual to achieve rational intentions; in other words, human dignity is equivalent to respected individual autonomy.[1]

This is only one example of how the idea that social rights are structurally different from civil 'liberty' rights underpins the stances of those who have opposed the recognition of social rights as genuine rights, whether moral, human or legal. Prominent among theorists of rights' minimalism and the exclusion of social rights from moral language is the anarcho-libertarian Robert Nozick. Nozick held that rights are 'side-constraints' on what can be done to persons.

Such side-constraints consist of precise entitlements to certain negative duties on the part of others: that is, to omissions. In this view, fundamental rights are all negative liberties.[2] This minimalist stance, apparently, is meant to deny the possibility of real conflicts between rights, which would allow for justified violations of the side-constraints. Those who embrace this view seem to think that, while positive actions can conflict, omissions (the content of negative duties) cannot. This position cannot be held on logical grounds, of course, so it must be supported by an empirical analysis. This is challenging, however, because we can easily think of cases in which two negative duties, referring to two different rights (or the rights of different persons), clash. Think, for instance, of a case in which a mentally unstable aggressor (who is supposed to be the innocent holder of a right to life) is killed in self-defence by the person whom he attacks (that is, another innocent holder of a right to life).[3]

Nonetheless, such minimalist views clearly display the widespread assumption that there is a substantial difference in structure between civil and social rights, and that this difference consists of the fact that the latter require the performance of positive duties, while the former do not. Other arguments for the exclusion of social rights from the catalogue of genuine human rights, which also draw on the assumption of a structural difference, include those presented by Onora O'Neill, who concludes that social rights cannot exist as universal entitlements previous to institutional allocation of the corresponding positive duties.[4]

It could be observed that, when we move from the realm of moral rights to that of legal rights – human rights being a hinge between the two – the debate around the minimalist option must be seen as decidedly prescriptive, rather than descriptive of the legal reality – the reason being that many national constitutions and other charters already include a number of social rights in their catalogues. As far as international charters and national constitutions that already expressly include social rights are concerned, we can rule out a minimalist stance that prescribes their abolition from the catalogues of fundamental entitlements. But in relation to countries that are contemplating constitutional reform, the entrenchment of social rights is still a live and pertinent normative question. Jeff King has offered a catalogue of the arguments used against such entrenchment, dividing them into what he considers to be bad and good arguments.[5] Most of these arguments make reference to presumptive differences in 'nature' between social and civil rights, like the above-mentioned active character of duties relating to social rights. An argument from conflict, for instance, is based on this view: social rights, so it goes, are more likely to give rise to rights conflicts, as they can both conflict with each other and with civil rights. For instance, one poor child's right to education can conflict with another's when the state financial resources cannot pay for both. Or, one person's civil rights of property can easily conflict with another's right to social security, whenever taxation is needed to afford a social security system. When austerity measures are required, limited resources will exacerbate these conflicts.

This brings King to a second argument, one from costs, implying that social rights, in contrast with civil and political ones, are costly: think of the right to health or to education, for instance, as contrasted with the right to free speech or the right to personal liberty. Public budget cuts in times of austerity would then require the sacrifice of social rights. Yet, constitutionalising social rights would tie the legislature's hands with respect to the possibility of cutting public expenditure. Other arguments he discusses rely less on the logical structure of rights (we could say, on their syntax), and more on aspects related to their interpretation (that is, to their semantics). Some hold that social rights are much more indeterminate than civil ones, in the sense that expressions like 'right to health' or 'right to work' can be interpreted in a vast variety of different ways. This, among other things, also makes it much more difficult both to assess their violations and to appeal to the judiciary – against the state or against other citizens – for their protection.[6] Yet, limitations to their justiciability will render them useless and lead to the delusion of citizens, especially in times of crisis when people need to entertain a realistic idea of their entitlements.

This last argument may also be seen as related to the idea that social rights are 'rights to' (a certain good, like education, health and the like) rather than 'rights against' someone, that is, a definite duty-bearer. While drawing upon the alleged semantic indeterminacy of social rights, the argument also involves a thesis regarding their pragmatics: namely, that social rights mainly have the 'expressive function' of giving voice to some of the most cherished values of the society that declares them, rather than offering a ground for judicial enforcement. Cass Sunstein, for instance, has argued that the European propensity to include social rights in national constitutional instruments derives from the prevalence of such expressive functions, with less regard for more practical worries concerning the possibility of their enforcement in courts.[7] This bears on the concept of 'programmatic' rights, to which I will return later.

II. Differences in political rhetoric for different rights

However, the idea of a difference in 'nature' between the two categories of entitlements does not lead to the discredit of social rights for all theorists. A recent, challenging article by Fernando Atria rather assumes such a difference as strategically preferable in the fight for their protection and implementation. Atria contrasts what he significantly calls 'individual' rights, that is, civil or liberty rights, with social rights. He boldly states that legal protection of social rights through their enforcement in courts does not actually uphold them, but rather sterilises and deprives them of their original meaning.

> Judicial institutions can protect individual rights more effectively than social rights because the latter imply an understanding of citizenship that is incompatible with bourgeois law, whilst the former are its most perspicuous manifestation. Thus, traditional forms of bourgeois law cannot contain social rights . . . bourgeois law can protect social rights through its traditional forms of legal protection, but in doing so, it will inevitably transform them

> into bourgeois (individual) rights. That is to say, the cost of subsuming social rights under bourgeois law is to de-socialize them.[8]

Atria rejects the self-appointed 'progressive' thesis that there are no structural, 'deep' differences between individual and social rights. In his view, there is a real difference that relates to their respective content and 'deep structure'. This difference is political in character and should be traced back to the Marxist critique of individual (natural) rights as indifferent to cooperation and reflecting the selfishness of individuals into bourgeois society. Social rights emerge from the socialist idea that human self-realisation can only be reciprocal and cooperative, rather than individual. They actually bring into bourgeois law something that does not belong originally to it, 'because the point of social rights is to subvert the idea of individual rights, to turn it against itself'; they are 'anomalous grafts in bourgeois law'.[9] In order to do so, social rights have had to be presented as the result of a coherent line of evolution, starting with the recognition of the first civil rights. But, Atria explains, the grafting has created an unstable situation. Stabilisation can only be achieved by one of two routes: either by normalising social rights and assimilating them into the category of individual rights (thereby neutralising their potential threat for bourgeois law) or, by transforming systems of law based upon individual rights, which are indifferent to cooperation, into systems based upon the ideas of reciprocal duty and cooperation, which are constitutive of authentic social rights.

The structural difference between individual and social rights, for Atria, can be explained as follows. For individual (negative freedom) rights, specifying their 'active aspect' (the right) implies specifying, at the same time, their 'passive aspect' (in Hohfeldian terms, their jural opposite, their duty). By specifying what the right-holder is entitled to (for instance, life), we specify at the same time the content of the right – that is, the dutiful action for the passive subject (in the case of the right to life, the duty to abstain from killing) – as well as the bearer of the duty.

> The active aspect of the right to life immediately reveals its passive aspect, thus fully specifying who has what duty. The passive subject must be universal because these rights are 'natural'. Their being natural rights is . . . a political claim: they are rights that do not presuppose any artificial (=non-natural, political) relations between individuals.[10]

However, in the case of social rights, according to Atria, specifying their active aspect does not sufficiently specify their passive content, that is, the correlative duty. In his view, the duty correlative to a social right stands in need of a 'grounding', which cannot be offered by the interest of the right-holder alone. There is a gap between the interest of the right-holder and the duty of the duty-bearer, which must be bridged. Finding an interest worth protecting is not enough to conclude that every human being has a right to the satisfaction of such interest, and that others bear a duty to promote such satisfaction.

Two paths to bridge the gap can be followed, in Atria's view. One is a contractualist view of social rights: the essential component of the social compact makes the condition of the less fortunate preferable to not adhering to the compact at all. Social rights thus become a mere protection against extreme poverty, 'and they ground not universal public services but strictly targeted (means-tested) programmes'.[11] The second path, which Atria ascribes to Marshall's *Citizenship and Social Class*, sees social rights, rather, as stemming from the reciprocal, cooperative duties that members of human communities bear, to enhance certain aspects of the well-being of one another. Under this second view, social rights cannot be seen as 'natural', nor as 'individual', because they presuppose responsibilities within a political society; in Marshall's terms, they are rights of citizenship. While the contractualist view neutralises social rights by downplaying the value of equality and rather focusing on poverty, thereby de-socialising them and 'transforming them into individual rights to a minimum provision of well-being',[12] the second, citizenship-related view expresses their meaning as a 'subversion' of the language of individual rights. Therefore, Atria rejects the contractualist ethical and political understanding of social rights and proposes to rescue the 'socialist idea' of social rights. He also adopts Charles Taylor's idea of a 'slow pedagogy' that sees humanity as a progressive goal of history, rather than as a sheer biological fact: everyone's rights and duties cannot be established once and for all, as if they were 'natural' and 'based on the most primitive aspects of human behaviour (which is why there is an intrinsic connection between liberalism and Neo-Darwinism)'.[13]

It is quite difficult to do justice to Atria's views from a purely legal-theoretical perspective. Suffice it to say, however, that his analysis seems to provide a re-definition of the language of social rights within the broader frame of moral and political language, rather than proposing a different understanding of them into legal language. After all, he anticipates the all-too-easy objection that existing ('bourgeois') legal systems do recognise and judicially enforce such rights, by contending that they deform them in order to fit them into the individualist values of bourgeois society.

The idea that rights language is originally laden with 'monadic' individualism and neglects the value of cooperation and mutual caring is not only Marxian or socialist in origin. The Italian nineteenth-century republican political thinker and nationalist agitator Giuseppe Mazzini criticised the exclusive reliance on the concept of 'the rights of man' on these very grounds, and especially from the progressive point of view of the fight for the liberation of all men from tyranny and injustice. He advocated the resort to the language of 'the duties of man' as more apt to the mobilisation of people and to sustain the association between them, as a matter of reciprocal duty.[14] More recently, Elizabeth Wolgast has criticised the resorting to rights language also in situations where right-holders are factually dependent on others and cannot claim their entitlements. Where the idea of self-interested, rational and factually autonomous individuals does not reflect reality, rights language is not the best tool for defending the weak and for doing them justice; instead, the language of care and responsibility towards them should be adopted.[15] Mary Ann Glendon has similarly pointed out that the excessive reliance on rights talk has completely erased concepts like the duty of aid to people in cases of emergency and the responsibility of government towards people in need.[16]

All these concerns bear on the use of rights language in general. Atria, then, has a strong point in claiming that social rights subvert the original functions of rights talk and seek to overcome its original selfish and individualist implications. But it is worth remarking that, although economic and social rights are often seen as a conceptual innovation stemming from the expansion of international human rights law, their origins can be traced back at least to the French Revolution and to Robespierre's proposal of an official recognition of the right to work and to social assistance as core individual rights.[17] It is very difficult to trace as sharp a distinction between the political (and moral) basis of civil and social rights as the one that Atria sees, both from the historical and conceptual points of view. An example of how the background political stances behind civil rights and social rights can easily merge is provided by Italian constitutional law, as shown by Albanese's chapter into this volume. While Art. 2 (recognising traditional 'inviolable' liberty rights) and Art. 3 (granting the active role of the Republic in enhancing positive freedom and equality) of the Italian Constitution were originally seen as being in an antagonistic relationship, a different understanding of them later prevailed: namely, that the values of liberty and equality expressed by the two articles should be seen in a synergistic relationship, linking individual development and human dignity to substantive equality. Rather than expressing a socialist perspective like the one embraced by Atria, this orientation reflects the relinquishment of the binary view that sees the liberal and the socialist states as two opposed and irreconcilable models.

Moreover, the apparent platitude that *all* rights are social should not be overlooked. In a response to Atria's article, Garland underlines that when merely aspirational claims become enforceable legal rights, this has an impact on the conduct of officials, the exercise of State power and the allocation of public resources. 'Private' rights are always also 'public'. The idea that, for instance, social rights are costly, while civil rights do not affect the public purse, is clearly incorrect and generally obscures undeclared ideological stances regarding how the State should spend public money.[18] Echoing Durkheim, Keat, in another response to Atria, contends that contractual exchange between individuals is always dependent on social institutions, and that these make possible market exchange and also the specification of all property rights. Market institutions are created by social cooperation and collective political choices.[19] A similar point had been made by Liam Murphy and Thomas Nagel, who criticised as ideological the idea of a free market as a virgin moral standpoint against which to assess the justifiability of fiscal levy. There is no free market without a strong legal architecture, financed by public expenditure: that is, without politics and the State. This holds all the truer in modern capitalism with its need for antitrust legislation and control on interest rates, on the monetary supply, and the like.[20]

However, while the contractualist foundation of rights probably is not guilty of the de-socialisation of social rights that Atria ascribes to it – but rather points to some reasonable form of rights conditionality, as we will see further on – there is some truth in the claim that those rights lose their meaning if seen merely as a safety net for the most disadvantaged. The idea that they only grant for a minimum of subsistence and are aimed at providing for the most basic necessities of life surely leads to social exclusion rather than inclusion.

III. Austerity, conditionality, and sanctions

Some of the national studies in this volume point at the above-mentioned loss of meaning of social welfare rights as instruments of equality and inclusion into national communities. The French case, as explained by Diane Roman, offers a clear example. Constitutional social rights in the French legal system seem originally to reflect the very same rhetoric of reciprocal duties and social bonds endorsed by Atria: social provisions are explicitly grounded in the principle of *solidarité*. National solidarity founds the protection of workers and their families and this principle has somehow helped to reduce the impact of the financial crisis on the poor. Nonetheless, not only has this not prevented French society from becoming increasingly unequal, but it also has given rise to phenomena of social exclusion rather than enhancing inclusion. Social benefits for the poor have been increasingly tied to a principle of desert, meant to minimise social security fraud and to implement a duty, rather than a right, to work. Unemployment benefits have been made dependent on the acceptance of job or training offers and the number of such offers that can be refused has been restricted. Sanctions like the suspension or cancellation of benefits have become harsher. French social welfare, explains Roman, has started to transform what before were rights into duties. Political rhetoric has started to target welfare scroungers and cheats and legislative choices have followed. The result is that social stigma has generated a non-take-up phenomenon: the poor are discouraged from applying for essential benefits.[21]

In Germany, the Hartz laws have introduced 'activation policies' aimed at pressuring the unemployed to re-enter the labour market as soon as possible: in this field, regulations have grown stricter and sanctions harsher.[22] Also, the UK case displays, with the Welfare Reform Act 2012, an increasing sanctions programme for unemployment benefits, aimed at promoting individual responsibility for welfare provision and at dis-incentivising benefit dependency. Moreover, for instance, the increment in Discretionary Housing Payments has added a layer of administrative discretion to the provision of social benefits, with the application of conditionality resulting in the denial of payments to those who smoke or have satellite television.[23]

Conditionality can be defined as the attachment of conditions to the receipt of public benefits. Conditions can be both *ex-ante* (eligibility conditions) and *ex-post* (such as the active search for work for recipients of unemployment benefits). Sanctions apply to those who do not comply with *ex-post* conditions.[24]

Now, the increasing tendency towards conditionality does not, by itself, mean that social rights are emptied of their meaning. Good normative frameworks in moral and political philosophy can be provided to account for the need of conditionality. Moreover, the very same ethics of reciprocity and social duties propounded by Atria can easily account for a minimum of conditionality in the enjoyment of social rights. However, when social rights cease to be seen as a means for the promotion of equality, and are rather regarded as a safety net for the poorest, their meaning as a common and social good is lost and their legitimacy within society starts to be questioned. In the French case, the focus on poverty makes the bulk of taxpayers feel increasingly excluded from the benefits of social security they are paying for. This also facilitates the use of arguments against scammers and scroungers in political propaganda. The sanctioning aspect of rights conditionality is emphasised, with a resulting stigmatisation and exclusion rather than inclusion. A similar trend can be observed in the UK: an increasing concern that social state support should be gained by meeting certain behavioural conditions has led to the application of excessively strict work-related conditionality to vulnerable groups. Disabled people, for instance, were affected by the application of reforms that made work-capability assessments intolerably distressing and humiliating.[25]

Much more than by contractualism, then, the de-socialisation of social rights is caused by a certain view of those rights as mere welfare claims for the most disadvantaged, who will receive social benefits as if they were yielded by the charity of taxpayers. The bulk of the community will not see themselves as possible beneficiaries of social assistance and will tend to be suspicious of those depending on it, who, in turn, will experience social stigma and marginalisation. Rights conditionality and sanctions will become dangerously akin to punishment for having to beg for society's help or compensation for society in granting it.

On the contrary, a refined and developed contractualist view on fundamental rights can provide convincing reasons for some forms of rights conditionality. Stuart White, for instance, has offered an account of welfare conditionality as a productive contribution, required by fair reciprocity in a society that meets a number of obligations required for the abolishment of the 'proletarian condition'. A society that protects all its members from immiseration, discrimination and exploitation (thereby defending them also against vulnerability to the free market) can rightfully ask for such contribution. The concern for equality, at least as equality of opportunities and as the correction of 'brute luck inequalities', is not lost within such a contractualist framework.[26] Political debate on how to meet such requirements of social justice and what can be expected from welfare recipients would surely help to devise forms of justified conditionality, without emptying rights of their social meaning. 'Punitive' and vastly discretionary forms of conditionality and sanctions, instead, will favour social exclusion and isolation.

Aside from the problem of the political and moral justification of rights conditionality, it is worth remarking that there is nothing in the concept of fundamental rights, both civil and social, that rules out their being conditional.

One way of seeing conditionality could be that of balancing: fundamental rights are subject to being weighed against, and limited by, other rights and principles. In this case, the duty to contribute with one's work to the life of the national community is a principle enshrined in many a constitutional charter. Another way of seeing rights conditionality is as part of the very definition of the right in question. If we embrace this last option, what is essential is that right-holders know in advance what can be expected of them in light of their entitlements. Again, open public discussion and political debate should be encouraged in order to reduce rights' indeterminacy by way of definition and to safeguard right-holders from uncertainty, discretionality and disappointment of legitimate expectations.

IV. The social dimension of dignity

The use of the principle of human dignity in legal interpretation, as an argumentative basis for the acknowledgement and protection of social rights, offers an interesting example of how differences in political rhetoric can impact on the meaning of fundamental rights, rather than the adoption of a developed contractualist political theory or the reduction of social rights to the model of civil rights.

A proper understanding of dignity would call for a level of social protection and security much higher than that of mere survival; when dignity is reduced to survival, there is much more room for proportionality and balancing against, for instance, a principle of financial stability. If the core of dignity is mere sustenance, almost all other constitutional protections shrink to irrelevance.

This phenomenon captures Atria's worry – unduly turned against contractualist political theories – about the de-socialisation of social rights. In Germany, the Federal Constitutional Court has used the principle of human dignity, enshrined into Art. 1 of the Basic Law, to found a fundamental right to minimum subsistence. However, as underlined in Lembke's chapter in this volume, this minimum subsistence is not understood as the mere sustenance of biological life: the court has identified its content as comprising both physical existence and the possibility of social relationships and participation in cultural and political life. This 'socio-cultural minimum' surely reflects an understanding of social rights – in this case, the right to minimum subsistence – as claims to inclusion into society's life. The safety net for the needy, here, is much more demanding and does not confine itself to the satisfaction of biological necessities.

This approach has been criticised for the significant legislative discretion allowed for by the court in the material realisation of the right to minimum subsistence. In this sense, the court has not departed from the tradition of leaving the social Welfare State principle (covered by Art. 20 of the Basic Law) highly undetermined. However, this kind of judicial deference – which represents, as King notes, a form of judicial incrementalism[27] – does not make the announcement of a constitutional right to minimum subsistence less revolutionary, nor deprive it of its impact on successive judicial review. For instance, it allowed the Federal Constitutional Court to declare the unconstitutionality of parts of the Asylum Seekers Benefits Act, on account of its failure to adjust benefits for asylum seekers to the level of social benefits designed to ensure minimum subsistence under the Social Codes.

Nonetheless, as Lembke points out, problems remain with regard to the justification of penalty deductions against benefit receivers. While German courts usually approve of welfare conditionality and sanctions, they fail to explain how sanctions affecting minimum subsistence (as defined by the legislature) could be justified. The constitutional principle of human dignity has always been interpreted as prohibiting the treatment of individuals as objects by the State. Thus, it poses serious questions about activation policies and sanctions in order to pursue goals regarding social security and the labour market. To overcome this contradiction, it has been argued that benefit awarding can be rightfully diminished as long as penalty reductions do not impede the pure physical existence of the benefit receiver. But, of course, this amounts to contradicting the idea that minimum subsistence also encompasses interpersonal relationships and participation into social, cultural and political life. The German case, then, both shows how the concept of human dignity can help mould a social understanding of the core of fundamental rights – thus avoiding their loss of meaning, even into the framework of a 'bourgeois' legal system – and how a shift in political rhetoric against benefit receivers can actually hinder the reception of a social understanding of dignity with its full implications.

The Spanish national case study also shows how the recognition of the minimal conditions for the development of a dignified human life (as required by Art. 10 of the Spanish Constitution) can effectively restrict legislative freedom, at least with regard to the restriction of existing social policies, even in a context where social rights are seen as leaving broad discretion to the legislature due to their semantic indeterminacy and their configuration as mere principles governing social and economic policy. This is due to the determination of the so-called 'Social State clause' embedded in Art. 1 of the Constitution, which requires the State to foster equality among citizens and allows it to ascribe rights to individuals in order to pursue social objectives.

The above cases show that the relationship between the ascription to social rights of a protective function regarding the most disadvantaged parts of society, and their losing their social character (reflecting the reciprocal duties that we bear towards one another, as members of a human community), is not so straightforward. Much depends on the prevailing political rhetoric (which influences both legislation and judicial review) and on the understanding of concepts such as that of human dignity. These concepts, in turn, are morality-laden and influenced by the prevailing political culture and public ethos. In the German case, a non-minimalistic understanding of dignity, including both biological necessities and the possibility of taking part in social and political life, has opened the way to a reshaping of the social Welfare State from Bismarckian paternalism to the social citizenship model, although this is still an ongoing process, hampered somewhat by public bias against benefit dependency.

In what follows, I will argue that differences in political rhetoric and ideology have a much more significant impact on the use of fundamental rights, and on their implementation in times of crisis, than pretended differences in their nature (be it their 'superficial grammar' or 'deep structure').

V. On the alleged 'programmatic' character of social rights

It has often been held that social rights, even when entrenched in constitutions and legally binding international charters, can only play a 'programmatic' role. The Italian case study in this volume reminds us that social rights explicitly mentioned in the Italian Constitution were long seen as purely programmatic in nature. It is not always easy to understand what is meant by 'programmatic' here. One sense seems to be, as Albanese explains, that they are seen as very general, non-specific goals assigned to public authorities, first and foremost to the legislature. This is sometimes presented as a denial of their 'subjective' character, meaning that they are 'objective' directives to the legislature and other State authorities, the content of which could not ground individual appeals to courts. The alleged non-specific nature of such rights and their non-subjective character constitute two different but related concepts, in the sense that semantic indeterminacy and lack of precision in establishing the content of social rights is sometimes offered as a reason to justify and recommend that they are not judicially enforced.

However, it is highly disputable whether rights of this kind could be seen as legal rights at all. They seem to have only the above-mentioned 'expressive function' of embodying the declaration of the nation's aspirations and values. They would be rights only in what Joel Feinberg has called the 'manifesto sense': therefore, they would not correlate to specific legal duties on the part of anyone, nor serve as their source.[28] A typical example of these rights is offered by the UN's 'Social Covenant' (International Covenant on Economic, Social and Cultural Rights (ICESCR), 1966), which seems to establish goals rather than binding entitlements. This was probably due to the fact that many countries, at the time that the Covenant was drafted, would not be able to accomplish those standards to an acceptable degree. However, it is very doubtful that these could be seen as legal rights at all. Human rights are akin to moral statements about human beings, and only become legal rights when made actually enforceable in national and international courts.

Merely programmatic rights are the closest equivalent of human rights at the national level and constitute moral statements rather than legal entitlements. Some would argue that they are moral rights still awaiting for their transformation into full-fledged legal rights. Such transformation would need the identification of particular agents with 'perfect duties' to fulfil those rights, and the possibility for individuals to seek judicial redress when such duties are not met. [29]

Now, the lack of specific duties on specific agents, individuated as correlative to (or grounded on) some rights, may be seen as a simple case of legal void. The Italian legal theorist Luigi Ferrajoli has contended that, when fundamental rights are stated but no guarantee has been established for them – namely, no duty or obligation to fulfil them, both on public authorities or citizens at large – such rights still represent an expectation of those guarantees and the legislature stands under an obligation (a second-level obligation, that is) to institute them. If the legislative power does not fill in this legal void, then the judiciary will have to do so.[30] If seen this way, fundamental rights still displaying a purely programmatic character could still be considered as legal rights, calling for the institution of some corresponding duties at the hands of the legislature (which stands under a duty to institute such duties: namely, a second-level duty). The legislator must make laws: this could be the legal sense of programmatic rights, transcending their simple moral meaning. Programmatic legal rights, lacking corresponding duties and obligations into the legal system, can be seen as mere 'rights on paper', but those paper rights still urge for their transformation into fully developed legal entitlements. If legislative inactivity delays this transformation, then courts will have to pursue it.

In Italian constitutional scholarship this last perspective has prevailed, as Albanese in this volume reminds us: fundamental social rights are no longer seen as mere directives to politics, devoid of any effect when no statutory laws embody them, but are rather considered as being directly enforceable by the courts. This is an aspect of a progressive 'constitutionalisation' of the legal system, which sees not only the Italian Constitutional Court, but also ordinary civil and administrative courts directly applying constitutional provisions embodying social rights in their decisions, thereby recognising their character of subjective rights.

Interestingly enough, the more recent Spanish Constitution seems to have solved this dispute in advance by distinguishing between fundamental rights in the broad and in the strict sense, and by further dividing fundamental rights from other constitutional rights that are seen as mere principles governing economic and social policy. As pointed out by Utrilla in this volume, rights seen as mere principles guiding legislation, judicial practice and public authorities enjoy a lower standard of judicial protection, since they may only be invoked before ordinary courts according to the legal provisions meant to develop them (Art. 53 of the Spanish Constitution). However, these are not simple paper rights: they do entail certain legal consequences, like the obligation for the legislature to meet some social objectives, subject to control by the Spanish Constitutional Court. Moreover, they can be balanced against other constitutional principles or rights, thereby entitling the legislature to restrict them. Nonetheless, only fundamental rights 'in the strict sense' (enshrined in Articles 14 to 30 of the Constitution) are granted the maximum constitutional protection, thanks to the possibility of an individual appeal.[31]

What some supporters of a strong distinction in nature between civil and social rights hold is not only that social rights, when constitutionally entrenched, risk remaining mere paper rights, but that they need to stay on paper. One of the arguments for this position has been mentioned above, namely the one from indeterminacy. Semantic indeterminacy is a matter of interpretation: a very indeterminate proposition is one that admits of a large number of different interpretations: that is, of different ascriptions of meaning. Expressions like 'right to work' or 'right to health' can be interpreted in a vast variety of different ways. Moreover, they are indeterminate not only regarding their scope and content, but also as to the bearers of the corresponding duties, which remain unspecified. Therefore – so goes the argument – this makes it extremely difficult to assess violations of social rights. If entrenched into national constitutions, they should remain programmatic in character, leaving the task of specifying their content to the legislature.

However, this looks like a very weak argument. First, it wrongly assumes that semantic indeterminacy only affects in a relevant degree constitutional provisions stating social rights. But we can have a hard time interpreting provisions expressing some of the most reputed members of the traditional catalogues of civil or liberty rights too. Think of the phrase 'Everyone has a right to freedom of expression' (Art. 10 ECHR): does that mean, for instance, that everyone should be granted equal access to the means that may be necessary for expressing themselves, such as the press and television? Or should it rather be interpreted as protecting a minimal core of freedom of expression, such as the possibility of expressing oneself with one's own voice? Moreover, does the right cover only possible interference at the hands of state authorities? Or, should it also hold against private interference? The written formulation of all fundamental rights, both civil and social, is very indeterminate. Such indeterminacy is often part of a strategy on the part of constitutional drafters to obtain flexibility and lowest-common-denominator consensus (regarding what I previously called the 'expressive function' of rights).[32]

Second, even if we concede that semantic indeterminacy is inherent to social rights more than civil ones, this by no means entails that the legislature should be under no legal (constitutional) obligation to fill them with specific content by legislation, nor that judges should not be allowed to adjudicate regarding them (thereby helping to progressively specify their import). It has been shown that even the 'expressive function' of constitutional rights, made easier by their imprecise formulations, can be used and is used indeed in judicial review to evaluate the expressive function of laws, which must not contradict the values inherent in constitutional declarations: this happens, for instance, in US constitutional practice.[33] Neither the identification of the legislature as an agent with a 'perfect duty' (corresponding to the rights in question), nor the possibility of individual judicial redress, stand impaired by semantic indeterminacy.

I would like to point out that the idea that '[f]or negative freedom rights . . . it is enough to specify that to which the holder is entitled in order to provide a full specification of the content of said right',[34] while the same does not hold for social rights, is both descriptively incorrect and problematic for the defence of social rights. First, it is descriptively incorrect, because all fundamental rights, both civil and social, are usually viewed under a 'dynamic' perspective, which means that they are not seen in a Hohfeldian fashion as strictly correlative (that is, logically equivalent) to certain precise duties and other 'jural positions', bore by strictly defined subjects. We should think of fundamental rights, not in terms of single jural positions, nor as aggregates of such positions, but rather as *sources* of them – which is how the courts usually see those rights. This is what the 'dynamic' view of fundamental rights amounts to.[35] One and the same right can serve as the justification for the creation or recognition of new duties, powers, immunities and the like. As new positions are created, old ones may be abolished. If we could take a picture of a right at a certain moment in time, we would see it as an aggregate of definite positions; but the picture is forever changing. In Jeremy Waldron's words, rights generate successive 'waves of duty'.[36] This holds both for civil and social rights. The example chosen by Waldron to illustrate this dynamic conception is one from the catalogue of civil rights, namely the right not to be tortured: it surely brings about a duty not to torture, but, according to the circumstances, it could also generate a duty on the part of state authorities to foster a culture of contempt for torture, a duty to be vigilant about the danger and temptation of torture, and so on.

Second, the above characterisation of the difference between civil and social rights is problematic for their defence because it reduces them to indeterminate and wishful declarations of needs and interests to be fulfilled, with no possible specification of who bears the duty to fulfil them – once again, it condemns them to the status of 'paper rights'. It also obscures the fact that, quite often, the problem with the protection of social rights is not their being merely on paper, that is, their lack of corresponding obligations meant to guarantee their enjoyment. Especially in times of economic or financial crises, those rights are already theoretically implemented by legislative provisions, but those provisions are simply not complied with. These are not 'paper rights', then, but may be called 'scam rights', since their guarantees are recognised by the legal system but still remain ineffective.[37] An example among many is offered by the French case of the Child Welfare Provisions, described in this volume: under them, local authorities are legally obliged to take care for migrant unaccompanied minors, but limited resources and lack of political will lead those authorities to find loopholes (like false determination of the age of the migrants) to turn minors away, or simply reject any new applications on illegal administrative orders.[38]

VI. Conclusions: ideology and the defeat of the democratic and social dimension of rights

Both the theory and practice of fundamental social rights in contemporary legal systems show us that their presumptive differences in structure and content with respect to civil rights are, at best, superficial and apparent. The fragility of social rights in times of crisis results from a shift in political rhetoric and from undeclared ideological assumptions, not from their structural characteristics. The above-mentioned arguments against social rights, which rely on their alleged propensity to give rise to conflicts or on their costly nature, bear on presumptive differences in their syntax, that is, in their logical structure. The main assumption here is that social rights ask for positive actions, while civil rights only correlate to negative duties. But the dynamic nature of fundamental rights falsifies this assumption. For instance, in cases involving traditional civil rights, like the right to due process and procedural fairness, and the rights to life, liberty and security of the person, international courts like the European Court of Human Rights (ECHR) have interpreted them as calling both for negative and positive duties on the part of the states.[39] Also civil rights, then, can involve costs and can conflict between them. Rights 'of protection', like those to life and to personal security – but also property rights – do require positive actions[40] and can be very costly.[41] Moreover, the positive duty of legal aid is usually associated to the civil right to a fair trial, as recognised by the ECHR (Art. 6) and the Charter of Fundamental Rights of the EU (Art. 47). In times of austerity, the right to legal aid is indeed threatened by measures aimed both at cost cutting and at protecting the executive from judicial review, with the pretext of inhibiting speculative claims at public expense.[42]

The impact of financial and economic crises on fundamental rights, then, is not predetermined by the differences in 'nature' between civil and social rights – that is, by their structure and content – but is rather directed by political rhetoric and action. Claiming that some rights are costly, while others are not, only helps to obscure the fact that privileging financial worries and the free market over public concern for social needs is a matter of political choice. The conflict is not between two kinds of rights, but between two options of resource allocation: one based on the free play of market choices, the other on social need and entitlement conferred by democratic choices.[43] Civil rights possess a strong social dimension; social rights impact on individual freedom and development. Which kind of political option will prevail will have consequences for both categories of fundamental rights. The defeat of the 'social' option will also affect civil rights. Utrilla's chapter in this volume, for instance, shows how crisis-driven welfare reforms in Spain have been accompanied by restrictions on freedoms of expression, assembly and demonstration, meant to limit the reactions of civil society. More generally, democratic deliberation has been bypassed or made impossible by the use of emergency legislation and budget acts. By conflating the concepts of urgency and of necessity, and by inappropriately referring to fiscal crises as national emergencies, the time required by truly democratic choices – time for study, reflection and discussion – is denied.[44] An undeclared political ideology, favouring unrestricted markets and the minimisation of public expense, is behind the erosion of the meaning and point of many fundamental rights, both civil and social. This same ideology is progressively overcoming the democratic allocation of resources, as well as emptying all fundamental rights, both civil and social, of their social dimension.

Notes

1 Michael Ignatieff, *Human Rights as Politics and Idolatry* (Princeton University Press, 2001).
2 Robert Nozick, *Anarchy, State, and Utopia* (Basic Books, 1974). This view is shared, among others, by Peter Jones, *Rights* (Basingstoke-New York, 1994) 108.
3 Judith J Thomson, *Rights, Restitution and Risk: Essays in Moral Theory* (Harvard University Press, 1986) 33–48.
4 Onora O'Neill, *Towards Justice and Virtue: A Constructive Account of Moral Reasoning*, (Cambridge: Cambridge University Press, 1996).
5 Jeff King, *Judging Social Rights* (Cambridge University Press, 2012) 3–8.
6 See Maurice Cranston, 'Are There Any Human Rights?' (1984) 112(4) *Daedalus* 1.
7 Cass R Sunstein, *The Second Bill of Rights: FDRs Unfinished Revolution and Why We Need It More than Ever* (Basic Books, 2004) 106–7.
8 Fernando Atria, 'Social Rights, Social Contract, Socialism' (2015) 24 *Social and Legal Studies* 598, 598–9.
9 Ibid 602.
10 Ibid 603–4.
11 Ibid 605.
12 Ibid 606.
13 Ibid 609.
14 Giuseppe Mazzini, 'On the Duties of Man' in Stefano Recchia and Nadia Urbinati (eds), *A Cosmopolitanism of Nations: Giuseppe Mazzini's Writings on Democracy, Nation Building, and International Relations* (Princeton University Press, 2009) 80.
15 Elizabeth Wolgast, 'Wrong Rights' (1987) 2(1) *Hypatia* 25.
16 Mary A. Glendon, *Rights Talk: The Impoverishment of Political Discourse* (The Free Press, 1991) 76–108.
17 Colm O'Cinneide, 'Austerity and the Faded Dream of a Social Europe', in A. Nolan (ed.), *Economic and Social Rights after the Global Financial Crisis*, (Cambridge University Press, 2014), 169–201.
18 David Garland, 'On the Concept of "Social Rights"' (2015) 24 *Social and Legal Studies* 622.
19 Russell Keat, 'Individual Rights as Social Rights' (2015) 24 *Social and Legal Studies* 618, 621.
20 Liam Murphy and Thomas Nagel, *The Myth of Ownership: Taxes and Justice* (Oxford University Press, 2002).
21 See D. Roman, Ch. 2 in this volume.
22 See U. Lembke, Ch. 3 in this volume.
23 See J Meers, *Shifting the Place of Social Security*, available at socialrights.co.uk.
24 See M. Adler and L.I. Terum, Ch. 7 in this volume.
25 Ellie Palmer, 'A Meaningful Right to Social Security in the United Kingdom: Beyond the Policies and Politics of Austerity?', in Marcin Wujczyk (ed.), *The Right to Social Security in the Constitutions of the World: Broadening the moral and legal space for social justice. An ILO Global Study, Volume 1: Europe* (International Labour Organization, 2016), 358–84.
26 Stuart White, *The Civic Minimum: On the Rights and Obligations of Economic Citizenship* (Oxford University Press, 2003).
27 See J. King, Ch. 10 in this volume.
28 Joel Feinberg, 'The Nature and Value of Rights' (1970) 4 *Journal of Value Enquiry* 243.
29 Suzanne Fitzpatrick, Bo Bengtsson and Beth Watts, 'Rights to Housing: Reviewing the Terrain and Exploring a Way Forward' (2014) 31(4) *Housing, Theory and Society* 1–17.

30 Luigi Ferrajoli, 'Fundamental Rights' (2001) 14 *International Journal for the Semiotics of Law* 1.
31 See D. Utrilla, Ch. 5 in this volume.
32 Katharine G Young, *Constituting Economic and Social Rights* (Oxford University Press, 2012) 29.
33 Richard H. Pildes, 'Why Rights Are Not Trumps: Social Meanings, Expressive Harms, and Constitutionalism' (1998) 27 *The Journal of Legal Studies* 725.
34 Atria, above n 7, 603.
35 Joseph Raz, *The Concept of a Legal System* (Oxford, 2nd edition, 1980) 199–200.
36 Jeremy Waldron, 'Rights in Conflict' (1989) 99 *Ethics* 503.
37 I am borrowing the expression and concept of 'scam rights' from the Italian equivalent *diritti-truffa*, originally found in Persio Tincani, 'Diritti-truffa' in Roberto Cammarata (ed.), *Chi dice universalità: i diritti tra teoria, politica e giurisdizione* (L'Ornitorinco, 2011) 108–12.
38 See D. Roman, Ch. 2 in this volume.
39 Craig Scott and Patrick Macklem, 'Ropes of Sand or Justiciable Guarantees? Social Rights in a New South African Constitution' (1992) 141 *University of Pennsylvania Law Review* 1.
40 Robert Alexy, *A Theory of Constitutional Rights* (Oxford University Press, 2002) 300–12.
41 Stephen Holmes and Cass R. Sunstein, *The Cost of Rights: Why Liberty Depends on Taxes* (Norton & Company, 1999).
42 One such example is provided by the *Legal Aid Sentencing and Punishment of Offenders Act 2012* (UK). However, the High Court has decided several times against the curtailment of civil legal aid.
43 See Christodoulidis and Goldoni, Ch. 11 in this volume.
44 Ibid.

Chapter 10

Social rights and welfare reform in times of economic crisis

*Jeff King**

I. Introduction – welfare reform in comparative analysis

All comparative legal work comes with a health warning, but nowhere more so than welfare reform does that warning deserve prominence. As the great comparative Welfare State scholar Gøsta Esping-Anderson has shown quite clearly, a Welfare State consists of much more than public spending.[1] There is public and private spending on welfare, different degrees of public ownership, different roles for collective bargaining and different endowments in natural resources. And all this is grafted on to different historical configurations. Welfare reform during economic crisis – our subject – typically engages public spending that addresses more than half a national budget, land reform, health and pharmaceutical regulation, pensions and retirement, natural resources management, health and safety oversight, international trade policy, investment management, labour market regulation, and taxation levels. It also addresses how to avoid inflation and ensure economic growth. In an interconnected global economy, generous spending on health and social security benefits can be destroyed in a couple of years by high inflation. We know, for example, that President Alan Garcia's well-intentioned actions to rescue Peru in the mid-1980s from the awful economic consequences of the country's debt crisis had the effect of creating hyperinflation – in real terms public spending plummeted under President Garcia and, paradoxically, it actually rose under Alberto Fujimori's brutal and authoritarian programme of neoliberal austerity. How so? Economic growth, control of inflation and macroeconomic stability, it turns out. [2] One need not be a fan of Fujimori, authoritarianism or neoliberalism to see that the experience suggests that the matter is complex.

The starting point of much comparative social policy work is that all of these different factors are interrelated. Your position on one question – such as labour-market regulation – will determine the right approach to another question – such as whether social security should be thick or thin, how much public, how much private, how much investment, how much taxation. The American legal theorist and lawyer, Lon Fuller, adapted an idea to describe such issues – the concept of polycentricity.[3] A problem is polycentric when the correct resolution of it depends on the resolution of a large number of other interrelated problems or issues. Such issues are related in a network of cause-and-effect relationships – when you change your position on one issue, it is like pulling the strand of a spider's web – you redistribute tensions elsewhere in the network of relationships. So setting a minimum wage affects prices, production costs, trade, taxation and so on. Having a strong social security system may reduce the need for a minimum wage. In these webs of relationships, the bigger the issue – and the closer it is to the centre of the network of relationships – the more interconnected it is with the other issues. Lon Fuller argued that the adjudicative process was not well adapted to resolving these problems. Fuller believed that the adjudication of polycentric disputes would (1) give rise to unintended consequences, (2) encourage judges to try unorthodox solutions such as consultations of non-represented parties and guessing at facts and (3) prompt the judge to recast the problem in a judicially manageable form.[4] These are prescient insights, and all three are visible in some constitutional social rights cases.[5] Fuller rather believed that the resolution of such problems requires bargaining, compromise, experimentation, flexibility, and constant adjustment as between a multitude of affected parties. Legislatures and large bureaucracies can offer that. Adjudication, by contrast, proceeds with the input of a relatively narrow range of actors – the parties to the litigation – and yes, of course, public interest interventions can help, but only so much.

Fuller's basic insight is correct. When you adjudicate heavily polycentric issues it creates unintended consequences. But the view that judges should not adjudicate *any* polycentric issue is clearly false. I have elaborated this argument with examples at depth in a book and in an article.[6] Despite that conclusion, however, I also admit and indeed elaborate upon why polycentricity and complexity are relevant and a good reason for restraint. And since *welfare reform* implicates everything, it is the very core of the web of social relationships itself. That implies as a very starting point a modest conception of the role of judges, *often even if the other branches are not doing their job properly.*

It may be noticed that although the topic of this collection concerns social rights, I have already focused the discussion on *constitutional* social rights as well as the role of judges in enforcing them. In my book, *Judging Social Rights*,[7] I distinguish between moral and legal senses of the expression 'social rights'. While I stipulate that 'social human rights' and 'social citizenship rights' are moral senses, 'constitutional social rights' are a legal sense. The book was chiefly a study and argument about the role of judges in enforcing the last of these. The reason for my focus on this aspect of social rights is that it is the peculiar competence of lawyers to speak to this dimension of social rights. That competence, rather than any legalistic myopia, not only explains my focus on constitutional social rights in this chapter, but will also figure in my arguments about the extent to which constitutional social rights can serve as a shield against austerity measures.

In *Judging Social Rights*, I argue that judges adjudicating constitutional social rights[8] in countries having background political conditions like those in Europe and the wealthier Commonwealth nations ought to give weight to four important principles of judicial restraint: democratic legitimacy, polycentricity, administrative expertise and administrative and legislative flexibility. These factors commend a default approach of judicial incrementalism. For the purposes of the present discussion, I will assume that it is accepted that these four principles of, or grounds for, judicial restraint, are sound. Any grasp of the complexity of the issues I referred to above should make that readily apparent. Yet what is also clear are the limitations of each of these reasons for judicial restraint: minorities need protection in democracies; expertise is often a lie and institutions are often disorganised or doing someone else's bidding; and administrative *inflexibility* is often the problem that takes litigants to court. Deciding hard cases in constitutional social rights adjudication requires considerable care and a distinct approach to judicial restraint.

II. The difference between emergencies and crises

Emergencies are a very important legal concept. The hallmark of a declared emergency is that the government 'claims the authority to operate outside the law'.[9] The concept of emergencies thus poses a direct threat to all constitutional and most human rights, for it represents the suspension of ordinary legal protections during what is often a struggle for national survival. The recent State responses to acts of purported Islamist terrorism against targets in North America, Europe and throughout the Middle East and Africa provide vivid illustrations of the precarious nature of ordinary civil liberties in situations regarded as a national emergency. In such circumstances, indefinite detention without trial, closed proceedings against suspects, extraordinary rendition and, in the United States, the institutional deployment of so-called 'enhanced interrogation techniques' – that were, in effect, torture – all took place with minimal obstruction from the highest courts of law in the respective lands. This was less the inauguration of a new period of institutional timidity than the resort to a well-known tradition. Both the United States and Great Britain interned civilians during World War II, and some of the most infamous civil rights cases in both jurisdictions are those in which the court failed to control what has come to be regarded as the draconian use of executive powers of detention during wartime.[10] It is not merely political practice, however, that manifests the willingness to suspend ordinary civil liberties in times of emergency and armed conflict. Most human rights conventions provide for the suspension of certain liberties during national emergencies and international law itself has grown out of a clear distinction between the law of war and the law of peace. In other words, the challenges presented by the concept of emergencies run deep both as a matter of legal and political doctrine and institutional practice.

The concept of a national *economic* emergency has been used very frequently in the twentieth century, by both left-wing and right-wing liberal democratic governments as well as authoritarian governments to justify limiting social provision.[11] Franklin Delano Roosevelt launched the New Deal in America under what he claimed were emergency powers at a time of national economic emergency. He used the language of war to describe his mission against want (later described as 'Freedom from Want' in his famous Four Freedoms speech), and many believed his actions in expanding the reach of federal jurisdiction in the United States were genuinely unconstitutional.[12] Similarly, the labour government of post-Second World War Norway used emergency 'state of exception' powers in the 1950s to pass 'enabling acts' to create one of the best Welfare States in the world.[13] The various Presidents under the Weimar Republic in Germany relied on Article 38 of the Weimar Constitution to use state of emergency powers to bypass the legislature in the effort to manage almost perpetual economic crisis.[14] In the early days of the twentieth century, emergency powers were often used in the United States and Great Britain to break strike actions by organised labour.[15] In Latin America, emergency powers were also used to deal with economic crisis. Due to the oil shock generated by the Organization of the Petroleum Exporting Countries (OPEC) nations in 1973 (oil prices quadrupled) and again in 1979 (prices doubled), the entire region was thrown into profound macro-economic turmoil, with nearly all countries defaulting on their externally held sovereign debt at the time. It generated enormous social upheaval. Real wages in Mexico were cut in half from 1980 to 1988; Brazil, Argentina and Peru experienced inflation rates near or exceeding 1,000 per cent per annum in the late 1980s, and there were riots leaving hundreds dead in Venezuela.[16] In fact, the coup d'état was a familiar occurrence prior to the oil crisis. General Augusto Pinochet's 1973 coup in Chile was yet another example of an unconstitutional change of government in a time of economic crisis followed by the implementation of a radical programme of neoliberal austerity. Nevertheless, once economic crises became pandemic in Latin America, the attraction to using emergency powers to implement economic reforms was unmistakable. Peru's Alberto Fujimori also used emergency powers to have the Peruvian Congress delegate broad discretionary authority to him in the early 1990s and, later, following his *autogolpe* (coup d'état against his own government), he suspended the Constitution and dismissed Congress altogether on precisely the same pretext.[17] These are just some of *many* examples. William Scheuermann has found that there were 'innumerable' declarations of economic emergency between the two world wars alone.[18]

Although the rhetoric of 'emergency' has been widespread in discussing financial crises, it can also be quite misleading. There is a difference between a national emergency and economic crisis. The concept of a national emergency has been well studied, particularly in the post-9/11 world of robust state action against terrorism.[19] A legal state of emergency normally has the following features: it is an extremely urgent situation – there is a need for rapid, decisive response that may preclude consultation and legislative debate; the threat is typically *existential* or comparable thereto – with Article 15 ECHR defining 'emergencies' as those events that 'threaten the life of the nation', although there are clearly other situations such as a natural disaster or serious or widespread breakdown in public order;[20] the executive or legislature proclaims the existence of the emergency, and the legal consequences that follow; it suspends the operation of ordinary law, potentially including the constitution; it is of a temporary or limited nature, and it is premised on a return to the status quo as soon as possible.[21]

While some financial crises may have these features, most do not. In particular, the recent round of fiscal crises in Europe have not been of this character. During the fundamental crises faced by Greece, Italy, Spain, Portugal and Ireland, the respective governments used the language of 'crisis', and 'emergency' and even 'national emergency', but did not suspend the operation of ordinary constitutional law nor exclude the legislature from the design of remedies and responses.[22] These cases set an important precedent by showing that in a well-functioning democracy, even in cases of fiscal crises, we do not suspend the ordinary process of law.

A fiscal crisis is a situation of urgency but it is not the same as a national emergency. The threat to public life, at least when a mature Welfare State is in place to provide a buffer, is ordinarily of a lower order of magnitude. The time-sensitivity is not as acute. There is a greater role for both legislative participation and broader consultation. And as other scholars have also noted,[23] a crisis is usually an event that betokens a change that is not only temporary, but that is often *permanent.* Hence we have good grounds for thinking about economic crises and austerity responses as something that ought to be addressed outside the emergency powers framework.

III. Crisis, austerity and social rights

Whatever the force of the distinction just drawn above, a great fiscal crisis is manifestly *not* business as usual. It is a crisis – it is serious, widespread and requires an abnormal and sometimes urgent response. In many cases, a crisis may be a prelude to catastrophe.

There is a clear question about whether, and if so how, judges ought to recognise the existence of a financial crisis. One thing is clear: in all the cases I have read, judges declined to quash executive or legislative determinations about *whether such a crisis exists*, and there are many cases in which they do recognise and give weight to its existence.[24] I think the thrust of the several cases before Greek, Italian, Spanish and Portuguese constitutional courts, as well as the Canadian Supreme Court, is that it is appropriate for a judge to recognise the existence of the crisis and *to give it weight* in the balancing exercise so common in rights adjudication. I think this is the correct approach. But that is manifestly not a licence to set rights or the constitution aside. Indeed, one can see a degree of what Simon Halliday has called 'legal conscientiousness' (although we may rather call it 'constitutional conscientiousness in the present situation')[25]. These approaches in Europe can be contrasted with experiences elsewhere where the rhetoric of 'emergency' is deployed to take extra-constitutional action. Such was evident in Pinochet's coup in Chile, Fujimori's coup in Peru and the invocation of constitutionally recognised state of exception powers to assert presidential power in Weimar Germany. The European experience surveyed in this volume and elsewhere in fact shows that constitutionalism has been a vehicle for implementing the rules of austerity rather than a paper tiger pushed aside in times of crisis.

The basic problem, however, is that when an economic crisis occurs the entire superstructure of the national economy is called into question and stands at serious risk. If inflation, unemployment and unsustainable debt levels are the key issues, then drastic measures may be defended – and are often defended – as necessary for the preservation (or introduction) of a system that itself provides the growth and fiscal stability required to provide social protection. The hard argument for advocates of constitutional social rights as general prophylaxis against neoliberal austerity is not the claim that social rights must bow to more efficiency or pure property rights, but rather that social welfare in the aggregate (which can be translated into the realisation of social rights) will be improved if austerity is swallowed. In the history of austerity arguments, this argument has played a very strong role. Among justifications for austerity, one can roughly divide between libertarian and welfarist theories. The libertarian arguments of writers such as Robert Nozick and, more importantly, Friedrich Hayek were quite influential in the 1980s.[26] Since they make arguments of principle about the permissible scope of taxation and expropriation, they are liable to rebuttal on principle alone. But these libertarian arguments have quite limited purchase in the realm of official political argument, because they reject not only social rights but the basic legitimacy of the Welfare State accepted throughout the Organisation for Economic Co-operation and Development (OECD) nations. So the fact that these arguments are manifestly contrary to the idea of social rights is rarely the actual point at issue in live disputes. They are certainly not the arguments offered by states in constitutional adjudication.

The welfarist (or, consequentialist) argument is much more challenging. It is that austerity is required for economic growth and employment, the attainment of which will solve the social problem rather than exacerbate it. This argument has an old pedigree, although it was first deployed as an argument for markets over central planning. It was the type of answer given by Walter Eucken, the famous German ordoliberal economist who thought free markets were the solution to Germany and Europe's 'social question':

> As a result of the general interdependence between all markets, the social question can only be resolved by means of an adequate and free economic system. Social reasons, in particular, indicate that there is no alternative to free competition.[27]

The argument may be old in pedigree, but it has much the same character today. Economic theorists developed models that claimed to demonstrate two crucial points that became part of the widespread justification for recent austerity:

(1) that, contrary to the Keynesian orthodoxy, 'expansionary fiscal consolidation' will actually promote growth[28] and (2) that evidence demonstrates that once a nation surpasses a 90 per cent debt-to-gross domestic product (GDP) threshold, growth is significantly curtailed.[29] These arguments were adopted enthusiastically and endorsed publically in the US, the UK and the EU.[30] Now, the arguments presenting both views have been comprehensively, indeed embarrassingly, refuted since the studies were undertaken.[31] However, they were refuted in ways that only trained social scientists could have carried out, and there is still a significant amount of ongoing disagreement about whether fiscal consolidation and low debt levels are important for job creation and growth. [32]

When austerity is genuinely justified with such an argument, the question becomes more about the effectiveness of competing policy measures for ensuring the enjoyment of social rights rather than about the moral validity of claims to social entitlements themselves. Although austerity in such situations purports to deprive some (now) in the name of others (down the line) – and in the process seems like the impermissible breach of a deontic core of a right – it is equally plausibly viewed as akin to a process of rationing resources in a context in which demand outstrips supply. The decision to adopt rationing policies in the life-and-death context of healthcare is not reasonably viewed as violating basic rights to life and health. It is a policy adopted with a view to maximising those rights in the aggregate for a population, each member of which lays the same basic claim against the state for a share of the resources that can fulfil that right. So, ultimately the large macro-level question here is whether the austerity programme will work or not. Such questions are matters of dispute among Nobel prize-winning economists, and the consequences of the wrong decision are utterly massive.

Nevertheless, although austerity and social rights are not *necessarily* in principled conflict, the issue does not end there. Austerity arguments are not always arguments about securing the recognition of a system that will protect social rights. While property rights or libertarian arguments may not be used much in legal argument in Europe, that may not always be the case elsewhere. Furthermore, and from a quite different direction, there is a risk that the welfarist or consequentialist arguments outlined above will ignore altogether the fact that the existence of rights does require treating each individual's dignity as an irreducible unit of value that is not susceptible to being bargained away or traded off except by the most carefully constructed scheme of rationing. To the extent that the argument for reform is couched entirely in consequentialist terms and disregards the existence of irreducible and individually held core rights claims in the process of reform, it would be prima facie incompatible with the idea of basic constitutional social rights. A reform policy that effectively sacrifices individuals is on its face incompatible with the notion of social human rights. But what is the upshot of recognising such a limit? It may in quite rare cases suggest that an entire or even substantial plank of a reform programme is on its face incompatible with the very idea of social rights. As I have argued elsewhere, I believe lifetime caps on eligibility for social assistance are such an example.[33]

Another may be where a reform programme virtually eliminates the basic social minimum indiscriminately for a large class of highly vulnerable beneficiaries.[34] Yet such examples are particularly rare, and are not in issue in the round of European austerity crises examined in this volume. It is more likely that the policy will cross the (judicially cognisable) line in elements of detail and implementation rather than at the level of general principle. This suggests space for the incrementalist role I defend below.

IV. What approach to social rights protection?

We now know that due to the proliferation of constitutional social rights, judges must give answer to the questions submitted. Ignoring the constitution is not an option, nor is it desirable. So what approach should they take? I want to suggest that there are three key strategies that judges *could* follow in giving protection to social rights in times of financial crisis and law reform. Ultimately, I only recommend one of them as a default position for adjudicating social rights in times of economic crisis.

A. Strong rights review: resources and the minimum core

One approach is to declare resources to be irrelevant. It is common in the realm of civil liberties for judges to say that the failure to protect a right cannot be justified by lack of resources. This approach has been taken in some of the earlier jurisprudence in Brazil on the right to health, and also in Colombia. A critique of these approaches is well-documented in the work of Octavio Ferraz, and Virgilio Afonso da Silva in Brazil,[35] and in Latin America more broadly in the book *Litigating Health Rights.*[36] At its peak, there were about 40,000 right-to-health cases in Brazil a year and the evidence shows *conclusively* that most of them were taken in the richer Brazilian states, that the claimants came from the richer neighbourhoods in these states, they overwhelmingly had referrals from private doctors rather than coming from the public system and the claims were for drugs that were experimental and expensive and so out of all proportion to the cost of primary-care services for the poor, which were desperately needed and presumably marginalised. Similar evidence is available in the experience with health *Tutelas* in Colombia. The more general problem here is that resources almost always do matter. If judges ignore them, they only ignore the impact of their decision on the rationing of resources in the system as a whole. Doing so produces two key problems. The first is unintended consequences. We just don't know what will happen or how to study it. Bureaucracies have often developed sophisticated ways of making rationing decisions, fair and transparent procedures, and they are tied to a political process that can provide more resources when they are needed or demanded. On the whole, these systems are better than adjudication. The second problem is access to justice. Once it becomes clear that the court will disregard scarcity, then lawyers engage in a race to the courthouse and those with the resources to get there come out on top. That means that those with the sharpest elbows get to the front of the queue.

It is relevant to address the minimum core content doctrine found in the jurisprudence of the UN Committee on Economic, Social and Cultural Rights and in the constitutional jurisprudence of certain countries.[37] The UN Committee's doctrine is in fact rather equivocal about whether a minimum core of subsistence rights is what one is entitled to. In the initial formulation, a failure to provide the minimum core triggers a more potent justificatory burden for the state.[38] Later formulations claim that there is a non-derogable core minimum, the failure to provide which is a clear violation of the Covenant. However, the Committee does not appear to take the consequences of such a doctrinal finding seriously in its reviewing of State party reports. Relatedly, its doctrine that retrogressive measures are impermissible is similar in doctrinal contour to the minimum core doctrine (that is, an augmented justificatory burden), and if pushed so far as to try to rule out austerity it quickly becomes absurd.

Other courts and institutions have been slightly truer to the basic idea – the doctrine of '*Existenzminimum*' (the 'social' or 'existential minimum') is recognised and applied in German constitutional jurisprudence and the idea of a minimum core is recognised in Germany, Italy and Portugal among potentially other states.[39] It is said that the state must ensure a minimum core existential existence of each person. The leading case on this principle is examined extensively by Ulrike Lembke elsewhere in this volume.[40] A brief examination is nevertheless appropriate for this particular discussion. In practice, the courts, including those in Germany, tend to pay judicial deference to legislative and executive attempts to define what the *Existenzminimum* is. In the most famous case on this question, the Hartz IV case[41] of the Bundesverfassungsgericht (Federal Constitutional Court), the court held that the government had the duty to recalculate the thresholds for the receipt of social assistance (*Arbeitslosengeld II*): it had not calculated them correctly because its methodology was flawed and thus the amounts calculated for assistance recipients were arbitrary and not strictly related to need.[42] The case is justly celebrated for asserting a durable core entitlement to a social minimum. However, the significance of the case can be and has been exaggerated. First, the court found explicitly that although it would determine in the abstract what the requirements of the existential minimum were, it was in practice the duty of the legislature to determine what the applicable thresholds were and that the courts should allow a margin of discretion (*Gestaltungsppielraum*) in the determination thereof. Ultimately, the court would insist on transparency in the determination of the thresholds. Indeed, there is a serious question of whether the only requirement effectively imposed by the decision is whether in determining the benefit levels they must do so transparently, or, and by contrast, whether there is a substantive limit that the determination must be comprehensible or make sense as well (*Nachvollziehbar*) [43] The legal standard at any rate does give significant latitude to the legislature to determine the benefit level. At the same time, the Federal Constitutional Court has made it clear that the State is constitutionally obliged to provide some form of general and ongoing basic social assistance benefit, something that some important countries such as Italy and the United States do not possess.

The political outcome of the decision was that the benefit rate was recalculated and a new level was adopted in the Bundestag, pursuant to a debate that generated more heat than light.[44] After taking account for the increases to the benefit level already made (in view of inflation) between the amount of the benefit in the Hartz IV case at the legislative debate of 2010, the actual increase to the benefit level was about 5 euros per month, what the government had allegedly been prepared to offer anyway in line with regular uprating of benefits to reflect higher costs of living.[45] The fact that the amount was exactly what would have resulted from virtually automatic increases, and that the increase was made pursuant to extensive political bargaining, in addition to the fact that the overall amount of social assistance was still woefully low (under 400 euros per month), gave rise to follow-up litigation in which the newly determined amount of *Arbeitslosengeld II* was challenged as a violation of the *Existenzminimum*. When the litigation reached the Federal Constitutional Court,[46] it found that an amount determined by political compromise, even behind closed doors in a parliamentary committee in which no minutes are kept or published, complied sufficiently with the constitutional duty. The case was dismissed (albeit with some important dicta). As Lembke clarifies in her discussion, litigation challenging benefit deductions (sanctions) may or may not have a chance of success.

The concept of the *Existenzminimum* has been used to greater effect in other cases. There is a line of jurisprudence that has held that the lowest taxation threshold may not fall below the *Existenzminimum* of a family – that is, that one may not tax the *Existenzminimum*.[47] While this may appear progressive at first, in fact its revenue implications can be quite substantial. This is not investigated in German public law at the time of writing, but it is acknowledged that the case raised the tax threshold across the board, benefiting all personal income taxpayers regardless of income.

The most significant case in this line of jurisprudence in Germany is that concerning asylum seekers.[48] In this well-known case, the Federal Constitutional Court found that the systematic failure to uprate social assistance benefits for asylum seekers violated the duty to provide the *Existenzminimum*. The case demonstrates the political and legal logic that can flow from the doctrinal recognition of the *Existenzminimum*. Once the government conceded in previous litigation that the social assistance rate was calibrated to the *Existenzminimum*, the failure to secure it to a group of lawfully present foreigners was a clear breach. The extent to which both the Hartz IV and asylum-seekers cases are compatible with the incrementalist approach set out in sub-section C is debatable. On the one hand, the former case did recognise a very wide margin of appreciation and in the latter case the holding was not substantially dissimilar from what UK courts found in respect of late-claiming asylum seekers under Article 3 of the European Convention of Human Rights.[49] On the other hand, in neither case was resource scarcity recognised as a legitimate ground for failing to secure the social minimum. Yet while this is true in theory, the definitional margin of appreciation accorded to the legislature is sufficiently wide to enable resource availability to factor into the decision-making process, whether it does or not. On the whole I take the view that these approaches, within European Welfare State structures, with due note taken of the reasonably clear constitutional commitment to both dignity and the social state, suggest that these cases are in line with the more incrementalist approach.

In the analysis above, I have explored why rationing in social rights policy will be important and an approach to adjudication that denies it is bound to be troublesome. But there is another, quite different but conceptually related ground for concern about a bold interpretive approach. It is the *Lochner* problem, namely that constitutional litigation may unintentionally have regressive effects in welfare reform strategies. Rights to property and contract as well as non-discrimination can be and have been asserted against welfare, economic or social policy reform. For instance, in 2008 the Parliament of Iceland passed the Emergency Act, which provided for the nationalisation of the three largest banks in response to the economic crisis there. The legislation was challenged as an unconstitutional deprivation of property rights as well as being discriminatory for giving Icelandic depositors priority over other creditors and even over foreign depositors.[50] The Supreme Court rejected the challenges and rightly found that 'The legislature . . . had not only a right but above all a constitutional duty to protect the welfare of the public and financial activity against the collapse of the banks'.[51] In a case of the German Federal Constitutional Court, employers challenged the German Worker Co-Determination Act (mandating worker representation on boards of large enterprises) arguing that it was a breach of constitutionally protected property rights. The Federal Constitutional Court rejected the claims and emphasised that it should show restraint in the area of social policy and that the German social state principle must be taken into account in determining the limits of property rights claims.[52] Even when social rights rather than property rights are asserted, and as with the Brazilian and Colombian cases examined above, the claimants may come from middle-class or other relatively well-off groups. In 2013, the Constitutional Court of Portugal quashed an aspect of the welfare reform programme on account of what it considered to be the disproportionate treatment of public sector pensions.[53] Litigation challenging pensions uprating policy was also successful before the Italian Constitutional Court,[54] and pensions were also a key aspect of earlier welfare reform litigation in Hungary.[55] It is beyond the scope of this chapter to assess whether these particular cases were rightly decided, or indeed whether they are compatible with the incrementalist approach defended below. Suffice it to say that they concerned the interests of the middle classes at least as much as those of the particularly vulnerable.

B. Structural reform injunctions

A structural injunction, roughly speaking, is one in which a judge issues an order to a defendant institution to undertake comprehensive structural reforms. The judge retains supervisory jurisdiction, requiring the defendant to report back to the court on success in satisfying judicially imposed benchmarks and timelines. The judge typically orders the appointment of an official (normally, a 'special master') who has technical proficiency in the area at issue.[56] The role of the master is to help devise and later supervise implementation of the decree, and to report to the court. They often supervise negotiations between claimants and defendants, steering them to an agreed remedial plan that the judge subsequently turns into a binding public law obligation by means of a 'consent decree', the violation of which will constitute contempt of court. Many such decrees remain in effect for several years, in some cases decades, and they are supplemented from time to time by court orders that may be aimed at aspects of administration or the legislature itself. The cases are episodic, better described as 'litigations' rather than court cases. Foreign courts other than those of India have largely been quite cautious about using these remedies; they are miles away from anything remotely as interventionist as the practice in the United States.[57] While structural injunctions grew out of the institutional reform litigation following *Brown v Board of Education*, they have been used subsequently in hundreds (or more) cases, many concerned with education, disability and mental health.

Structural reform injunctions are not a panacea for dealing with the institutional competence of courts in constitutional social rights adjudication, least of all with the macro process of welfare reform. First, the experience in the United States and India has been decidedly mixed, and it represents a serious departure from the ordinary conception of the separation of powers.[58] I have elsewhere reviewed the experience of education litigation in particular in the United States, and despite the astonishingly interventionist measures of the courts there, including judicial orders to legislatures that they raise taxation levels, the results have been mixed and viewed with great ambivalence among progressive commentators on the American Welfare State.[59] The experiences in Latin American countries are mixed though some commentators see significant potential. Second, where successful, these remedies were born out of a political situation in which the breach of the constitutional standard was patent, and the bureaucracy refused to comply with the court judgment. They arose out of the desegregation litigation in the United States but also dealt with problems in prisons where officials simply refused to provide a modicum of humane conditions. There were real and serious rule of law problems in these cases. The clarity of the constitutional breach in most social rights cases is not ordinarily as clear, and certainly not in mature Welfare States of the sort in Europe and North America. Such conditions may well arise in some Latin American or other countries, although the experience thus far is somewhat mixed.[60] Furthermore, the political situation in countries where there is patent and chronic institutional failure may lead to bold steps being met with a powerful push back on judicial independence, generating knock-on effects for the rule of law on other key issues. At any rate, the point is that welfare reform and financial crises are not normally, for reasons discussed above in section III, nearly as clear cut as the patent executive disobedience of a judicial order in the desegregation cases in which these remedies found their origin. I believe there is a role for this remedy – but it is a residual role best reserved for egregious cases.

C. Incrementalism – a focus on the process of decision-making

In *Judging Social Rights*, I argue that the best role for courts in adjudicating constitutional social rights is to adopt a default strategy of judicial incrementalism. Under such an approach, the courts recognise that it is the primary duty of the legislature and executive to define and create the enabling statutory and administrative framework for securing social rights. The role of the court is to exercise supervisory jurisdiction over this process, sometimes prodding it into action.[61] Although the default approach is judicial incrementalism, I nevertheless outline principles of judicial restraint that indicate where restraint and hence incrementalism may not be indicated. Yet even under the incrementalist strategy, the role for courts can be important. The present question is: what sorts of decisions may we expect from courts adjudicating austerity under such an approach? In what follows, I offer a list of approaches or principles that emerge from comparative jurisprudence of various constitutional and supreme courts.

Legislative oversight: In all the recent structural reforms taken in Europe (Greece, Italy, Spain, Portugal, Ireland) there was active involvement of the legislature in the design of the policies. True, there was on some occasions a significant delegation of power to the executive, but the experience collectively shows that it is manageable to involve the legislature in devising responses to acute financial emergencies. The Italian experience in particular, at least in this round, has tended to show a distinct preference for legislative law-making over executive orders or decrees.[62] This is entirely compatible with the general principle that interferences with rights ought only to be conducted under clear legislative authorisation.[63]

Evidence-based policies: Often enough, administrative and some legislative decisions are taken in a rushed manner, and are based on gut instincts rather than real evidence. This is above all during a period of crisis. In the Hartz IV decision, the Federal Constitutional Court found that some of the rates for the standard social assistance benefit were 'plucked out of the blue' (*ins Blaue hinein*) and had no connection to the actual existential needs of the persons. Someone in government had just made a best guess of what the benefit should be. The court ordered the government to reassess it. In the South African Constitutional Court's *Treatment Action Campaign* case,[64] which was a challenge against the government's decisions to restrict the availability of an HIV antiretroviral drug on health grounds, the court found that the government had ignored its own health agency's determination of the safety of the drug Nevirapene. The court ordered the restriction removed and that the drug – which was provided cost-free by the company – be made available. In her chapter on Spain in this volume, Utrilla notes a case where the decision of the High Court of Justice of Castilla-Lamancha struck down a measure that modified the availability of medical staff without an adequate plan that took account of how to provide services without such staff.[65] In the chapter on the UK, Meers illustrates both the promise and, more notably, the limitations of an approach based on process. Although some aspects of the welfare reform programme were successfully quashed on account of the failure to consider public sector equality duties sufficiently, the subsequent decision to reaffirm the programme was challenged unsuccessfully. These cases seem to be a lost opportunity but are perhaps not surprising given the UK's failure to give formal recognition to constitutional or international social rights in its public law.

Focus on vulnerable groups: The democratic legitimacy of the court in times of constitutional review is at its peak when it is seeking to protect the interests of politically marginalized groups.[66] One can both recognise where such attention to vulnerable groups is not given, and where it is given. In Portugal, the measures taken to reduce public sector wages only applied to those in the higher income bracket. Commentators have shown that this attempt to make the better off bear a greater share of the burden was blocked by the Portuguese Constitutional Court's decision to strike down the tax on them. Those earning less than 600 euros a month received no cuts.[67] Canada's welfare reform in the 1990s, although representing a brutal set of cuts at first, ultimately employed specific concrete and targeted measures aimed at the vulnerable; it ended up showing that, despite considerable reform and savings, the relative poverty did not increase substantially – in marked contrast to the reforms under Reagan and Thatcher in the 1980s.[68] While it would be easy to whitewash a brutal programme of austerity by making some token gesture for the most vulnerable, the bona fides and adequacy of such measures can be precisely what is under review in such cases. There are a number of cases discussed in the national studies chapters in this volume that manifest this pattern. In the chapter on Spain, Utrilla notes the protection of mortgage debtors at risk of foreclosure; in the chapter on Italy, Albanese refers to the SIA (sostegno per l'inclusione attiva) to support the poorest families in cities with more than 250,000 people in the effort to promote social inclusion, as well as the willingness of the Italian Constitutional Court to be more assertive at protecting the social rights of disabled children. Nevertheless, the use of Discretionary Housing Payments in the United Kingdom is shown by Meers to effectively function as a discretionary pot of funds to legitimate deep and otherwise discriminatory cuts to social services for the most vulnerable personsin Britain. Under an incrementalist approach to constitutional social rights adjudication, a scheme that is patently unable to meet the demands for securing the social minimum would rightly be declared unconstitutional. (Alternatively, the courts may read discretionary payments as functionally mandatory where need can be demonstrated.)

Transparent and Consultative process: In the Irish financial crisis, there was the so-called 'Croke Park Agreement' in which the Irish Government consulted and reached an agreement with public employees to cooperate with wide-scale reforms of the public sector, but in so doing agreed not to reduce civil servants' pay rates beyond the reductions decided in 2009–10.[69] In Portugal, the scholar Manuel Nogueira de Brito shows that civil society groups were allowed to express a view but not engage in a social contract of this sort.[70] Enforceable participation rights in such reform initiatives are fully compatible with the incrementalist approach, for they do not impose finality on the resolution of the social problem.[71] In the United Kingdom during the Second World War, there was a coalition government of all the parties. There was an explicit agreement with the labour unions that they would take no industrial action during the period of the war. In return their wages were legally protected. The unions wholly supported this outcome and were hostile to the few wildcat strikes that took place.[72]

Transitional measures: Courts can insist that there must be transitional measures between the old and new policy that give some relief to those who suffer from the policy change, whether because they had legitimate expectations of the old policy's continuation, or because they are particularly vulnerable to the change. There are many examples in the recent cases highlighting that the programmes had transitional measures. This is especially evident in the Italian and Portuguese decisions.[73] The Hungarian welfare reform cases notably found that sudden cuts to various means-tested programmes without transitional arrangements were not compatible with the constitutional right to social security.[74]

Sunset or renewal provisions: If the rationale for the emergency action is truly time sensitivity, then it is possible and desirable to use 'sunset provisions' that are essentially expiration dates on laws. These are commonly used in emergency legislation, in Britain especially with anti-terrorism legislation. It is also possible and indeed common to use renewal provisions such that a law's continued operation requires a parliamentary intervention.[75] In the context of welfare reform, depending on whether the justification for an extreme measure is to deal with an acute crisis, it may be plausible for the adjudicating court to insist that sunset clauses be used to give effect to the more drastic policies. Such is consistent with the idea of using a measure that is least restrictive of the right.

V. The failed promise of incrementalism, process and social rights?

A number of chapters in the present book suggest that social rights have failed to prevent the onset of austerity, the implication in some cases being that they have failed to live up to their potential. For example, in his analysis of UK law, Meers draws attention to the 'blunt' role of adjudication in addressing austerity. In the analysis of Spain, Utrilla shows that the Spanish Constitutional Court repeatedly deferred to the austerity programme and indeed oversaw with some vigilance the constitutionally adopted austerity measures relating to finance. Alessandra Albanese demonstrates that the Italian Constitutional Court adopted a policy, contrary to the approach of the German system, whereby the constitutional social rights principles and guarantees would be dependent on the availability of resources. The essay by Christodoulidis and Goldoni goes furthest in suggesting that constitutional social rights have not only failed to protect any defensible notion of real social rights but have in some ways become part of the enabling framework for the advancement of a capitalist and highly financialised mode of economic organisation.

There is considerable truth in all these views. But in my view the conclusions are at times put more starkly than is warranted by the evidence. First, we can notice that the willingness of courts to intervene to protect social interests does tend to track somewhat the level of constitutional recognition of social rights. The UK has none. Germany's affirmative protection is limited chiefly to findings about the *Existenzminimum* (although the role of the social state principle in defending social policy against rights challenges is in fact considerable). Spain has some principles, but largely located outside the justiciable chapter of the Constitution. The Italian Constitution treats the social rights provisions as principles, further read down by the courts. Yet it nevertheless has the most overt coverage for social rights and it is not surprising that the courts there have been among the most active (even if they have not undertaken to stop austerity measures).

Second, each country's approach to adjudication will reflect its political and legal history. The willingness of German courts to read strong protection into dignity rights is well known. And notably, the German economy was not rocked by any financial crisis during the Hartz IV reform, which was, incidentally, initiated by the Social Democratic Party Chancellor (Gerhard Schroeder) and was endorsed by a majority of the country's trade unions. The Anglo-Saxon aversion to judicial meddling in policy is well known, as is its commitment to economic liberalism and the stingy liberal welfare model. Legal obstruction within so liberal a legal and political order was bound to be weak. Spain and Italy were rocked by extremely profound economic crises, and the need for desperate measures was accepted by the constitutional courts there much as it was by a substantial number of its politicians. In the case of France, while unemployment remained high, the impact of the crisis on social rights was comparatively light and it was among the few countries to raise taxes. Third, and most importantly, these arguments probably expect more from courts and constitutionalism than any reasonable account of them can support. Would they really have thought that the constitution should bar welfare reform measures in a time of crisis?

I do not dispute all of the claims made in the essay by Christoloudis and Goldoni. I also agree with them that the financial constitutionalisation of austerity and balanced budgets is misguided – this is so for all the reasons I have explored in my book, *Judging Social Rights*. However, the tenor of the piece suggests that austerity is a straightforward product of a misguided neoliberal ideology that is patently in conflict with the idea of social rights. That fact, furthermore, is necessary and sufficient proof of the claim that constitutional social rights have been no barrier to austerity policies. I believe the argument is considerably more complicated than their analysis suggests. For one thing, the tax revenue *as a proportion of GDP* increased markedly in Italy and Spain, and doubled in Greece, from 1980 to 2007 (before the crisis) and increased significantly after 2008.[76] Furthermore, public social spending as a percentage of GDP in these three Southern states also significantly increased from 1980 to the present, in some cases nearly doubling.[77] Also, as the data presented in the chapter by Adler and Terum in this volume demonstrates, although the level of benefit generosity declined, when compared to the precipitous drop in growth (nearing 10 per cent in Spain and more than that in Italy), and bulging costs of social protection, at a time when borrowing was particularly difficult, it must be admitted that the macroeconomic constraints were severe. If anything, the figures presented in Adler and Terum's chapter suggest quite a success story for the resilience of the Welfare State under extremely severe economic conditions. None of this is an apology for austerity in such countries. It is meant to show that the picture is hardly a straightforward downward spiral towards neoliberalism that their and other accounts present.

Perhaps the view is that fiscal consolidation should have been met entirely by tax increases instead of spending cuts. This may well be the case, and is certainly the policy option I would be inclined to advocate. But, in fact, Italy's increase in revenue exceeded its reduction in benefit generosity, although Spain arguably had greater room to increase taxes.[78] Indeed, Italy's tax revenue as a percentage of GDP exceeded that of Norway and Sweden in 2014.[79] At any rate, is deciding where the tax to spending ratio should come in, at a time of collapsing growth and ballooning unemployment and debt, something that judges should do with the constitution at their elbows? Both institutional humility and plain common sense suggest otherwise.

So, to the more pessimistic accounts in the chapters I have briefly addressed, and to those who deride more incrementalist or catalytic approaches more generally, the point here is that (1) the story of austerity and social rights is more complex than suggested, and (2) the types of policy decisions that ultimately shaped social policy in this period were complex and, at the macro- rather than micro-level, typically not the kinds that courts could reasonably have been asked to intervene in much further than they did.

If we return to considering the merits of a more incrementalist approach more generally, it is to ask, *Is there any substance behind all this process*? Can't the government just jump through the hoops, pretending to care but in reality just ticking the boxes? Well, law may also provide a remedy for this type of issue. In fact, labour tribunals in some countries have long assessed *good faith negotiations* in collective bargaining. They can see when one party's action is mere box ticking, and when there is genuine and meaningful engagement. Now it is true, they will be unlikely to stop a government that is highly aggressive and has half a good argument. But at the same time they can certainly raise the political costs for adverse political action, and ensure that the political decision-making process takes social rights as seriously as possible along the way. This is a more potent judicial control than one may at first think – and it relies on a mode of control that judges happen to be good at.

On the whole, if the techniques alluded to in the previous section were applied by courts, and if they stood ready to move beyond incrementalism when the principles of restraint commend that course, then constitutional social rights adjudication does have the potential for making an important contribution to the humanisation of welfare reform. Whether it has done so in Europe during the present crisis is hard to say in the round. The litmus test, it seems to me, is not whether it stopped austerity, but whether commentators both think that the courts should have gone much farther (due note taken of the risks I have identified in this chapter) and whether they thought it made no difference and hence would have been as happy without the social rights litigation. On my reading, each country was better off with the adjudication, and the most substantial legal failure (Britain) was the country with the least formal recognition of social rights. To me, the glass remains half full.

Notes

* Professor of Law, Faculty of Laws, University College London. This paper is a revised and extended version of a paper prepared for the Venice Commission for Democracy through Law, presented in Ouro Preto Brazil in 2014. I would like to thank the participants in the seminar held at the University of York in September 2015 for helpful comments on the chapter, and in particular those of Marco Goldoni and Emilios Christodoulidis, neither of whose objections are answered fully in this chapter.

1 Gøsta Esping-Anderson, *The Three Worlds of Welfare Capitalism* (Polity Press, 1990).

2 Stephan Haggard and Robert R Kaufman, *Development, Democracy and Welfare States: Latin America, East Asia, and Eastern Europe* (Princeton University Press, 2008) Ch. 7, appendix A6.7.

3 Lon L Fuller and Kenneth I Winston, 'Forms and Limits of Adjudication' (1978) 92(2) *Harvard Law Review* 353.

4 Ibid 401. On the last of these, see also Jerry L Mashaw, *Bureaucratic Justice* (Yale University Press, 1983) 6. '[T]here are . . . ways of translating many claims for more affirmative protection into a negative, and therefore more judicially manageable form. "Give me a healthful environment" can thus become "Do not proceed without attending to my legislatively validated demand for a more healthful environment".'

5 See, e.g., *Residents of the Joe Slovo Community* v. *Thubelisha Homes and Others* 2010 (3) SA 454 (CC) and the discussion of its extended context in Kirsty McLean, 'Meaningful Engagement: One Step Forward, Two Steps Back' (2010) 3 *Constitutional Court Review* 223.

6 Jeff King, *Judging Social Rights* (Cambridge University Press, 2012), Ch. 4; Jeff King, 'The Pervasiveness of Polycentricity' (2008) *Public Law* 101.

7 Ibid.

8 The present essay is concerned chiefly with constitutional social rights, and not with statutory social rights nor with the protection of social rights in administrative law.

9 David Dyzenhaus, 'States of Emergencies' in Robert E Goodin, Philip Pettit and Thomas W Pogge (eds), *A Companion to Contemporary Political Philosophy* (Blackwell, 2012) 804.

10 *Korematsu v United States* 323 US 214 (1994); *Liversidge v Anderson* [1941] UKHL 1.

11 See W Scheuermann, 'The Economic State of Emergency' (2000) 21 *Cardozo Law Review* 1869 for a superb historical and theoretical overview.

12 See G E White, *The Constitution and the New Deal* (Harvard University Press, 2000); J O Freedman, *Crisis and Legitimacy: The Administrative Process and American Government* (Cambridge University Press, 1978).

13 Scheuermann, above n 11.

14 Cindy Skach, *Borrowing Constitutional Designs: Constitutional Law in Weimar and the French Fifth Republic* (Princeton University Press, 2005). See also, Clinton Rossiter, *Constitutional Dictatorship: Crisis Government in the Modern Democracies* (Princeton University Press, 1948); Hans Mommsen, *From Weimar to Auschwitz* (Princeton University Press, 1992). Although reliance on such powers to manage economic crisis was begun under the Social Democratic Party President Friedrich Ebert, far-reaching emergency powers were used by President Paul Hindenberg to implement Chancellor Heinrich Brüning's austerity budget in 1930. The budget caused a sharp rise in public discontent and surge in support for both the NSDAP and the Communists, and reduced further the influence of more moderate parties in the Weimar Reichstag.

15 Scheuermann, above n 11, 1868–9.

16 Jeffrey Sachs, 'Making the Brady Plan Work' (1988) 68 *Foreign Affairs* 87, 91–2; Klaus Friedrich Veigel, *Dictatorship, Democracy and Globalization: Argentina and the Cost of Paralysis 1973–2001* (Pennsylvania State University Press, 2009); Carmen M Reinhart and Kenneth S Rogoff, *This Time is Different: Eight Centuries of Financial Folly* (Princeton University Press, 2009); David E Spiro, *The Hidden Hand of American Hegemony: Petrodollar Recycling and International Markets* (Cornell University Press, 1999).

17 Haggard and Kaufman, above n 2, Ch. 7.

18 Scheuermann, above n 11, 1867.

19 Oren Gross, 'Chaos and Rules: Should Responses to Violent Crises Always Be Constitutional?' (2003) 112 *Yale Law journal* 1011; Bruce Ackerman, *Before the Next Attack: Preserving Civil Liberties in a Time of Terrorism* (Yale University Press, 2006); David Dyzenhaus, *The Constitution of Law: Legality in a Time of Emergency* (Cambridge University Press, 2006).

20 See also, Constitution of Portugal art 19(2) – a 'state of siege' may only be declared in cases of actual or imminent aggression by foreign forces, a serious threat to or disturbances of constitutional democratic order or public disaster. See also, art 48 of the Constitution of Greece, which applies only to situations of war, general mobilisation due to external dangers or immediate threats to national security, or armed insurrection or overthrow of the democracy. Both constitutions also limit the range of rights that can be suspended. In practice, governments sometimes invoke emergencies such as terrorism to deal with situations that clearly do not threaten either a breakdown in social order or a national emergency: see *A & Others v Secretary of State for the Home Department* [2004] UKHL 56. The majority of the UK Law Lords accepted the Secretary of State's assessment of the existence of a national emergency but Lord Hoffmann famously rejected this argument in his brief concurring speech.

21 There is some discussion in the terrorism context about whether an 'emergency' is in fact temporary or meant to be more permanent: see Gross, above n 19, 1069–96. At any rate, Gross also distinguishes 'economic emergencies' and considers that his analysis does not extend to them since the urgency of response time is of a different order: Gross, above n 19, 1025–6.

22 See the excellent collection of essays in Claire Kilpatrick and Bruno De Witte (eds), *Social Rights in Times of Crisis in the Eurozone: The Role of Fundamental Rights' Challenges* (Working Paper No 5, European University Institute, 2014). One exception may be Spain, which adopted a 'Royal Decree Law', 'which is adopted by government in exceptional circumstances and emergency', however this law is concerned with giving the executive sweeping powers rather than suspending ordinary law or the Constitution: see M Gonzalez Pascual, 'Welfare Rights and the Euro Crisis – The Spanish Case' in Claire Kilpatrick and Bruno De Witte (eds), *Social Rights in Times of Crisis in the Eurozone: The Role of Fundamental Rights' Challenges* (Working Paper No 5, European University Institute, 2014).

23 Jennifer Rubenstein, 'Distribution and Emergencies' (2007) 15 *Journal of Political Philosophy* 296.

24 The essays throughout this volume give examples of where courts have taken notice of the existence of a crisis without suggesting that rights are entirely suspended. For an illustrative example outside of the European context, see *Newfoundland (Treasury Board) v N.A.P.E.* [2004] 3 SCR 381 [64] (Binnie J, for the Supreme Court of Canada): 'It is true, as the Court recently affirmed in *Nova Scotia (Workers' Compensation Board) v Martin* [2003] 2 SCR 504 [109] that "[b]udgetary considerations in and of themselves cannot normally be invoked as a free-standing pressing and substantial objective for the purposes of s. 1 of the Charter". The spring of 1991 was not a "normal" time in the finances of the provincial government. At some point, a financial crisis can attain a dimension that elected governments must be accorded significant scope to take remedial measures, even if the measures taken have an adverse effect on a Charter right, subject, of course, to the measures being proportional both to the fiscal crisis and to their impact on the affected Charter interests. In this case, the fiscal crisis was severe and the cost of putting into effect pay equity according to the original timetable was a large expenditure ($24 million) relative even to the size of the fiscal crisis.'

25 Simon Halliday, *Judicial Review and Compliance with Administrative Law* (Hart Publishing, 2004) Ch. 3.

26 Robert Nozick, *Anarachy, State and Utopia* (Wiley-Blackwell, 2001); Frederich A Hayek, *Law, Legislation and Liberty* (University of Chicago Press, 1978).

27 Walter Eucken, '*The Social Question*' (Derek Ruter trans) reprinted in Horst Friedrich Wunsche, Wolfgang Stutzel and Derek Rutter (eds), *Standard Texts on the Social Market Economy: Two Centuries of Discussion* (Gustav Fischer, 1982) 275. See also, Alan Peacock and Hani Willgerodt (eds), *Germany's Social Market Economy: Origins and Evolution* (Macmillan, 1989). For a succinct summary of the influence of these views at a critical juncture in post-war Germany, see H F Zacher, *Social Policy in the Federal Republic of Germany: The Constitution of the Social* (T Dunlop trans, Nomos, 2013) 146–52.

28 Alberto Alesina and Silvia Ardagna, 'Large Changes in Fiscal Policy: Tax versus Spending' in Jeffrey R Brown (ed.), *Tax Policy and the Economy* (National Bureau of Economic Research, 2010) Vol. 24.

29 Carmen M Reinhart and Kenneth S Rogoff, 'Growth in a Time of Debt' (2010) 100 *American Economic Review: Papers and Proceedings* 573.

30 Suzanne J Konzelmann, 'The Political Economics of Austerity' (2014) *Cambridge Journal of Economics* 1, 25.

31 Ibid. See further Paul Krugman, *How the Case for Austerity has Crumbled* (6 June 2013) New York Review of Books <www.nybooks.com/articles/2013/06/06/how-case-austerity-has-crumbled/>: 'At this point, then, austerity economics is in a very bad way. Its predictions have proved utterly wrong; its founding academic documents haven't just lost their canonized status, they've become the objects of much ridicule'; Mark Blyth, *Austerity: The History of a Dangerous Idea* (Oxford University Press, 2013). On the IMF's admission of the failure of the austerity policies, see Oliver Blanchard and Daniel Leigh, 'Growth Forecast Errors and Fiscal Multipliers' (Working Paper No 13/1, International Monetary Fund, January 2013).

32 I have considered the circumstances under which a claim to expertise can be dismissed as a failure of expertise in constitutional adjudication, one of which is the contradiction of established social-scientific evidence: see King (2012), above n 6, 240–8. The threshold stated there is that there will be a failure of expertise where the proposition asserted by the state conflicts with a proposition that, inter alia, is 'met with general acceptance in the relevant scientific community'. It is certainly arguable that we are now reaching the point where a substantial majority of economists take the view that austerity in fact promotes the opposite of what governments claim when relying on it to guide economic policy. Where this threshold to be crossed, I admit that the case for incrementalism must be substantially qualified if not abandoned. See, e.g., King (2012), above n 6, 240–9 where I refer to the limits of incrementalism when failures of expertise are at issue. While arguable, I do not think that the proposition has yet met with 'general acceptance'.

33 See, ibid, 279, considering the *Personal Responsibility and Work Opportunity Reconciliation Act 1996* (US), which ushered in Temporary Assistance for Needy Families.

34 As appeared to be the case with the IMF-inspired Hungarian welfare reform of 1995, which was struck down by the Hungarian Constitutional Court. See Kim Lande Scheppele, 'A Realpolitik Defense of Social Rights' (2004) 82 *Texas Law Review* 1921, 1941–9. Even so, as the author points out, contributory social insurance rights were given greater protection over means-tested social assistance interests due to their property-like character.

35 Octavio Luiz Motta Ferraz, 'The Right to Health in the Courts of Brazil: Worsening Health Inequities?' (2009) 11 *Health and Human Rights: An International Journal* 33; Ottar Mæstad, Lise Rakner and Octavio Ferraz, 'Assessing the Impact of Health Rights Litigation: A Comparative Study of Argentina, Colombia, Costa Rica, India and South Africa' in Alicia Ely Yamin and Siri Gloppen (eds), *Litigating Health Rights: Can Courts Bring More Justice to Health?* (Harvard University Press, 2011); V Afonso da Silva and F Vargas Terrazas, 'Claiming the Right to Health in Brazilian Courts: The Exclusion of the Already Excluded?' (2011) 36 *Law & Social Inquiry* 825.

36 Yamin and Gloppen (eds), above n 35.

37 See Committee on Economic, Social and Cultural Rights, *General Comment No 3: The Nature of States Parties' Obligations (Art. 2, Para 1, of the Covenant)*, 5th sess., UN Doc E/1991/23 (14 December 1990); Committee on Economic, Social and Cultural Rights, *General Comment No 12: The Right to Adequate Food (Art. 11)*, 20th sess., UN Doc E/C.12/1999/5 (12 May 1999); Committee on Economic, Social and Cultural Rights, *General Comment No 13. The Right to Education (Article 13 of the Covenant)*, 21st sess., UN Doc E/C.12/1999/10 (8 December 1999); Committee on Economic, Social and Cultural Rights,

General Comment 14: The Right to the Highest Attainable Standard of Health (Art. 12), 22nd sess., UN Doc E/C.12/2000/4 (11 August 2000). I analyse some of these in King, above n 6, chs 4 and 9, and together with Malcolm Langford in our essay on the ICESCR: Jeff King and Malcolm Langord, 'The Committee on Economic, Social and Cultural Rights' in Malcolm Langford (ed.), *Social Rights Jurisprudence: Emerging Trends in Comparative and International Law* (Cambridge University Press, 2009) 477. See also K Young, 'The Minimum Core of Economic and Social Rights: A Concept in Search of Content' (2008) 33 *Yale Journal of International Law* 113; David Bilchitz, *Poverty and Fundamental Rights: The Justification and Enforcement of Socio Economic Rights* (Oxford University Press, 2007).

38 Committee on Economic, Social and Cultural Rights, *General Comment No 3: The Nature of States Parties' Obligations (Art. 2, Para 1, of the Covenant)*, 5th sess., UN Doc E/1991/23 (14 December 1990).

39 For a short overview of the German jurisprudence in English, see H M Heinig, 'The Political and the Basic Law's Sozialstaat Principle – Perspectives from Constitutional Law and Theory' (2011) 12 *German Law Journal* 1887; Jeff King, 'Social Rights, Constitutionalism, and the German Social State Principle (2014) 3 *E-Pública: Revista Electrónica De Direito Público* 1. In German, see A Voßkuhle, 'Der Sozialstaat in der Rechtsprechung des BverfG' (2011) 4 *Die Sozialgerichtsbarkeit* 181–6 and the classic if dated examination in H F Zacher, 'Das Soziale Staatsziele' in J Isensee und P Kirschhof (eds), *Handbuch des Staatsrechts der Bundesrepublik Deutschland* (C F Mueller Juristische Verlag, 1987) Vol. 1, Ch. 25.

40 See Lembke, Ch. 3 in this volume.

41 Bundesverfassungsgericht [German Constitutional Court], 1 BVL 1, 3, 4/09, 9 February 2010 reported in (2010) 125 BVerfGE 175 (2010) ('Hartz IV').

42 There were three important holdings in the case, but for simplicity's sake I will focus on two of them – both had to do with the court finding the methods for calculating the benefits unsound. First, the court declared the Standard ALG II Benefit to be unconstitutional. The key problem was that the formula used to up-rate the benefits from 1998 to 2005 were based on pension values, which track wages, salaries and other data that is logically unrelated to the subsistence minimum, rather than on factors such as net income, cost of living and consumer behaviour. Second, the social allowance for children was determined to be 40% of the Standard Benefit. This meant that it fell with the unsound Standard Benefit, but the court also found that the figure was determined entirely without any empirical or methodological foundation, which should have taken into account children's costs of schooling and living. A schooling supplement of €100 per year was likewise held to be determined without any empirical basis. Each of these findings in my view fits the approach of judicial incrementalism outlined in my book – it shows the merit of a careful forensic investigation of the process by which this key benefit was determined.

43 I am in a minority in advocating the latter position. The most prominent commentators on the doctrine, and leading judges, take the former view.

44 The debate is reported in the Federal Parliament (Bundestag), *Stenographic Report* 79 (3 December 2010) Plenary Protocol 17/79, 8739.

45 Despite the mismatch between the notoriety of the Hartz IV judgment and its impact on the basic Unemployment Benefit II rate, there were other political responses to the judgment such as the increase in funding for an educational allowance (the '*Bildungspaket*') whose repercussions may be important. The *Bildungspaket* is discussed in the Bundestag debate, above: see Federal Parliament

(Bundestag), *Stenographic Report* 79 (3 December 2010) Plenary Protocol 17/79, 8739, 8740, 8748.

46 Bundesverfassungsgericht [German Constitutional Court], 1 BvL 10/12, 1 BvL 12/12, 1 BvR 1691/13, 23 July 2014 reported in (2014) BVerfG 3425. (The social state principle mandates an existential minimum in conjunction with Art. 1 para. 1 Basic Law, but allows for generalisations unless there are systematic deficits in the calculation of the amounts or serious concerns as to their adequacy to cover living expenses. It also allows for political compromise in the determination of benefits levels.)

47 Bundesverfassungsgericht [German Constitutional Court], 2 BvL 14/91, 25 September 1992 reported in (1992) 87 BVerfGE 153.

48 Bundesverfassungsgericht [German Constitutional Court], 1 BvL 10/10, 18 July 2012, reported in BVerfG Absatz-Nr. (1–220).

49 *R. v Secretary of State for the Home Department, ex parte Limbuela* [2005] UKHL 66. For discussion, see Sandra Fredman, 'Human Rights Transformed: Positive Duties and Positive Rights' (2006) *Public Law* 498.

50 The legislation is *Emergency Act* (Act No. 125/2008) (Ice.), the Supreme Court case is ISC No. 340/2011 (Oct. 28, 2011) (Ice.). I am indebted for these references and penetrating analysis of them to Ragnhildur Helgadóttir, 'Economic Crises and Emergency Powers in Europe' (10 March 2012) *Harvard Business Review Online* <www.hblr.org/2012/03/eu-economic-emergency-powers/>.

51 Ibid 18–19. Notably, and consistent with the analysis above, the court did not view the issue as being an emergency suspension of the constitution but rather fully compliant with the ordinary constitutional regime.

52 Bundesverfassungsgericht [German Constitutional Court], 1 BvL 21/78, 1 March 1979 reported in 50 BVerfGE 290.

53 Judgment of the Portuguese Constitutional Court 353/12, 3 July 2012; Judgment of the Portuguese Constitutional Court 396/11, 21 September 2011. See also M G De Brito, 'Putting Social Rights in Brackets? The Portuguese Experience with Welfare Challenges in Times of Crisis', in Claire Kilpatrick and Bruno De Witte (eds), *Social Rights in Times of Crisis in the Eurozone: The Role of Fundamental Rights' Challenges* (Working Paper No 5, European University Institute, 2014).

54 Italian Constitutional Court, 30 April 2015, decision no 70. For discussion, see Albanese, Ch. 4 in this volume; S Civitarese, 'Austerity and Social Rights in Italy: A Long Standing Story' on UK Constitutional Law Association Blog (17 December 2015) <https://ukconstitutionallaw.org/>.

55 Scheppele, above n 34.

56 See D L Horowitz, 'Decreeing Organizational Change: Judicial Supervision of Public Institutions' (1983) 32 *Duke Law Review* 1265, 1272–6, 1297–1302.

57 See King, *Judging Social Rights*, above n 6, 271–5 for a comparative overview.

58 In the US, see Ross Sandler and David Schoenbrod, *Democracy by Decree* (Yale University Press, 2003); cf the critical review in Susan Rose-Ackerman, 'Review of R Sandler and D Schoenbrod, Democracy by Decree' (2003) 118 *Political Science Quarterly* 679. See also Jeff King, 'Two Ironies about American Exceptionalism over Social Rights' (2014) 12 *International Journal of Constitutional Law* 572. For a more upbeat appraisal, see C F Sabel and W H Simon, 'Destabilization Rights: How Public Law Litigation Succeeds' (2004) 117 *Harvard Law Review* 1016. In India, see Ashok H Desai and S Muralidhar, 'Public Interest Litigation: Potential and Problems' in B Kirpal (ed.), *Supreme but Not Infallible: Essays in Honour of the Supreme Court of India* (Oxford University Press, 2000); P Singh, 'Promises and Perils of Public Interest Litigation in Protecting the Rights of the Poor and the Oppressed' (2005) 27 *Delhi Law Review* 8.

59 See King, above n 57.

60 César Rodriguez-Garavito and Diana Rodriguez-Franco, *Radical Deprivation on Trial: The Impact of Judicial Activism on Socioeconomic Rights in The Global South* (Cambridge University Press, 2015) Ch. 2, which examines in detail and even-handedly the experience of the rights-claimants in a structural reform litigation concerning internally displaced persons in Colombia. See further, David Landau, 'The Reality of Social Rights Enforcement' (2012) 53 *Harvard International Law Journal* 190, 257–61, offering both ambivalence and confidence about the potential for structural remedies to give social rights their potential.

61 A very important qualification of my argument is that it applies to countries that have similar specified background social conditions to the United Kingdom, including much of northern Europe. While this does not apply in countries such us those throughout Latin America or in India, the principles of restraint identified would often also apply wherever the epistemic constraints of adjudication are a factor in deciding upon the best way to resolve a social problem. See further the review of my book by T Khaitan and F Ahmed, 'Constitutional Avoidance in Social Rights Adjudication' (2015) 35 *Oxford Journal of Legal Studies* 607.

62 Diletta Tega, 'Welfare Rights in Italy' in Claire Kilpatrick and Bruno De Witte (eds), *Social Rights in Times of Crisis in the Eurozone: The Role of Fundamental Rights' Challenges* (Working Paper No 5, European University Institute, 2014) 50. However, note the contribution by Albanese, Ch. 4 in this volume in which, at text to note 30, she observes that significant budget cuts were passed in Law 78/2015 to health services without any parliamentary debate.

63 I argue that an absence of legislative focus eliminates democratic accountability as a ground for judicial restraint: see King, above n 6, Ch. 6.

64 *Minister of Health and Others v. Treatment Action Campaign and Others* 2002 (10) BCLR 1033 (CC).

65 High Court of Castilla-La Mancha (Administrative Division), Judgment of 26 June 2013.

66 John Hart Ely, *Democracy and Distrust: A Theory of Judicial Review* (Harvard University Press, 1980). See King, above n 6, Ch. 6 for a critical analysis and integration of these insights into a theory of adjudication for social rights.

67 M Nogueira de Brito, 'Putting Social Rights in Brackets? The Portuguese Experience with Welfare Challenges in Times of Crisis' in Claire Kilpatrick and Bruno De Witte (eds), *Social Rights in Times of Crisis in the Eurozone: The Role of Fundamental Rights' Challenges* (Working Paper No 5, European University Institute, 2014).

68 Paul Pierson, 'Coping with Permanent Austerity: Welfare State Restructuring in Affluent Societies' in Paul Pierson (ed.), *The New Politics of the Welfare State* (Oxford University Press, 1999).

69 See the essay by A Kerr, 'Social Rights in Crisis in the Eurozone: Work Rights in Ireland' in Claire Kilpatrick and Bruno De Witte (eds), *Social Rights in Times of Crisis in the Eurozone: The Role of Fundamental Rights' Challenges* (Working Paper No 5, European University Institute, 2014).

70 Nogueira de Brito, above n 67.

71 See King, *Judging Social Rights*, above n 6, 298–9.

72 Rossiter, above n 14.

73 Nogueira de Brito, above n 67.

74 Constitutional Court Decision No. 43/1995 (VI. 30), MK 56/1995, translated in L Solyom and G Brunner (eds), *Constitutional Judiciary in a New Democracy: The Hungarian Constitutional Court* (University of Michigan Press, 2000) 327. I am again indebted to the analysis in Scheppele, above n 34.

75 See, Ackerman, above n 19 on the 'supermajoritarian escalator' as a further mechanism for such legislative approval.

76 See OECD Stat, *Revenue Statistics: OECD Countries, Comparative Tables* <https://stats.oecd.org/Index.aspx?DataSetCode=REV>. In 1980, the tax revenue as a percentage of GDP for Spain was 22% and for Italy 28.7%; by 2008 it was 32.3% and 41.6% respectively, both increasing to 33.2% and 43.6% by 2014.

77 OECD Stat, *Social Expenditure – Aggregated Data* <https://stats.oecd.org/Index.aspx?DataSetCode=SOCX_AGG>. As at 6 October 2016, as a percentage of GDP, the figures in 1980 for Spain were 15.4% and for Italy 18%, increasing to 20.9% and 24.9% respectively by 2005, and on to 26.8% and 28.6% respectively by 2014. Notably, the GDP also rose significantly during this period.

78 Spain's revenue from 2005 to 2007 was quite atypical for OECD countries, dropping precipitously as a percentage of GDP.

79 OECD Stat, above n 76. The figures are 43.6% (Italy), 39.1% (Norway) and 42.7% (Sweden).

Chapter 11

The political economy of European social rights

Emilios Christodoulidis and Marco Goldoni

I

In the wake of the 2008 crisis it is surprising, but also perhaps instructive, how much ink is still being spilt on the question of whether social rights are better protected through legislative, administrative or judicial channels, or a mix of these.[1] *Better* protected? What is *surprising* about the unabated ink-spilling is that social rights constitutionalism has been all but defeated, clearly the first victim of the regime of economic austerity rolled out to contain sovereign debt crisis. Where they have not been hollowed to the point of extinction by austerity programmes, systems of social and labour protection have been thrown into the vicious circle of competitive alignment, with the devastating effects the race to the bottom has had on social rights. Alain Supiot refers in this context to the 'Matthew effect',[2] where the very commitment of national economies to political redress of the social costs of globalisation becomes self-defeating because the logic of globalisation weakens the State's ability to deliver it. Accordingly, those most in need of protection are those most bereft of it due to the economic freedom afforded to capital to circumvent the costs of social protection by relocating to cheaper sites – whether it is the reality, or merely the threat, of relocation. With the European Court's sustained attack on syndicalism and trade union protection of social rights, a position that has a wall of immunity built around it, unchallengeable in effect through the threat of bankruptcy of any European trade union inviting it to revisit the barbarity of its Laval/Viking jurisprudence, the separation of economic from social constitutionalism creates the conditions of a staggering asymmetry between the damage that markets wield in the field of labour protection and the remedies available in terms of social rights jurisprudence. In the light of all this what counts as the better channel of institutional protection becomes at best a question of secondary significance. At the national level, the State, as we will see, is forced into competitive pressure at the European level because 'social Europe', as Draghi had no qualms pronouncing, is 'finished', a closure that the Luxembourg Court judges are falling over themselves to secure.[3]

As we write this, the French National Assembly has twice heard the 'Loi Travail', the notorious 'El Khomri' Law (named after the French Minister of

Labour responsible for it), finally approving it on 21 July 2016, following the use of Article 49.3 of the Constitution.[4] Since its first presentation of the draft legislation in February 2016, the Act, drafted without any prior consultation with trade unions and rushed through emergency procedures, is now part of a series of labour markets reforms adopted in many European countries.[5] It, to give some examples, offers a new regulation of working time with a priority given to collective agreements at enterprise level; modifies the rules concerning collective agreements; de–'rigidifies' economic dismissal; and covers issues of occupational health, discrimination, vocational training and posting of workers. In a country accustomed to industrial action and unrest, the response has been unprecedented; a new social movement has emerged in the form of Nuit Debout ('Up All Night' or 'Standing Night') that began in February 2016; important strikes in the energy sector have involved blocking oil refineries; there have been strikes in transport, garbage and in universities; and there has been the *Confédération générale du travail* (CGT) in arms. And yet it appears impossible to resist this relentless march of market thinking – the Labour Act is an unqualified endorsement of the EU's flexibilisation agenda[7] – to the detriment of labour and social protection.

But why, then, *instructive*? Because the continuing rhetorical relevance of social rights is a mark of their powerful symbolic currency, in the way that they have underwritten what was arguably unique about the venture of social Europe. We will revisit some of these aspirations below; suffice it now to point to the centrality of dignity, solidarity and security as collective goods, as constitutive dimensions even, of the common good of the European 'community'. It is this symbolic significance that raises the stakes of the debate over social rights, and why the discussion of their continuity or discontinuity with the securely entrenched property and negative rights (or 'freedoms') is so vitally important if we are to draw on the language of social rights as a valuable political resource and means of articulation of claims to just allocations of the burdens and yields of production and distribution.

Let us look at one powerful articulation of continuity, something akin to a basic consensus even, in the idea that while their content may be different, the basic *grammar* of rights is the same across the three 'generations' of property/civil, political and social/economic rights. (A note of clarification: while 'property' and 'civil' rights are clearly distinct, they are often coupled in our discussion in both constitutively entailing an exercise of *negative* freedom – freedom, that is, not to be interfered with.) The discussion over the best institutional forum for their enforcement often builds on this common assumption. The theorising here departs from a commonality of normative structure. Of course, different justifications may be available, and rights can be conceived as interest-based claims, as means of empowerment, as expression of the autonomy of will and so forth.[8] The discussion rather turns 'downstream' on the continuity between normative structure and institutional realisation. And what matters is that once the common, core normative structure has been established, then it is continuous with its institutional manifestations across categories of rights. Joseph Raz's conception of rights as collective goods is a sophisticated and refined statement of this version of the 'continuity thesis'. On his account, all fundamental rights are at once responsive to *both* individual *and* collective interests.[9] His is an irenic and 'conciliatory' account of rights as collective goods. Under this description, rights are protected reasons and, given how reasons are understood by Raz, it is necessary for a right to be a collective good. A clear example, according to Raz, is freedom of speech: this is an individual good that, when protected, is also collective because it enhances the democratic life of a polity. *Vice versa* a collective right is also in the interest of each individual. The assumption undergirding this perfectionist view of rights is that, contrary to the classic liberal understanding of natural or fundamental rights, the subject of rights is a social individual. In full perfectionist mode, the well-being of the individual is dependent on the normative (social) environment, and Raz, consistently since his important *Morality of Freedom*,[10] is a committed advocate of a liberalism that constitutively implicates the embeddedness of individual life, identity and capacity in their social context.

This is admirable stuff, but it elides an important juncture. It is one thing to say that individual goods and the exercise of negative freedoms must be conceptualised *in tandem* with the positive freedoms, which, in the guise of social rights, undergird any meaningful exercise of freedom by any individual. It is quite another to establish on that basis a smooth passage between individual and social rights where, under conditions of liberal economic arrangements, capitalist control over social resources trumps redistributive demands of social justice, and the problem is how to manage that discontinuity *institutionally*. In other words, under capitalist conditions, individual and social rights name two opposing, rather than mutually reinforcing, principles of resource allocation, the first based on entitlement, the second on need. To argue the confluence on conceptual grounds (laudable as the political sentiment is) smooths over difficult institutional questions over managing discontinuity and incongruence. The difficult questions concern the institutional moments of selective coupling and de-coupling that realise the continuity institutionally, the dynamics of selective alignment on which so much of the theoretical casting of continuity in fact hangs *and falters*.

More direct, and refreshingly unapologetic, is Fernando Atria's recent challenge to the deep tension between individual and social rights. For Atria, social rights, unlike individual rights, are particularly sensitive to cooperation in a way that cannot be easily reduced to their individual content.[11] If Atria's is an argument about discontinuity, it is emphatically not because individual rights are not social or sensitive to social context. On the contrary, for him, '[s]ocial rights arise as a way of affirming – in terms of justice – the importance of understanding human self-realization as reciprocal rather than individual'.[12] This is therefore not to deny that individual rights always entail some sort of relation; it is to draw attention to the correlative duty that is attached to each right. For individual rights, the duty is a general or universal one, therefore not strictly relational because it does not apply to concrete subjects. Think of the case of the right to life, which is usually conceived as the right to not have one's life taken. The correlative duty is addressed, abstractly, to everyone. In the case of social rights, the duty concerns identifiable and specific subjects: institutions. The correlative duty of the right to education is the duty of the government to organise an educational service. This being the case, it is central to the very idea of social rights to preserve the distinction between them and individual rights. On the understanding that freedom is a relationship that develops *between* people rather than a good that needs to be protected *from* them, its institutionalisation in social rights is constitutively geared to sustaining solidarity in cooperation. Intriguingly, Atria invites us to think of social rights as 'anomalous grafts'.[13] The grafting aims to create an uncertain relation between (categories of) rights because, in the long term, either the host will be transformed or the guest will be co-opted. In other words, the social dimension of rights carries with it a generative potential for transformation or disruption. To the contrary, when reduced to the claim of individual access to services, then social rights completely lose this potentially productive quality.

We pursue Atria's insight in the context of social rights protection in contemporary Europe, with a special emphasis on the re-formation (and de-formation) of welfare provision and the organisation of social services.[14] We explore the question at two levels, *historical* and *conceptual*, and at both our points of departure is the acknowledgement of a particular configuration of the Welfare State that frames social rights as subject to a different status than liberal individual rights.[15] Historically, social rights are embedded in institutional histories and are associated with a particular set of legal and political orders; in Europe the Welfare State emerged in particular form,[16] was stabilised in the second post-war period and spread across the Western part of the Continent.[17] Conceptually, our emphasis is on the *material* content of social rights, that is, the substantial governing arrangements that regulate them as essential building blocks of societal reproduction. Our *methodological* assumption is that each regime of social rights is always associated with a particular political economy, that is, each regime crystallises around specific and *politically* organised relations of production and reproduction of the societal order. In other words, the enactment and the provision of social rights are defining moments of the dynamics of social reproduction. Their regulation impacts directly on the self-understanding and the political capacity of social actors, their relative positions and class relations. Atria's discontinuity thesis helps us open the enquiry into possible lines of conflict in the processes of social interaction and cooperation. We argue that it is not possible to have an accurate understanding of social rights without a proper analysis of their material dimension. Of course, in theory it is still possible to conceive of social rights as individual rights, adjudicated in adversarial form, and pitted against the public interest. These are familiar forms of domesticating them to orders of individual right. But it is only by looking at how a society materially reproduces itself through work, healthcare, education and housing, can we obtain a proper grasp of the nature and conditions of operation of social rights. The 'discontinuity' between civil and social rights, then, links social rights to collective goods and services while it allows individual rights to be conceived mostly as means of protection of fundamental liberties.

While the emphasis on the material substratum of social rights in the Welfare State is a necessary condition for understanding their function, we need to return to their developing history in order to appreciate the conjuncture that confronts us today in the society of debt. The material premise of the class dynamic of the developing story of social rights constitutionalism, whose earlier chapters were told with exceptional clarity by, among others, Claus Offe in the *Contradictions of the Welfare State*,[18] Fritz Scharpf, Wolfgang Streeck and others, takes a decisive turn in the society of debt.[19] This is the focus in this chapter. We hold on to our methodological commitment to thematise public debt as the stake and outcome of social and political struggle over the organisation of production and the distribution of wealth. And it is at this point that the unfolding story of 'social Europe' as a society of debt confronts us with a crucial displacement; it is the displacement that we chart here. The national Social State's debt is – or rather *was* – a site for class conflict. The unstable relation between civil/property and social rights created a field of struggle over the control of public debt, a struggle that is eminently political even when it appears to concern purely economic issues. Public expenditures are not conceived as something external to society but as the material field of political intervention. As remarked by Alain Supiot, the development of the Social State is not tantamount to a totalising grip over society as political philosophers such as Carl Schmitt and Hannah Arendt would have it.[20] As long as social rights are not completely reduced to individual entitlements subject to processes of adjudication vis-à-vis the State, a space is left open for political challenges over the appropriation and distribution of resources. The crucial new development that confronts us is the mutation of the tax state into the debt state under conditions of sovereign debt. And for this we must turn to what makes social rights radically different in the European context in the political economy of the EU, as we analyse the main tenets of the new Euro economic governance.

II

The trajectory of European integration, in the decisive way in which it encroaches on social rights, has been punctuated by two key moments. The first, providing the imprint to the European Community itself, the legal (and only in an indirect sense, the political) DNA, so to speak, of the European project is *market integration*, with competition law its linchpin. The creation of a common market represents the keystone of the whole project of integration. It is not necessary to rehearse it here. Suffice to say that a clear division of labour was established at the inception of the process of integration that would leave to the National States full competences on all matters of social policy and protection, while the integration of the market would take place at the transnational level, with competition law underpinning freedom of movement and guaranteeing standards of the product's circulation.[21] Welfare States were relatively isolated from the pressure coming from market integration – so much so that it was extremely difficult to subject social expenditures to 'market-oriented' criteria. In a sense, the severing off of the operation of the common market from the regulative priorities of national Welfare States functioned as a shield against the centrifugal forces of the common market, and at the time there was no suggestion that the latter would be conceptualised in terms of market access.[22] However, the situation would quickly change during the 1970s, and in particular after the oil crisis of 1973; the type of commodities by now circulating within the common market were far from being limited to industrial products.[23] In what marks the beginning of a process of transformation of the market itself, which is crucial for understanding the dismantling of Member States' welfare systems and the neutralisation of social rights, the massive influx of *financial products* into the common market forced a restructuring of capital relations along different and socially more pervasive lines. This is part of a general restructuring of the global political economy that situates market rationality as the main arbiter for managing States' welfare systems.

The second decisive moment is the launch of the single currency project with the Maastricht Treaty. One cannot overestimate the importance of this turning point for our discussion of social rights, because the introduction of the Euro required, for political and economic reasons, an agreement upon a series of governing objectives among the participating countries. The convergence of basic economic indicators led to a *self*-imposed pressure upon the political economy of the Member States. It impacted upon the State's governing activities with gravitational force, pushing governments to steer their policies in ways that would 'please' markets. Economic and financial policies had to be reconfigured in order to meet the standards of a common currency without a State.[24] The founding assumption introduced with Maastricht is that in the absence of a lender of last resort, self-imposed frugality will ensure that the currency will function smoothly and will be harboured from financial speculation. The pillars of Euro governance are, from the outset, the reduction of the deficit and public debt vis-à-vis the national gross domestic product (GDP), coupled with an entrenched objective of keeping inflation relatively low.[25] This forces States into the contraction of public expenditure in order to appear as virtuous actors before international financial markets. Otherwise, so goes the narrative, it won't be possible to attract investors to buy the national bonds.[26] It should be added, for the sake of accuracy, that the standards of governance of the common currency have been set according to the wishes of the centre and against the interests of the periphery. In this way, the monetary government of the Eurozone freezes relations of power in the form of creditor–debtor relations, where creditors are mostly financial investors (such as banks, insurances and funds) and debtors are Member States (some more than others). The 2008 crisis transformed public debts into sovereign debts. Sovereign debts were to be managed according to the principles of austerity because only in this way, near-defaulting states were told, would they regain the confidence of markets. Here was the politics of the common currency clearly and fully unfolding: and with it, the space for political conflict over public debt closed down and was sealed.

Let us pause here to take another look at the trajectory taken by 'Euro governance'. Our reference to the material dimension of social rights sheds light on new orchestrated forms of invalidation of their content or, in subtler ways, of their hollowing-out and depletion. A material analysis allows us to understand that social rights are not just violated, but their shrinkage is actually pre-empted by the current 'Euro' form of government, centrally oriented, as it is, toward austerity.[27] The objective of Euro governance is to ensure the stability (at this point in time, the survival) of the common currency that would in turn secure the viability of the internal market and then the solidity of Member States' finances, all under the imperative that markets are 'reassured'. According to this approach, sound financial policy consists in cutting back public expenditure.

The political economy holds the key to explaining the different understanding of social rights in the two epochs. Antonio Negri, in a series of articles, has identified a significant change in the way that the political economy undergirds social rights constitutionalism. A financial convention is grafted on the European material constitution in a way that allows capital as a social relation to play a commanding role. The difference couldn't be more striking: 'Whereas the labour-measure, in the Fordist constitution, was hard and relatively stable, and depended directly on the relation of forces between classes (this was the situation of any constitutional arrangement during the "short century"), the financial convention, when it takes a constitutional form, that is, when it comes to constitute capitalist political relations hegemonically, presents itself as an independent and super-venient power.'[28] Note that formally social rights are still recognised by national constitutions. The change has taken place at a different level.[29]

Make no mistake: the State remains the main constitutional unit upon which European integration develops, but the point of the latter is precisely to impose specific 'reforms' upon national economies with a view to containing and limiting social rights.[30] Compared to the age of the Welfare State, a counter-movement is at play here, but this is no Polanyian 'double-movement' by society to reclaim some form of embeddedness against market excess. Quite the opposite: the movement now is toward a re-'patrimonialised' State,[31] which ensures the extraction of value from social labour and cooperation (that is, wealth generated through both living labour and subsumed labour) through a variety of processes (symmetrical and asymmetrical) of European integration. While the *Welfare State* is a State form whose material constitution centres on social conflict and aims at its regulation and containment, the form of the *Member State*[32] (in particular of those within the Eurozone) elides conflict altogether and displaces its centrality to the constitution and reproduction of the social order. The latter (and the cooperation necessary to reproduce it) is primarily seen as a condition of debt.[33] The subtraction of public and social debt from the mediating role of sovereignty (a scheme that was at the heart of Fordist constitutionalism) sets the scene for the exercise of commanding power by financial capital. Again, Negri is particularly insightful on this point: 'Public debt has been removed from public regulation . . . and subjected to value mechanisms which are determined on global markets by financial capitalists.'[34]

We would suggest that the main gist of this impressive transformation had already been glimpsed in an insightful manner by Nicos Poulantzas in the mid-1970s. His intuition was that the onset of European integration was transforming the relations between different factions of the capitalist class *within* individual States, rather than leading to the formation of a pan-European capitalist class, of the type that, as was thought, would be able to compete with the US. In fact, contrary to Mandel, who believed that the crisis of the 1970s was leading to a convergence of interests among national capitalist classes in Europe, Poulantzas remarked that:

> certain distensions are currently manifested between the State and the nation, but not in the sense generally meant by the 'supranationalization' of the State. It is not the emergence of a new State over the nations that we are witnessing but rather ruptures in the national unity underlying the existing national states.[35]

Poulantzas based his understanding of the development of integration on the rise of a new kind of bourgeoisie, which he defined as 'interior bourgeoisie'. In place of coherent and self-identifying national bourgeois classes of the kind that mobilised on a nationalist basis and had fought against one another in the two World Wars, European states were increasingly structured around this new kind of bourgeoisie, social class formations 'imbricated by multiple links of dependence, with the processes of international division of labour and international concentration of capital under the domination of American capital'.[36]

In this light, the celebrated principle of constitutional tolerance that Joseph Weiler saw at work in European integration[37] begins to look rather more sinister, less of an openness to the 'other' and more of a laying bare of the State's public wealth to supranational financial forces. The meaning of tolerance then moves away from signifying the role of the State as standing above, and mediating, antagonistic social forces, and towards the acceptance of norms and rules issued by other legal orders. More concretely, a series of institutional interventions ensure that the monetary area is actually governed through strict criteria of budgetary austerity. These include the State's financing of great infrastructure projects, the privatisation of public services or, more ambiguously, the promotion of horizontal forms of subsidiarity through European projects, cuts to pensions independently from the supporting social structures and, of course, the mother of all reforms, salary moderation obtained through the creation of an asymmetric labour market and subjected to a currency whose formal value is insensitive to local dynamics.

There has been, therefore, a transformation of the role of the State vis-à-vis social rights because the State itself has to resort to financial markets in order to fund social services. The problem is that once this move is entrenched, as it is de facto in the European material constitution, the debt of the State is judged according to a strict understanding of market rationality.[38] Member States' debt is assessed by rating agencies and kept under review by the European Commission, and despite the fact that the approach may vary (think of the swing of the European Central Bank (ECB) toward a milder monetarist position), it is clear that public services that are run according to public and non-profit principles are deemed to be inefficient.[39]

In this way, the decoupling of social rights from European citizenship is fully realised.[40] In a crucial sense, the standard narrative put forward by T H Marshall is here completely denied if not reversed. As is well known, Marshall thought that the history of citizenship unfolds in successive, interrelated, waves of acquisition of rights.[41] For Marshall, the widening of the franchise, to give one important example, would lead to demands for access to socially generated wealth. Note the reversal: in the New Economic Governance, it is no longer true that the recognition of political rights of citizenship leads in the longer term to access to social rights though the political process. The political condition of the European citizen is structurally severed from the promotion of social rights. What is exercised through the marketisation of public debts is a form of governing of contemporary societies with a view to depleting social rights. The pillars of this type of governance will be illustrated in the following sections. For now, let us stop and take stock: we have argued that the whole 'philosophy' of Euro governance is geared toward the entrenchment of austerity policies that entails a dramatic compression of social rights and a re-structuring of the societal orders of Member States. Public debts are transformed into sovereign debts, which is to say: from being sites of social conflict, debts become financial products. As aptly remarked by Negri, financial capital and its monetary translation is the linchpin of the European material constitution.[42] Its capacity for extraction of surplus value corresponds to a strong commanding power, one that imprints itself into the new material constitution. The new economic governance has triggered a new 'original appropriation' or, better, a series of new original appropriations. As we are reminded by Carl Schmitt, every legal order begins with an original taking, after which distribution and production follow.[43] The appropriation of social wealth is followed by a new distribution of resources and a new cycle of valorisation of capital. The main target of the financial convention is to extract value from (or, in different words, to valorise) social cooperation and interaction. This process operates directly against a conception of irreducible social rights for the reasons previously explained. Note that such a financial convention is not a denial of social rights tout court but it is a *reduction* of these rights to something else. In addition to the financial convention ruling over States' public debts there is a second staple that further depletes the political space available to European citizens: the reform of labour markets. The severing off of the economy from the political space is strengthened by the assault on labour rights and the disempowering of social actors representative of those rights, like trade unions and social movements. All of this is in the name of competitiveness on the European and global markets. In a nutshell, Europe's material constitution forces a re-signification of social rights as instruments of market access or market competition.

III

A new functionality pervades EU law and justifies what in effect cannot but be seen as a weakening of legality, an undercutting even. Take the deluge of *Ersatz* law of the last few years, the 'six-packs' and 'two-packs', the aborted Monti regulation and its successor, the European Financial Stabilisation Mechanism (EFSM) and the European Financial Stability Facility (EFSF) – the full range of measures that sovereign debt loan assistance has assumed in order to shore up the Euro, as blatant an exercise of what Walter Benjamin identified as 'police power' with the emphasis on the ad hoc, the exceptional, a responsiveness tailored to particularity, the abandonment of formal justice.

To appreciate the scale and reach of the new economic governance one needs to unpack the complexity of the measures introduced to cope with either the reduction of public debt and the cutting of public expenditure or with access to credit under strict conditionality. In both cases, the undergirding philosophy is austerity and its constitutionalisation. The reaction to the crisis of the common currency has been to 'reassure' financial markets by cutting further classic provisions given by the Welfare State (such as labour, pensions and education). The European semester, built on EU law, is geared on the cycle of national budgetary drafting with the explicit aim to harness it to strict financial goals.[44] The European semester creates, so to say, a dialogue between supranational and national institutions in order to patrol the latter's discretionary budgetary policies and nudge them toward a convergence upon certain fiscal outcomes. The Commission plays an important role in this cycle, but the same goes for the Council as it is to the latter that the final decision on sanctions is allocated.[45] The European Stability Mechanism (ESM), which is also based on international law, establishes a fund, through an agency based in Luxembourg, for providing credit to Member States that are not capable of financing themselves on financial markets at reasonable interest rates.[46] The ESM is constituted through funding provided by all Member States in different proportions, with Germany being the biggest contributor. Decisions are taken by majority voting but the votes are calculated according to financial contribution. In other words, the wealthiest States count in a disproportionate way while those financially more vulnerable are even more marginalised. It is an evident overcoming of the principle of political equality. In order to be eligible, a Member State has to accept a number of conditionalities that are supposed to ensure that the State won't spend the supplied credit in excessive or unnecessary public expenditures. The conditionalities attached to the memoranda are a clear demonstration of the extractive power of a debt-based political economy: credit is provided at the condition of restructuring the Member States' welfare systems.

A key element that grants Euro governance predominance and displaces the budgetary sovereignty of States is the coupling between the common currency and the necessity, for Member States, to finance their public debt directly through financial markets. On the one hand, the separation between treasury and central banks and the opening up of sovereign financing to global financial markets, forces Euro Member States to abide to market requirements (or what is presented as desirable and convenient from the perspective of market rationality) if they want to issue their bonds successfully. On the one hand, the common currency works as a straightjacket for monetary leverage applied to each Member State, empowering, in light of the separation between central bank and treasury, the European Central Bank as a key institutional actor in determining access to credit lines for States and their banking systems. It should be remembered, to avoid any misunderstanding at this point, that the ECB is not the only institution responsible for granting access to credit to legal and physical persons. In reality, the whole banking system is responsible for that and its function is therefore crucial for the reproduction of the crucial division of labour within society.[47] Significantly, the Euro as a currency does not represent only a unit of account, but its legal tender consolidates a creditor–debtor relation. This is why the loss of monetary sovereignty through subjection to financial markets (which, note, was already in place *before* the entry into force of the Euro) and delegation to the ECB of key monetary policies imply an entrenchment of the established conditions of creditors and debtors. It is important to insist on this point. Issuing currency (in multiple forms, from coining to issuing bonds through private banks) within the context of the European Monetary Union consolidates a relation of debt that is then discounted by forcing Member States to intervene upon their public finances. As a consequence, social rights become the main target of the process of State transformation. In this way, a constitutional drive is established, with the aid of established State structures, in order to bend social rights to the logic of efficiency and competitiveness.[48]

We will not press further the analysis of the *deconstituent* effect of the new economic governance. It is perhaps an indication of how desperate the effort to shore up what is becoming the European *mis*-adventure, that the erratic and largely mistaken efforts of the European Court to lend legitimacy to these usurpations has attracted the praise of academic commentators. Take the cases (*OMT* and *Thomas Pringle*,[49] heard by the Court of Justice of the European Union (CJEU) in 2012) decided by the CJEU in clear contravention of what the Treaty on the Functioning of the European Union (TFEU) (in Art 125) establishes with clarity as the no-bail-out clause, the absolute prohibition of debt-financing between Member States. In the Irish case of *Pringle,* the court argued that conditionalities within the ESM secure the prime purpose of price stability within the EMU in ensuring that debtor Member States will be subject to market discipline in maintaining sound budgetary policy. Paul Craig, one of the most influential voices in the academy, concurs with the decisions on the grounds that 'economic reality renders the neat juncture between purpose and interpretation of Art 125 a great deal more tenuous'.[50] 'The blend of text, background purpose and teleology that constitutes the very essence of legal reasoning',[51] is what *Pringle* exhibits for him. Other scholars are lending their weight to this line of argument so that the dominant position, as insightfully argued by Michelle Everson in a recent paper,[52] praises the efforts of the CJEU to maintain monetary stability. The European common interest, the endorsement of which becomes a requirement for assistance, is tied to the principle of sound fiscal policy as measured on the axis of stability, discipline and austerity.

The functionalist reading of this Euro-securing decision harnesses the European constitutional imaginary to the leitmotif of conditionality against current and future political democratic alternatives. 'A sadly diminished legal discourse',[53] is how Everson puts it, one that surrenders the constitutional imaginary to the faits accomplis of economic science. Here is her comment:

> *Pringle* fails on all counts. In a Europe of uproar and revolt against austerity regimes, as well as of counterpart fiscal trepidation, or popular unwillingness to commit to a European community of solidaristic fate, the *fait accompli* judgement, expounded without reference to social context, and unfolded only within the technical minutiae of a sadly diminished European legal discourse forecloses potential for proper evolution of a socially-responsive European constitutional tradition. At the same time, in all of its manic vacillation between formalism, literalism, teleological referencing and purposive re-statement of that referencing, the judgment similarly fails to connect with any form of constitutional-legal tradition, leaving itself open to the accusation of legal trickery in the politicised service of a brute functionalist rescue of the Euro.[54]

IV

We return to social rights in the wake of the 'brute functionalist rescue of the Euro'. We have looked at how the logic of Euro governance – in terms of both political expedience and judicial law-making – has bent social rights to the logic of efficiency and competitiveness. We looked at the key tenets of new governance as *an order of policing*, extending forms of managerial legal thinking that are hurriedly enacted to shore up stability to the detriment of social rights. We will end with a comment on that modality and that effect. We will look at how in the modality of ad hoc responsiveness and under the sign of emergency, urgency and necessity are treated as interchangeable.[55]

Under the sign of 'exceptionality' a certain equivocation sets in between urgency on the one hand and necessity on the other. These are very different concepts and their mutual collapse serves nothing except political expediency. Urgency refers to the need to take decisions outside of the normal timeframes and procedural requirements that secure adequate deliberation. Necessity, on the other hand, refers to the absence of alternatives: what is 'necessary' visits us with the compulsion of a natural disaster; to carve out alternatives – to project other options – becomes the task of political rationality. In fact, it would not be an exaggeration to say that political reflexivity coincides with the resistance to false necessity. Naturally, when we refer to the closure and the undercutting of reflexivity we are talking about the 'philosophy' of austerity.

What happens when urgency and necessity collapse into each other around the notion of exceptionality? For one thing, the horizon of political decision-making recedes. The need to act at once to avoid calamity (urgency) meets the diminishing or elimination of options (necessity); the circumvention of democratic deliberation becomes the way in which emergency is managed. Democratic deliberation involves learning processes, and requires the presence of differences, the negotiation of those differences and the mutual adjustment of expectations: it requires *time*. Time is what we can no longer afford.

Look at how the discourses of the economic, the political and the juridical compete over and around the organisation of time, and how, in effect, the *speed* of decision-making comes to occupy the centre of ideological battle, assuming that it is seen as a battle at all. The political demand for the democratic organisation of the economy is pitted against the endless acceleration and rapidity of free markets so that it is forever presented as outmoded, outmanoeuvred by a different temporality that has no time for mutual learning processes and that has instead moved beyond a critical point of de-synchronisation. As a result, the public, political or common interest can only be conceptualised as fiscal salvation, and that is precisely how the courts see it. How surprising that courts couch their reasons in the apocalyptic language of fiscal salvation, understood predominantly against the acceleration, promiscuity and unpredictability of markets as stability. The constitutional coupling between the political and the legal has surrendered to a new constellation where both become harnessed to the non-negotiable outcomes of market veridiction.

Few have written so intelligently about the *outpacing* of democracy by the economy as Hartmut Rosa.[56] The thrust of his critique of dialogic forms of democratic theory is that they neglect the temporal preconditions of democracy and therefore fail to grasp the current crisis of democratic self-determination under conditions of globalisation. Rosa's main argument is that while the 'acceleration' of society was at first enabling of democratisation, beyond a certain critical threshold, a 'speed-frame' of social change, as he calls it, the speed of socio-economic development, threatens the proper functioning of democracy. He says:

> [T]he speed of change, or the dynamics of society, has to be slow enough for democratic and deliberative political processes of will formation and decision-making to actually be effective, or for politics to actually control (or steer) social developments and set the pace. Beyond a certain temporal threshold, the dynamic forces of society are too strong for democratic political self-determination, . . . collective will-formation, deliberation and action.[57]

Society's *self-propelling* forward thus occurs despite any form of steering or even an adequate sense of self that would have required time, embeddedness and the unfolding of layers of reflection.

If such are the temporal preconditions of democracy, then we can see how the subjection of societal processes to economic processes involves a constitutive loss of political control. What is lost is the possibility of thinking the economy politically and the European Union as a political society of our making.[58] The problem, as is so often the case where battles are won by default, is in the difficulty of discerning and establishing the battle lines. The loss of language becomes clear in the constitutionalisation of austerity. With each decision is renewed the judicial resort to the standard reference of price stability and with it the denial of the politically integrative nature of the European project. The givens of market integration prevent any politically mediated evolution of the European polity that remains neither adapted nor adaptable to the variable steering demands of the core and the periphery of the Eurozone. If the very idea of constitutionalism involved, in its conception and development, a co-evolution of the political and the economic around the organizing concepts of the juridical, a sadly diminished European constitutional discourse under the sign of emergency now forecloses the potential for a responsive constitutional sensibility. And with this we return to where we started: emergency comes to stand for the time frame within which society must be reproduced and necessity becomes the other side of the coin, since any form of resisting that necessity has come undone under the temporal dimension and the pace of market choices.

V

It is time to take stock and come to a conclusion. We will do it by going back to the starting point in order to illustrate how the material dimension of social rights has been subjected to 'government by numbers'[59] under the aegis of austerity. The main objective of the new European Economic Governance is to close down the space opened by social rights for the political articulation of social conflicts and this has been realised by collapsing that space into market thinking. The *Loi travail* is a perfect illustration of the effects produced by the instrumental use of the web of rules cast by the economic governance over social rights across Europe. In fact, labour and pensions have been especially affected by the European measures adopted after the crisis. And this applies not only to France. It is possible to observe a wave of 'structural reforms' of labour markets across the Euro-zone as part of a deal for obtaining flexibility over deficits and public debts.[60] The aim in this case is to constrain (if not simply to eradicate) key rights attached to labour protection (strike and bargaining are the most targeted). Moreover, one can observe that labour and pension reforms are often offered by national governments in exchange for more flexibility on public deficit and debt. In fact, the approval of the controversial *Loi travail* through emergency means has been obtained as a consequence of European pressure, coming in particular from the Commission and the Council.[61] France has been under strict scrutiny since the inception of the new rules of Euro governance because its deficit has exceeded the ratio of 3% between annual deficit and GDP since 2009. While the jury is still out on its concrete impact, it is clear that the European Semester,[62] in conjunction with the sanctions introduced by the Two-packs, have produced a serious 'nudging' effect on the French Government.[63] The logic behind this type of governance is evident: under the preventive arm of the Macroeconomic Imbalance Procedure (MIP) and the terms of the Stability and Growth Pact (SGP), a Member State faces severe financial sanctions by the Council if it violates fiscal rules or presents excessive macroeconomic imbalances.[64] This is not the place to discuss whether the threat of these sanctions makes what was supposed to be soft law into (extremely) hard law.[65] For the purposes of this chapter, it will suffice to say that the French example shows how the mix of austerity, fiscal discipline, labour marketisation and the rhetoric of emergency and necessity has bent French labour policies towards closing down the space originally opened up by the recognition of the materiality of social rights. In a crucial sense the French case represents a classic instantiation of the current political economy of European social rights.

Notes

1 See, e.g., Mark Tushnet, *Weak Courts, Strong Rights* (Princeton University Press, 2008); Katherine G Young, *Constituting Economic and Social Rights* (Oxford University Press, 2012); Jeff King, *Judging Social Rights* (Cambridge University Press, 2012); K Klare and L Williams (eds), *Social and Economic Rights in Theory and Practice* (Routledge, 2015).

2 Alain Supiot, *L'esprit de Philadelphie: la justice sociale face au marché total* (PUF, 2010) 45.

3 Draghi hinted at the end of the European social model during a press conference at the ECB on 4 April 2012. See the transcript of the press conference here: www.ecb.europa.eu/press/pressconf/2012/html/is120404.en.html (last accessed 3 March 2017).

4 Article 49.3 of the French Constitution stipulates the emergency procedure that allows the government to pass a Bill into law *without a vote*, unless a majority of deputies pass a motion of non-confidence, thus forcing the prime minister to resign.

5 Notably, Spain and Italy adopted deeply impactful reforms of their labour markets respectively in 2012 and 2014.

6 The Labour Act provides that collective agreements must be made by majority agreement, i.e. approved by trade unions representing at least 50% of the recorded vote (currently, only 30% is needed but trade unions representing 50% of the recorded vote can oppose a minority agreement and specific agreements like the employment continuity agreement need to be signed by a majority of trade unions).

7 This decentralisation of collective bargaining (Article 2 of the Bill) is at the heart of the debates and of the contestations. It proposes a 'new' articulation of norms, a fundamental change in the construction of labour law in which company-wide collective bargaining could prevail over industry-wide collective agreements (which is still an important level of collective bargaining in France), and over the law, even in cases where these decentralised agreements result in less protection for employees. In fact, what is really new, is that the exception (the possibility for collective agreement at company level to deviate from the law or from the sectoral level) is becoming the rule.

8 For a reconstruction of this debate, and also as general introductions to the topic, see Tom Campbell, *Rights: An Introduction* (Routledge, 2006).

9 Joseph Raz, *Ethics in the Public Domain* (Clarendon, 1994) 321.
10 Joseph Raz, *Morality of Freedom* (Clarendon, 1986) Ch. 13.
11 Fernando Atria, 'Social Rights, Social Contract, and Socialism' (2015) 24(2) *Social and Legal Studies* 598.
12 Ibid 602.
13 Ibid 605.
14 For a powerful reconstruction based on the same view, see Wolfgang Streeck, *Buying Time* (Verso, 2014).
15 Our intervention is limited to the European Union and in particular to the Eurozone. But the enforcement of social rights on an individual basis is a common feature in many contemporary constitutional orders. See, e.g., David Bilchitz, *Poverty and Fundamental Rights: The Justification and Enforcement in Socio-Economic Rights* (Oxford University Press, 2007). There is a growing literature enquiring precisely into the potential of social rights adjudication to bring about social change, in particular in South America: Roberto Gargarella (ed.), *Courts and Social Transformation in New Democracies: An Institutional Voice for the Poor?* (Routledge, 2006); Varun Gauri and Daniel Brinks (eds), *Courting Social Justice: Judicial Enforcement of Social and Economic Rights in the Developing Countries* (Cambridge University Press, 2010).
16 Esping-Andersen's important work remains the key point of reference here: see Gøsta Esping-Anderson, *The Three Worlds of Welfare Capitalism* (Polity Press, 1990).
17 For a succinct but effective account see Tony Judt, *Ill Fares the Land* (Penguin, 2009) Ch. 3.
18 Claus Offe, *Contradictions of the Welfare State* (MIT Press, 1984).
19 Streeck, above n 14; Fritz W Scharpf, 'After the Crash: A Perspective on Multilevel European Democracy' (2015) 21(3) *European Law Journal* 384.
20 Alain Supiot, *Homo Juridicus* (Verso, 2007) 102–4. For an application of this idea to EU law making, see M Dani, 'Rehabilitating Social Conflicts in European Public Law' (2012) 18 *European Law Journal* 621.
21 For one of the best accounts of this 'division of labour' see S Giubboni, *Social Rights and Markets* (Cambridge University Press, 2005).
22 For the 'shift' in EU Law thinking in this direction, see Catherine Barnard, *EU Employment Law* (Oxford University Press, 4th edn, 2012).
23 Daniel K Tarullo, 'Law and Governance in the Global Economy' (1999) 21 *American Society of International Law* 106. It should be added that in the stalemate due to the political situation, the European Court of Justice played an aggressive role in expanding market integration. A key decision, *Cassis de Dijon*, was delivered by the court precisely at the end of the 1970s: *Rewe-Zentral AG v Bundesmonopolverwaltung für Branntwein* (European Court of Justice, C-120/78, 20 February 1979).
24 Costas Lapavitsas, *Profiting without Producing* (Verso, 2010).
25 The Board of the European Central Bank (ECB) has identified the level of a healthy inflation at 2%.
26 A key passage here is the detachment of the Central Bank from national government because Member States cannot self-finance themselves any longer.
27 Cf Mark Blyth, *Austerity* (Oxford University Press, 2013).
28 Antonio Negri, 'On the Constitution and Financial Capital' (2015) 32 *Theory, Culture and Society* 35.
29 Cf, the analyses offered in chs 2-6 in this volume.
30 The work of the 'new intergovernmentalists' is insightful on this point: cf Chris Bickerton, *European Integration* (Oxford University Press, 2012); Uwe Puetter, *The European Council and the Council: New Intergovernmentalism and Institutional*

Change (Oxford University Press, 2014); C J Bickerton, D Hodson and U Puetter (eds), *New Intergovernmentalism* (Oxford University Press, 2015).

31 Chris Thornhill has put forward a powerful argument for explaining the rise of the modern State as a moment in the functional differentiation of modern society that allows to de-patrimonialise a huge amount of resources through the constitution of public institutions: Chris Thornhill, *A Sociology of Constitutions* (Cambridge University Press, 2011) 8–10. The thesis advanced in this chapter is that the condition of Member Statehood signals a new process of re-patrimonialisation through the financial discipline imposed upon public debts.

32 See the definition given by Bickerton, above n 30, 10–12.

33 A clarification is necessary at this point. We do not subscribe to the view that debt is immanent to the formation of human societies, an assumption that is taken almost for granted by Graeber: see David Graeber, *Debt* (Melville Publishing, 2011). The transformation of social cooperation and wealth into debt is a political operation.

34 Negri, above n 28, 27–8.

35 N Poulantzas, 'Internationalization of Capitalist Relations and the Nation-State' in James Martin (ed.), *The Poulantzas Reader* (Verso, 2008) 242.

36 Ibid 244. According to Poulantzas, attempts at regional cooperation of the kind like the EEC were therefore as much expressions of continued US hegemony as they were challenges to it. Cafruny and Ryner build on Poulantzas' argument their thesis that European monetary union is not a challenge to US hegemony so much as a confirmation of it. Europe's attempts at challenging US power with the introduction of the Euro are read by Cafruny and Ryner as self-limited strategies, meaning that they deepen the very bonds they were set out to break: see Alan W Cafruny and J Magnus Ryner, *Europe at Bay* (Lynne Rienner Pub, 2007).

37 J H H Weiler, 'In Defence of the Status Quo: Europe's Constitutional Sonderweg' in J H H Weiler and Marlene Wind (eds), *European Constitutionalism beyond the State* (Cambridge University Press, 2003) 7.

38 On the centrality of total market rationality for the contemporary European constitutional order, see E Christodoulidis, 'The European Court of Justice and Total Market Thinking' (2014) 14(10) *German Law Journal* 2005.

39 On the governing function driven by economic statistics see Alain Supiot, *La gouvernance par les nombres* (PUF, 2015).

40 But, for a different take, cf the enquiry into the possible spaces for a re-coupling attempted by Giubboni, Ch. 13 in this volume.

41 T H Marshall, *Citizenship and Social Class* (Cambridge University Press, 1950).

42 Negri, above n 28.

43 Cf the use of Schmitt made by Maurizio Lazzarato, *Governing by Debt* (MIT Press, 2014) 85–9.

44 Francesco Bilancia rightly notes that this is part of a process of juridification of the economic governance of the Euro-zone: see Ch. 12 in this volume.

45 Federico Fabbrini, *European Economic Governance* (Oxford University Press, 2016) 88–90.

46 The European Stability Mechanism was preceded by a transitional measure called The European Financial Stability Mechanism.

47 See Nigel Dodd, *The Social Life of Money* (Princeton University Press, 2014).

48 Cf, the reconstruction of the European Union material constitution put forward by Michael Wilkinson, 'Political Constitutionalism and the European Union' (2013) 76(2) *Modern Law Review* 191.

49 *Gauweiler and Others* (European Court of Justice, C-62/14, 16 June 2015); *Thomas Pringle v Government of Ireland, Ireland and the Attorney General* (European Court of Justice, C-370/12, 27 November 2012).

50 Paul Craig, 'Pringle: Legal Reasoning, Text, Purpose and Teleology' (2013) 20 *Maastricht Journal of Law* 1, 9.
51 Ibid.
52 Michelle Everson, 'An Exercise in Legal Honesty: Rewriting the European Court of Justice and the *Bundesverfassungsgericht*' (2015) 21(4) *European Law Journal* 474.
53 Ibid 482.
54 Ibid.
55 For an analysis of the differences between emergency and exception, see Mariano Croce and Andrea Salvatore, 'After Exception' (2016) 29(3) *Ratio Juris* 410.
56 Hartmut Rosa, 'The Speed of Global Flows and the Pace of Democratic Politics' (2005) 27(4) *New Political Science* 445; cf William E Scheuermann, *Liberal Democracy and the Social Acceleration of Time* (John Hopkins University Press, 2004).
57 Hartmut Rosa, 'The Speed of Global Flows and the Pace of Democratic Politics' (2005) 27(4) *New Political Science* 445 at 450.
58 This is one of the key insights offered by the works by Alexander Somek: see Alexander Somek *Individualism* (Oxford University Press, 2008); Alexander Somek, *The Cosmopolitan Constitution* (Oxford University Press, 2014).
59 See Supiot, above n 39.
60 See European Commission, *Labour Market Reforms Database* <https://webgate.ec.europa.eu/labref/public/>, which contains all labour reforms adopted since 2000.
61 See, e.g., the recommendations issued by the Council in 2013: *Council Recommendation with a View to Bringing an End to the Situation of an Excessive Government Deficit in France*, SWD (2013) 384, 29 May 2013 <http://ec.europa.eu/economy_finance/economic_governance/sgp/pdf/30_edps/126-07_commission/2013-05-29_fr_126-7_commission_en.pdf>.
62 For a first assessment of the European Semester see the forthcoming 2017 special of the *Journal of European Public Policy* edited by Jonathan Zeitlin. For an analysis of the legal bindingness of the European Semester and in particular of the Country Specific Recommendations (CSRs) see Claudia Wutscher, 'Coordination by Coercion: On the Legal Status of European Semester Instruments' (copy on file with author).
63 For an effective reconstruction of the role of EU institutions in the approval of the *Loi travail 2016* (Fr), see Corporate Europe Observatory, 'How the EU Pushed France to Reforms of Labour Law' (27 June 2016) <http://corporateeurope.org/eu-crisis/2016/06/how-eu-pushed-france-reforms-labour-law>.
64 Alexandre De Streel, 'The Confusion of Tasks in the Decision-Making Process of the European Economic Governance' in F Fabbrini and H Somsen (eds), *Which Form of Government for the European Union and the Eurozone?* (Hart, 2015) 79.
65 For a recent analysis, see Fabien Terpan, 'Soft Law in the EU: The Changing Nature of EU Law' (2015) 21 *European Law Journal* 68.

Chapter 12

Economic crisis and territorial asymmetrical effects on the guarantee of social rights within the European Economic and Monetary Union (EMU)

Francesco Bilancia

1. Introduction

Two preliminary points of clarification are required in relation to the analysis of this chapter. First, although its context is the whole European Common Market and constitutional system, it deals essentially with problems within the Euro system. Second, although not written by an economist, the analysis is based on an 'economically informed'[1] point of view. Thus, a complex approach will be used, one that tries to place constitutional law alongside economic and financial questions, given that they have recently started to change the legal foundations of the Welfare State. The main topics at stake are the common currency (Euro) and monetary policies, considered both in their own right and as they relate to democracy and the guarantee of social rights.

Some concepts, despite being drawn from a common language, have different meanings and functions when used respectively in law and economics. This immediately leads us to a methodological issue: what is the best approach for understanding fundamental aspects of the Euro crisis and their implications for European and national constitutional systems, for social rights guarantees especially? The approach adopted in this chapter is that of a 'legal analysis'[2] of economic and financial questions within the Euro crisis. The aim is to interpret the connections between legal rules and economic facts both at an institutional level and in relation to the functioning of the Single Market. On the one hand, we need to understand the actual meaning, the correct interpretation of European legal rules dealing with these subjects; on the other, we must understand the influence of material economic events on the constitutional system[3] and its legal rules.

Such an approach is all the more important now that, following monetary integration under the Treaty of Maastricht of 1992, economic policies within the European legal system have become more rule-bound. Indeed, such policies – both monetary and economic – have recently become increasingly *juridified*[4] in the wake of the financial and sovereign debt crisis that began in 2008. This has considerably reduced the opportunities for member states to manage their own social and economic issues by way of their discretionary political powers.[5] As a consequence of these institutional and legal constraints, national governments are no longer in practice permitted to deal with social and economic questions in isolation, bound as they are by what we will now investigate and explain. The fundamental point of this chapter, then, is to argue that member states in conditions of financial instability and budget deficit – at least within the Eurozone – have lost any power to combat regressive social policy as 'suggested' by European institutions.

II. On Welfare State legitimacy: some remarks

The questions to be addressed here are how much legitimacy, accountability and transparency of economic policies remain following the economic crisis, and the extent to which these questions now depend on a different constituency from democracy. These questions are especially pertinent, it is suggested, with respect to distributional justice within constitutional systems that are inspired by principles of the Welfare State, such as Italy.

The argument is not simply that finance has replaced democracy. Rather, the European institutional system as a whole bears responsibility. The European financial legal framework, the economic system, the Common Market rules and financial systems are all now working together to determine the very background and settings of any decisions regarding State regulation or economic management by national governments.

We must investigate the ways in which these materials and legal relations work together within the Euro system, looking for its legal faults and substantive drawbacks. This will allow us to adopt a critical stance towards the European financial legal framework, assuming a normative, constitutionally oriented approach to the interpretation of the European legal system.

By 'European legal system' is meant the Treaties from which a legal theory can be deduced for constructing the constitutional dimension[5] of the EU and its member states, founded on justice and equality among member states. Following the general decline of constitutional scrutiny by national parliaments, this should be an important objective for legal scholars within Europe.

III. The macroeconomic dimension of the so-called 'European economic constitution'

The main question here – indeed, the starting point of this analysis – concerns monetary policies.[7] The dimension of the problem is a very specific one: currency and financial stability after the financial crisis within a system where monetary policies are divided from economic and social policies along States' borders.

To understand the real core of the question we have to use a very specific approach to analyse the European economic constitution – at least as it relates to the Eurozone. Public law scholars traditionally speak about economic constitutionalism – or public regulation – in a microeconomic sense. This sense is used when discussing regulation, competition, market, free-movement, economic liberties and so on. But after the entry into force of the Maastricht Treaty, a new concept must be developed to understand how the legal system interferes in the (Eurozone) economic system: a 'constitution of macroeconomics', dealing with aggregate economic objectives.[8] K. Tuori and K. Tuori, for instance, speak of the Eurozone crisis as one of the Maastricht economic constitution, because this crisis has highlighted the macroeconomic side of the European economic constitution.[9] This is self-evident, indeed, in the way we speak about anti-inflationary monetary policy, the currency's stability, exchange-rate fluctuations, cyclical or anti-cyclical policies, economic and financial imbalances, price stability and so on.

Within the Common Market, the key issue is the separation of responsibilities with regard to monetary, fiscal and macroeconomic policies. No stable harmony has yet been realised between the EU and member states' positions. The Euro system has left the responsibility for issues of financial stability to member states, while monetary policy is reserved to the European Central Bank (ECB). So, within the Euro system the reaction to country-specific economic shocks is a matter for state fiscal and economic policy. The so-called 'fiscal adjustments' are now completely dependent on States' policy-making. Central Bank intervention, in turn, is strictly bound by the no-bail-out clause, precluding shared liability for national debts across member states.[10]

So, in order to manage national government deficits and debt and promote financial stability, member states can only use traditional counter-cyclical policies to alter revenues and expenditures, including welfare spending. Monetary instruments are banned. Within the Single Market, without monetary aid by the Central Bank, employment, national income, rate of growth, gross domestic product (GDP) and inflation are now dependent on only a limited number of levers.

National adjusting measures are primarily achieved via labour mobility and flexibility within the Common Labour and Goods Market. Where fiscal and financial imbalances among member states are at stake, to improve exporting performance and reduce the weight of importation on national financial systems, policies are then adopted to reduce salaries and the cost of workers' rights. This leads to a shrinking of the cost of the production of goods and services, which in turn makes it possible to fix cross-border imbalance of payments. But this then leads to a redistribution of the economic targets of the member states, where, however, a European common economic policy is still lacking. In order to manage the price of goods and services to strengthen national competitiveness within the Single Market, member states further reduce labour costs by way of salary cuts and casualisation. This is the only way to face, on the one hand, the structural differences between the financial markets of member states and, on the other, the still very significant asymmetries between common European monetary policy and national fiscal policies, although they are now strongly intertwined. As we are going to see below, financial market asymmetries are also relevant as regards the determination of the performance of each national economic system: measures of monetary policy adopted by the European Central Bank produce different effects on national financial systems depending upon the deficit and debt situation within any of them.

At the same time, the said attempts by the single member states to adjust the system via wage flexibility and inter-state fiscal transfer could affect the Common Market as a whole, further threatening the stability of the Eurozone. This is why any financial and fiscal adjustment is of great significance for intra-market trade. In fact, the different forms of financial adjustment adopted by various member states, as any monetary policy decision taken by the ECB, closely match the separation between borrower countries and saver/lender countries. Such different forms also determine different fiscal transfers among member states, as well as measures of national social policy financed by taxes that are levered according to the economic cycle. In other words, when the ECB decides to expand money supply through the system, the effect of such a policy of 'monetary transmission' is good for debtors because monetary inflation reduces the weight of their debts. At the same time, it is bad for creditors. Hence, in a way it amounts to an asymmetrical financial assistance in favour of debtors. Indeed, the so-called Outright Monetary Transactions (OMT) programme of the ECB – that is to say the decision to implement extraordinary money supply measures in order to reduce the weight of public debt interest rates of single states within the Euro system – prompted the German Federal Constitutional Court to raise[11] a preliminary reference to the European Court of Justice (ECJ).[12] Along the same lines, the German Federal Constitutional Court (CC) could do the same in reaction to the Quantitative Easing (QE) programme of the ECB,[13] that is, the decision to increase the *quantity* of money within the financial system through low-cost lending in favour of the banking system.

Outside the Eurozone, improving liquidity in order to increase market confidence in financial stability is a completely different matter. There, we find considerable room for discretionary and flexible national policy-making,[14] including use of the budget.[15] By way of contrast, inside the Eurozone, member states are bound by strict legal (even constitutional) constraints on economic decision-making, particularly after the sovereign debt crisis. This is especially the case in the form of budgetary constraints, as in the Italian Constitution after an important reform in 2012.[16]

As Tony Prosser puts it, these new constitutional provisions may lead to even more imbalances among member states within the Eurozone Single Market: 'This is one of the greatest inconsistencies of the Euro as a whole.'[17] It also leads to an asymmetric reduction of public expenditure in order to control the different levels of public deficit and debt in various states. To achieve value for money, the different States' policies are likely to cause, among other inconsistencies, asymmetric adjustments on levels of guarantees of social rights, breaking constitutional solidarity within the EU. Although my analysis is more concerned with building a normative argument than making an empirical claim, there is already enough evidence that deficit countries are getting worse off in terms of social welfare protections than the surplus ones. This can be deduced, for example, by looking at the figures relating to social expenditure in the EU[18] and comparing, for example, Italy and Spain, on the one hand, with Germany, on the other. At first glance, very small annual rates of change have occurred, but one has to be especially cautious in interpreting such data as they measure social expenditure relative to GDP. The latter has, significantly, fallen in some countries much more than in others after the financial crisis (see Figure 12.1). This means that in the face of the downsizing of GDP, social expenditure in countries where economic growth was poor has in fact dwindled. This is also reflected in the figures regarding social indicators deterioration, and in comparative scores regarding social inclusion and poverty.[19]

This leads us to the core issue: social rights, caught in this new normative dimension that obliges States to alter the guarantees of social rights while reforming their financial and budgetary system, are becoming more of a macroeconomic systemic question than an individual, personal one. The need to find a new harmony between monetary, fiscal and macroeconomic policies reduces individual social rights and their economic guarantees to a systemic macroeconomic stability question.

Indeed, no longer can we conceive of the problem as simply one of social rights being financially driven, conditional on the availability of public resources,[20] as it is anyway. Rather, social rights are now even losing their fundamental character as individual rights. Labour mobility and wage flexibility within Common Labour and Goods Markets are now becoming the crux of the matter for European economic policies, reallocating financial balance targets among member states. Within a monetary area where member states have very different financial market structures and values, this produces significant asymmetries between *common* European monetary policies and *national* economic and fiscal policies, that is, important inequalities, as will now be explained further.

IV. European monetary policy versus national economic and fiscal policies: asymmetries among Eurozone states

The analysis above sets out what is meant by the macroeconomic dimension of the European 'constitutional' system. Indeed, we may frame it as European 'constitutional law', but only if we adopted a critical perspective based on a series of theoretical assumptions that we do not have room to address here.[21]

By managing public budgets towards deficit and debt stability, in a way that produces measurable macroeconomic effects, the policies of the financial crisis opted for spending cuts. This approach was pursued without much consideration of the constitutional tensions regarding social rights. The economic responsibilities that fell to individual States (reduction of public borrowing, the elimination of structural current deficits, the reduction of public sector debt) have led to serious inequalities among different member states.

Real GDP growth rate - volume

Percentage change on previous year

geo / time	2004	2005	2006	2007	2008	2009	2010	2011	2012	2013	2014	2015
EU (28 countries)	2.5	2.1	3.3	3.1	0.5	–4.4	2.1	1.8	–0.5	0.2	1.4	2
EU (27 countries)	:	:	:	:	:	:	:	:	:	:	:	:
Euro area (changing composition)	2.2	1.6	3.2	3	0.5	–4.5	2.1	1.6	–0.9	–0.3	0.9	1.7
Euro area (19 countries)	2.3	1.7	3.2	3.1	0.5	–4.5	2.1	1.6	–0.9	–0.3	0.9	1.7
Euro area (18 countries)	2.3	1.7	3.2	3	0.5	–4.5	2.1	1.6	–0.9	–0.3	0.9	1.7
Euro area (17 countries)	:	:	:	:	:	:	:	:	:	:	:	:
Belgium	3.6	2.1	2.5	3.4	0.7	–2.3	2.7	1.8	0.2	0	1.3	1.4
Bulgaria	6.6	7.2	6.8	7.7	5.6	–4.2	0.1	1.6	0.2	1.3	1.5	3
Czech Republic	4.9	6.4	6.9	5.5	2.7	–4.8	2.3	2	–0.8	–0.5	2.7	4.5
Denmark	2.6	2.4	3.8	0.8	–0.7	–5.1	1.6	1.2	–0.1	–0.2	1.3	1
Germany	1.2	0.7	3.7	3.3	1.1	–5.6	4.1	3.7	0.4	0.3	1.6	1.7
Estonia	6.3	9.4	10.3	7.7	–5.4	–14.7	2.5	7.6	5.2	1.6	2.9	1.1
Ireland	4.4	6.3	6.3	5.5	–2.2	–5.6	0.4	2.6	0.2	1.4	5.2	7.8
Greece	5.1	0.6	5.7	3.3	–0.5	–4.3	–5.5	–9.1 (p)	–7.3(p)	–3.2(p)	0.7(p)	–02(p)
Spain	3.2	3.7	4 2	3.8	1.1	–3.6	0	–1	–2.6(p)	–1.7(p)	1.4(p)	3,2(p)
France	2.8	1.6	2.4	2.4	0.2	–2.9	2	2.1	0.2	0.6	0.6(p)	1.3(p)
Croatia	4.1	4.2	4.8	5.2	2.1	–7.4	–1.7	–0.3	–2.2	–1.1	–0.4	1.6
Italy	1.6	0.9	2	1.5	1.1	5.5	1.7	0.6	–2.8	–1.7	–0.3	0.8
Cyprus	4.6	3.9	4.5	4.9	3.7	–2	1.4	0.4	–2.4	–5.9	–2.5(p)	1.6(p)
Latvia	8.3	10.7	11.9	10	–3.6	–14.3	–3.8	6.2	4	3	2.4	2.7
Lithuania	6.6	7.7	7.4	11.1	2.6	–14.8	1.6	6	3.8	3.5	3	1.6
Luxembourg	4.4	3.2	5.1	8.4	–0.8	–5.4	5.7	2.6	–0.8	4.3	4.1	4.8
Hungary	4.9	4.4	3.8	0.4	0.8	–6.6	0.7	1.8	–1.7	1.9	3.7	2.9
Malta	04	3.8	1.8	4	3.3	–2.5	35	1.9	2.9	4.3	3.5	64

Netherlands	2	2.2	3.5	3.7	1.7	–3.8	1.4	1.7	–1.1	–0.2	1.4	2 (p)
Austria	2.7	2.1	3.4	3.6	1.5	–3.8	1.9	2.8	0.8	0.3	0.4	0.9
Poland	5.1	3.5	6.2	7	4.2	2.8	3.6	5	1.6	1.3	3.3	3.6
Portugal	1.8	0.8	1.6	2.5	0.2	–3	1.9	–1.8	–4	–1.1	0.9(e)	1.5(e)
Romania	8.4	4.2	8.1	6.9	8.5	–7.1	–0.8	1.1	0.6	3.5	3(p)	3.8(p)
Slovenia	4.4	4	5.7	6.9	3.3	–7.8	1.2	16	–2.7	–1.1	3	2.9
Slovakia	5.3	6.4	8.5	10.8	5.7	–5.5	5.1	2.8	1.5	1.4	2.5	3.6
Finland	3.9	2.8	4.1	5.2	0.7	–8.3	3	2.6	–1.4	–0.8	–0.7	0.5
Sweden	4.3	2.8	4.7	3.4	–0.6	–5.2	6	2.7	–0.3	1.2	2.3	4 2
United Kingdom	2.5	3	2.7	2.6	–0.5	–4 2	1.5	2	1.2	2.2	2.9	2.3
Iceland	8.2	6	4.2	9.5	1.5	–4.7	–3.6	2	1.2	4.4	2	4
Liechtenstein	:	:	:	:	:	:	:	:	:	:	:	:
Norway	4	2.6	2.4	2.9	0.4	–1.6	0.6	1	2.7	1	2.2	1.6
Switzerland	2.8	3	4	4.1	2.3	–2.1	3	1.8	1.1	1.8(p)	1.9(p)	:
Montenegro	:	:	:	:	:	:	:	:	–2.7	3.5	1.8	:
Former Yugoslav Republic of Macedonia, the	4.7	4.7	5.1	6.5	5.5	–0.4	3.4	2.3	–0.5	2.9	3.5(p)	3.7(e)
Albania	:	:	:	:	:	3.4	3.7	2.5	1.4	1.1	2(p)	:
Serbia	9	5.5	4.9	5.9	5.4	–3.1	0.6	1.4	–1	2.6	–1.8	0.7(p)
Turkey	:	:	:	:	:	:	:	:	:	:		:
Kosovo (under United Nations Security Council Resolution 1244/99)	9	:	:	:	:	3.6	3.3	4.4	2.8	3.4	1.2	:

:-not avaliable p-provisional e-estimated
Source or Data: Eurostat
Last update: 01.07.2016
Date of extraction: 02 Jul 2016 19:15:17 CEST
Hyperlink to the table: http://ec.europa.eu/eurostat/tgm/table.do?tab=table&init=1&plugin=1&language=en&pcode=tec00115
General Disclaimer of the EC website: http://ec.europa.eu/genifo/legal notices en.htm

Figure 12.1 Real GDP growth rate percentage change in EU, Euro Area and single member states.

Source - Eurostat, *General Statistics* (2 July 2016) http://ec.europa.eu/eurostat/tgm/table.do?tab=table&init=1&plugin=1&language=en&pcode=tec00115

National crisis policies were driven by two different goals: to reduce national budget imbalances, correcting their instability and to adjust financial and monetary imbalances among Eurozone states. In relation to the Eurozone states in *deficit*, both these goals were pursued through labour law reforms, reducing social and work-related rights guarantees, or more generally by managing the level of social welfare protections in order to reduce public expenditure.[22]

These goals represent the so-called macroeconomic balancing measures, both at national and EU level – within the Eurozone in the first instance, but looking also towards the Single Market as a whole. Market, financial and monetary stability are considered to have cross-border relevance. That is why social rights and labour law became so relevant for EU Law – as a balancing question among Member States. So, for instance, Ireland, Italy, Portugal, Spain and Greece had to deal with wage-freezing measures such as the suspension of wage rises (despite the fact that workers were already entitled to them following previous commitments), pay and pensions cuts, increased flexibility in labour-market rules, as well as considerable reductions in welfare spending.[23] Thus, the welfare question became a Common Market and a monetary question, as is also evident by thinking of the competitive position acquired by Germany within the Common Market thanks to the introduction of similar measures well before the financial crisis officially kicked off, compounded in the so-called Hartz reforms of 2005.[24]

Taking a step back, it is important to recall that within the common monetary area it is no longer possible to manage financial imbalances among member states through monetary exchange rate adjustments. Equally, the ECB, acting independently as the body with exclusive responsibility for common monetary policy, has to fulfil monetary and price stability against inflation as a fundamental duty, the treaties having neutralised monetary leverage as a tool of economic policy. The ECB can now use monetary policy tools to keep inflation risks at bay and to combat the lack of liquidity within the Euro system to let the payment mechanism work, but not to provide financial support for public expenditure.

Eurozone member states are no longer permitted to enjoy monetary expansion through either the creation of currency or the purchase of government bonds by national Central Banks. This restricts their options to raising more tax revenue or borrowing money from private financial markets and savers. Yet, in order to secure financial and monetary stability within the Eurozone, the European Treaties and fiscal pacts[25] have now prescribed significant limits to public debt and deficit – respectively 60% and 3% of the GDP.[26]

As was stressed above, the Euro system has proved to be characterised by important drawbacks and inconsistencies, especially as regards the considerable asymmetries in the transmission of the effects, through national financial systems, of monetary policy issued by the ECB.[27] Here, we are referring to the financial effects of this transmission on the different national financial and economic systems, which react in different ways depending on the structural situation of national budget stability, deficit and debt. For example, because monetary policy decisions affect interest rates, as already set out above, monetary expansion will produce redistributive consequences – from savers to borrowers or vice versa – via the interest-rate exposure instruments.[28] Thus, where inflation increases due to monetary expansion, a redistribution occurs from savers/lenders to borrowers on the debt market.

These kinds of asymmetric financial effects lead to a structural dysfunction between monetary policies and national budget situations within the Common Market, causing serious imbalances of the Common Capital Financial Market within the Eurozone. In this context, as described above, social measures and benefits and any other economic decisions taken by any Member State will produce important cross-border macroeconomic externalities, because of the systemic interrelations between currency and market, on the one hand, and national public budgets and sovereign debt, on the other.

This boosts, in turn, cross-border inequalities on social rights guarantees, labour law costs,[29] employment and unemployment rates, wealth redistribution through social measures and so forth. Where cross-border imbalances cannot be compensated by the quantitative movement of goods and currency, the only option for national economies in acting on real inflation is to work on price and salaries fluctuations, taxes, labour costs and productivity and social expenditure.[30] This is why these factors are now better regarded as tools for redressing financial and commercial imbalances among Eurozone Member States, rather than policies to satisfy individual social rights.

Here, as a result of the economic logic put down by the Euro institutions as country-specific normative commitments, a kind of paradox lies: States with a budget *surplus* – we could also say richer States with very low unemployment rates – should expand their social expenditure in order to increase domestic demand to redress Euro system cross-border imbalances;[31] while states with a budget *deficit* – with higher needs because of the economic crisis and higher rate of unemployment – should reduce their social expenditure.

This amounts to a new constitutional system of fiscal rules, one that has tangible implications for welfare restrictions. We can see these in the European Commission's year-by-year Overview of the 'Stability and Convergence Programmes' for each Eurozone country.[32] And, in my opinion, it would even be possible to investigate the correlation between Eurozone countries' 'wealth' and 'poverty' imbalances and the extent of their welfare spending cuts.[33]

All this is likely to bring about more inequalities among the citizens of Europe. These kinds of imbalances are normal and tolerable if just temporary – but they become critical and dangerous if stabilised.[34] One of the most important ambitions of the contemporary Euro crisis is simply to create *stable* commercial imbalances between importing and exporting countries, rather than redressing those imbalances.[35] This is often presented in terms of *necessary* social spending reforms within the well-known austerity framework.[36] However, the question remains of whether, when applying these new fiscal rules, it would be possible for States to cut *non-social welfare* expenditure with a view to minimising the impact of the 'compulsory austerity' on the poorest, thus giving rise to social rights protection, which is still a crucial constitutional commitment for the majority of member states.

The way that States come to terms with such commitments is often conceived as a matter of legislative discretion in allocating the available financial resources between social policy and other areas of public spending.[37] However, the fundamental point we are making here is that national institutions no longer have the rule-making power to determine that, instead of saving on social policy, they want to cut back on, for example, national security, the military, the cost of politics and so forth. As explained above, this is because the philosophy set forth in the European fiscal rules, especially as implemented by the recommendations of the European Commission, tends to blame traditional labour law and 'expensive' social rights for the unwelcome cross-border financial and economic consequences that we have depicted above.[38]

We may confirm this loss of autonomous national policy-making regarding the fundamental factors of the European social model, by looking at an apparently specific aspect of the governance of the Eurozone, which is the system of *clearing* of monetary transactions among Eurozone member states. Any financial transaction between two economic agents in the Single Market needs cross-border money transfer. Due to the huge number of these kinds of operations within the currency area (Euro), every time a corporation or a bank sends or receives money as payment for trading goods or services, an indefinite number of transactions need to be managed. In order to work out all these cross-border operations with the aim of guaranteeing the right settlement of the quantity of money circulating throughout the market, a specific set of rules and technical instructions has been laid down. They amount to the so-called 'clearing system' managed by a technical platform, named Target2,[39] within the ECB institutional framework. Its task is to compensate any imbalance and to ensure there is enough liquidity in any part of the Market. To do so, cross-border currency movements as a consequence of monetary and good transactions among private corporations operating in import/ export businesses are constantly monitored. This platform should be able to record both positive and negative assets in the balance sheet among national systems in order to compensate them in the medium term. In addition, the platform is expected to assure that any national financial system (banks first) is provided with the currency quantity that it needs if necessary, also by lowering cross-border transactions fees. Since the beginning of the 2008 financial crisis, however, a significant stable imbalance of quantitative currency movements in favour of exporting countries over importing countries has occurred, with the risk of jeopardising the functioning of the payment system itself (see Figure 12.2).

This led again to a consolidated financial imbalance between States in *surplus* and States in *deficit*, imbalances that are not absorbable in the medium term. This could have led to a quantitative bubble and a consequent paralysis of the cross-border payment system, had the ECB not intervened by injecting an important, albeit unconventional, amount of liquidity into the financial market.[40]

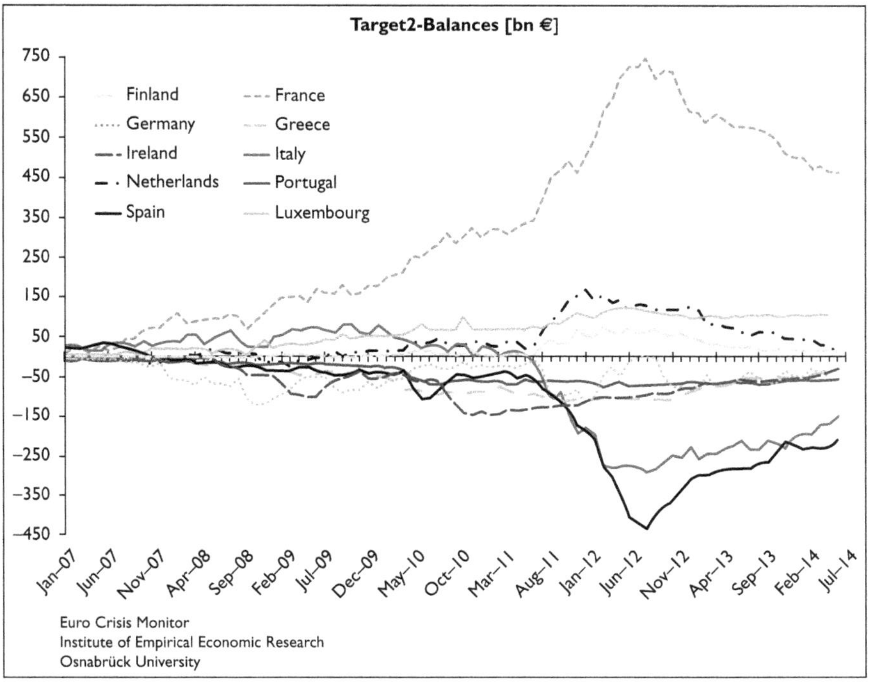

Figure 12.2 Target2 registering imbalances among member States during the Euro crisis years

Source - Euro Crisis Monitor, *Target2 – Balances* <http://intermarketandmore.finanza.com/target2-una-eurozona-piu-equilibrata-si-puo-62339.html>

This clearly shows how difficult it would be for a single state to try to set out adequate compensation for such imbalances[41] by just manoeuvring its own economic and social policy. Commercial and financial imbalances[42] within the Euro system are so much deeper – indeed, systemic – than what a single government can manage on its own. Accordingly, it is virtually impossible to disregard the guidelines offered by the European Institution as to how to cope with the objective of financial stability and sound budget. The endemic, European and common dimension of managing social policies is then evident. They have the same structural complexity and reciprocal embeddedness as the common currency system itself, which is absolutely not manageable from a single national point of view.[43]

V. Conclusion

This is the background of what we could call 'territorial fractures on cross-border monetary policy transmission', meaning the distributional effects of ECB monetary policy decisions due to the country-specific differences in any national financial system. Taking into account the debt/deficit situations of any national public budgets, the deficit/surplus divide among national systems in the cross-border economic transactions within the Single Market (import/export stable divide), produces asymmetric redistributive effects in different countries. Due to the lack of common economic and fiscal policies and without redistributive federal policies[44] among different territories, the destiny of the Euro system is to co-exist with these imbalances. This, in turn, brings about a significant crisis of the EU political system and a serious decline in its democratic legitimacy.[45] This is what we are witnessing in this historical period where, for the first time since the 1950s, we have to consider national political conflicts between EU States and a new, horrible season of nationalism.

Within this framework, currency, monetary policies, spending reviews and social rights represent a privileged perspective from which to explore such a crisis of legitimation. The analysis presented above shows that economic policies have become more rule-bound since the European Fiscal Pacts imposed a particular model of economic management, at least as regards the Eurozone member states. This model of economic management has gone as far as imposing on member states reforms to their national constitutions. There are now different constitutional frameworks at different levels, it is suggested: one is the Euro System level; another is the one constituted by national constitutions.

They promote conflicting principles,[46] and no legal solution can succeed in harmonising them. We now have a conflict between at least two competing concepts of distributional justice: equality among citizens within the European social system, and equality among the States themselves across the European territory, meant both as the Eurozone and the EU as a whole. As financial stability and sound budgets have become the new goal of European integration, the declining constitutional scrutiny both by national parliaments and the European Parliament has led to a tangible weakening of constitutional commitments on social rights.

No doubt this is why we are witnessing European citizens exercising their rights of free movement in order to seek more generous social rights provision. It amounts to an actual territorial shopping of their guarantees. In turn, of course, governments try to implement measures to prevent this.[47] The consequence is the creation of more and more serious inequalities among citizens and territories. Within the Common Market we are building a very fragmented European territory – especially fragmented at the level of enjoyment of fundamental rights and equality in the delivery of social services.

Notes

1 These are the words used to describe the analytical approach of Kaarlo Tuori and Klaus Tuori, *The Eurozone Crisis: A Constitutional Analysis* (Cambridge University Press, 2014).
2 T C Daintith, 'Legal Analysis of Economic Policy' (1982) 9(2) *Journal of Law & Society* 191, 192.
3 See the theoretical approach in Tony Prosser, *The Economic Constitution* (OUP, 2014).

4 European Commission, *Stability and Growth Pact* (6 July 2016) <http://ec.europa.eu/economy_finance/economic_governance/sgp/index_en.htm>; *Treaty on Stability, Coordination and Governance in the Economic and Monetary Union between the Kingdom of Belgium, the Republic of Bulgaria, the Kingdom of Denmark, the Federal Republic of Germany, the Republic of Estonia, Ireland, the Hellenic Republic, the Kingdom of Spain, the French Republic, the Italian Republic, the Republic of Cyprus, the Republic of Latvia, the Republic of Lithuania, the Grand Duchy of Luxembourg, Hungary, Malta, the Kingdom of the Netherlands, the Republic of Austria, the Republic of Poland, the Portuguese Republic, Romania, the Republic of Slovenia, the Slovak Republic, the Republic of Finland and the Kingdom of Spain*, T/SCG/en 1 (entered into force 1 May 2013) ('*Fiscal Compact*') and so on.

5 For well-founded examples, see Albanese, Ch. 4 in this volume; Christodoulidis and Goldoni, Ch. 11 in this volume; Lembke, Ch. 3 in this volume.

6 Gunther Teubner, 'Transnationale Wirtschaftsverfassung: Franz Böhm und Hugo Sinzheimer jenseits des Nationalstaates' (2014) 74 *ZaöRV* 733, speaks about not an organic transnational 'economic constitution,' but of a 'fragmentierte Kollisionsverfassung'.

7 The Euro system and its problems, more than global currency questions, are the focus, although cross-border transactions are always involved.

8 See Tuori and Tuori, above n 1.

9 Ibid 35, 181.

10 See the interesting analysis and the proposed approach of Armin Steinbach, 'The Mutualisation of Sovereign Debt: Comparing the American Past and the European Present' (2015) 53(5) *Journal of Common Market Studies* 1110–25.

11 Bundesverfassungsgericht [German Constitutional Court], 2 BvR 2728/13, 14 January 2014, reported in BVerfGE, Order of the Second Senate of 14 January 2014, requiring financial scrutiny of expenditure by the Bundestag's Budget Committee.

12 *Peter Gauweiler and Others v Deutscher Bundestag* (European Court of Justice, C-62/14, 16 June 2016).

13 Gregory Claeys, Alvaro Leandro and Allison Mandra, 'European Central Bank Quantitative Easing: The Detailed Manual' (2015) 2 *Bruegel Policy Contribution* 1.

14 See, e.g., Prosser, above n 3.

15 Which is still lacking, indeed, in the European Union's Budget: see Gabriele Cipriani, *Financing the EU Budget: Moving Forward or Backwards?* (Rowman & Littlefield, 2014) 75. Having said that, while non-Eurozone countries develop new financial instruments to increase liquidity, such as new categories of exchequer bonds, they too must control systemic risks. In this sense, they share with the Eurozone Member States the same risk of creating monetary instability and financial shocks.

16 *Constitutional Law 1/2012* (Italy) on the so-called 'balanced budget rule'. The same occurred, e.g., in Germany and Spain after the Fiscal Compact entered into force: above n 4. See Paul Craig, 'The Stability, Coordination and Governance Treaty: Principle, Politics and Pragmatism' (2012) 3 *European Law Review* 231; Federico Fabbrini, 'The Fiscal Compact, the "Golden Rule", and the Paradox of European Federalism' (2013) 36(1) *Boston College International & Comparative Law Review* 1, in a comparative and critical dimension. See also, F Bilancia, 'Spending review e pareggio di bilancio. Cosa rimane dell'autonomia locale?' (2014) 1 *Diritto pubblico* 45.

17 Prosser, above n 3, 243.

18 See Eurostat, *General Statistics* <http://ec.europa.eu/eurostat>.

19 Ibid.

20 Albanese, Ch. 4 in this volume, for instance, talks about a transformation of the Italian welfare model as it is not anymore centred 'around the protection of rights' as it is shifting to a model based on a 'theory of social rights as conditional on finance'.
21 I refer here to the debate evoked, for instance, by the approach of Jurgen Habermas, 'So, Why Does Europe Need a Constitution?' (2001) 11 *New Left Review* 1.
22 See Albanese, Ch. 4 in this volume; Christodoulidis and Goldoni, Ch. 11 in this volume; Lembke, Ch. 3 in this volume; and Meers, Ch. 6 in this volume about the effects of these policies on individual social rights protection levels in actual fact (cumulative impact of austerity measures, discrimination and so on).
23 Upon request by the Committee on Civil Liberties, Justice and Home Affairs of the European Parliament, a study has been published presenting a synthesis of researches conducted in seven member states 'regarding the impact of financial and economic crises, and austerity measures imposed in response thereto, on fundamental rights of individuals'. See the Policy Department, Citizens' Rights and Constitutional Affairs, *The Impact of the Crisis on Fundamental Rights across Member States of the EU – Comparative Analysis* (13 March 2015) <www.europarl.europa.eu/thinktank/en/document.html?reference=IPOL_STU(2015)510021>.
24 About Hartz legislation, see Lembke, Ch. 3 in this volume; European Commission, *Communication from the Commission to the European Parliament, the Council, the European Central Bank, the Economic and Social Committee, the Committee on the Regions and the European Investment Bank: Making the best of the flexibility within the existing rules of the stability and growth pact* (13 January 2015) <http://ec.europa.eu/economy_finance/economic_governance/sgp/pdf/2015-01-13_communication_sgp_flexibility_guidelines_en.pdf>.
25 *Treaty on European Union*, opened for signature 7 February 1992, [1992] OJ C 191/1 (entered into force 1 November 1993) annex ('*Protocol on Excessive Deficits*'); European Commission, above n 4; *Fiscal compact*, above n 4. See also the 'Six-Pack': European Commission, 'EU Economic Governance "Six Pack" Enters into Force' (Press Release, Memo/11/98, 12 December 2011).
26 Not taking into account, at the moment, the more and more complicated fiscal rules and control procedure set forth in the treaties and other normative acts by the EU.
27 Especially through unconventional measures to react to financial shocks, see Stefano Micossi, 'The Monetary Policy of the European Central Bank' (Special Report No 109, Centre for European Policy Studies, May 2015) 9; see also F Koulischer, 'Asymmetric Shocks in a Currency Union: The Role of Central Bank Collateral Policy' (Working Paper No 554, Banque de France, May 2015); Andrew Hallet, 'Quantitative Easing: Side Effects in the Financial Markets' in Policy Department – Economic and Scientific Policy, 'ECB Quantitative Easing (QE): What are the Side Effects' (Report, European Commission, June 2015); Karl Whelan, 'Does QE have Unpleasant Side Effects' in Policy Department – Economic and Scientific Policy, 'ECB Quantitative Easing (QE): What are the Side Effects' (Report, European Commission, June 2015).
28 A very deep analysis on these topics in Anton Brender, Florence Pisani and Emile Gagna, *Money, Finance and the Real Economy: What Went Wrong?* (Report, Centre for European Policy Studies, 2015).
29 See, e.g., Anastasia Poulou, 'Austerity and European Social Rights: How Can Courts Protect Europe's Lost Generation?' (2014) 15(6) *German Law Journal* 1145.
30 See European Commission, above n 25. These measures had been already taken by the German Government, in 2003 and 2010, before the gravity of the crisis

became so evident, as well analysed by Lembke, Ch. 3 in this volume, especially about the Hartz labour market and insurance system reforming process.

31 This can be read as a country-specific duty for Germany: see *Council Recommendation of 8 July 2014 on the National Reform Programme 2014 of Germany and Delivering a Council opinion on the Stability Programme of Germany*, 8 July 2014 OJ C 247/20. See also the analysis and critical commentaries in Simon Tilfor, 'Germany Rebalancing: Waiting for Godot' (Policy Brief, Centre for European Reform, March 2015).

32 The yearly Stability or Convergence Programme for each country, with the yearly National Reform Programmes and the Commission's Country-specific Recommendations, which are, among others, very detailed 'suggested' measures on welfare rights protection system reforms and cuts.

33 See, e.g., Patrick Diamond, Roger Liddle and Daniel Sage, *The Social Reality of Europe after the Crisis: Trends, Challenges and Responses* (Rowman & Littlefield, 2015).

34 Another question being the reallocation of power among member states through European financial governance. See Federico Fabbrini, 'States Equality v. States Power: The Euro-Crisis, Inter-State Relations and the Paradox of Domination' (2015) 17(1) *Cambridge Yearbook of European Legal Studies* 3.

35 On a critical perspective, see David Guerreiro, 'Is the European Debt Crisis a Mere Balance of Payments Crisis?' (Working Paper No 118, Forschungsschwerpunkt Internationale Wirtschaft, April 2013).

36 See the interesting approach and critical analysis carried out by Tony Prosser, 'Constitutionalising Austerity in Europe' (2015) *Public Law* 111.

37 See again, for instance, the chapter written by Albanese, Ch. 4 in this volume.

38 See Mario Draghi, 'The Governance of Structural Reforms' (Speech delivered at European Central Bank Memorial Lecture in honour of Tommaso Padoa-Schioppa, London, 9 July 2014).

39 European Central Bank, *Trans-European Automated Real-time Gross Settlement Express Transfer System* (18 November 2016) <www.ecb.europa.eu/paym/t2/html/index.en.html>. See also, European Central Bank, *TARGET Annual Report* (June 2015) <www.ecb.europa.eu/pub/pdf/other/targetar2014.en.pdf> 43.

40 On European Central Bank monetary policies, see generally, C Randall Henning, 'The ECB as a Strategic Actor: Central Banking in a Politically Fragmented Monetary Union' (Research Paper, No 2015-1, American University School of International Service, 11 January 2015). On ECB monetary policies see, in general, Anthoy Delivorias, 'Monetary Policy of the ECB: Strategy, Conduct and Trends' (Paper, European Parliamentary Research Service, February 2015).

41 See comments by the European Central Bank Governor in Mario Draghi, 'Unemployment in the Euro Area' (Speech delivered Annual European Central Bank Symposium, Jackson Hole, 22 August 2014) 9.

42 Which can also be, of course, surplus imbalances, Daniel Gros and Matthias Busse, 'The Macroeconomic Imbalance Procedure and Germany: When is a Surplus an "Imbalance"?' (Policy Brief No 301, Centre for European Policy Studies, 13 November 2013) 302.

43 Mark Dawson and Floris de Witte, 'Constitutional Balance in the EU after the Euro-Crisis' (2013) 76(5) *Modern Law Review* 817.

44 See the interesting analysis promoted by Celine Allard *et al.*, 'Toward a Fiscal Union for the Euro Area' (Staff Discussion Note SDN/13/09, International Monetary Fund, September 2013).

45 Cf Agustin Jose Menendez, 'The Existential Crisis of the European Union' (2013) 14(5) *German Law Journal* 453, 470; P Leino and J Salminen, 'Should

the Economic and Monetary Union Be Democratic After All? Some Reflections on the Current Crisis' (2013) 14(2) *German Law Journal* 844.

46 See Sergio Fabbrini, 'The Constitutional Conundrum of the European Union' (2016) 23(1) *Journal of European Public Policy* 84.

47 See, e.g., *Elisabetta Dano and Florin Dano vs. Jobcenter Leipzig* (European Court of Justice, C-3337/13, 11 November 2014); *Jobcenter Berlin Neukölln vs Alimanovic N., S., V., V* (European Court of Justice, C-67/14, 15 September 2015); *European Commission vs. UK* (European Court of Justice, C-308/14, 14 June 2016). On this case-law, analysed among many other important decisions, see Giubboni, Ch. 12 in this volume. The discussion could then move through the recent events after the result of the UK referendum to 'leave' the EU, held 23 June 2016, as the vote campaign was deeply involved with the 'question' of free movement of European citizens within the Market and social rights costs, but this is not possible in the circumstances.

Chapter 13

Free movement of persons and transnational solidarity in the European Union

A melancholic eulogy

Stefano Giubboni

But people loved darkness instead of light

John, III, 19

1. Prologue

For almost fifteen years, the saga of the constitutionalisation of European citizenship has been based on the famous promise of 'a certain degree of financial solidarity'[1] between the nationals of different member states. The idea that a Union citizen could have access to a new 'status of social integration',[2] directly defined at the supranational level, and derived from the fundamental freedom of movement, actually seemed to be able to open up a new constitutional dimension to European citizenship, finally destined to transcend the nation-States' particularistic allegiances in order to revive and expand the universal and 'omniinclusive'[3] promise of a society of free and equal individuals built on the jus-naturalistic foundations of modern citizenship.

The process of constitutionalisation of the weak provisions on citizenship introduced by the Maastricht Treaty[4] has been carried out by the European Court of Justice (ECJ) along two convergent trajectories, beginning with the *Martínez Sala*[5] path-breaking case.

On the first trajectory, a new universal status for transnational access to social rights on an equal footing with the nationals of the host country was progressively attached to the freedom of the European citizen to move and establish residence in another member state, irrespective of his status of economic activity. As a result of this, the main feature of this first jurisprudential movement can be identified in the fact that the Court of Justice has progressively extended those same powerful mechanisms of de-nationalisation (and partly of de-territorialisation) of social citizenship rights to every citizen of the Union *qua talis*.

These mechanisms had originally been reserved by the Treaty of Rome for economically active persons, and to workers in particular, as a fundamental means for the functional integration of the Common Market.[6] The fragility of this first ideational-pillar, in such a sophisticated endeavour of making European citizenship the fundamental status of the individual in the European Union's constitutional order, is probably due to the intrinsic contradiction pervading the conceptual categories used by the court for such an ambitious purpose. The attempt to overcome the functionalistic logic and the mercantile *ratio*, historically underpinning the guarantee of social security rights to migrant workers,[7] actually took place through a sort of radicalisation and generalisation of those same conceptual premises under the new universalistic and unifying rhetoric of European citizenship.

However, for this very same reason the pseudo-universal allure of transnational social solidarity, expected to stem from European citizenship, could not (and cannot) sever the original connection with the market citizen construct,[8] which has overbearingly re-emerged (and re-surfaces) during the hard times of EU crisis. The 'resilience' of such a model[9] – and the reappearance of its intrinsic limits – is therefore actually due to the contradictions underlying the attempt to promote the status of social integration of European (economically inactive) citizens over and above an individual freedom of movement built in the image and likeness of the transnational economic actor.[10]

The other trajectory for constitutionalisation was even more ambitious as, in *Zambrano*,[11] it was looking at an even greater attempt of overcoming the transnational perspective in a view of 'disconnecting citizenship from mobility'.[12] The integration-loop potentially envisioned by such a move would have actually brought the constitutional trajectory of European citizenship to a sort of federal completion, in so far as the Union would no longer be seen simply as 'the sum of the physical territories of the Member States' but as 'a new common space, a space of distribution of rights and common values'.[13] But this second trajectory, based on even more fragile assumptions, was soon interrupted, even before the new territories of the common space of distribution of rights and political values could be explored by their unknowing and disoriented holders. The great crisis has, rather, precipitated the Union towards a new *terra incognita*, which is exactly the opposite of the land promised by the Maastricht Treaty. Instead of welcoming the 'magnificent and progressive destinies'[14] of an ever-closer union among the peoples of Europe, tightened by the political project of common citizenship and currency, the great crisis has created deep rifts of division and reciprocal distrust between the member states, threatening the disintegration of the whole project, above all beginning with the recurring risk of the fracture of the Euro zone.

This chapter gives a critical overview of the rapid rise and equally sudden decline of the normative ideal of European citizenship as a status of transnational social integration. The tipping points can be quite easily identified with the great changes that have diverted the course of European integration since the mid-2000s; the cumulative effect of the big-bang Eastern enlargement and the great political-financial crisis of the Euro zone have totally altered the political economy of European integration and irreversibly degraded the optimistic and neo-illuminist assumptions underpinning the normative ideal.

The court's case law – especially with the much discussed *Brey*,[15] *Dano*[16] and *Alimanovic*[17] judgments – has shown a clear retreat, or maybe a retrenchment, in the discourse on EU citizenship as a source for transnational social solidarity, with an indisputable step back to a strict functional interpretation of the Treaty provisions in their relationship with secondary law (Directive 2004/38/EC and Regulation No. 883/2004). If predictions on possible future directions appeared risky and probably premature[18] in the aftermath of *Brey* and *Dano,* the effective meaning of the two judgments being sufficiently ambiguous to leave alternative interpretative paths open, the *Alimanovic* and *Garcìa-Nierto*[19] rulings have in the meanwhile definitely dismissed the long-standing ambition for a socially inclusive notion of European citizenship.

It is no coincidence that the overall regressive itinerary of the ECJ's case law seems to be perfectly in line with the political dynamics within the so-called new Union reform agenda, which are simply dismantling even the rhetoric of the European space of transnational solidarity.

II. Transnational solidarity in its ascending phase

As already mentioned, 'during the golden era of the Welfare State a concrete freedom of movement was inconceivable without the guarantee of the right to social security'.[20] This is why the right to the free movement of workers and, even before that, the social security coordination system, introduced in 1958, could be considered as an embryo of European citizenship.[21] The Court of Justice's case law played a decisive role during the founding phase of the constitutionalisation of the Community legal order, especially in relation to the freedom of movement and social rights of migrant workers.[22]

During this 'heroic' original phase of integration, when the constitutional bases of the Common Market were set, the freedom of movement of workers had been intended in a broader sense than the one suggested by the mere functional logic of market integration.[23]

We should not forget that the court has, on the one hand, accepted an extremely broad definition of worker, as far as it encompasses all activities having any effectiveness and a minimum of economic consistency, that are performed under the direction of a different person in return for remuneration. On the other hand, it allowed the holders of the fundamental freedom of movement, and their family members, to have access to the whole panoply of social rights guaranteed to the nationals of the host member state under conditions of full equal treatment. As for the first aspect, the court was able to extend the guarantee of equal treatment in the host member state – according to the current Art. 45 of the Treaty on the Functioning of the European Union (TFEU) – to workers holding employment contracts that differ from the standard model of the permanent full-time job, already undermined during the early eighties by the gradual spread of atypical work-relations. As for the second, the court assigned an important integrative function to the guarantee of equal treatment, generally extended to social advantages by Art. 7 of Regulation No. 1612/68 into the domain of social assistance and welfare rights, thus opening up the inner circles of national solidarity systems to migrant workers and their families.[24]

In this case law,

> social integration into the host society is seen by the ECJ as an instrument for promoting participation within the EU internal market and within its economic objective of free movement of factors of production, even when their productivity may be rather low. The rationale behind this case law has more to do with the internal market than with combating social exclusion, even if this actually contributes to the latter.[25]

The model of integration endorsed by the court is certainly based on the idea that the migrant worker (and their family members) should be included, from the beginning and without exceptions, in the social protection system of the host member state, in its entirety, as they contribute to the well-being of the society that is hosting them through their (albeit reduced) economic activity.[26]

An outcome of social integration in the migrant's elected country of residence – extended to all persons whose contribution to the internal market is actually only potential or at the very best only indirect – had thus been already firmly secured by the court's historical case law on the freedom of movement of workers and their families. If read in light of this *acquis*, it can be said that the judgments, through which the court has extended the principle of equal treatment in the access to social and welfare rights acknowledged by the host country, must also be extended to economically inactive European citizens. These judgments, from the leading case *Martínez Sala* to *Zambrano*, have done nothing but generalise a status of social integration already widely acquired, although within a more limited perimeter.

This case law was supposed to have the merit of universalising the logic of social integration originally anchored to the functioning of the internal market, as free movers not carrying out an activity of economic nature were included in the equal-protection status based on European citizenship. The innovative feature of this case law was to be found in the universalistic projection of the model of transnational social solidarity, already pre-envisaged by the Treaty of Rome in favour of economic migrants. Some have thus recognised a change in the very normative paradigm of European social solidarity; where access to the social-protection systems of member states was previously functional to the internal market's full effectiveness, according to such case law, it has now become an autonomous constitutive element of Union citizenship, widely codified by Directive 2004/38, and it is seen as a fundamental status of social integration totally unrelated to the mercantile *ratio* and the original idea of *homo œconomicus*. In this view, a constitutional citizenship-status of transnational value was hence created[27] and – overcoming the old category-based model of market-justice and occupational-solidarity – it underpins a general claim for social integration within the host member state, which is not very different from the functioning of federal-type polities.

However, the fragility of this conceptual construction has been brutally exposed by the great EU crisis. Such an idea of compassionate transnational solidarity was built, in fact, on a huge misunderstanding,[28] whose hypocrisy has been mercilessly revealed by the drama of the European crisis. The great crisis has quite inevitably dissolved any propensity of the Northern European core Member States to host EU foreigners in need in their (still relatively) generous welfare systems: as social chauvinism ineluctably resurfaced in face of the well-cultivated *spectre* of 'benefit tourism', the swift political reaction has been everywhere nothing but the closing of the porous borders of the so-called transnational solidarity.

Hypocrisy has indeed its shortcomings: in our case, such limits are all included in a post-modern model of abstract solidarity, which – in so far as it relies not on a common welfare and fiscal system but on the disposition of selected member states towards the hosting migrants in social need – by definition cannot ensure for economically inactive European citizens either an unconditional freedom of residence, nor equal access to the system of social protection of the host country, at least until the status of long-term resident has been acquired according to Art. 16 of Directive 2004/38/EC. In concrete terms, the right to take up residence in another member state for a period exceeding three months remains conditional on the reverse means test of having comprehensive health-insurance coverage, as well as sufficient resources to prevent the economically inactive citizen from becoming a burden for that State's social assistance system (Art. 7 of Directive 2004/38/EC). And the unfortunate accident of becoming such an unreasonable burden on the host Welfare State system gives the national authorities the power of expelling the unwelcome parasitic EU citizen, although without making use of rude automatisms and in compliance with the principle of proportionality (Art. 14, par. 3). Moreover, transnational access to the social solidarity system of a Member State under conditions of equal treatment with its nationals is subject in any case to an incremental criterion, since the inactive Union citizen must show proof of a sufficient degree of integration into the society of the host country.

Such limitations have a specific *ratio*, which has reverted to showing all its selective duress and disciplining power following the great crisis.[29] The very roots, at least of the Euro zone crisis, lie indeed in the total lack of any real European solidarity, and it is not by accident that the most prominent structure of the new crisis-management law of Europe is that authentic tribute to the de-solidarisation un-popularly known as Fiscal Compact.[30] As there is no form of Europeanisation or sharing of national social-protection systems, each member state may legitimately require that access to its welfare system has to depend on a given substratum of social integration already legitimately acquired by the European citizen.

By necessity, the exclusively transnational dimension of social solidarity connected to European citizenship is confronted with this underlying tension,[31] which inevitably re-emerges any time a freedom of movement not functional to the needs of the market ends up impinging on the finances of the national Welfare State.[32] And, if such a tension can easily be disguised behind a vaguely cosmopolitan and post-modern rhetoric of transnational solidarity in times of economic growth, more or less equally distributed among the Member States,[33] in times of crisis all of the illusory and dangerous fragility of the rhetoric is revealed. This is especially true when the new highly asymmetrical Euro zone economic-governance rules trace a non-negotiable line between the self-proclaimed financial virtues of the northern countries and the irresponsibility of the southern ones, dismantling any resemblance of isonomy within the Union.[34]

In essence, this is the lesson learned from *Brey* and *Dano*.

III. Brey and Dano

It is worth remembering that thanks to one of the most acrobatic (and indeed most discussed)[35] passages in the *Martínez Sala* ruling, the Court of Justice had already come to infer that economically inactive European citizens may enter the scope *ratione materiae* of Art. 18 of the TFEU, derived from the simple exercise of the freedom of movement, even outside the conditions defined by Art. 7, par. 1, letter b) of Directive 2004/38/EC. That very fact could indeed be capable of attracting the mobile EU citizen within the perimeters of the principle of equal treatment, if not otherwise, at least for the sake of having full access to the non-contributory social benefits in the host member state. In *Martínez Sala*, as well as in other later cases, the residence permit held by the economically inactive European citizen was actually granted not on the basis of EU law but according to national law.[36] Nevertheless, the effective exercise of the freedom of movement and subsequent residency by Mrs Martínez Sala was sufficient to include her situation in the scope of the principle of equal treatment, regardless of nationality.[37]

However, while certainly daring, the passage appeared in line with the overall political meaning of the interpretative efforts conducted at the time by the Court of Justice, which openly acted – both with that ground-breaking judgment as well as with other paradigmatic rulings of the same period[38] – within a bold perspective of the constitutionalisation of the freedom of movement attributed to the European citizen by the Maastricht Treaty.[39] In such a perspective, the conditions or limits posed by secondary law to the freedom of movement of the EU (economically inactive) citizen must be – coherently – very restrictively considered, while the maximum *effet utile* must be accorded to the rules of the Treaty in guaranteeing equal treatment in all relevant situations in order to effectively exercise that right *magis ut valeat*.[40]

Michael Dougan has observed that, at least since the *Förster*[41] judgment of 2008, the Court of Justice's constitutional narrative has gradually undergone some reshaping with an undeclared 'backtrack from the technique of indirect judicial review previously cultivated by its case law on Union citizenship'.[42] Nonetheless, in its essence such a constitutional path had not been systematically abandoned by the court, at least until *Brey*. The *Brey* judgment marks in our opinion the first essential separation from the expansive logic of Union citizenship as a fundamental status of member states nationals, since it marks a paradigmatic retreat to a sort of interpretative legalistic-minimalism, according to which secondary law rules – strictly – determine the applicative limits of the Treaty, and not conversely.

While *Brey* has an irresistible ambiguity,[43] it seemingly does not as yet imply a significant retreat from the old judicial course in respect of the degree of social solidarity 'among strangers'. In the judgment, in fact, the court confirms that EU law – requiring a certain degree of transnational solidarity – does not consider the application for social assistance, made by an economically inactive citizen of a member state, to be sufficient to prove that they have become an unreasonable burden for the welfare system of the host country, therefore depriving them of the right to reside in that country. The court also states that the competent national authorities are entrusted with the task, and the duty, to carry out a careful assessment of the specific characteristics of each individual situation according to the principle of proportionality, without there being any automatic consequence attributable to the request of enjoyment of welfare benefits by the citizen of another member state.

However, at the same time the *Brey* judgment prepared the ground that was soon after explored by *Dano* for the return to a tight functional interpretation – and a true de-constitutionalisation – of the freedom of movement and residence of the Union (economically inactive) citizen, in two important aspects: first, because the judgment anticipates that the focus-point of the argumentative line carried out in *Dano* is the relationship between Directive 2004/38/EC and Regulation No. 883/2004 and it essentially attributes an improper hierarchical prevalence of the former over the latter. As stated in *Brey*, and then repeated in *Dano*, the main issue is whether the recourse to social assistance, and the request of a special non-contributory benefit according to Regulation No. 883/2004 by the economically inactive citizen who has exercised her freedom of movement, would imply that the same European citizen risked losing the right to reside in the host country, as provided for by Directive 2004/38/EC under the conditions defined by Art. 7. And the court's response was exactly that, although seen through the filter of the proportionality test, such a request for social assistance may actually endanger the status of legal residence under the Directive, due to the loss of the condition of economic self-sufficiency imposed by the latter in order to safeguard the financial stability of the welfare systems of the host member states.

Second, because, among the possible configurations of the assessment of the alleged existence of an unreasonable burden on the public finances of a member state, *Brey* accepts the most rigorous version, effectively defined by Daniel Thym as a 'systemic' evaluation-type as opposed to an 'individual' one.[44] As elusive as it can be, the systemic type of assessment in fact tends to privilege the importance of the overall implications that may impact on national public finances by the effective or potential increasing mobility of economically inactive Union citizens in need, therefore strengthening the protection of member states' purses against – the real or imaginary – malpractices of 'benefit tourism'.

Following the pathway opened by *Brey*, in *Dano* the Court of Justice took the decisive step to overturn the constitutional dynamic that, from *Martínez Sala* onwards, has essentially promoted the access of economically inactive citizens to the welfare systems of the host countries based on conditions of equal treatment with their nationals.

First, only the fulfilment of the conditions of economic self-sufficiency (and of comprehensive health-insurance coverage) imposed by Art. 7, par. 1, letter b) of Directive 2004/38/EC would grant the European economically inactive citizen the right to reside in the host Member State, and therefore to benefit from equal treatment in the access to social-assistance benefits in the territory of the latter. And, second, only a prior condition of legal residence, under the requirements strictly set out by Art. 7 of the Directive, would allow the economically inactive citizen (who can prove also a sufficient degree of integration in the society of the host country) to access the welfare system of the latter, without putting in jeopardy the right of that citizen to reside in that State (Art. 24, par. 1, of Directive 2004/38, read in conjunction with Arts 4 and 70 of Regulation No. 883/2004). This therefore does not prohibit member states from excluding economically inactive European citizens from the enjoyment of a special non-contributory benefit that is acknowledged to their nationals, when those Union citizens do not enjoy the right to legally reside under Art. 7 of the Directive.

This is in fact a spectacular retreat from the 'magnificent and progressive destinies' of transnational solidarity towards the nationals of other member states, that the court has performed with sublime ease in name of a new European *Realpolitik*, which evidently urges for further reassurances to the hegemonic countries of the far North, both continental and insular.[45] This new case law reintroduces a sharp line of demarcation in the European *status civitatis*, which goes back to obeying to a strict mercantile logic or, rather, to a new census model of citizenship.

Hence, 'Two citizenships' re-emerge,[46] characterised by totally different protection statuses: first and second class.[47] First-class citizenship is reserved to persons who are active in the internal market (as workers or simply as providers or merely as individuals receiving services in return for remuneration) and to those who, while not being economically active, can nonetheless prove their economic self-sufficiency. Second-class citizenship, essentially devoid of any transnational protective status, is for the indigent. The latter, in fact, are trapped within a classic *Catch-22* situation,[48] since in order to claim for social assistance in the host member state this would almost automatically require, for them, giving evidence of not satisfying the requirements provided for by Directive 2004/38/EC in order to legally reside for a period exceeding three months.

From a technical point of view, the keystone of what, in hindsight, appears as the restoration of the system prior to the Maastricht Treaty, needs to be identified once again in the re-construction of the relationship between Directive 2004/38/EC and Regulation No. 883/2004. And in relation to this, *Dano* falls firmly in the conceptual wake traced by *Brey*.

As Rob Cornelissen and Herwig Vershueren have shown,[49] the interpretation adopted by the court in *Dano* in fact overturns the terms of the political compromise behind the contextual adoption of the Regulation and the Directive in 2004. This compromise reaffirmed the political balance already achieved in 1992,[50] with the introduction of a special system of coordination for non-contributory cash benefits, characterised by the express and exceptional provision of a derogation to the general principle of exportability, albeit offset by the attribution of the responsibility of the payment of such benefits to the member state of actual residence of the beneficiary according to the *lex loci domicilii*.

Yet, the notion of residence to this end, also used by Regulation No. 883/2004 for this very reason, is based on parameters that are inherently and essentially factual, as opposed to Directive 2004/38/EC, which gives a much stricter legal definition instead, anchored as it is to requirements of legal-substantial nature. Therefore, the original idea was precisely that, as often as the merely factual situation of habitual residence in the host country recurred,[51] the EU economically inactive citizens covered by the Regulations on social security would certainly be entitled to non-contributory benefits provided for by the legislation of the host member state in which that citizen placed their centre of interests. Thus, at least within the semi-universal scope of application *ratione personae* of Regulation No. 883/2004, the right to have access to non-contributory benefits in the country of actual/factual habitual residence would certainly allow, or at least legitimately help, the European economically inactive citizen to meet the requirement of economic self-sufficiency set forth by Art. 7 of Directive 2004/38/EC.

Evidently, that compromise was overwhelmed by the interpretation of the relationship between the social security Regulation and the citizenship Directive endorsed by the court in *Brey* and even more boldly in *Dano*. Only the status of legal residence – in full compliance with the Directive[52] – would allow access to special non-contributory/social assistance benefits under the specific conditions of equal treatment with the nationals of the host member state. However, this reintroduces a decisive cleavage within the status of Union citizenship, with a retreat from the previous deeply held normative ideal that aimed at making EU citizenship the main constitutional vehicle for transnational social integration, in the name of solidarity 'among strangers'.

IV. Alimanovic

This erosion of the constitutional meaning of European citizenship, witnessed by the shift from the primacy of the Treaty to a straightforward application of Directive 2004/38/EC, seems to reflect the political concerns captured by the media-metaphor of 'welfare tourism'. *Alimanovic* clearly echoes those concerns, in so far as the Court of Justice considers the abstract assessment made by the Directive as an a priori complaint with the Treaty, without the necessity to submit the national rules limiting the access to social benefits to a contextual and concrete proportionality scrutiny.

The Directive is re-interpreted according to a sort of teleological reduction: the objectives pursued by the legislator have been identified with the need to prevent economically inactive citizens from using the host member states' welfare system, whereas in the recent past they were construed as intended to facilitate the exercise of the fundamental right to move and reside freely within the EU.

Such a construction of the *telos* of the Directive explains also the re-alignment between Regulation No. 883/2004 and Directive 2004/38/EC around the meaning of social assistance: as a result of this, the non-contributory social benefits as defined by the Regulation are to be considered as social assistance for the (prevailing) purposes of Directive 2004/38/EC. In fact, although containing some social-security flavour (and for this reason falling within the scope of Regulation No. 883/2004), these benefits are paid by the State out of general taxation. Thus, insofar as they involve the public largesse, they should fall within the notion of social assistance within the meaning of the Directive, whose precise aim is to prevent individuals who have not made any contribution to financing the national social-security schemes from becoming an unreasonable burden for the receiving State.[53]

In *Alimanovic*,[54] indeed, the court denied two Swedish citizens, who had very recently come back to Germany, where they had lived and worked briefly in the past (before leaving that country for a number of years), special non-contributory benefits such as subsistence allowances for long-term unemployed people. Specifically, the court argued that persons who became unemployed after short periods of work (less than one year) should not be considered former workers within the meaning of Art. 7, par. 3, b), of Directive 2004/38/EC[55] and consequently admitted to retain access to social assistance benefits by virtue of Art. 24, par. 1. Indeed, after the expiry of the period provided for in Art. 7, par. 3, c), of Directive 2004/38/EC (six months after the last employment had ended), it is assumed that the rules on first-time job-seekers apply by analogy. In this regard, the individuals concerned might establish a right of residence under Directive 2004/38/EC on the basis of Art. 14, par. 4, letter b) thereof,[56] but "the host Member State may rely on the derogation in Art. 24, par. 2 of that Directive in order not to grant that citizen the social assistance sought".[57]

Hence, once again, any claim of equal treatment from persons qualified as economically inactive (due to the loss of the status of workers or due to the status of job-seekers) must be subject to what has been called the 'right-to-reside-under-Directive 2004/38-test'.[58] Residence pursuant to legal instruments other than Directive 2004/38/EC is definitely immaterial in order for those persons to fall within the scope of the equal treatment principle, even when the claimant has not exercised the migratory rights 'solely to obtain another Member State's social assistance',[59] as in the case at issue of residence arising out of the search for an employment.

It is quite clear that the rough solution adopted in *Alimanovic* is inconsistent with the old 'progressive' ECJ's case law in several respects. First of all, the simple acceptance of the Directive's notion of former worker is in contrast with the previous court's insistence on the concept of worker referred to in Art. 45 TFEU, as a matter of primary law.[60]

Second, the embarrassing disappearance from the scene of the contextual proportionality test collides with the old and consistent jurisprudence on indirect discriminations previously developed. In this regard, the court clearly stated that national legislations – as the German one at issue – which do not allow access to social benefits like subsistence allowances for the long-term unemployed *under any circumstance*, irrespective of their link to the host State, should not be subject to any individual assessment. Contrary to the opinion of the Advocate General,[61] whereby the demonstration of a real link to the labour market of the State would prevent the automatic exclusion from those benefits, the court dismissed the case-by-case approach according to which it had been considering the welfare claims of economically inactive EU citizens in the past.

Third, it should be noted how the special non-contributory benefit at issue, namely the subsistence allowance for the long-term unemployed, provided for in the pertinent Annex of Regulation No. 883/2004, has been encompassed once again in the notion of social assistance under Art. 24 Directive 2004/38/EC. Indeed, even if the allowance in question formed part of a scheme aimed at facilitating the search for employment, nevertheless it was intended to cover minimum subsistence costs necessary to lead a life in conformity with human dignity and for this reason financed through the tax revenue. The latter function was found to be predominant, and this explains the benign neglect reserved to the very different approach developed in *Vatsouras and Koupatantze*.[62]

However, even after *Alimanovic* the picture remains rather unclear.

It is not entirely clear if the Member States will be allowed to refuse to pay any social benefits, including *social security* benefits, to *all* Union citizens who do not have the right to reside under Directive 2004/38/EC because they do not possess sufficient means of subsistence. Admittedly, this new line of case-law is *per se* limited to first-job seekers and purely non-active citizens, but an extension of this doctrine to those citizens who could find themselves in need prior to the acquisition of permanent residence cannot be excluded. The kaleidoscope of factual situations related to non-economic migration, in fact, can encompass subjects so disparate as not to form a unitary category of economically non-active citizens.

Hence, the rationale underpinning the conservative drift of the ECJ's case law – namely the protection of national welfare systems from abusive claims – does not always fit into situations in which the reasons behind free movement have nothing to do with obtaining another Member State's social assistance. A radical and over-encompassing understanding of the reach of the new case-law would generate quite paradoxical outcomes. If any claim to social assistance was to be considered to be predestined to constitute an unreasonable burden for the host State thanks to an almost indisputable presumption, that would lead to the paradoxical result that only those who have sufficient resources (not being in need of social assistance) are entitled to rely on public welfare mechanisms.

This kind of reading is now clearly foreshadowed by the Conclusions of the European Council of 18-19 February 2016. According to the Decision in Annex 1 of the Conclusions, free movement of EU citizens is to be exercised if it is subject to the conditions and limitations laid down in the Treaties and the measures adopted to give them effect. For this very reason, Member States have the possibility of refusing to grant social benefits to persons who exercise their right to freedom of movement solely in order to obtain host States' social assistance while not having sufficient resources to claim the right of residence. Member States may as well reject claims for social assistance by EU citizens from other Member States who do not enjoy a right of residence or are entitled to reside on their territory solely because of their job-search. And this includes claims by EU citizens from other Member States for benefits whose predominant function is to cover the minimum subsistence costs, even if such benefits are also intended to facilitate access to the labour market of the host Member State.[63]

At the same time, the *de facto* abandonment of the proportionality test, in this regard, would make the provision set out in Art. 8, par. 4 of Directive 2004/38/EC simply irrelevant. According to that provision, Member States, when acknowledging the right to reside, may not lay down a fixed amount regarded as indicating 'sufficient resources', but must take into account the personal situation of the person concerned. And yet, the findings of the court in *Alimanovic* postulate that the Directive, by establishing a gradual system as regards the retention of the worker's status, takes into consideration various factors characterising the individual situation of each applicant for social assistance, and, in particular, the duration of the exercise of any economic activity.[64] Accordingly, although member states may indicate a certain sum as a reference amount, they may not impose a minimum income level below which it will be presumed that the person concerned does not have sufficient means of subsistence, irrespective of the specific examination of the situation of each claimant.

As rightly observed, another unfair result would be to turn Union citizens into illegal migrants,[65] unable to rely on the Treaty provisions, in particular on Art. 21 TFEU, and for this reason likely to be expelled due to the unlawful residence in the territory of the member state concerned. In this regard, Art. 14, par. 3, of Directive 2004/38/EC states that expulsion measures shall not be the automatic consequence of a Union citizen's recourse to the social-assistance system of the host State.

The necessity of the proportionality test has been remarked in *Brey*,[66] where the court reminded how it is clear from recital 16 in the preamble of Directive 2004/38/EC that, before adopting an expulsion measure, the host member state should examine whether the person concerned is experiencing temporary difficulties and take into account the duration of his residence, his personal circumstances and the amount of aid that has been granted to the applicant. In this respect, and at least in those circumstances at issue in the main proceeding, it seems that *Alimanovic* has dropped the individual assessment concerning not only whether the person concerned is placing an unreasonable burden on the social-assistance system but also whether an expulsion measure is to be adopted.[67] That solution would be definitely inconsistent with the traditional teaching according to which every expulsion decision must comply with the principle of proportionality and the procedural safeguards of Arts 30 and 31 of Directive 2004/38/EC.

Moreover, when a deportation order is not issued by the national authorities, citizens without a European entitlement to reside may continue to stay (unlawfully) in the host State but national authorities can try to effectively 'starve them out'[68] by denying access to social benefits: a very perverse strategy that would be openly in contrast with the Union commitments towards fighting poverty and social exclusion, as enshrined in Arts 9 and 151, par. 1, TFEU.

IV. Epilogue

Even after *Alimanovic*, many uncertain and controversial aspects still remain, needing to receive a conclusive answer from the court. The jurisprudential framework is still developing and the darkest scenarios, although clearly visible on the horizon, do not, it is hoped, necessarily need to take place, as Leopardi's insuperable pessimism on the unhappiness of the human condition would predict.

However, our fear is that the most likely outcome, in line with the new neurotic and intolerant European Zeitgeist, is towards a creeping return to the grim logic of the *Poor Laws*, with a post-modern rediscovery of the classical remedy of the expulsion of the undeserving poor, by sending them back to the parish (or, in our case, to the country) of origin.[69] It is no coincidence that, among the different hypotheses of reforms there are some that are impressively similar to the old 'non-resident relief', which under the *Law of Settlement* from the Elizabethan period exceptionally allowed for the prevention of the expulsion of the poor stranger if the parish of origin accepted to take on the burden of his assistance.[70]

The hypothesis according to which, at least partially or even temporarily, such a burden is to be transferred to the State of origin of the migrant European citizen, perhaps unwittingly (but no less clearly) echoes back to that historic tradition. And if this were to be actualised in the new context of the Union, the deep asymmetries already created by the great crisis between core and periphery countries would be exacerbated, again to the detriment of the Member States at the outer (Mediterranean or eastern) borders of the EU and to the benefit of the northern block under the German track (as well as the motherland of the *Poor Laws*, of course).

Pessimism is justified by the increasingly explicit and disturbing signs of an even more broad and general, not to say 'systemic', questioning of the postulates of the freedom of movement of persons and workers within the Union.[71] One of these is now well-discernible within the case-law of the Court of Justice, which more and more frequently – in a sort of reverse cross-fertilisation – demands that economic migrants, especially frontier workers, give proof of a certain degree of integration in the society of the host country in order to have access to social advantages and benefits on par with the nationals of that State.[72] If this trend were to be consolidated, such an interpretative reorientation, or detour, would evidently undermine one of the pillars of the free movement within the internal market and of the model of social integration that it embodied: that is to say, the unconditional right for migrant workers to have access to all the social benefits guaranteed by the host country (Art. 7 of Regulation n. 1612/68 and Regulation n. 492/2011).[73]

Moreover, the UK prospective deal on EU membership definitely goes even more blatantly in this same devastating direction. In the above-mentioned conclusions of the European Council of 18–19 February 2016, and especially in the legally binding decision drawing a new settlement for the United Kingdom within the EU adopted therein, the new architecture of the restrictive free-movement law is already outlined in great detail. If overriding reasons of public interest make it necessary, free movement of workers may be restricted by measures proportionate to the legitimate aim pursued. Encouraging recruitment, reducing unemployment, protecting vulnerable workers and averting the risk of seriously undermining the sustainability of social-security systems are expressly considered to be reasons of public interest in such a perspective.[74]

The European Council Decision goes even further along the slippery line of such a regressive drift of EU free movement (of workers) law. Through the provision of an 'emergency brake',[75] member states will be allowed to limit the access of newly arriving EU workers to in-work benefits for a period of up to four years from the start of employment, although such a safeguard mechanism will be graduated from an initial complete exclusion to a progressive assimilation, taking account of the growing connection of the worker with the labour market of the host State.[76] This would be an inglorious step back to the nineteen fifties, but without any prospective hope for an ever-closer union among Europeans.

If these scenarios of counter-reformation were to be consolidated in the new regressive law of the dis-Union, we would be witnessing, as lost and disoriented as ever, not only the final and inglorious sinking of any misplaced hope of trans-national social solidarity, but the deletion of an entire history of achievements of civilisation in the long march towards the freedom of movement of persons in the EU. Not only would it be a return to a de-socialised idea of market citizen, but a stronger premonition of the forthcoming disintegration of the whole European project.

Notes

1 *Rudy v Grzelczyk v Centre public d'aide sociale d'Ottignies-Louvain-la-Neuve* (European Court of Justice, C-184/99, 20 September 2001) [44].
2 Loic Azoulai, 'La citoyenneté européenne, un statut d'intégration sociale' in Gérard Cohen-Jonathan (ed.), *Chemins d'Europe: Mélanges en l'honneur de Jean-Paul Jaqué* (Dalloz, 2010) 1.
3 Costanza Margiotta, *Cittadinanza europea: Istruzioni per l'uso* (Editori Laterza, 2010) 7.
4 'Little more than a cynical exercise in public relations on the part of the High Contracting Parties,' as was famously said by J H H Wieler, 'The Selling of Europe: The Discourse of European Citizenship in the IGC 1996' (Working Paper, Jean Monnet Series No. 3, Harvard Law School, 1996) 1.
5 *María Martínez Sala v Freistaat Bayern* (European Court of Justice, C-85/96, 12 May 1998).

6 Stefano Giubboni, 'European Citizenship and Social Rights in Times of Crisis' (2014) 15(1) *German Law Journal* 935.
7 Giuseppe Federico Mancini, 'The Free Movement of Workers in the Case Law of the European Court of Justice' in Giuseppe F Mancini (ed.), *Democracy and Constitutionalism in the European Union* (Hart Publishing, 2000) 123.
8 See, e.g., M Everson, 'The Legacy of the Market Citizen' in J Shaw and G More (eds), *New Legal Dynamics of European Union* (Oxford, 1995) 73.
9 Niamh Nic Shuibhne, 'The Resilience of EU Market Citizenship' (2014) 47(6) *Common Market Law Review* 1605.
10 Alexander Somek, 'Solidarity Decomposed: Being and Time in European Citizenship' (2007) 32(6) *European Law Review* 787; Alexander Somek, 'From Workers to Migrants, from Distributive Justice to Inclusion: Exploring the Changing Social Democratic Imagination' (2012) 18(5) *European Law Journal* 711. See also Augustín José Menéndez, 'European Citizenship after Martínez Sala and Baumbast: Has European Law Become More Human but Less Social?' in Miguel Poiares Maduro and Loic Azoulai (eds), *The Past and Future of EU Law. The Classics of EU Law Revisited on the 50th Anniversary of the Rome Treaty* (Hart Publishing, 2010).
11 *Gerardo Ruiz Zambrano v Office national de l'emploi* (European Court of Justice, C-34/09, 8 March 2011).
12 Margiotta, above n 3, 150.
13 Loic Azoulai, 'Euro-Bonds. The Ruiz Zambrano Judgment or the Real Invention of Union Citizenship' (2011) 3(2) *Perspectives on Federalism* 34.
14 To the benefit of the non-Italian reader, I would like to remind that this is the verse of one of Giacomo Leopardi's most famous poems, *La ginestra*, composed in 1836. The citation from John's Gospel, appearing in exergue, is also taken from Leopardi's poetry.
15 *Pensionsversicherungsanstalt v Peter Brey* (European Court of Justice, C-140/12, 19 September 2013).
16 *Elisabeta Dano and Florin Dano v Jobcenter Leipzig* (European Court of Justice, C-333/13, 11 November 2014).
17 *Jobcenter Berlin Neukolln v Nazifa Alimanovic* (European Court of Justice, C-67/14, 15 September 2015).
18 Niamh Nic Shuibhne, 'Limits Rising, Duties Ascending: The Changing Legal Shape of Union Citizenship' (2015) 52(4) *Common Market Law Review* 889.
19 *Vestische Arbeit Jobcenter Kreis Recklinghausen v Jovanna García-Nieto and Others* (European Court of Justice, C- 299/14, 25 February 2016).
20 Margiotta, above n 3, 55.
21 Lionello Levi Sandri, 'La sicurezza sociale dei lavoratori migranti nell'ambito della Comunità economica europea' in L Riva Sanseverino and G Mazzoni (eds), *Nuovo trattato di diritto del lavoro* (Cedam, 1971) Vol. 3, 941. See also Stefano Giubboni, 'L'azione comunitaria in materia di sicurezza sociale in prospettiva storica: Omaggio a Lionello Levi Sandri' in Antonio Varsori and Lorenzo Mechi (eds), *Lionello Levi Sandri e la politica sociale europea* (Franco Angeli, 2008) 175.
22 J H H Weiler, 'The Transformation of Europe' (1991) 100(8) *Yale Law Journal* 2403.
23 Eleanor Spaventa, *Free Movement of Persons in the European Union: Barriers to Movement in their Constitutional Context* (Alphen aan den Rijn, 2007) 2.
24 Maurizio Ferrera, *The Boundaries of Welfare. European Integration and the New Spatial Politics of Social Protection* (Oxford University Press, 2005) 53.
25 Herwig Verschueren, 'Union Law and the Fight against Poverty: Which Legal Instruments?' in Bea Cantillon, Herwig Verschueren and Paula Ploscar (eds),

Social Inclusion and Social Protection in the EU: Interaction between Law and Policy (Intersentia, 2012) 217.
26 M Dougan and E Spaventa, 'Wish You Weren't Here . . . New Models of Social Solidarity in the European Union' in M Dougan and E Spaventa (eds), *Social Welfare and EU Law* (Hart Publishing, 2005) 181.
27 Azoulai, above n 2, 8.
28 Catherine Barnard, 'EU Citizenship and the Principle of Solidarity' in M Dougan and E Spaventa (eds), *Social Welfare and EU Law* (Hart Publishing, 2005) 157.
29 Almost prophetic was the analysis dedicated to German Ordo-liberalism by Michael Foucault, *Nascita della biopolitica: Corso al Collège de France (1978–1979)* (Feltrinelli, 2005) 113.
30 Alain Supiot, 'Introduction' in Alain Supoit (ed.), *La Solidarité: Enquête sur un principe juridique* (Odile Jacob, 2015) 8; Stefano Rodotà, *Solidarietà. Un'utopia necessaria* (Laterza, 2014) 126.
31 Stefano Giubboni, 'Free Movement of Persons and European Solidarity' (2007) 13 *European Law Review* 360.
32 See also Floris de Witte, 'Transnational Solidarity and the Mediation of Conflicts of Justice in Europe' (2012) 18(5) *European Law Journal* 694.
33 Richard Bellamy, 'The Liberty of Post-Moderns? Market and Civic Freedom within the EU' (Discussion Paper LEQS No 01/2009, London School of Economics and Political Science, May 2009).
34 On the importance of isonomy in the Aristotle's philosophy of justice classically see Chaim Perelman, *Justice et Raison* (Presses Universitaires de Bruxelles, 1963) 9; Alessandro Giuliani, *Giustizia ed ordine economico* (Giuffrè, 1997) 3.
35 See in particular the sharp criticism in Kay Hailbronner, 'Union Citizenship and Access to Social Benefits' (2005) 42(5) *Common Market Law Review* 1245.
36 Herwig Verschueren, 'EU Free Movement and Member States' Solidarity Systems: Searching for a Balance' in Elspeth Guild and Paul Minderhoud (eds), *The First Decade of EU Migration and Asylum Law* (Martinus Nijhof Publisher, 2012) 47, 62.
37 A P Van Der Mei, 'EU Law and Education: Promotion of Student Mobility versus Protection of Education Systems' in M Dougan and E Spaventa (eds), *Social Welfare and EU Law* (Hart Publishing, 2005) 225–6.
38 See especially *Baumbast and R v. Secretary of State for the Home Department* (European Court of Justice, C-413/99, 17 September 2002), in which, for the first time, the court explicitly states the direct effect of the fundamental right to reside in the territory of another member state granted to the European citizen by Art. 21 of the Treaty on the Functioning of the European Union.
39 K Lenaerts, 'European Union Citizenship, National Welfare Systems and Social Solidarity' (2011) 18(2) *Jurisprudencija/Jurisprudence* 397.
40 Stefano Giubboni, *Diritti e solidarietà in Europa* (il Mulino, 2012) 186.
41 *Jacqueline Förster v Hoofddirectie van de Infromatie Beheer Groep* (European Court of Justice, C-158/07, 18 November 2008).
42 M Dougan, 'The Bubble that Bursts: Exploring the Legitimacy of the Case Law on the Free Movement of Union Citizens' in M Adams *et al.* (eds), *Judging Europe's Judges: The Legitimacy of the Case Law of the European Court of Justice* (Hart Publishing, 2013) 127, 141.
43 Herwig Verschueren, 'Free Movement and Benefit Tourism: The Unreasonable Burden of Brey' (2014) 16(2) *European Journal of Migration and Law* 147.
44 Daniel Thym, 'The Elusive Limits of Solidarity: Residence Rights of and Social Benefits for Economically Inactive Union Citizens' (2015) 52(1) *Common Market Law Review* 17, 28–9.
45 The bold political position expressed by the governments of Austria, Germany, the Netherlands and the United Kingdom in the conjunct letter addressed by the

competent ministers of those countries to the presidency of the Union in April of 2013 is evidently perceivable. The main theme abruptly put on the political table was that limitations of the freedom of movement apply only to economically inactive citizens meeting the legal requirements set by Directive 2004/38/EC.

46 J M Berlorgey, 'La protection sociale dans une union de citoyens' (1998) 2 *Droit social* 159, 160.

47 Cf Herwig Verschueren, 'Free Movement of EU Citizens: Including the Poor?' (2015) 1 *Maastricht Journal of European and Comparative Law* 1.

48 Paul Minderhoud, 'Sufficient Resources and Residence Rights under Directive 2004/38' (Paper presented at *Where do I belong? EU law and the Adjudication on the Link between Individuals and Member States*, Antwerp, 7–8 May 2015) 15. The reference is of course to the famous paradox/dilemma of Joseph Heller's 1961 novel *Catch-22*. Here, in order to avoid war service, a combatant can claim insanity, but such a claim, being the act of a rational person, would negate the effect of the claim and mean the combatant had to fight.

49 R Cornelissen, 'EU Regulations on the Coordination of Social Security Systems and Special Non-Contributory Benefits: A Source of Never-Ending Controversy' in E Guild, S Carrera and K Eisele (eds), *Social Benefits and Migration: A Contested Relationship and Policy Challenge in the EU* (Centre for European Policy Studies, 2013) 82; Herwig Vershueren, 'Preventing Benefit Tourism in the EU: A Narrow or a Broad Interpretation of the Possibilities Offered by the ECJ in Dano?' (2015) 52(2) *Common Market Law Review* 363.

50 Through Regulation No. 1247/92, that modified Regulation No. 1408/71 by introducing the new sub-system for the coordination of special non-contributory cash benefits. Cf Stefano Giubboni, 'Cittadinanza comunitaria e sicurezza sociale: un profilo critico' (1997) 6 *Argomenti di diritto del lavoro* 67.

51 See *Kelvin Albert Snares v Adjudication Officer* (European Court of Justice, C-20/96, 4 November 1997); *Vera A Patridge v Adjudication Officer* (European Court of Justice, C-297/96, 11 June 1998); *Robin Swaddling v Adjudication Officer* (European Court of Justice, C-90/97, 25 February 1999).

52 Further, see the judgment delivered by the Court in the joined *Tomasz Ziolkowski and Barbara Szeja and Others v Land Berlin* (European Court of Justice, Joined Cases C-424/10 and C-425/10, 21 December 2011).

53 See *Pensionsversicherungsanstalt v Peter Brey* (European Court of Justice, C-140/12, 19 September 2013) [24], where in relation to a compensatory supplement for pensioners the court expressly stated that 'the concept of social assistance could be given its own particular meaning based on the objectives pursued by Directive 2004/38, which is intended, inter alia, to prevent persons who have not made any contribution to financing the social security schemes of a host Member State from becoming an excessive burden on that State's budget'. Cf also the clear-cut conclusion in *Elisabeta Dano and Florin Dano v Jobcenter Leipzig* (European Court of Justice, C-333/13, 11 November 2014) [63], where it was held that 'special non-contributory cash benefits, as referred to in Article 70(2) of Regulation No. 883/2004, do fall within the concept of "social assistance" within the meaning of Article 24(2) of Directive 2004/38'.

54 *Jobcenter Berlin Neukölln v Nazifa Alimanovic and Others* (European Court of Justice, C-67/14, 15 September 2015).

55 This Article provides for the unlimited retention of the status of worker after employment for more than a year, contrary to Article 7, par. 3, b), which provides for a retention of such a status for a period no less than six months.

56 According to which the Union citizen who entered the territory of the host member state in order to seek employment may not be expelled for as long as s/he can provide evidence that s/he is continuing to seek employment, having a genuine chance of being engaged.

57 *Jobcenter Berlin Neukölln v Nazifa Alimanovic and Others* (European Court of Justice, C-67/14, 15 September 2015) [57].
58 Verschueren, above n 49.
59 *Elisabeta Dano and Florin Dano v Jobcenter Leipzig* (European Court of Justice, C-333/13, 11 November 2014) [78].
60 See, e.g., *Jessy Saint Prix v Secretary of State for Work and Pensions* (European Court of Justice, C-507/12, 19 June 2014).
61 *Jobcenter Berlin Neukölln v Nazifa Alimanovic and Others* (European Court of Justice, C-67/14, 15 September 2015).
62 *Athanasios Vatsouras and Josif Koupatantze v Arbeitsgemeinschaft (ARGE) Nürnberg 900* (European Court of Justice, Joined Cases C-22/08 and C-23/08, 4 June 2009).
63 See *Conclusions of the European Council Meeting 18–19 February 2016*, EUCO 1/16, 19 February 2016, annex 1, s D(b).
64 *Jobcenter Berlin Neukölln v Nazifa Alimanovic and Others* (European Court of Justice, C-67/14, 15 September 2015) [60].
65 Cf Daniel Thym, 'When Union Citizens Turn into Illegal Migrants: The Dano Case' (2015) 40 *European Law Review* 6.
66 *Pensionsversicherungsanstalt v Peter Brey* (European Court of Justice, C-140/12, 19 September 2013) [69].
67 *Jobcenter Berlin Neukölln v Nazifa Alimanovic and Others* (European Court of Justice, C-67/14, 15 September 2015) [59].
68 Thym, above n 65.
69 Kees Groenendiik, 'Access for Migrants to Social Assistance: Closing the Frontiers or Reducing Citizenship?' in E Guild, S Carrera and K Eisele (eds), *Social Benefits and Migration* (Centre for European Policy Studies, 2013) 1.
70 N Landau, 'The Regulation of Migration, Economic Structures and Definitions of the Poor in Eighteenth-Century England' (1990) 33 *Historical Journal* 541; Lynn Hllen Lees, *The Solidarities of Strangers: The English Poor Laws and the People (1700–1948)* (Cambridge University Press, 2007).
71 Cf Editorial Comments, 'The Free Movement of Persons in the European Union: Salvaging the Dream while Explaining the Nightmare' (2014) 51 *Common Market Law Review* 729.
72 Cf *Wendy Geven v Land Nordrhein-Westfalen* (European Court of Justice, C-213/05, 18 July 2007); *Cavse Krier Frères Sàrl v Directeur de l'Administration de l'emploi* (European Court of Justice, C-379/11, 13 December 2012); *Elodie Giersch and Others v État du Grand-Duché de Luxembourg* (European Court of Justice, C-20/12, 20 June 2013).
73 Herwig Verschueren, 'Being Economically Active: How it Still Matters' (Paper presented at *Where do I belong? EU law and the adjudication on the link between individuals and Member States*, Antwerp, 7–8 May 2015) [5].
74 See *Conclusions of the European Council Meeting 18–19 February 2016*, EUCO 1/16, 19 February 2016, annex 1, s D(a).
75 See *Conclusions of the European Council Meeting 18–19 February 2016*, EUCO 1/16, 19 February 2016, annex 1, s D(b).
76 Another noteworthy provision regards the option to index child benefits to the conditions of the member state where the child resides, with a spectacular counter-reform of Regulation No. 883/2004: see *Conclusions of the European Council Meeting 18–19 February 2016*, EUCO 1/16, 19 February 2016, annex 1, s D(b).

Index

For Product Safety Concerns and Information please contact our EU
representative GPSR@taylorandfrancis.com
Taylor & Francis Verlag GmbH, Kaufingerstraße 24, 80331 München, Germany

www.ingramcontent.com/pod-product-compliance
Ingram Content Group UK Ltd.
Pitfield, Milton Keynes, MK11 3LW, UK
UKHW020018200926
475702UK00014B/1947
9780367191801